SUPPLEMENT TO

ERNEST HEMINGWAY:

A COMPREHENSIVE BIBLIOGRAPHY

SUPPLEMENT TO

ERNEST

HEMINGWAY

A COMPREHENSIVE

BIBLIOGRAPHY

BY AUDRE HANNEMAN

PRINCETON, NEW JERSEY

PRINCETON UNIVERSITY PRESS

1975

FOR MY GRANDNEPHEW

SHAWN MICHAEL HANNEMAN

AND ALL THE FUTURE GENERATIONS
OF HEMINGWAY STUDENTS, SCHOLARS,
AND CRITICS

PREFACE

This supplement mainly comprises work by and about Ernest Hemingway published between 1966 and 1973. It also includes omissions in the first volume of my Hemingway bibliography and a few entries that have been repeated from the bibliography in order to give more complete information. The most notable omission was *Fact*, the monograph published in London, in July 1938, containing Hemingway's Spanish Civil War dispatches under the title "The Spanish War." While this item was known to me, and inadvertently omitted, other omitted items have been called to my attention by Hemingway students and collectors, mentioned in reviews and addendas, or located through new reference sources. I welcome this opportunity to make these additions toward a definitive bibliography of the greatest writer of the twentieth century.

During the eight years covered by this supplement, Charles Scribner's Sons published four new books by Hemingway: *By-Line: Ernest Hemingway* edited by William White, *The Fifth Column and Four Stories of the Spanish Civil War*, *Islands in the Stream*, and *The Nick Adams Stories*. Although only the last two contain previously unpublished work, all four books received extensive critical attention. Whenever possible I have selected excerpts from the reviews to indicate both the reviewer's opinion of the work and of Hemingway's present literary standing. The extended appearance of *By-Line* and *Islands in the Stream* on the best-sellers lists attest to his continued wide popularity. Two collections of Hemingway's early work, both edited by Matthew J. Bruccoli, were also published during this period: *Ernest Hemingway, Cub Reporter: Kansas City Star Stories*, containing twelve articles attributed to Hemingway after a fifty-year interim in which none of his work on the *Kansas City Star* during 1917-1918 was positively identified, and *Ernest Hemingway's Apprenticeship: Oak Park, 1916-1917*, containing his writings from the *Trapeze* and the *Tabula*. Work by and about Hemingway during his high school years was also edited by Daniel Reichard and made available on microfilm by the Oak Park and River Forest High School. A new book, *The Enduring Hemingway: An Anthology of a Lifetime in Literature* edited by Charles Scribner, Jr., is scheduled for publication in June 1974. It will include the first appearance in book form of "Miss Mary's Lion" from the "African Journal," which was serialized in *Sports Illustrated* in December 1971 and January 1972.

It is interesting to note that the number of principal books on Hemingway has more than doubled in the last eight years. I listed twenty-one, published between 1931 and 1966, in the bibliography and I have listed twenty-five, published between 1966 and 1974, in this supplement. The outstanding book on the recent list is, of course, Carlos Baker's *Ernest Hemingway: A Life Story*, a brilliant *tour de force* whose large section of Sources and Notes contributed numerous items to this supplement. Another book on this list, *Hemingway at Auction: 1930-1973* compiled by Matthew J. Bruccoli and C. E. Frazer Clark, Jr., was largely responsible for the long list of published letters in Section F. *The Hemingway Manuscripts: An Inventory* by Philip Young and Charles W. Mann served to partially satisfy scholarly curiosity concerning the unpublished work until it is made available to researchers. Work-in-progress includes *Essays on the Short Stories of Ernest Hemingway* edited by Jackson J. Benson, a collection of twenty-nine reprinted essays and two original ones, "The Dark Snows of Kilimanjaro" by Gennaro Santangelo and "Ernest Hemingway as Short Story Writer" by Professor Benson, to be published by Duke University Press in 1974; *Hemingway: Last Days of the Lion* by William F. Nolan, to be published by Capra Press in Santa Barbara, California, in September 1974; a long critical book by Wirt Williams, titled *The Tragic Art of Ernest Hemingway*, to be published in 1975; and Mary Hemingway's memoirs (one has only to recall her vivid account of life at Finca Vigia in *Flair* magazine, in January 1951, to look forward with keen anticipation to her forthcoming reminiscences).

Besides the growing number of book-length studies of Hemingway's work there has been a noticeable increase in doctoral dissertations, critical essays, and textual studies. Hemingway scholarship has been furthered by two new publications. Four volumes of the *Fitzgerald/Hemingway Annual*, edited by Matthew J. Bruccoli and C. E. Frazer Clark, Jr., have been published since its first appearance in 1969. And six issues of *Hemingway notes*, edited by Taylor Alderman and Kenneth Rosen, have been published biannually since the Spring of 1971.

The prefix S- has been used in numbering the entries in this supplement in order to distinguish them from entries in the first volume of the bibliography. The number of the entry is given in all cross-references to items before 1966 if they appear in the supplement.

Where the text of Hemingway's books is referred to, the reference is always to the first edition.

I am again greatly indebted to Mrs. Mary Hemingway, Charles Scribner, Jr., and Carlos Baker. I owe a special debt of gratitude for information and assistance from Charles W. Mann, Jr. of University

Park, Pennsylvania, C. E. Frazer Clark, Jr. of Bloomfield Hills, Michigan, Donald St. John of Franconia, New Hampshire, Mrs. Morris Buske of Oak Park, Illinois, Mrs. Fred Colin of Roslyn Estates, New York, William F. Nolan of Woodland Hills, California, and Stanley A. Carlin of Melrose, Massachusetts.

I would also like to express my appreciation for the information I received from Yeatman Anderson, III of Cincinnati, Ohio, Robert L. Beare of College Park, Maryland, Kurt Bernheim of New York City, Matthew J. Bruccoli of Columbia, South Carolina, Robert B. Carowitz of Grand Rapids, Michigan, Mrs. Louis Henry Cohn of New York City, Donald Gallup of New Haven, Connecticut, Walter Goldwater of New York City, George Hocutt of Westminster, California, David V. Koch of Carbondale, Illinois, Mrs. Sally Leach of Austin, Texas, Ms. Elizabeth M. Lintner of Boise, Idaho, Kenneth A. Lohf of New York City, Mrs. Russell McKay of Logan, Iowa, George Monteiro of Providence, Rhode Island, Mrs. Caroline Moon of Des Moines, Iowa, David L. O'Neal of Milton, Massachusetts, Mrs. Maria Pelikan of Riverdale, New York, John Milton Price of Natchitoches, Louisiana, Mrs. Wanda Randall of Princeton, New Jersey, Alfred Rice of New York City, J. Albert Robbins of Bloomington, Indiana, Bertram D. Sarason of New Haven, Connecticut, William W. Seward, Jr. of Norfolk, Virginia, Mrs. Joan P. Smith of Charlottesville, Virginia, Donald D. Teets of Grand Rapids, Michigan, John E. Via of Charlottesville, Virginia, William White of Franklin Village, Michigan, Wirt Williams of Studio City, California, Donald C. Woods of Milwaukee Wisconsin, and Philip Young of University Park, Pennsylvania.

And, lastly, I would like to express my deep gratitude to my sister, Marjorie Hanneman, for the constant encouragement and support she has given me during these past twenty years of Hemingway research.

Audre Hanneman

March 5, 1974
New York, New York

CONTENTS

ABBREVIATIONS
USED IN THIS WORK

AMF	A Moveable Feast
ARIT	Across the River and Into the Trees
Baker anthology	Hemingway and His Critics: An International Anthology edited by Carlos Baker
By-Line	By-Line: Ernest Hemingway edited by William White
DIA	Death in the Afternoon
First 49	The Fifth Column and the First Forty-nine Stories
FTA	A Farewell to Arms
FWBT	For Whom the Bell Tolls
GHOA	Green Hills of Africa
iot	in our time (Paris, 1924)
IOT	In Our Time
Islands	Islands in the Stream
MWW	Men Without Women
NANA	North American Newspaper Alliance
NAS	The Nick Adams Stories
OMATS	The Old Man and the Sea
SAR	The Sun Also Rises
TDS	Toronto Daily Star
TFC	The Fifth Column
TFC & 4 Stories	The Fifth Column and Four Stories of the Spanish Civil War
THAHN	To Have and Have Not
TOS	The Torrents of Spring
TSTP	Three Stories & Ten Poems
TSW	Toronto Star Weekly
WTN	Winner Take Nothing

PART ONE
THE WORKS
OF ERNEST HEMINGWAY

CHRONOLOGICAL LIST
OF HEMINGWAY'S BOOKS

1923 *Three Stories & Ten Poems*. Short stories and poems

1924 *in our time*. Short chapters

1925 *In Our Time*. Short stories and inter-chapters

1926 *Torrents of Spring*. Novel

1926 *The Sun Also Rises*. Novel

1927 *Men Without Women*. Short stories

1929 *A Farewell to Arms*. Novel

1932 *Death in the Afternoon*. Treatise on bullfighting

1933 *God Rest You Merry Gentlemen*. Short story

1933 *Winner Take Nothing*. Short stories

1935 *Green Hills of Africa*. Nonfictional account of big game hunting

1937 *To Have and Have Not*. Novel

1938 *The Spanish Earth*. Commentary for the film of the same name

1938 *The Fifth Column and the First Forty-nine Stories*. Play and short stories

1940 *For Whom the Bell Tolls*. Novel

1942 *Men at War*. Anthology. Edited by Hemingway

1950 *Across the River and Into the Trees*. Novel

1952 *The Old Man and the Sea*. Novella

BOOKS PUBLISHED POSTHUMOUSLY

1962 *The Wild Years*. *Toronto Star* articles. Edited by Gene Z. Hanrahan

1964 *A Moveable Feast*. Nonfictional sketches of Paris in the twenties

1967 *By-Line*: *Ernest Hemingway*. Journalism. Edited by William White

1969 *The Fifth Column and Four Stories of the Spanish Civil War*. Play and short stories

CHRONOLOGICAL LIST

1970 *Ernest Hemingway, Cub Reporter: Kansas City Star Stories.* Journalism. Edited by Matthew J. Bruccoli

1970 *Islands in the Stream.* Novel

1971 *Ernest Hemingway's Apprenticeship: Oak Park, 1916-1917.* High school juvenilia. Edited by Matthew J. Bruccoli

1972 *The Nick Adams Stories.* Short stories

SECTION A

BOOKS AND PAMPHLETS

The books in this section are listed chronologically according to the date of their first publication. This arrangement allows for the six new books to be placed appropriately at the end of the section. While the entry numbers do not correspond with those in the bibliography, the alphabetical designations for the various editions are a continuation of those used in the bibliography; e.g., in the bibliography the various editions of *The Old Man and the Sea* are numbered and lettered A24A to A24E, in this supplement they are S-A9F to S-A9H. The English editions, which follow the American editions, are keyed in a similar manner.

In the following descriptions, the endpapers are white and the lettering is black unless otherwise noted. Notes on additional information or corrections to earlier entries appear at the end of the entries.

The bibliographer gratefully acknowledges her debt to Charles Scribner, Jr. for information regarding the various editions of Hemingway's books.

The Torrents of Spring

c. Reprint edition:

THE | TORRENTS | OF SPRING | A Romantic Novel in Honor of the | Passing of a Great Race | by | ERNEST HEMINGWAY | *And perhaps there is one reason why a comic writer should of* | *all others be the least excused for deviating from nature, since it* | *may not be always so easy for a serious poet to meet with the* | *great and the admirable; but life everywhere furnishes an accu-* | *rate observer with the ridiculous.* | HENRY FIELDING | CHARLES SCRIBNER'S SONS | NEW YORK | 1972

8 x 5 3/8. Published August 17, 1972, at $5.95. Issued in orange cloth lettered in black on the backstrip only. Backstrip, reading downward: HEMINGWAY The Torrents of Spring SCRIBNERS. All edges trimmed.

COLLATION: [i]-[vi] + [1]-90, as follows: [i] half title; [ii] BOOKS BY; [iii] title page as above; [iv] notices of copyright, reservation of rights, Scribner's code "A-7.72 [C]," note of origin, Library of Congress catalog card number, and SBN numbers; [v] CONTENTS; [vi] blank; [1] title for PART ONE and quotation from Henry Fielding; [2] blank; [3]-90 text.

NOTE: The dust jacket, designed by Hal Siegel, is orange, lettered in black and white. A list of books by Hemingway is on the back cover. A photograph of Hemingway and a short biographical note appear on the front inside flap. The back flap is blank.

d. Paperback edition:

The title page and pagination of the paperback edition of *The Torrents of Spring* are identical to the hard-cover edition described above. Scribner's code "A-7.72[C]" appears on both copyright pages. 8 x 5 3/8. Published August 17, 1972, at $2.45, as No. SL 373 in the Scribner Library Contemporary Classics series. Issued in orange stiff paper covers, lettered in black and white. The cover design, by Hal Siegel, is the same as the dust jacket of the hard-cover edition.

2 Men Without Women

G. First paperback edition:

Men | Without Women | ERNEST HEMINGWAY | CHARLES SCRIBNER'S SONS | New York

8 x 5 3/8. Published August 5, 1970, at $1.95, as No. SL 217 of the Scribner Library Contemporary Classics series. Issued in stiff paper covers. Front cover: [in white on a black horizontal strip:] ERNEST | HEMINGWAY | [in orange at the top of a painting by James and Ruth McCrea:] Men Without Women. The white backstrip and back cover are printed in black, gray, and brown.

COLLATION: [i]-[viii] + 1-232, as follows: [i] half title; [ii] *Books by*; [iii] title page as above; [iv] dedication, notices of copyright of the short stories and the cover painting, reservations of rights, Scribner's code "A-6.70 [C]," and note of origin; [v] CONTENTS; [vi] blank; [vii] half title; [viii] blank; 1-232 text.
NOTE: For contents, see (A7A).

NOTE: For new information on the concealed printings, see Jean Muir Rogers and Gordon Stein's "Bibliographical Notes on Hemingway's *Men Without Women*," *Papers of the Bibliographical Society of America*, LXIV, ii (April-June 1970), 210-213. Eight copies dated 1927 and one copy each dated 1928, 1932, 1946, 1955, the London first printing of 1928, and the 1938 first printing of *The Fifth Column and the First Forty-nine Stories* were examined for differences in weight, states of the dust jacket, and textual changes. Foremost in their conclusions is the fact that the "first printing of the first edition (1927) can be most clearly identified by the presence of a perfect folio '3' on page three of the text, and by a weight of approximately 15.8 ounces as contrasted with an average weight of 13.7 ounces and a broken folio '3' on page three of the text in the second printing."

3 A Farewell to Arms

P. Second uniform edition:
A FAREWELL | TO ARMS | BY | ERNEST HEMINGWAY | CHARLES SCRIBNER'S SONS | NEW YORK
8 x 5 1/2. Published in [1965?], at $5.95. Issued in rose-red cloth. Stamped in gold on the front cover: [ornament] A FAREWELL TO ARMS [ornament]. Backstrip: the title is stamped in gold on a black block; the author's name and the publisher's name are stamped in black on gold blocks. All edges trimmed.
COLLATION: [i]-[iv] + [1]-332, as follows: [i] title page as above; [ii] notices of copyright, reservation of rights, Scribner's code, and note of origin; [iii] dedication; [iv] blank; [1] BOOK ONE; [2] blank; 3-332 text.
NOTE: This typesetting, with the text on pp. 3-332, first appeared in *Three Novels of Ernest Hemingway* published in 1962, see (A29). Since then it has become Scribner's standard text, corrected from time to time, as typographical errors are called to their attention.
NOTE: The dust jacket is the same as the first uniform edition, see note under A8M. It was later changed to gray-green, white, red, and gray, with a painting by James and Ruth McCrea on the front cover.

Q. School edition:
A FAREWELL | TO ARMS | BY | ERNEST HEMINGWAY | [drawing] | CHARLES SCRIBNER'S SONS | NEW YORK

8 x 5 1/2. Published February 2, 1967, at $3.60. Issued in beige cloth covers, lettered and illustrated in black and red. Front cover: [in black:] ERNEST HEMINGWAY | [below the author's name on the left-hand side:] [drawing in red of a soldier, signed Gil Walker] [in black, at the bottom of the right-hand side:] A | FAREWELL | TO | ARMS. Backstrip: [reading downward, in two lines:] HEMINGWAY [in red] | A FAREWELL TO ARMS [in black] | [horizontal, in red:] SCHOOL | EDITION | [reading downward, in black:] SCRIBNERS. Back cover: [drawing in red of a Red Cross ambulance]. All edges trimmed. Map endpapers printed in brown.

COLLATION: [i]-x + [1]-358, as follows: [i] half title; [ii] Introduction and Study Guide by | JOHN C. SCHWEITZER | *English Department* | *Rye High School, Rye, N.Y.*; [iii] title page as above; [iv] notices of copyright for the text, introduction, and study guide, reservations of rights, Scribner's code "A-1.67 [C]," note of origin, and Library of Congress catalog card number; [v] dedication; [vi] blank; vii-x INTRODUCTION by John C. Schweitzer; [1] BOOK ONE; [2] blank; 3-332 text; 333-353 text of the study guide; 354-355 Topics for Writing and Research; 356-358 Glossary.

R. Large-type edition:
A FAREWELL | TO | ARMS | BY | ERNEST HEMINGWAY | NEW YORK | CHARLES SCRIBNER'S SONS
11 x 8 1/2. Published June 15, 1968, at $7.95, as an aid to the visually handicapped. Issued in white cloth covers, lettered and illustrated on the front and back covers in blue, brown, and black, enclosed in a black border. Decorative first letter at beginning of each chapter.

COLLATION: [i]-[viii] + [1]-[344], as follows: [i] blank; [ii] BOOKS BY; [iii] half title; [iv] blank; [v] title page as above; [vi] notices of copyright, reservation of rights, Scribner's code "A-5.68 [c]," and note of origin; [vii] dedication; [viii] blank; [1] *BOOK ONE*; [2] blank; 3-[343] text; [344] blank.

NOTE: *The Old Man and the Sea* was also published in a large-type edition. See (S-A9H).

S. Paperback school edition:
A FAREWELL | TO ARMS | BY | ERNEST HEMINGWAY | [drawing] | CHARLES SCRIBNER'S SONS | NEW YORK
8 x 5 3/8. Published February 4, 1969, at $2.36, as No. SSP 23 in the Scribner School Paperbacks series. Issued in brown stiff paper covers, lettered in black and white, with a montage-type painting by Victor Mays extending over the front and back covers and the backstrip.

COLLATION: [i]-x + [1]-358 + 8 blank leaves. Same pagination as the hard-cover edition, see (S-A3Q), except for the additional eight blank leaves at the end of the book. Scribner's code "A-1.69 [M]" on the copyright page, p. [iv].

NOTE: The title page of this edition is identical to the hard-cover edition. This edition also contains the Study Guide by John C. Schweitzer.

NOTE: *A Farewell to Arms* was published in Moscow, in 1969, by Progress Publishers, with the text and notes in English. 320 pages. Hemingway's introduction to the 1948 edition is reprinted in English. An introduction, by M. Mendelson, is printed in Russian.

4 Death in the Afternoon

E. First paperback edition:
DEATH IN THE | AFTERNOON | By | Ernest Hemingway | [silhouette of a black bull] | CHARLES SCRIBNER'S SONS | NEW YORK

8 x 5 3/8. Published January 20, 1969, at $2.95, as No. SL 175 in the Scribner Library Lyceum Editions series. Issued in black stiff paper covers printed in white, yellow, black, and gray. The painting, by Roberto Domingo, on the front cover appeared on the dust jacket of the first edition.

COLLATION: [i]-[viii] + 1-[488], including 96 pages of photographs, as follows: [i] half title; [ii] Books by; [iii] title page as above; [iv] notices of copyright, Scribner's code "A-1.69 [MC]," SBN numbers, note of origin, and reservation of rights; [v] dedication; [vi] blank; [vii] CONTENTS; [viii] blank; 1-278 text; [279] ILLUSTRATIONS; [280] blank; [281]-[375] photographs; [376] blank; [377] AN EXPLANATORY GLOSSARY; [378] blank; 379-463 glossary; [464] blank; 465-471 SOME REACTIONS OF A FEW INDIVIDUALS TO THE INTEGRAL SPANISH BULLFIGHT; [472] blank; 473-476 A SHORT ESTIMATE OF THE AMERICAN, SIDNEY FRANKLIN, AS A MATADOR; 477-485 dates of bullfights; [486] blank; 487 BIBLIOGRAPHICAL NOTE (signed "E.H."); [488] blank.

NOTE: The complete contents of the first edition are included in this paperback edition. Only the photograph credits to Vandel and Rodero (on p. 408 of the first edition) are omitted.

5 Winner Take Nothing

D. First paperback edition:
WINNER TAKE | NOTHING | *by* | *Ernest Hemingway* | "Unlike all other forms of lutte or | combat the conditions are that the | winner shall take nothing; neither | his ease, nor his pleasure, nor any | notions of glory; nor, if he win far | enough, shall there be any

reward | within himself." | CHARLES SCRIBNER'S SONS [dot] NEW YORK

8 x 5 3/8. Published August 15, 1968, at $1.65, as No. SL 155 of the Scribner Library Contemporary Classics series. Issued in stiff paper covers. Front cover: [in white on gray horizontal strip:] ERNEST | HEMINGWAY | [in black at the top of a painting by Ruth and James McCrea:] Winner Take Nothing. The white backstrip and back cover are printed in black and gray.

COLLATION: [i]-[x] + [1]-[246]. Same pagination as the first edition. See (A12A).

NOTE: For contents, see (A12A). In "A Clean, Well-Lighted Place," the dialogue between the waiters, on p. 20, has not been emended. See (S-A7F).

6 To Have and Have Not

H. Second paperback edition:
TO HAVE | AND | HAVE NOT | ERNEST | HEMINGWAY | NEW YORK | CHARLES SCRIBNER'S SONS

8 x 5 3/8. Published August 15, 1966, at $1.65, as No. SL 132 in the Scribner Library Contemporary Classics series. Issued in stiff paper covers. Front cover: [in white on a green horizontal strip:] ERNEST | HEMINGWAY | [in orange at the top of a painting by James and Ruth McCrea:] To Have and | Have Not. The white backstrip and back cover are printed in black, gray, and gray-green.

COLLATION: [i]-[viii] + [1]-[264]. The same pagination as the first edition. See (A14A).

NOTE: The artists' surname is misspelled "McCrae" in the notice of copyright, on p. [vi], for the cover painting by James and Ruth McCrea.

7 The Short Stories

F. First paperback edition:
THE SHORT | STORIES | of Ernest Hemingway | [ornament] | NEW YORK | CHARLES SCRIBNER'S SONS

8 x 5 3/8. Published August 15, 1967, at $2.95, as No. SL 141 of the Scribner Library Omnibus Volumes series. Issued in stiff paper covers printed in bands of gold and olive-green. Lettered in white and black on the front cover and backstrip.

COLLATION: [i]-viii + [1]-[504]. Same pagination as the 1954 uniform edition, see (A16D).

CONTENTS: Same stories as in *The Fifth Column and the First Forty-nine Stories*, see (A16A).

NOTE: The dialogue between the two waiters in "A Clean, Well-

Lighted Place" has been emended, on p. 381/lines 4 and 5, to read: "His niece looks after him. You said she cut him down." | "I know." This editorial correction was previously made in the June 1965 printing of the uniform edition of this collection (Scribner's code "H-6.65"). It had been suggested by John V. Hagopian in "Tidying Up Hemingway's 'Clean Well-Lighted Place,'" *Studies in Short Fiction*, 1 (Winter 1964). For L. H. Brague's letter to Dr. Hagopian, regarding Scribner's decision to make this emendation, see *Studies in Short Fiction*, 1 (Summer 1964), ii. For Nathaniel M. Ewell's suggestion that further corrections are necessary, see "Dialogue in Hemingway's 'A Clean, Well-Lighted Place,'" *Fitzgerald/Hemingway Annual: 1971*. Essays and notes regarding the illogical sequence of the dialogue are listed in a footnote to Ewell's article, on p. 306. For Scott MacDonald's arguments for reverting to Hemingway's original text, see "The Confusing Dialogue in Hemingway's 'A Clean, Well-Lighted Place': A Final Word?" *Studies in American Fiction*, 1 (Spring 1973).

8 Across the River and Into the Trees

E. Second paperback edition:
ACROSS THE RIVER | AND | INTO THE TREES | BY | *ERNEST HEMINGWAY* | *CHARLES SCRIBNER'S SONS* | *NEW YORK*

8 x 5 3/8. Published January 28, 1970, at $1.95, as No. SL 202 in the Scribner Library Contemporary Classics series. Issued in stiff paper covers. Front cover: [in white on a Venetian-red horizontal strip:] ERNEST | HEMINGWAY | [in black at the top of a painting by James and Ruth McCrea:] Across the River | and into the Trees. The white backstrip and back cover are printed in black, gray, and light brown.

COLLATION: [i]-[xii] + 1-308. Same pagination as the first edition. See (A23A). Scribner's code "A-1.70 [C]," Library of Congress catalog card number, and SBN numbers are on the copyright page, p. [vi].

9 The Old Man and the Sea

F. Second paperback edition:
THE | OLD MAN | AND | THE SEA | ERNEST HEMING-WAY | [publisher's device encircled by:] [dot] BANTAM BOOKS [dot] TORONTO NEW YORK LONDON

7 x 4 1/4. Published in September 1965, by Bantam Books, Inc., in New York, at sixty cents, as A Bantam Sixty, No. H 3136. Issued in

blue-green stiff paper covers with an illustration of a fisherman on the front cover.

COLLATION: [i]-[viii] + 1-118 + [119]-[120]. The last leaf is blank.

NOTE: The printing history on the copyright page lists twenty-eight printings for the Scribner edition, as of April 1965.

G. Paperback school edition:

The Old Man and The Sea | *ERNEST HEMINGWAY* | [drawing] | CHARLES SCRIBNER'S SONS [dot] NEW YORK

8 x 5 3/8. Published January 18, 1968, at $1.20, as No. SSP 6 in the Scribner School Paperbacks series. Issued in green stiff paper covers, lettered in black and white, with a painting by Victor Mays extending over the front and back covers and the backstrip.

COLLATION: [i]-[iv] + [1]-[124], as follows: [i] half title; [ii] blank; [iii] title page as above; [iv] notices of copyright for the text, study guide, and cover painting, reservation of rights, Scribner's code "A-1.68 [M]," and note of origin; [1] dedication; [2] blank; [3] half title; [4] blank; 5-94 text; [95] *STUDY GUIDE* | *by* | MARY A. CAMPBELL; [96] blank; 97-111 text of the study guide; [112] blank; 113-118 NOTES ON THE TEXT; 119-121 QUESTIONS FOR STUDY AND DISCUSSION; 122 THE NOVEL AS A WHOLE—TOPICS FOR DISCUSSION AND WRITING; 123 BOOKS ABOUT HEMINGWAY; [124] blank.

NOTE: For the hard-cover edition of this book, see (A24D).

NOTE: A Canadian school edition was published in Toronto by S. J. Reginald Saunders, in November 1961. Issued in light-blue cloth, lettered and illustrated in blue and black on the front cover and backstrip. The collation is the same as the first American edition, see (A24D), except for p. [2], opposite the title page. Instead of being blank, it reads: *STUDY GUIDE* | *by* MARY A. CAMPBELL, M. A. | HEAD OF THE ENGLISH DEPARTMENT | PARK-DALE COLLEGIATE INSTITUTE | TORONTO. For a more detailed description, see William White's article in *Hemingway notes*, III (Spring 1973), 14-15.

H. Large-type edition:

[Drawing] | The Old Man | and the Sea | BY ERNEST HEMING-WAY | ILLUSTRATED EDITION | CHARLES SCRIBNER'S SONS | *New York*

11 x 8 1/2. Published June 15, 1968, at $6.95, as an aid to the visually handicapped. Illustrated by Raymond Sheppard and C. F. Tunnicliffe. Issued in beige cloth covers, lettered and illustrated on the front and back covers in beige, blue, green, and black, enclosed in a black border.

COLLATION: [1]-[140] + 2 blank leaves, as follows: [1] blank; [2]

Books by; [3] half title and drawing; [4] frontispiece drawing; [5] title page as above; [6] notice of copyright, reservation of rights, Scribner's code "A-5.68 [c]," and note of origin; [7] dedication; [8] blank; [9] PUBLISHER'S NOTE on the drawings; [10] blank; 11-138 text; [139] drawing; [140]-[144] blank.

NOTE: *A Farewell to Arms* was also published in a large-type edition, see (S-A3R).

NOTE: There is a descriptive error in A24A. All edges are trimmed in Scribner's first edition of *OMATS*. It is the Book-of-the-Month Club edition that has untrimmed fore edges. See John M. Meador's "Addendum to Hanneman: Hemingway's *The Old Man and the Sea*," *Papers of the Bibliographical Society of America*, LXVII, iv (Oct.-Dec. 1973), 455. Also, Meador's comparison of the book club edition with Scribner's first on the Hinman collator showed two different typesettings. Additional information is given on the two states of the dust jacket, and textual changes are noted.

NOTE: An abridged version of *The Old Man and the Sea* was published in English as a textbook for Dutch students, in Amsterdam, in 1955, by J. M. Meulenhoff. 72 pages. Adapted, with a 16-page "Vocabulary," by J. M. Terlingen. A description of the eighth edition, 1966, is given by William White in the *Papers of the Bibliographical Society of America*, LXII (Oct.-Dec. 1968), 613-614. The book was also published in English in Amsterdam, in 1964, by Van Ditmar. 127 pages. 6 1/2 x 4 1/8.

NOTE: *The Old Man and the Sea* was published in Moscow, in 1963, with the text in English and the introduction, by R. Samarin, in Russian. The introduction, "Ernest Kheminguei i ego *Starik i more*" [EH and his *OMATS*], is on pp. 3-19. Reissued in 1967 and 1969. The book was also published in Moscow, in [1970?], by Nakladatelstvi Progress, with the text in English and the introduction, by Radoslav Nenadal, and the commentary, by Vladimir Varecha, in Czech. 128 pages.

10 The Collected Poems

D. Fourth pirated edition:
ORIGINALLY | PUBLISHED IN PARIS | The | COLLECTED | POEMS | of | Ernest Hemingway | PIRATED EDITION | SAN FRANCISCO | 1960

9 x 6. According to the publisher's catalogue, published by Haskell House, in New York, in [1967?], as No. MS44 of the Monograph Series, at $1.95. Issued in slick gray stiff paper covers. A duplication of the title page is printed in black on the front cover.

COLLATION: [1]-28 + 2 blank leaves. The same pagination as A26c, except for the addition of two blank leaves at the end of the pamphlet. The title page is identical to A26c.

CONTENTS: [Part One:] ULTIMATELY | THE LADY POET WITH FOOTNOTES | THE AGE DEMANDED | THE ERNEST LIBERAL'S LAMENT | THE SOUL OF SPAIN | NEO-THOMIST POEM. [Part Two:] MITRAIGLIATRICE | OKLA-HOMA | CAPTIVES | CHAMPS D'HONNEUR | RIPARTO D'ASSALTO | MONTPARNASSE | OILY WEATHER | T. ROOSEVELT | ALONG WITH YOUTH | CHAPTER HEADING | VALENTINE. Note: The poems in the second pirated edition (A26B) and in all subsequent editions are in this order.

E. First hard-cover edition:
ORIGINALLY | PUBLISHED IN PARIS | The | COLLECTED | POEMS | of | Ernest Hemingway | PIRATED EDITION | SAN FRANCISCO | 1960 | [publisher's device] | HASKELL HOUSE PUBLISHERS Ltd. | *Publishers of Scarce Scholarly Books* | NEW YORK, N.Y. 10012 | 1970

8 3/8 x 5 1/2. Published as No. 150 in the American Literature Series, at $3.95. Issued in pink-violet cloth covers, stamped in gold on the backstrip only. Backstrip, reading downward: COLLECTED POEMS Hemingway.

COLLATION: [i]-[ii] + [1]-[30], as follows: [i] half title; [ii] frontispiece: drawing of Hemingway by [John Blomshield]; [1] title page as above; [2] notice of first publication in 1960, publisher's address, Library of Congress catalog card number, SBN number, and note of origin; [3] blank; [4] designed by Brayton; [5] contents; [6] blank; [7] divisional title; [8] blank; 9-16 text; [17] divisional title; 18-28 text; [29]-[30] blank.

NOTE: The first ten lines of the title page are identical to A26c.

F. Reprint paperback edition:
ORIGINALLY | PUBLISHED IN PARIS | The | COLLECTED | POEMS | of | Ernest Hemingway | Gordon Press | NEW YORK | 1972

9 x 6. Published May 2, 1972, in the American Poets Series, at $2.25. Issued in white stiff paper covers, with a duplication of the first seven lines of the title page printed in black on the front cover.

COLLATION: [1]-28 + 2 blank leaves, as follows: [1] half title; [2] frontispiece: photograph of Hemingway; [3] title page as above; [4] ISBN and Library of Congress catalog card numbers, publisher's address, and note of origin; [5] contents; [6] blank; [7] divisional title; [8] blank; 9-16 text; [17] divisional title; 18-28 text; and two blank leaves.

NOTE: The frontispiece is a photograph of Hemingway in the court-

yard of 113 rue Notre Dame des Champs, in 1924. This photograph
is No. 45 in Carlos Baker's *EH: A Life Story.*

NOTE: Placement of the page numbers indicates that the plates for
the third pirated edition (A26c) were used for the first three editions
listed here.

G. Reprint hard-cover edition:

NUMBER ONE OF | The Library of Living Poetry | THE COL-
LECTED POEMS | *of* | Ernest Hemingway [the title and au-
thor's name are enclosed in a ruled border with a thick second rule
at the top and a broken thick rule and ornamental design at the bot-
tom] | ORIGINALLY | PUBLISHED IN PARIS

8 x 5 3/8. Published by [Ridgeway Books, in Philadelphia, in 1971],
at $4.00. Issued in black "library binding," stamped in gold on the
backstrip only. Backstrip, reading downward: THE COLLECTED
POEMS OF HEMINGWAY.

COLLATION: 24 unnumbered pages, plus two blank leaves in the
front and two blank leaves at the end of the book. Identical with
the second pirated edition (A26B), except for the larger page size, the
four blank leaves, and the omission of the photograph on the back
cover of the pamphlet, leaving p. [24] blank. The front cover of the
pamphlet serves as the title page in this edition.

NOTE: A variant copy of the pamphlet, titled *The Suppressed Poems
of Ernest Hemingway,* in the collection of Stanley Carlin, of Melrose, Massachusetts, is described by William White in *American
Notes & Queries,* VII (May 1969). Professor White notes that this
copy, possibly unique, differs from the second pirated edition
(A26B) in title, size (it is 6 3/4 x 4 3/4), and the addition of a white
margin around the photograph on the back cover. The poems are
in the same order as the second edition. See the correction under
(S-A10D).

11 Three Novels of Ernest Hemingway

B. Paperback edition:

THREE NOVELS OF ERNEST HEMINGWAY | *The Sun Also
Rises* | WITH AN INTRODUCTION BY | MALCOLM COW-
LEY | *A Farewell to Arms* | WITH AN INTRODUCTION BY
| ROBERT PENN WARREN | *The Old Man and the Sea* | WITH
AN INTRODUCTION BY | CARLOS BAKER | CHARLES
SCRIBNER'S SONS | [graduated line] | NEW YORK

8 x 5 3/8. Published August 17, 1972, at $4.95, as No. SL 394 of the
Scribner Library Contemporary Classics series. Issued in stiff paper
covers printed in yellow and gray bands lettered in black and white.

COLLATION: [752] pages (each of the three novels is folioed separately). Same pagination as the first edition. See (A29A). Scribner's code "A.8-72 [C]" is on the copyright page, p. [iv].

12 The Wild Years

B. Second paperback edition:
THE WILD YEARS | *ERNEST HEMINGWAY* | *Edited and Introduced by* GENE Z. HANRAHAN | A DELL BOOK

7 x 4 1/4. Published by Dell Publishing Co., Inc., New York, in September 1967, at seventy-five cents, as Dell No. 3577. Issued in white stiff paper covers printed in red and black. Front cover: DELL [dot] 3577 [dot] 75¢ | THE GREATEST EVER | UNDER THE BY-LINE—[first three lines in black] | ERNEST | HEM-INGWAY [author's name in red] | THE WILD YEARS [in black] [a photograph of Hemingway is between, and partially covered by, the last two lines]. All edges stained blue.

COLLATION: [1]-288. Same pagination and contents as the first edition. Contains seventy-three articles from the *Toronto Star Weekly* and the *Toronto Daily Star*. See (A30).

NOTE: A notice on the copyright page, p. [iv], states: New Edition. The plates for the first edition were apparently used; the only discernible differences are the larger size, the new cover, and the higher price.

13 A Moveable Feast

C. Second paperback edition:
ERNEST HEMINGWAY | *A Moveable Feast* | [ornament] | If you are lucky enough to have lived | in Paris as a young man, then wherever you | go for the rest of your life, it stays with | you, for Paris is a moveable feast. | ERNEST HEMINGWAY | *to a friend, 1950* | CHARLES SCRIBNER'S SONS, *New York*

8 x 5 3/8. Published February 4, 1971, at $2.95, as No. SL 260 of the Scribner Library Contemporary Classics series. Issued in stiff paper covers. Front cover: [on a gray horizontal strip:] [in white:] ERNEST | HEMINGWAY | [in yellow:] A Moveable Feast [in blue in two lines:] Sketches of the Author's | Life in Paris in the Twenties | [painting of Pont Neuf, Paris, by Hildegard Rath]. The painting on the front cover appeared on the dust jacket of the first edition. The white backstrip and back cover are printed in black, gray, and blue.

COLLATION: [i]-[xii] + [1]-[212] + 4 leaves. Same pagination as the first edition, see (A31A), except for the addition of four blank leaves at the end of the book. Scribner's code "A-1.71 [C]" and the SBN number are on the copyright page, p. [vi].

NOTE: The title page of this edition is identical to the first edition. The second appearance of Hemingway's name should have been in small capital letters in the transcription of the title page under A31A. NOTE: The omitted part of a sentence on p. 198 in the first edition has been included in this edition, on p. 198/line 28. On p. 199/line 10, Tchagguns has been changed to Tschagguns. It remains Tchagguns on line 13.

NOTE: Carlos Baker notes in *EH: A Life Story*, p. 588, that there is reason to believe that in preparing the manuscript for *AMF* material was transposed on p. 125, so that Hemingway seemed to be saying that Ernest Walsh was one of the editors of the *Dial*, "whereas the reference to 'this quarterly' (line 11) was actually to *This Quarter*, of which (as EH well knew) Walsh was 'one of the editors.'"

NOTE: The first paperback edition was reissued by Bantam Books, Inc., October 1, 1970, at $1.25. Seventh printing. Issued in white stiff paper covers, lettered in black, with a red, black, and white photomontage of Paris on the front cover. See (A31B).

14 By-Line: Ernest Hemingway

A. First edition:

BY-LINE: | ERNEST | HEMINGWAY | [long rule] | *Selected Articles and Dispatches of Four Decades* | EDITED BY WILLIAM WHITE | CHARLES SCRIBNER'S SONS [dot] NEW YORK

6 x 9. Published May 8, 1967, at $8.95. Issued in red cloth with the author's signature stamped in black on the front cover. Backstrip, reading downward: BY-LINE: ERNEST HEMINGWAY [in gold on a black background] | [gold rule running length of backstrip to:] SCRIBNERS [in black letters]. Scribner's device stamped in gold on back cover. All edges trimmed. Black endpapers.

COLLATION: 1 leaf + [i]-[xvi] + [1]-[494], as follows: blank; BOOKS BY; [i] half title; [ii] blank; [iii] title page as above; [iv] notices of copyright, notice of simultaneous publication in Canada, reservation of rights, Scribner's code "A-3.67 [V]," note of origin, and Library of Congress catalog card number; v-x Contents; xi-xiv Hemingway needs no introduction . . . by WILLIAM WHITE | FRANKLIN VILLAGE, MICHIGAN | *February 16, 1967*; [xv] half title; [xvi] blank; [1] divisional title: ONE | [decoration] *Reporting, 1920-1924*; [2] blank; [3]-478 text; [479] INDEX; [480] blank; 481-489 index; [490]-[494] blank.

CONTENTS: Part One: Reporting, 1920-1924

    pp. 3-4: "Circulating Pictures," *TSW* (Feb. 14, 1920). See (C33).

pp. 5-8: "A Free Shave," *TSW* (March 6, 1920). See (C34).

pp. 9-12: "The Best Rainbow Trout Fishing," *TSW* (Aug. 28, 1920). See (C47).

pp. 13-15: "Plain and Fancy Killings, $400 Up," *TSW* (Dec. 11, 1920). See (C53).

pp. 16-17: "Tuna Fishing in Spain," *TSW* (Feb. 18, 1922). See (C63).

pp. 18-19: "The Hotels in Switzerland," *TSW* (March 4, 1922). See (C67₁).

pp. 20-22: "The Swiss Luge," *TSW* (March 18, 1922). See (C70₁).

pp. 23-25: "American Bohemians in Paris," *TSW* (March 25, 1922). See (C72₁).

pp. 26-29: "Genoa Conference," *TDS* (April 13, 1922). See (C77).

pp. 30-32: "Russian Girls at Genoa," *TDS* (April 24, 1922). See (C80).

pp. 33-35: "Fishing the Rhone Canal," *TDS* (June 10, 1922). See (C92).

pp. 36-40: "German Inn-Keepers," *TDS* (Sept. 5, 1922). See (C102).

pp. 41-44: "A Paris-to-Strasbourg Flight," *TDS* (Sept. 9, 1922). See (C103).

pp. 45-48: "German Inflation," *TDS* (Sept. 19, 1922). See (C104).

pp. 49-50: "Hamid Bey," *TDS* (Oct. 9, 1922). See (C108).

pp. 51-52: "A Silent, Ghastly Procession," *TDS* (Oct. 20, 1922). See (C112).

pp. 53-55: " 'Old Constan,' " *TDS* (Oct. 28, 1922). See (C116).

pp. 56-60: "Refugees from Thrace," *TDS* (Nov. 14, 1922). See (C120).

pp. 61-65: "Mussolini: Biggest Bluff in Europe," *TDS* (Jan. 27, 1923). See (C122).

pp. 66-69: "A Russian Toy Soldier," *TDS* (Feb. 10, 1923). See (C123).

pp. 70-75: "Getting into Germany," *TDS* (May 2, 1923). See (C130).

pp. 76-82: "King Business in Europe," *TSW* (Sept. 15, 1923). See (C135).

pp. 83-89: "Japanese Earthquake," *TDS* (Sept. 25, 1923). See (C136₂).

pp. 90-98: "Bull Fighting a Tragedy," *TSW* (Oct. 20, 1923). See (C143).

pp. 99-108: "Pamplona in July," *TSW* (Oct. 27, 1923). See (C144).

pp. 109-114: "Trout Fishing in Europe," *TSW* (Nov. 17, 1923). See (C146₁).

pp. 115-119: "Inflation and the German Mark," *TSW* (Dec. 8, 1923). See (C149).

pp. 120-123: "War Medals for Sale," *TSW* (Dec. 8, 1923). See (C149₁).

pp. 124-131: "Christmas on the Roof of the World," *TSW* (Dec. 22, 1923). See (C151₁).

pp. 132-133: "Conrad, Optimist and Moralist," *Transatlantic Review* (Oct. 1924). See (C160₁).

Part Two: *Esquire*, 1933-1936

pp. 137-143: "Marlin off the Morro: A Cuban Letter," *Esquire* (Autumn 1933). See (C209).

pp. 144-152: "The Friend of Spain: A Spanish Letter," *Esquire* (Jan. 1934). See (C215).

pp. 153-158: "A Paris Letter," *Esquire* (Feb. 1934). See (C216).

pp. 159-161: "A.D. in Africa: A Tanganyika Letter" (Nairobi, January 18, 1934), *Esquire* (April 1934). See (C218).

pp. 162-166: "Shootism versus Sport: The Second Tanganyika Letter," *Esquire* (June 1934). See (C219).

pp. 167-172: "Notes on Dangerous Game: The Third Tanganyika Letter," *Esquire* (July 1934). See (C220).

pp. 172-178: "Out in the Stream: A Cuban Letter," *Esquire* (Aug. 1934). See (C221).

pp. 179-185: "Old Newsman Writes: A Letter from Cuba," *Esquire* (Dec. 1934). See (C224).

pp. 186-191: "Remembering Shooting-Flying: A Key West Letter," *Esquire* (Feb. 1935). See (C227).

pp. 192-197: "The Sights of Whitehead Street: A Key West Letter," *Esquire* (April 1935). See (C229).

pp. 198-204: "On Being Shot Again: A Gulf Stream Letter," *Esquire* (June 1935). See (C232).

pp. 205-212: "Notes on the Next War: A Serious Topical Letter," *Esquire* (Sept. 1935). See (C235).

pp. 213-220: "Monologue to the Maestro: A High Seas Letter," *Esquire* (Oct. 1935). See (C237).

pp. 221-228: "The Malady of Power: A Second Serious Letter," *Esquire* (Nov. 1935). See (C238).

pp. 229-235: "Wings Always over Africa: An Ornithological Letter," *Esquire* (Jan. 1936). See (C240).

pp. 236-244: "On the Blue Water: A Gulf Stream Letter," *Esquire* (April 1936). See (C243).

pp. 245-254: "There She Breaches! *or* Moby Dick off the Morro," *Esquire* (May 1936). See (C244).

Part Three: Spanish Civil War, 1937-1939

pp. 257-258: "The First Glimpses of War," NANA dispatch (March 18, 1937). See (C255).

pp. 259-261: "Shelling of Madrid," NANA dispatch (April 11, 1937).

pp. 262-267: "A New Kind of War," NANA dispatch (April 14, 1937). Note: The NANA dispatch of this title, entered as C260, is the same dispatch published in the *New York Times* (April 25, 1937), entered as C261.

pp. 268-274: "The Chauffeurs of Madrid," NANA dispatch (May 22, 1937). See (C264).

pp. 275-276: "A Brush with Death," NANA dispatch (Sept. 30, 1937). See (C271).

pp. 277-280: "The Fall of Teruel," NANA dispatch (Dec. 23, 1937). See (C275).

pp. 281-283: "The Flight of Refugees," NANA dispatch (April 13, 1938). See (C280).

pp. 284-286: "Bombing of Tortosa," NANA dispatch (April 15, 1938). See (C286).

pp. 287-289: "Tortosa Calmly Awaits Assault," NANA dispatch (April 18, 1938). See (C287).

pp. 290-293: "A Program for U.S. Realism," *Ken* (Aug. 11, 1938). See (C303).

pp. 294-297: "Fresh Air on an Inside Story," *Ken* (Sept. 22, 1938). See (C306).

pp. 298-300: "The Clark's Fork Valley, Wyoming," *Vogue* (Feb. 1939). See (C312).

Part Four: World War II

pp. 303-314: "Hemingway Interviewed by Ralph Ingersoll," *PM* (June 9, 1941). See (H481). Note: William White explains in a prefatory note, on p. 303, that this interview served as an introduction to Hemingway's seven articles on the Far East. "It was corrected and revised by Hemingway after having been transcribed and hence might be called an authenticated interview."

pp. 315-319: "Russo-Japanese Pact," *PM* (June 10, 1941). See (C320).

pp. 320-322: "Rubber Supplies in Dutch East Indies," *PM* (June 11, 1941). See (C321).

pp. 323-324: "Japan Must Conquer China," *PM* (June 13, 1941). See (C322).

pp. 325-328: "U.S. Aid to China," *PM* (June 15, 1941). See (C323).

pp. 329-331: "Japan's Position in China," *PM* (June 16, 1941). See (C324).

pp. 332-334: "China's Air Needs," *PM* (June 17, 1941). See (C325).

pp. 335-339: "Chinese Build Air Field," *PM* (June 18, 1941). See (C326).

pp. 340-355: "Voyage to Victory," *Collier's* (July 22, 1944). See (C330).

pp. 356-363: "London Fights the Robots," *Collier's* (Aug. 19, 1944). See (C331).

pp. 364-373: "Battle for Paris," *Collier's* (Sept. 30, 1944). See (C332).

pp. 374-383: "How We Came to Paris," *Collier's* (Oct. 7, 1944). See (C334).

pp. 384-391: "The G.I. and the General," *Collier's* (Nov. 4, 1944). See (C335).

pp. 392-400: "War in the Siegfried Line," *Collier's* (Nov. 18, 1944). See (C336).

Part Five: After the Wars, 1949-1956

pp. 403-416: "The Great Blue River," *Holiday* (July 1949). See (C351).

pp. 417-424: "The Shot," *True* (April 1951). See (C363).

pp. 425-469: "The Christmas Gift," *Look* (April 20, 1954) and (May 4, 1954). See (C381).

pp. 470-478: "A Situation Report," *Look* (Sept. 4, 1956). See (C395).

NOTE: William White notes in his introduction, on p. xiv, that where he has shortened the title of an article, he has included the original headline in the table of contents. He also notes that he has "corrected obvious misspellings and typographical errors, regularized capitalization and some punctuation. These are accepted practices for a reading text."

NOTE: In "Errors in *By-Line: Ernest Hemingway*," *American Book Collector*, XVIII (June 1968), 28, William White lists three errors in this book: on p. xii/line 15, "before" should be "during"; on p. 267/line 19, "as what Jay Raven" should be "as that what Jay Raven"; on p. 436/line 5, "incidently" should be "incidentally."

NOTE: The dust jacket, designed by Victor Mays, is white, red, and black with sketches of various modes of transportation on the front cover. Four quotations from the book, under the heading: ERNEST HEMINGWAY OBSERVES, appear on the back cover. The date APR. '67 appears on the front flap. A list of Hemingway's books is on the reverse of the dust jacket.

PRINTING HISTORY: Second printing in May 1967. Third printing in June 1967. With its third printing, copies in print totaled 45,000 according to *Publishers' Weekly*, CXCII (Aug. 7, 1967), 112.

NOTE: *By-Line* was on the *Publishers' Weekly* nonfiction Best-Sellers list from June 26, 1967 to August 7, 1967.

NOTE: Scribner's distributed an eight-page promotional booklet containing nineteen short excerpts from *By-Line*. 6 x 9. Issued in white stiff paper covers printed in red and black. A photograph of Hemingway during the Spanish Civil War, by Robert Capa, is on the back cover.

NOTE: A Literary Guild edition was published in 1967. 5 1/2 x 8 1/4. The binding, title page, and pagination are the same as the first edition. The dust jacket is identical except for the notation on the lower right corner of the front flap: *Book Club* | 594 *Edition.*

B. Paperback edition:

BY-LINE: | ERNEST | HEMINGWAY | [single-ruled line under Hemingway] | SELECTED ARTICLES AND DISPATCHES OF | FOUR DECADES EDITED BY WILLIAM WHITE | [publisher's device encircled by:] [dot] BANTAM BOOKS [dot] TORONTO NEW YORK LONDON 7 x 4 1/8. Published in July 1968, by Bantam Books, Inc., in New York, at $1.25. No. Q3788. Issued in white stiff paper covers lettered in black. Drawings of Hemingway and characters from the movie versions of his novels in pale brown, pink, and orange on the front cover, backstrip, and back cover. All edges stained yellow.

COLLATION: [i]-[xviii] + [1]-[430], as follows: [i]-[iii] excerpts from reviews of the hard-cover edition; [iv] blank; [v] title page as above; [vi] note regarding the printing from new plates: NOT ONE WORD HAS BEEN OMITTED, arrangement for publication, printing history, notices of copyright, reservation of rights, publisher's address, and note of origin; vii-xii Contents; xiii-xvii Hemingway needs no introduction . . . WILLIAM WHITE | FRANKLIN VILLAGE, MICHIGAN | *February 16, 1967*; [xviii] blank; [1] divisional title; [2] blank; 3-419 text; [420] blank; 421-428 index; [429] ad for Bantam Book edition of *AMF*; [430] ad for BANTAM BEST SELLERS (including *By-Line*).

NOTE: Reissued by Bantam Books, October 1, 1970, at $1.25.

15 The Fifth Column and Four Stories of the Spanish Civil War

A. First edition:

The | Fifth Column | and Four Stories | of the Spanish Civil War | [ornament] | ERNEST HEMINGWAY | CHARLES SCRIBNER'S SONS [dot] NEW YORK
8 1/4 x 5 1/2. Published August 13, 1969, at $4.95. Issued in red-orange cloth with the author's signature in gold on the front cover. Printed in gold on the backstrip, reading downward: [in two lines:] Ernest | Hemingway [ornament] [in two lines:] The Fifth Column | AND FOUR STORIES OF THE SPANISH CIVIL WAR SCRIBNERS. All edges trimmed.

COLLATION: [i]-[vi] + [1]-[154], as follows: [i] half title; [ii] *Books by*; [iii] title page as above; [iv] notices of copyright, reservation of rights, Scribner's code "A-8.69 (C)," note of origin, and Library of Congress catalog card number; [v] CONTENTS; [vi] blank; [1] half title; [2] blank; 3-151 text; [152]-[154] blank.

CONTENTS: *The Fifth Column*, "The Denunciation," "The Butterfly and the Tank," "Night Before Battle," and "Under the Ridge."

PREVIOUS PUBLICATION: The four stories are collected for the first time. Two of the stories, "The Denunciation" and "Night Before Battle," appear for the first time in book form. For previous publication of *The Fifth Column*, see (A16) and (A17). "The Denunciation" first appeared in *Esquire*, x (Nov. 1938), see (C307). "The Butterfly and the Tank" first appeared in *Esquire*, x (Dec. 1938), see (C308). For first book publication, see (B58). "Night Before Battle" first appeared in *Esquire*, xi (Feb. 1939), see (C311). "Under the Ridge" first appeared in *Cosmopolitan*, cvii (Oct. 1939), see (C317). For first book publication, see (B37).

NOTE: The black dust jacket, designed by Michèle Maldeau, is printed in red, white, and black. The title on the front cover reads: THE | FIFTH | COLUMN | and four unpublished | stories of the | Spanish Civil War. (The stories were, of course, uncollected not unpublished.) There is a photograph of Hemingway on the back cover with an inscription below it in his handwriting: Ernest Hemingway | Madrid | May 1937.

NOTE: Second printing in September 1969, third printing in November 1969. An item in *Publishers' Weekly*, cxcvi (Sept. 15, 1969), 49, reported that a second printing was ordered prior to publication date. "There are now 15,000 copies in print."

B. First paperback edition:

THE FIFTH | COLUMN | and Four Stories | of the Spanish Civil War | [ruled line under the fourth line of type] | ERNEST HEMINGWAY | [publisher's device encircled by:] [dot] BANTAM BOOKS [dot] TORONTO NEW YORK LONDON | A NATIONAL GENERAL COMPANY

7 x 4 3/16. Published by Bantam Books, Inc., in New York, in October 1970, at $1.25. No. Q5645. Issued in white stiff paper covers, lettered in black with a photograph in color on the front cover.

COLLATION: [i]-[viii] + [1]-[216], as follows: [i] brief excerpts from reviews of the hard-cover edition; [ii] Bantam Books by Ernest Hemingway; [iii] title page as above; [iv] note regarding the reprinting from new plates: NOT ONE WORD HAS BEEN OMITTED, arrangement for publication, printing history, notices of copyright, reservation of rights, address of the publisher, and note of origin; [v] CONTENTS; [vi] blank; [vii] half title; [viii] blank; [1] THE FIFTH COLUMN; [2] blank; 3-215 text; [216]

advertisement for books by and about Hemingway published by Bantam Books.

c. Second paperback edition:
The | Fifth Column | and Four Stories | of the Spanish Civil War | [ornament] | ERNEST HEMINGWAY | CHARLES SCRIBNER'S SONS [dot] NEW YORK
8 x 5 3/8. Published February 14, 1972, at $2.45, as No. SL 329 of the Scribner Library Contemporary Classics series. Issued in stiff paper covers. Front cover: [in white on a blue horizontal strip:] ERNEST | HEMINGWAY | [in orange at the top of a painting by James and Ruth McCrea:] The Fifth Column | and Four Stories of | the Spanish Civil War. The white backstrip and back cover are printed in black, white, gray, and blue.
COLLATION: [i]-[vi] + [1]-[154]. Same pagination as the first edition. Scribner's code "A-1.72 [M]" and SBN numbers are on the copyright page, p. [iv].
NOTE: The title page of this edition is identical to the first edition.

16 Ernest Hemingway, Cub Reporter

A. First edition:
ERNEST | HEMINGWAY, | CUB | REPORTER | [next four lines in single-ruled box:] *Kansas* | *City* | *Star* | Stories | Edited by | MATTHEW J. BRUCCOLI | University of | Pittsburgh Press
8 x 5 1/2. Published May 4, 1970, at $4.95. Issued in dark gray cloth, stamped in bronze on the backstrip only. Backstrip, reading downward: Bruccoli ERNEST HEMINGWAY, CUB REPORTER Pittsburgh. All edges trimmed. A fold-out facsimile (7 3/4 x 14 1/2) of the *Kansas City Star* style sheet for 1925 is pasted onto the loose end paper facing the back cover.
COLLATION: [i]-[xiv] + [1]-66, as follows: [i] half title; [ii] facsimile: The *Kansas City Star* assignment sheet for 3 January 1918 showing Hemingway's daily routine; [iii] title page as above; [iv] ISBN number, Library of Congress card number, notice of copyright, note of origin, and acknowledgments for illustrations; [v] dedication; [vi] blank; [vii] Hemingway is quoted, regarding his newspaper work versus his creative writing, from Louis Henry Cohn's *A Bibliography of the Works of Ernest Hemingway*, p. 112, followed by a note by the editor; [viii] blank; [ix] Contents; [x] blank; xi-xiii Preface by the editor; [xiv] blank; [1] half title; [2] blank; 3-11 "With Hemingway Before *A Farewell to Arms*" by Theodore Brumback, excerpt from the *K.C. Star* (Dec. 6, 1936); [12] blank; [13] half title; [14] blank; 15-58 text; [59] half title for Appendices; [60] blank; 61-66 Appendices.

CONTENTS: The *Kansas City Star* Stories: "Kerensky, the Fighting Flea" (Dec. 16, 1917). See (S-C2). "Battle of Raid Squads" (Jan. 6, 1918). See (S-C3). "At the End of the Ambulance Run" (Jan. 20, 1918). See (S-C4). "Throng at Smallpox Case" (Feb. 18, 1918). See (S-C5). "Laundry Car Over Cliff" (March 6, 1918). "Six Men Become Tankers" (April 17, 1918). "Big Day for Navy Drive" (April 17, 1918). "Navy Desk Jobs to Go" (April 18, 1918). "Would 'Treat 'Em Rough'" (April 18, 1918). "Recruits for the Tanks" (April 18, 1918). "Dare Devil Joins Tanks" (April 21, 1918). "Mix War, Art and Dancing" (April 21, 1918). See (S-C9). Appendices: Possible Hemingway Stories.

NOTE: The facsimile, on p. 20, of a portion of page one of the *K.C. Star* (Jan. 6, 1918) is reproduced on the front cover of the limited edition.

NOTE: For information on the type face of this edition, see the colophon of the limited edition.

NOTE: The dust jacket, designed by Gary Gore, is white with black, red, and gold lettering and drawing. A black-and-white photograph of Hemingway is incorporated in the drawing.

NOTE: 200 copies of a limited edition were published by the University of Pittsburgh Press, at $15.00. The size, title page, and pagination are the same as the trade edition. Issued in dark gray back cover and backstrip over brown front cover. The lettering on the backstrip is identical to the trade edition. Ornamental design in bronze on the gray section of the front cover. A portion of page one of the *Kansas City Star* for January 6, 1918 is reproduced on the brown section of the front cover. This facsimile is also reproduced on p. 20. Tan end papers.

Colophon on the loose endpaper opposite p. 66: This limited printing of | ERNEST HEMINGWAY, CUB REPORTER | has been set in the Linotype | version of Times Roman, a type face | first cut for the *London Times*. | The printing was done directly from | the type on Warren's Olde Style | Antique Wove paper. | Of the 200 copies | specially printed and bound, | this is number | signed by the editor: | [decoration].

17 Islands in the Stream

A. First edition:

ISLANDS | IN THE | STREAM | Ernest Hemingway | New York | CHARLES SCRIBNER'S SONS

9 x 6. Published October 6, 1970, at $10.00. The first printing consisted of 75,000 copies. Issued in green cloth stamped in gold on the front cover and backstrip. Front cover: Author's signature stamped in gold in a blind-stamped oblong box. Backstrip, reading down-

ward in two lines: [in gold in a blind-stamped oblong box:] ISLANDS IN THE STREAM | [in gold on a black oblong box:] Ernest Hemingway [in gold:] *Scribners*. All edges trimmed. Yellow endpapers printed in green with a map, by Samuel H. Bryant, of Cuba and the Bimini Islands.

COLLATION: [i]-[x] + [1]-[470], as follows: [i] blank; [ii] Books by; [iii] half title; [iv] blank; [v] title page as above; [vi] notices of copyright of text and end paper map, reservation of rights, Scribner's code "A-9.70 (V)," note of origin, and Library of Congress catalog card number; [vii] NOTE regarding preparation of the manuscript by Mary Hemingway; [viii] blank; [ix] CONTENTS; [x] blank; [1] divisional title: Part I | BIMINI; [2] blank; 3-466 text; [467]-[470] blank.

NOTE: The NOTE on p. [vii] reads: Charles Scribner, Jr. and I worked together preparing this | book for publication from Ernest's original manuscript. Be- | yond the routine chores of correcting spelling and punctua- | tion, we made some cuts in the manuscript. I feeling that | Ernest would surely have made them himself. The book is | all Ernest's. We have added nothing to it. | MARY HEMINGWAY

NOTE: *Islands in the Stream* was written at intervals in 1946-1947 and 1950-1951. For dates of the composition of the three parts, see Carlos Baker's *EH: A Life Story*, p. 652, and *Hemingway: The Writer as Artist*, 4th edition, pp. 379-380. For information on the manuscripts and typescripts of the three parts of the book, see [No.] 17 "Sea Novel" in Philip Young and Charles Mann's *The Hemingway Manuscripts: An Inventory*, pp. 21-25. See (S-B11).

NOTE: Part I, "Bimini," on pp. 3-200, was originally titled "The Sea When Young." Another tentative title was "The Island and the Stream." A 34,000-word excerpt from Part I was published in *Esquire*, LXXIV (Oct. 1970). See (S-C64). Part II, "Cuba," on pp. 203-327, was originally titled "The Sea When Absent." A long excerpt from this section was published in *Cosmopolitan*, CLXX (March 1971). Part III, "At Sea," on pp. 331-466, was originally titled "The Sea-Chase." Hemingway read an excerpt from this section on Ernest Hemingway Reading, Caedmon Record, TC 1185, issued in 1965. See (F154). Fredric March read an excerpt at a reception at the White House, on April 29, 1962, for Nobel prize recipients. See (H1392). For a discussion of the original titles, see Carlos Baker's *Hemingway: The Writer as Artist*, 4th edition, pp. 381, 384.

NOTE: The green dust jacket, designed by Paul Bacon, is printed in black with a U.S. Coast and Geodetic Survey map of the Gulf Stream currents. It is lettered in yellow and white on the front cover and backstrip. A list of Hemingway's books is printed in black and green on the reverse side of the dust jacket.

NOTE: *Islands* was the "Special Fall Selection" of the Book-of-the-Month Club in October 1970. The front flap of the dust jacket has the notation: B-O-M-C Selection*. A footnote explains the trademark.

NOTE: *Islands* was on the Best-Seller list of the *N.Y. Times Book Review* for 24 weeks (Oct. 18, 1970 to March 28, 1971). It was in second place for ten weeks. It was in first place on the "Best sellers" list in *Publishers' Weekly*, CXCIX (Jan. 4, 1971), 82, with the comment: "New leader of fiction best sellers. Has sold over 100,000 copies. The *San Francisco Chronicle* reports it as the number 1 seller in the Bay Area." It was on *PW's* list for over six months (Oct. 26, 1970 to May 10, 1971).

B. First paperback edition:
ISLANDS | IN THE | STREAM | ERNEST HEMINGWAY | [publisher's device encircled by:] [dot] BANTAM BOOKS [dot] TORONTO NEW YORK LONDON | A NATIONAL GENERAL COMPANY
7 x 4 1/4. Published in February 1972 by Bantam Books, Inc., in New York, at $1.50. No. T6999. Issued in white stiff paper covers printed in brown, red, and pale yellow on the front cover, and lettered in black. A blurb about the book appears on the inside of the front and back covers.

COLLATION: [i]-[xii] + [1]-[436], as follows: [i]-[iii] brief excerpts from reviews of the hard-cover edition; [iv] Books by; [v] title page as above; [vi] note regarding the printing from new plates: NOT ONE WORD HAS BEEN OMITTED, arrangement for publication, printing history, notices of copyright for the text and the map, reservation of rights, publisher's address, and note of origin; [vii] NOTE by Mary Hemingway; [viii] blank; [ix] CONTENTS; [x]-[xi] map of Cuba and the Bimini Islands by Samuel H. Bryant; [xii] blank; [1] divisional title: Part 1 | BIMINI; [2] blank; 3-435 text; [436] blank.

NOTE: A special report on paperback sales in the *N.Y. Times Book Review* (Feb. 11, 1973), Part II, pp. 30-31, reported that Bantam Books had a print order of 900,000 copies of *Islands* for 1972.

18 Ernest Hemingway's Apprenticeship

A. First edition:
ERNEST | HEMINGWAY'S | APPRENTICE- | SHIP | Oak Park, 1916-1917 | Edited by | Matthew J. Bruccoli | [series device] *A Bruccoli Clark Book* [first eight lines enclosed in single-ruled box] | N C R [in white on gray squares] Microcard Editions [in gray]
9 x 6. Published July 2, 1971, at $6.95, by Microcard Editions, a

division of the National Cash Register Company, in Washington, D.C. Issued in blue-gray cloth, stamped in gold on the backstrip only. Backstrip, reading downward: ERNEST HEMINGWAY'S APPRENTICESHIP [small solid square] Bruccoli [in single-ruled joined squares:] N C R. All edges trimmed. Facsimile of the *Trapeze* for December 8, 1916 on front endpapers. Facsimile of the *Trapeze* for November 3, 1916 on back endpapers.

COLLATION: [i]-[xviii] + [1]-122, as follows: [i] half title; [ii] photograph: *Hemingway back from the war, 1919*; [iii] title page as above; [iv] notice of copyright, Library of Congress card number, ISBN number, note of origin, and address of publisher; [v] dedication; [vi] blank; [vii]-[viii] Contents; ix-xi Foreword by Russell J. Fuog, Superintendent, Oak Park and River Forest High School, Oak Park, Illinois; [xii] blank; xiii-xv Introduction by the editor; [xvi] photograph of Hemingway and list of his activities in high school reproduced from the *Senior Tabula* (June 1917); [xvii] Hemingway is briefly quoted from a letter to Charles Fenton; [xviii] blank; [1] half title; [2] blank; 3-117 text; 118-122 Appendix.

CONTENTS: Thirty-nine articles, editorials, and columns from the *Trapeze* (January 20, 1916 to May 25, 1917), and three short stories, five poems, and the class prophecy from the *Tabula* (February 1916 to June 1917). See (C1) to (C31). "Junior Debates," on p. 22, an editorial reprinted from the *Trapeze* (May 4, 1916), was omitted in *EH: A Comprehensive Bibliography*. See (S-C1). Facsimiles of full-pages of the *Trapeze* with articles by Hemingway: pp. 10-11: *Trapeze* (Feb. 10, 1916), p. 1. pp. 14-15: *Trapeze* (Feb. 17, 1916), p. 4. pp. 70-71: *Trapeze* (March 30, 1917), p. 1. pp. 74-75: *Trapeze* (April 20, 1917), p. 1. The Appendix is a checklist of material about Hemingway in the *Trapeze* and the *Tabula* compiled by Daniel Reichard.

NOTE: For information on the type face of this edition, see the colophon of the limited edition.

NOTE: 200 copies of an extra-illustrated collector's edition were published by Microcard Editions, at $12.50. The size, title page, and pagination are the same as the trade edition. Issued in blue-gray cloth backstrip over olive-green covers. Stamped in gold on the front cover and the backstrip. Front cover: 1916 / 1917. The lettering on the backstrip is identical to the trade edition. The endpapers with facsimiles from the *Trapeze* are the same as in the trade edition. Two additional facsimiles are inserted between the front loose endpaper and p. [i]: the back of an envelope (8 3/4 x 4) with Hemingway's holograph signature and return address: Lieut. Ernest M. Hemingway | A. R. C. Hospital | Milano | Italia; and a fold-out leaf (8 3/4 x 11) printed on both sides with pages one and three of the

Trapeze for March 31, 1919, which contain an article about Hemingway and a photograph. See (H15).

Colophon on the loose end paper opposite p. 122: This limited printing of | ERNEST HEMINGWAY'S APPRENTICESHIP | has been set in the Photon | version of Times Roman, a type face | first designed for the London Times. | Of the 200 copies of this special | edition which were printed and bound, | this is number | signed by the editor:

19 The Nick Adams Stories

A. First edition:

THE | Nick Adams | STORIES | *BY* | ERNEST HEMINGWAY | PREFACE BY PHILIP YOUNG | *NEW YORK* | CHARLES SCRIBNER'S SONS

9 x 5 7/8. Published April 17, 1972, at $7.95. The first printing consisted of 25,000 copies. Issued in blue cloth stamped in gold on the front cover and backstrip. Front cover: Author's signature stamped in gold. Backstrip, reading downward in three lines: ERNEST HEMINGWAY | THE NICK ADAMS STORIES | [on third line, but not below the other two:] SCRIBNERS. All edges trimmed. Rust-brown endpapers.

COLLATION: [i]-[ii] + [1]-[270], as follows: [i] decoration by Walter Ferro and half title; [ii] blank; [1] BOOKS BY; [2] blank; [3] title page as above; [4] notices of copyright for the text and the preface, note regarding the unpublished pieces, reservation of rights, Scribner's code "A-4.72 (V)," note of origin, Library of Congress catalog card number, SBN number, and credit line for the half title page decoration; 5-7 PREFACE by Philip Young; 7 list of four biographical studies; [8] blank; 9-10 CONTENTS; [11] divisional title: THE NORTHERN | WOODS; [12] blank; 13-268 text; [269]-[270] blank.

NOTE: A note on the copyright page reads: Publication of the eight previously unpublished pieces in this book is the | result of a gift of the English language rights by Mary Hemingway to The | Ernest Hemingway Foundation.

CONTENTS: 24 stories. [Part] I The Northern Woods: "Three Shots," "Indian Camp," "The Doctor and the Doctor's Wife," "Ten Indians," and "The Indians Moved Away." [Part] II On His Own: "The Light of the World," "The Battler," "The Killers," "The Last Good Country," and "Crossing the Mississippi." [Part] III War: "Night Before Landing," "Nick sat against the wall . . . ," "Now I Lay Me," "A Way You'll Never Be," and "In Another Country." [Part] IV A Soldier Home: "Big Two-Hearted River," "The End of Something," "The Three-Day Blow," and "Summer People." [Part] V Company of

Two: "Wedding Day," "On Writing," "An Alpine Idyll," "Cross-Country Snow," and "Fathers and Sons."

PREVIOUS PUBLICATION: The eight previously unpublished stories are: "Three Shots," "The Indians Moved Away," "The Last Good Country," "Crossing the Mississippi," "Night Before Landing," "Summer People," "Wedding Day," and "On Writing." "On Writing" is the deleted conclusion to "Big Two-Hearted River." Excerpts are quoted in Carlos Baker's *EH: A Life Story*, pp. 131-132; see also Notes, p. 585. "Nick sat against the wall . . ." was published in *in our time* (1924). Seven of the stories were published in *In Our Time* (1925): "Indian Camp," "The Doctor and the Doctor's Wife," "The Battler," "Big Two-Hearted River," "The End of Something," "The Three-Day Blow," and "Cross-Country Snow." Five of the stories were published in *Men Without Women*: "Ten Indians," "The Killers," "Now I Lay Me," "In Another Country," and "An Alpine Idyll." Three of the stories were published in *Winner Take Nothing*: "The Light of the World," "A Way You'll Never Be," and "Fathers and Sons."

NOTE: Philip Young notes in the Preface, on p. 7, "To distinguish them from previously published works, all the new materials in this book have been printed in a special 'oblique' type."

NOTE: The woodcut by Walter Ferro on the dust jacket is printed in blue, brown, orange, and black. The lettering on the front cover and backstrip is white and yellow. A list of Hemingway's books is printed in black and blue on the reverse of the dust jacket.

NOTE: For information on the manuscripts and typescripts of the previously unpublished pieces, see Philip Young and Charles Mann's *The Hemingway Manuscripts: An Inventory* (S-B11). [No.] 71: "Three Shots," the rejected opening to "Indian Camp." [No.] 76: "The Indians Moved Away." [No.] 62: "The Last Good Country." [No.] 59: "Crossing the Mississippi." [No.] 5 D: "Night Before Landing," the discarded opening to *FTA*. [No.] 85: "Summer People," probably the first Nick Adams story written. [No.] 46: "Wedding Day." [No.] 27 B and [No.] 57: "On Writing," an early draft for the end of "Big Two-Hearted River."

NOTE: The working title for this collection was "The Adventures of Nick Adams," see Philip Young's *Three Bags Full*, New York, 1972, p. 73. For Professor Young's comments on the editing of the new material in this collection (only "The Last Good Country" required any substantial editing, which was done by Scribner's), see " 'Big World Out There': *The Nick Adams Stories*," *Novel*, VI (Fall 1972). A footnote, on p. 5, explains that this essay was initially conceived as an introduction to *NAS*.

NOTE: This book was an alternate selection of the Book-of-the-Month Club and the Literary Guild, in June 1972.

B. First paperback edition:

THE | NICK ADAMS | STORIES | BY | ERNEST HEMING-
WAY | PREFACE BY PHILIP YOUNG | [publisher's device
encircled by:] [dot] BANTAM BOOKS [dot] TORONTO NEW YORK
LONDON | A NATIONAL GENERAL COMPANY

7 x 4 3/16. Published March 1973, by Bantam Books, Inc., in New
York, at $1.75. No. X7250. Issued in stiff paper covers. A painting of
a tall boy leaning against the trunk of a large tree is on the front
cover, which is lettered in white; a small portion of the painting is
reproduced on the back cover. The backstrip and back cover are
white, lettered in black.

COLLATION: [i]-x + [1]-[246], as follows: [i] blurb about the book
and brief excerpt from the *Minneapolis Tribune* review; [ii] Books
by; [iii] title page as above; [iv] note regarding the printing from
new plates: NOT ONE WORD HAS BEEN OMITTED, publish-
er's numbers, arrangement for publication, printing history, note
regarding the publication of the previously unpublished pieces,
notices of copyright, publisher's address, and note of origin; [v]-vii
PREFACE by Philip Young; vii list of four biographical studies;
[viii] blank; [ix]-x CONTENTS; [1] divisional half title: THE
NORTHERN | WOODS; [2] blank; [3]-245 text; [246] advertise-
ment for Bantam Books, including *Islands in the Stream.*

ENGLISH

EDITIONS

20 I. First English edition with commentary:
ERNEST HEMINGWAY | [long graduated line] | *A Farewell to Arms* | WITH A COMMENTARY | BY | TONY TANNER | [publisher's device] | HEINEMANN EDUCATIONAL | BOOKS LTD : LONDON
7 1/4 x 4 3/4. Published in September 1971, at 75p, in The Modern Novel Series. Issued in brown covers, lettered in black and white on the front cover and in black on the backstrip. A drawing, in brown, black, and white, of two ambulances and a soldier with a Red Cross armband is on the front cover. All edges trimmed. Signatures are in 32s with printer's marks.
COLLATION: [1]-[320], as follows: [1] half title; [2] list of titles in THE MODERN NOVEL SERIES; [3] title page as above; [4] list of publisher's international locations, ISBN number, notice of first publication of *FTA* in 1929, notice of copyright of the Commentary, arrangement for publication, publisher's address, and notes on printing and binding; [5] dedication; [6] legal disclaimer (signed) E.H.; [7] half title; [8] blank; 9-[287] text; [288] blank; 289-315 Commentary; [316] blank; 317 Suggested Further Reading; [318]-[320] blank.
NOTE: The Commentary, by Tony Tanner, includes "Biographical Background," on pp. 289-292; "The Title and the Structure," on pp. 292-293; "The Style," on pp. 293-296; and "The Book," in which each chapter is discussed individually, on pp. 297-315.

21 F. First English hard-cover edition:
THE | FIFTH | COLUMN | ERNEST HEMINGWAY | [publisher's device] | JONATHAN CAPE | THIRTY BEDFORD SQUARE LONDON
7 3/4 x 5. Published in January 1968, at 18s. Issued in black cloth, stamped in gold on the backstrip only. All edges trimmed; top edges stained purple. Signatures are in 16s with printer's marks.
COLLATION: [1]-106, as follows: [1]-[2] blank; [3] half title; [4] *Books by*; [5] title page as above; [6] notice of first publication in 1939, notes on printing and presswork; 7-8 PREFACE (signed) Ernest Hemingway; [lacks pp. 9-10]; [11] half title; [12] blank; 13-106 play script.
NOTE: Hemingway's preface, regarding the play, is reprinted from the *First 49*. See (A41A).
NOTE: The black dust jacket is printed in purple and white.

22 A. First English edition:
Men at War | [long graduated line] | EDITED | *with an Introduction* | BY | ERNEST HEMINGWAY | *Collins* | FONTANA BOOKS
7 x 4 1/8. 384 pages. Published in London and Glasgow, in December 1966, at 5s. Issued in green stiff paper covers, lettered in black and red, with an illustration of a skeleton in color on the front cover.

CONTENTS: This "shortened version" contains 26 of the original 82 stories. See (A19). Two of Hemingway's three selections are included: "The Fight on the Hilltop," from *For Whom the Bell Tolls*, on pp. 84-99; and "The Retreat from Caporetto," from *A Farewell to Arms*," on pp. 244-261.

NOTE: Hemingway's Introduction, on pp. 7-19, has been "Edited for the 1966 Fontana edition."

23 c. Second English edition:

For Whom the Bell Tolls. Published by The Reprint Society, London, in 1942. 7 1/2 x 5 1/4. 443 pages. Issued in beige cloth with gold-tooled black leather label on the backstrip. Top edges stained black. Bottom and fore edges trimmed.

NOTE: This edition was published before the Penguin edition, see (A42B).

24 D. Third English edition:

The Essential Hemingway. Published by The Companion Book Club, London, in 1962. 7 3/4 x 5. 447 pages.

NOTE: Printed by offset in The Netherlands by 'Jan de Lange,' Deventer, 1961.

NOTE: This edition was published before the Penguin edition, see (A43C).

25 D. First English paperback edition:

The Old Man | and the Sea | Ernest Hemingway | [publisher's device] Penguin Books

7 1/8 x 4 3/8. iv + 114 pages + 10 pages of advertisements. Published by Penguin Books Ltd., Harmondsworth, in 1966. Issued in stiff paper covers.

NOTE: The dedication has been changed to "Charles" Scribner from "Charlie" in the American edition.

26 A. First English edition:

By-Line: | Ernest Hemingway | [long double rule] | *Selected articles and* | *dispatches of four decades* | EDITED BY WILLIAM WHITE | WITH COMMENTARIES BY PHILIP YOUNG | *Collins* | ST JAMES'S PLACE | LONDON 1968

8 1/2 x 5 5/8. Published in March 1968, at 45s. Issued in orange cloth, stamped in gold on the backstrip, with the title and author's name on black. All edges trimmed. Signatures are in 16s with printer's marks.

COLLATION: [1]-[480] as follows: [1] half title; [2] *other books by*; [3] title page as above; [4] notices of copyright, first English publication, reservation of rights, printing, and presswork; 5-12 Contents; 13-17 Hemingway needs no introduction . . . by WILLIAM WHITE | FRANKLIN VILLAGE, MICHIGAN | *16 February*

1967; [18] blank; 19-24 Foreword by PHILIP YOUNG | UNIVER-
SITY PARK, PENNSYLVANIA | *26 May 1967*; 25-479 text; [480]
blank.

CONTENTS: The contents differ from the Scribner's edition as follows: two articles have been omitted, the first one in the book, "Cir-
culating Pictures," *Toronto Star Weekly* (Feb. 14, 1920), and "The
Clark's Fork Valley, Wyoming," *Vogue* (Feb. 1939); the addition
of a Foreword by Philip Young; and the omission of an Index.

NOTE: The blue, black, and pale gray dust jacket, designed by Brian
Russell, is printed in white, red, and black.

SUBSEQUENT EDITION: (B) Issued by Penguin Books Ltd., Harmondsworth, in 1970, at 40p, as No. 00.3063 8. 7 1/16 x 4 5/16. 446 pages.
Same contents as the first English edition except for the addition of
an index, on pp. [443]-446.

27 A. First English edition:

ISLANDS IN | THE STREAM | *A Novel by* ERNEST | HEM-
INGWAY | COLLINS | ST JAMES'S PLACE, LONDON | 1970
8 1/2 x 5 3/8. Published October 12, 1970, at 40s. Issued in blue
cloth, stamped in gold on the backstrip only. All edges trimmed.
Blue map endpapers by Samuel Bryant.

COLLATION: [1]-[400], as follows: [1] half title; [2] *by the Same Author*; [3] title page as above; [4] First published 1970, ISBN number, notices of printing, copyright, and presswork; [5] CONTENTS;
[6] blank; [7] divisional title: *Part I* | BIMINI; [8] blank; [9]-398
text; [399]-[400] blank.

NOTE: Mary Hemingway's Note in the Scribner edition regarding
the editing of the manuscript does not appear in this edition.

NOTE: The dust jacket, designed by Paul Bacon, is green lettered in
yellow and white with a map printed in black. It is the same design
as the Scribner edition. A 1 1/4-inch wide black band, lettered in
yellow with drawings of Hemingway in white, was wrapped around
the dust jacket. On the front of the band: The only Hemingway |
novel you can't have read. On the back of the band: 'A story about
action, about loneliness, containing much | humour, as good as any-
thing he ever wrote' | Mary Hemingway 1970. On the inside back
flap of the band: Collins [small circle] London.

NOTE: The publisher distributed a "press kit," which included a promotional booklet with 30 pages of extracts from the text.

SUBSEQUENT EDITION: (B) Issued by Penguin Books Ltd., Harmondsworth, in April 1972, at 40p, as No. 00.3479 X. 405 pages.

SECTION B
CONTRIBUTIONS AND FIRST APPEARANCES IN BOOKS AND PAMPHLETS

S-B1 The Twelfth Anniversary Playboy Reader

THE TWELFTH ANNIVERSARY | PLAYBOY READER | [long line] | EDITED BY HUGH M. HEFNER | [long line] | [publisher's device] | PLAYBOY PRESS | CHICAGO, ILLINOIS | DISTRIBUTED BY TRIDENT PRESS

9 1/2 x 6 7/8. ix + 876 pages. Published in 1965, at $9.95. Issued in beige cloth with the publisher's device (a bunny's head) in light brown on the front cover. Lettered in light brown on the backstrip: HEFNER | [reading downward in two lines:] THE TWELFTH ANNIVERSARY | PLAYBOY READER [publisher's device]. Top and bottom edges trimmed. Fore edges untrimmed.

"Advice to a Young Man," on pp. 736-744, is reprinted from *Playboy*, XI (Jan. 1964). See (C419). A headnote appears on p. 735. See also (S-G187).

NOTE: An English edition was published by Souvenir Press, London, in 1966.

2 50 Great American Short Stories

50 | GREAT | AMERICAN | SHORT STORIES | Edited and with an introduction by | MILTON CRANE | Professor of English Literature | The George Washington University | [publisher's device encircled by:] [dot] BANTAM BOOKS [dot] TORONTO NEW YORK LONDON

7 x 4 1/4. x + 502 pages. Published by Bantam Books, Inc., in New York, in March 1965, as a Bantam Classic, No. WC 265, at 95 cents. Issued in white stiff paper covers printed in blue, red, gold, and black.

"A Man of the World," on pp. 308-312, is reprinted from the *Atlantic*, CC (Nov. 1957). See (C398). Bibliographical note on p. 500.

NOTE: Reissued for the tenth printing, in September 1971, in a Bantam Literature edition, No. QM 6663, at $1.25. Same pagination.

3 Ezra Pound: 22 Versuche über einen Dichter

EZRA POUND | 22 Versuche über einen Dichter | Herausgegeben und eingeleitet von Eva Hesse | 1967 | Athenäum Verlag [dot] Frankfurt am Main [dot] Bonn

9 x 6. 456 pages. Issued in light brown cloth, stamped in gold on the backstrip only.

No. 21: "Huldigung an Ezra" on pp. 398-400. Hemingway's "Homage to Ezra," translated into German from *This Quarter*, I (Spring 1925). See (C165₁).

NOTE: References to Hemingway on pp. 142*n.*, 358, 366, 430, 433.

₄ Three Great American Novels

[On the left-hand page:] Three | Great | American | Novels | [On the right-hand page:] The Great Gatsby | F. SCOTT FITZ-GERALD | WITH AN INTRODUCTION BY MALCOLM COWLEY | A Farewell to Arms | ERNEST HEMINGWAY | WITH AN INTRO-DUCTION BY ROBERT PENN WARREN | Ethan Frome | EDITH WHARTON | WITH AN INTRODUCTION BY EDITH WHARTON | MOD-ERN STANDARD AUTHORS | CHARLES SCRIBNER'S SONS | NEW YORK

8 1/4 x 5 1/2. vi + 570 pages. Published October 9, 1967, at $4.95, in the Modern Standard Authors series. Issued in smooth black cloth backstrip and covers with a 1 3/4-inch panel of red cloth at the fore edges. The signatures of the three authors are stamped in gold on the black section of the front cover. Backstrip: [title in red:] Three | Great | American | Novels | [individual titles in gold:] THE GREAT | GATSBY | A FAREWELL | TO ARMS | ETHAN | FROME | [in red:] SCRIBNERS. All edges trimmed. The dust jacket, designed by Ronald Clyne, is black, white, red, blue, and purple. The date: Sept. '67 appears on the bottom of the front flap.

A Farewell to Arms is reprinted in its entirety on pp. 189-471. Robert Penn Warren's introduction, on pp. 153-186, is reprinted from Scribner's Modern Standard Authors edition of *FTA* (1949). See (A8L).

₅ The Last Will and Testament

THE LAST WILL | AND TESTAMENT | Copyright, 1968, Robert A. Farmer & Associates, Inc.

7 1/8 x 4 1/4. 184 pages. No place of publication given. RAF Books, 103N, Unabridged Historical Series, 95¢. Issued in white paper covers, with black borders, lettered in black and red. Lettered in white on the black backstrip, reading downward: THE LAST WILL *and* TESTAMENT R. A. Farmer & Assoc., Inc.

"The Will of Ernest Hemingway," on p. 51, is dated (within the text of the will) September 17, 1955, and signed Ernest Miller Hemingway. Note: A facsimile of this will was reproduced in the *New York Times* (Aug. 25, 1961). A facsimile is also reproduced in Billie Pesin Rosen's *The Science of Handwriting Analysis*, New York, 1965, p. 216.

NOTE: This book contains the last wills and testaments of 27 famous people, from Shakespeare to John F. Kennedy.

6 Hemingway, entre la vida y la muerte

J. L. CASTILLO-PUCHE | HEMINGWAY, | ENTRE LA VIDA | Y LA MUERTE | [series device] | EDICIONES DESTINO | TALLERS, 62 - BARCELONA

8 1/8 x 5 1/2. 467 pages. Published in May 1968, in the SER O NO SER Biografias series. Issued in blue cloth, stamped in gold on the front cover and the backstrip. All edges trimmed. The black dust jacket, lettered in light purple and white, has a photograph of Hemingway on the front cover.

"Fragmento inédito de 'El Verano Peligroso' de E. Hemingway," on pp. [9]-10. An excerpt from "The Dangerous Summer" translated into Spanish.

NOTE: For facsimiles of letters, see (S-F141), (S-F145), and (S-F161). See also (S-G74).

7 New Masses An Anthology of the Rebel Thirties

NEW MASSES | An Anthology of | the Rebel Thirties | *Edited with a Prologue* | *by* JOSEPH NORTH | *Introduction by* MAXWELL GEISMAR | [publisher's device] | INTERNATIONAL PUBLISHERS | New York

8 x 5 1/4. 318 pages. Published in 1969, at $7.50. Issued in red cloth. Lettered in gold on the backstrip, reading downward: *NEW MASSES: Anthology* [slash] *North* | [publisher's device] | [horizontal:] INTERNATIONAL | PUBLISHERS. All edges trimmed. The dust jacket is white, black, and red.

"Who Murdered the Vets?" (A First-Hand Report On The Florida Hurricane), on pp. 181-187, is reprinted from *New Masses*, XVI (Sept. 17, 1935). See (C236).

"On the American Dead in Spain," on pp. 306-307, is reprinted from *New Masses*, XXX (Feb. 14, 1939). See (C313). The Editor's Note, on p. 308, briefly quotes a letter from Hemingway, which states he had worked on the article for five days.

NOTE: For work on Hemingway, see (S-G317).

8 Ernest Kheminguei

Ernest Kheminguei by S. S. Shvedov. Published in Moscow, in 1969, in paper covers. 35 pages.

Contains the following excerpts and short stories, in English: pp. 13-18: Excerpt from *FWBT*, pp. 466-471. pp. 19-22: Excerpt from *SAR*, pp. 157-160. pp. 23-24: Excerpt from *FTA*, pp. 352-355. pp. 25-27: "Old Man at the Bridge." pp. 27-30: "Cat in the Rain."

9 Hemingway's African Stories

JOHN M. HOWELL | Southern Illinois University, Carbondale | HEMINGWAY'S AFRICAN STORIES: | The Stories, Their Sources, Their Critics | [series device] SCRIBNER | RESEARCH | ANTHOLOGIES | CHARLES SCRIBNER'S SONS New York
9 1/4 x 6 1/2. x + 169 + ix pages. Published January 17, 1969, as a Scribner Research Anthology, at $2.95. Issued in light brown stiff paper covers, printed in black, white, beige, and olive. Frontispiece facsimile of a page from the typescript of "The Snows of Kilimanjaro," see (S-F29₂).

pp. 5-22: "The Short Happy Life of Francis Macomber." pp. 23-36: "The Snows of Kilimanjaro." p. [37]: Excerpt from the Introduction to *Men at War*, p. xv. pp. 39-42: Excerpt from *GHOA*, pp. 19-27. pp. 43-44: Excerpt from *AMF*, pp. 12-13. pp. 45-49: "Monologue to the Maestro," *Esquire*, IV (Oct. 1935). pp. 50-51: Excerpts from *DIA*, pp. 2-3, 191-192. p. [53]: Hemingway is quoted from George Plimpton's interview in the *Paris Review*, V (Spring 1958). pp. 63-65: Excerpt from *AMF*, pp. 3-8. p. 66: Excerpt from *DIA*, pp. 232-233. pp. 67-68: "A.D. in Africa: A Tanganyika Letter," *Esquire*, I (April 1934). pp. 69-71: "Shootism vs. Sport: The Second Tanganyika Letter," *Esquire*, II (June 1934). pp. 71-73: "Notes on Dangerous Game: The Third Tanganyika Letter," *Esquire*, II (July 1934). pp. 74-88: Excerpts from *GHOA*, pp. 34-43, 64-66, 68-73, 96-107, 111-118, 148-150, 283-285. p. 89: Excerpt from the Introduction to *Men at War*, pp. xiii-xiv, xxvii. p. [111]: Hemingway's Nobel prize acceptance speech.

NOTE: For critical essays, see (S-G203).

NOTE: "Guide to Research," on pp. i-ix at the back of the book, by Martin Steinmann, Jr., the general editor of the Scribner Research Anthologies.

10 Ernest Hemingway: A Life Story

Ernest | Hemingway | A LIFE STORY | [graduated line] | *By* | CARLOS BAKER | "To live, to err, to fall, to triumph, | to re-create life out of life . . ." | —JAMES JOYCE, *A Portrait of the Artist as a Young Man* | *New York* | CHARLES SCRIBNER'S SONS
9 1/4 x 6. xviii + 697 pages. Published April 21, 1969, at $10.00. Issued in dark blue cloth covers, lettered in gold in a blind-stamped box on the front cover, and lettered in gold with decorations in red on the backstrip. All edges trimmed. Blue endpapers. The brown dust jacket, designed by Greta Franzen, is printed in beige, orange, and dark brown. The portrait of Hemingway on the front cover was painted by Henry Strater, in 1930, in Key West.

Previously unpublished work by Hemingway: p. 12: "My First Sea Vouge" [sic]. A four-paragraph short story, written April 17, 1911, for his sixth-grade English class. "EH's first extant short story" (p. 568).

p. 15: "The Opening Game." Six lines from a poem, written April 12, 1912.

p. 35: Character sketch of Lionel Moise "from an undated, unpublished holograph MS" (p. 570).

p. 60: "The Passing of Pickles McCarty." The lead paragraph of a short story, probably written in "the spring of 1919" (p. 574).

pp. 65-66: "Wolves and Doughnuts." Fragment of a short story, written in Petoskey (on the back of a letter dated Dec. 20, 1919) (p. 575).

p. 88: "Blood is thicker than water." Five-line poem, "composed ca. Feb., 1922" (p. 577).

pp. 90-91: "Paris 1922." Six "one-sentence sketches, probably composed ca. late May, 1922" (p. 578).

p. 101: Character sketch of Dave O'Neil, "composed probably spring, 1923" (p. 579).

pp. 120-121: Sketch of Robert Reade and Gregory Clark, written in the "fall, 1923" (p. 582).

pp. 131-132: "Some observations on esthetic principles" from the deleted conclusion of "Big Two-Hearted River," "composed Aug., 1924" (p. 585). [Excerpts from "On Writing," published in *The Nick Adams Stories*, pp. 237-240.]

pp. 166-167: Plans for "a picaresque novel for America" and a "discourse on death and suicide," written "ca. late March, 1926" (p. 591).

p. 235: A "public statement" regarding his service in the ambulance corps during World War I and his boxing ability, written [ca. Dec. 1932] to counteract the press releases for Paramount's production of the film *A Farewell to Arms*.

p. 261: "List of earthly pleasures." Deleted passage from the holograph manuscript of *Green Hills of Africa* (p. 611).

p. 263: "Dialogue on courage and allied powers." Deleted passage from the holograph manuscript of *Green Hills of Africa* (p. 611).

p. 428: Three lines of a poem "on battle in forest," written Sept. 24, 1944 (p. 642).

p. 593: Deleted passage about "the rich" from the manuscript version of the last chapter of *A Moveable Feast*, "composed ca. 1958" (p. 592).

p. 609: Canceled passage "about courage and cowardice" from the holograph manuscript of *Green Hills of Africa*.

NOTE: Parts of this book first appeared in the *Atlantic Monthly*, CCXXIII (Jan. and Feb. 1969). A Book-of-the-Month Club edition was published in April 1969. A Literary Guild edition was published in

July 1969. And a Bantam paperback edition was published in October 1970. See also (S-G15).

11 The Hemingway Manuscripts

The | HEMINGWAY | Manuscripts | An Inventory | Philip Young | and | Charles W. Mann | The Pennsylvania State University Press | University Park and London

8 x 5. xiv + 138 pages + 6 pages of illustrations. Published in October 1969, in a trade edition of 3500 copies, at $5.95. Issued in faded-rose cloth, stamped in gold on the backstrip only. Backstrip, reading downward: *Young & Mann* The HEMINGWAY Manuscripts *Pennsylvania State*. All edges trimmed. Gray endpapers. The dust jacket is printed in light brown, dark brown, and white. The last page of the notebook draft of *The Sun Also Rises* is reproduced on the front cover.

A facsimile of the first page of the holograph manuscript of "Summer People" is reproduced following p. 18. [Published in *The Nick Adams Stories*, p. 217.]

A facsimile of the first page of the typescript of the discarded opening of "Fifty Grand" is reproduced opposite p. 19. Pages two and three of the discarded opening are reproduced, along with page one, in the limited edition described below. Note: For additional facsimiles, of previously published work, see (S-F33).

NOTE: This book contains an inventory of 332 items, including manuscripts of published and unpublished work, letters, and miscellaneous items, in the possession of Mary Hemingway.

NOTE: Also published in a limited edition, at $20.00, in December 1969. 8 x 6 1/8. Issued in beige cloth covers with a brown leather spine. Stamped in gold on the backstrip: The HEMINGWAY Manuscripts *Pennsylvania State*. Issued in a gray board slip-case with a beige paper label, printed in dark brown, on one side only.

Same pagination as the trade edition except this edition contains two additional facsimiles of manuscript pages from the discarded opening of "Fifty Grand."

The colophon, on p. [iv], states: This is a limited edition of three hundred specially printed | and bound copies, of which this is number

12 Fishing with Hemingway and Glassell

Fishing | with | Hemingway | and Glassell | by | S. Kip Farrington, Jr. | DAVID McKAY COMPANY, INC. | *NEW YORK*

8 x 5 3/8. x + 118 pages. Published in March 1971, at $5.95. Issued in black cloth covers stamped in gold on the front cover and

44

the backstrip. Geodetic map endpapers of Cuba and Peru. All edges trimmed. The blue dust jacket is printed in black and white. A small photograph of Hemingway is on the front cover.

Hemingway's Introduction to S. Kip Farrington's *Atlantic Game Fishing* is reprinted, with substantive emendations, on pp. 9-14. First published in 1937, see (B27).

NOTE: For material on Hemingway, see (S-G121).

13 A Hemingway Selection

LONGMAN IMPRINT BOOKS | A Hemingway Selection | compiled by Dennis Pepper | [publisher's device] | Longman

7 1/4 x 4 3/4. vi + 211 pages. Published in 1972 by Longman Group Limited, in London. Issued in black stiff paper covers, printed in white, with a blue and red portrait of Hemingway. The back and front covers are identical.

in our time and seventeen short stories from the *First 49* are reprinted on pp. 1-161. The stories are: "My Old Man," "Out of Season," "Indian Camp," "The Doctor and the Doctor's Wife," "Ten Indians," "The End of Something," "The Three-Day Blow," "The Battler," "The Killers," "Now I Lay Me," "Big Two-Hearted River," "Cross-Country Snow," "A Day's Wait," "The Undefeated," "Fifty Grand," "On the Quai at Smyrna," and "Old Man at the Bridge." Excerpts from *DIA* and "Monologue to the Maestro," *Esquire*, IV (Oct. 1935), on pp. 193-194, under the general heading "Hemingway on Writing."

NOTE: There are brief glossary footnotes to the short stories. A map of "North Michigan | Nick Adams country" is on p. [vi].

NOTE: For introductory essays and excerpts from reviews and interviews, see (S-G326).

14 Authors on Film

Authors on Film | edited by Harry M. Geduld | [broken line under the second line of type] | INDIANA UNIVERSITY PRESS | *Bloomington and London*

7 7/8 x 5 1/4. xiii + 303 pages. Published in November 1972, at $5.95. Issued in black cloth, lettered in silver on the backstrip only. [Horizontal:] Geduld | [reading downward:] Authors on Film | [horizontal:] INDIANA. Red endpapers. All edges trimmed. The white dust jacket is lettered in black and red.

"A Tribute to Mamma from Papa Hemingway," commentary on Marlene Dietrich, on pp. 283-284, is reprinted from *Life*, XXXIII (Aug. 18, 1952). See (C367).

₁₅ Selected Short Stories

F. S. Fitzgerald e E. Hemingway | SELECTED SHORT STORIES | *A CURA DI* | P. COSTA e D. CALDI | [publisher's device] | 1973 | G. B. PETRINI | *TORINO*

8 x 5 1/4. ii + 288 pages. 1.700 lire. Issued in green and white stiff paper covers, printed in black, white, yellow, and brown.

Five short stories by Hemingway are printed, in English, on pp. 159-282. The stories are: "The Short Happy Life of Francis Macomber," "Old Man at the Bridge," "Cat in the Rain," "The Undefeated," and "In Another Country." Footnotes in English and Italian.

NOTE: "Introduzione," in English, on pp. 153-157. "Bibliografia critica" on pp. 157-158. Notes on vocabulary and exercises at the end of each story.

NOTE: The first half of this study text is comprised of six short stories by F. Scott Fitzgerald and related material.

₁₆ Hemingway's Craft

Hemingway's Craft | Sheldon Norman Grebstein | WITH A PREFACE BY | *Harry T. Moore* | SOUTHERN ILLINOIS UNIVERSITY PRESS | *Carbondale and Edwardsville* | FEFFER & SIMONS, INC. | *London and Amsterdam*

8 1/4 x 4 7/8. xvii + 245 pages. Published in February 1973, at $8.95, in the Crosscurrents/Modern Critiques series. Issued in orange cloth, lettered in gold on the backstrip only: [decoration] | [reading downward:] Hemingway's Craft | [horizontal:] Sheldon | Norman | Grebstein | Southern | Illinois | University | Press. All edges trimmed. Top edges stained orange. The dust jacket is black and lavender, printed in white, with a drawing of Hemingway, by Dani Aguila, on the back cover.

The textual differences between the published novels and the manuscripts of *A Farewell to Arms* and *For Whom the Bell Tolls* are examined in the Appendix. The manuscripts are on deposit at Harvard University. See (S-F4). Three passages deleted from *FTA* before publication are quoted on pp. 212-215. A passage deleted from *FWBT* before publication is quoted on pp. 216-217. See also (S-G166).

₁₇ A Fly Fisher's Life

CHARLES RITZ | A Fly Fisher's Life | REVISED AND ENLARGED EDITION | *prepared in collaboration with* | JOHN PIPER | CROWN PUBLISHERS, INC. | NEW YORK

9 3/4 x 6 7/8. viii + 285 pages. Published in March 1973, at $7.50.

Third edition. Issued in green cloth covers stamped in dark green on the backstrip only. All edges trimmed. The black dust jacket is printed in white, gray, and blue, with a photograph of the author in color on the front cover. The first two lines of Hemingway's Foreword are quoted on the back cover: "Charles Ritz is one of the very finest | fly fishermen I know. He is not only a | great fly fisherman for trout and salmon | but he is an articulate writer and splen- | did technician. . ."

Hemingway's Foreword, on p. 1, is undated. In the first English translation, in 1960, it is dated December 12, 1954. See (B57).

NOTE: A photograph of Hemingway and Charles Ritz appears opposite p. 11.

NOTE: In the second English edition, published by Winchester Press, New York, in 1969, only two lines of Hemingway's foreword were quoted (on the copyright page).

18 Hemingway at Auction

HEMINGWAY | *AT* | *AUCTION* | *1930-1973* | Compiled by | Matthew J. Bruccoli | C. E. Frazer Clark, Jr. | Introduction by | Charles W. Mann | [series device] A Bruccoli [ornament] Clark Book | Gale Research Company, Book Tower, Detroit

10 x 6 3/4. xxii + 286 pages. Published November 1, 1973, in the Authors at Auction Series, at $25.00. Issued in dark green cloth, stamped in gold on the front cover and backstrip. All edges trimmed. Front endpapers: Photograph of two shelves of boxed and slip-cased Hemingway first editions and inscribed copies. Back endpapers: Twelve pages of Hemingway letters are completely or partially reproduced.

A facsimile of page seven of the typescript, with holograph corrections, of "Black Ass at the Cross Roads" is reproduced, on p. 129, from the Charles Hamilton auction catalogue, No. 19 (May 24, 1967). The 26-page unpublished manuscript is described on p. 128.

NOTE: This book contains reproductions of pages from sixty auction sale catalogues and fifty-five dealer catalogues issued from 1930 to 1973. For facsimiles of manuscript pages, see (S-F40). See also entries under published letters in Section F.

NOTE: Introduction, on pp. vii-xi, by Charles W. Mann. Compilers' Note, on p. xiii, by C.E.F.C., Jr./M.J.B.

SECTION C
CONTRIBUTIONS TO NEWSPAPERS AND PERIODICALS

This section comprises both first appearances and reprinted work in newspapers, periodicals, and hardcover serial publications. It includes "The Spanish War," nineteen of Hemingway's NANA dispatches on the Spanish Civil War, which was published in *Fact* (London), No. 16 (July 1938). This item was inadvertently omitted from the bibliography.

The December 1920 issue of the *Co-operative Commonwealth* (C52) is still the only issue that has been located containing work by Hemingway. However, since publication of the bibliography, twelve *Kansas City Star* stories, written during 1917-1918, have been attributed to Hemingway by Donald Hoffman, Mel Foor, Matthew J. Bruccoli, and C. E. Frazer Clark, Jr. They have been collected in *Ernest Hemingway, Cub Reporter: Kansas City Star Stories* edited by Matthew J. Bruccoli, Pittsburgh, 1970.

Two other notable Hemingway items that have recently been located are a review of Sherwood Anderson's *A Story Teller's Story*, in *Ex Libris*, II (March 1925), and a review of two plays, which were performed in Schruns, Austria, printed in a German translation in the *Vorarlberger Landes-Zeitung* (Jan. 13, 1926). The reviews appeared in the *Fitzgerald/Hemingway Annual* in 1969 and 1971 respectively.

S-C1   Editorial. "Junior Debates," *Trapeze*, v, xvi (May 4, 1916), 2. Signed: E.M.H.

A short item on the benefits of debating in high school. Reprinted in *Ernest Hemingway's Apprenticeship* edited by Matthew J. Bruccoli, Washington, D.C., 1971, p. 22. See (S-A18).

2   Article. "Kerensky, the Fighting Flea," *Kansas City Star* (Dec. 16, 1917), p. 3 C. Unsigned.

Attributed to Hemingway by Donald Hoffman, and reprinted in the *K.C. Star* (Jan. 28, 1968). See (S-C53). Also reprinted in Mel Foor's article in the *K.C. Star* (July 21, 1968), see (S-C56); in *Ernest Hemingway, Cub Reporter* edited by Matthew J. Bruccoli, Pittsburgh, 1970, pp. 15-19, see (S-A16).

3   Article. "Battle of Raid Squads," *Kansas City Star* (Jan. 6, 1918), p. 1. Unsigned.

Attributed to Hemingway by Matthew J. Bruccoli, and reprinted in *Esquire*, LXX (Dec. 1968). See (S-C57). Reprinted in *Ernest Hemingway, Cub Reporter* edited by Bruccoli, Pittsburgh, 1970, pp. 20-26. See (S-A16).

4   Vignettes. "At the End of the Ambulance Run," *Kansas City Star* (Jan. 20, 1918), p. 7 C. Unsigned.

Attributed to Hemingway by Mel Foor, and reprinted in the *K.C. Star* (July 21, 1968). See (S-C56). Reprinted in *Ernest Hemingway,*

Cub Reporter edited by Matthew J. Bruccoli, Pittsburgh, 1970, pp. 27-33. See (S-A16).

5   Article. "Throng at Smallpox Case," *Kansas City Star* (Feb. 18, 1918), p. 3. Unsigned.

Reprinted in Mel Foor's article in the *K.C. Star* (July 21, 1968), see (S-C56), with commentary on Theodore Brumback's version of Hemingway's experience as related in the *K.C. Star* (Dec. 6, 1936). Both Hemingway's article and Brumback's reminiscences are reprinted in *Ernest Hemingway, Cub Reporter* edited by Matthew J. Bruccoli, Pittsburgh, 1970. See (S-A16).

6   Article. "Laundry Car Over Cliff," *Kansas City Star* (March 6, 1918), p. 1. Unsigned.

Reprinted in *Ernest Hemingway, Cub Reporter* edited by Matthew J. Bruccoli, Pittsburgh, 1970, pp. 37-39. See (S-A16). This story was phoned in to the *Star*. For background on the story, see Mel Foor's article in the *K.C. Star* (July 21, 1968).

7   Article. "Big Day for Navy Drive," *Kansas City Star* (April 17, 1918), p. 6. Unsigned.

Reprinted in *Ernest Hemingway, Cub Reporter* edited by Matthew J. Bruccoli, Pittsburgh, 1970, pp. 45-46. See the headnote, on p. 40, regarding Hemingway sending a copy of this article to his family as a sample of his work. See (S-A16).

7₁ Article. "Six Men Become Tankers," *ibid.*, p. 7. Unsigned.

Reprinted in *Ernest Hemingway, Cub Reporter* edited by Matthew J. Bruccoli, Pittsburgh, 1970, pp. 41-44. See the headnote, on p. 40, for authentication of this article. See (S-A16).

8   Article. "Would 'Treat 'Em Rough,' " *Kansas City Star* (April 18, 1918), p. 4. Unsigned.

Article on the U.S. Army recruiting office for the Tank Corps. Reprinted in *Ernest Hemingway, Cub Reporter* edited by Matthew J. Bruccoli, Pittsburgh, 1970, pp. 49-51. See the headnote, on p. 40, for authentication of this article. See (S-A16).

8₁ Article. "Recruits for the Tanks," *ibid.*, p. 6. Unsigned.

Reprinted in *Ernest Hemingway, Cub Reporter* edited by Matthew J. Bruccoli, Pittsburgh, 1970, pp. 52-53. See the headnote, on p. 40, for authentication of this article. See (S-A16).

8₂ Article. "Navy Desk Jobs to Go," *ibid.*, p. 17. Unsigned.

Reprinted in *Ernest Hemingway, Cub Reporter* edited by Matthew J. Bruccoli, Pittsburgh, 1970, pp. 47-48. See the headnote, on p. 40, for authentication of this article. See (S-A16).

9 Article. "Mix War, Art And Dancing," *Kansas City Star* (April 21, 1918), p. 1. Unsigned.

Although not mentioned by title or date, this story is attributed to Hemingway by Charles A. Fenton in *The Apprenticeship of Ernest Hemingway*, New York, 1954, p. 46. Reprinted in Mel Foor's article in the *K.C. Star* (July 21, 1968), see (S-C56); in *Ernest Hemingway, Cub Reporter* edited by Matthew J. Bruccoli, Pittsburgh, 1970, pp. 56-58. See (S-A16).

9₁ Article. "Dare Devil Joins Tanks," *ibid.*, p. 3 A. Unsigned.

A "possible" article by Hemingway, reprinted in *Ernest Hemingway, Cub Reporter* edited by Matthew J. Bruccoli, Pittsburgh, 1970, pp. 54-55. See (S-A16).

10 Article. "Buying Commission Would Cut Out Waste," *Toronto Daily Star* (April 20, 1920), p. 3. Unsigned.

Regarding Ralph Connable's part in the War Purchasing Commission's investigation of the system of buying supplies for the various departments of the Dominion Government. A facsimile of this article, and authentication by C. E. Frazer Clark, Jr., appears in the *Fitzgerald/Hemingway Annual: 1971*, pp. 209-211.

11 Book review. Review of Sherwood Anderson's *A Story-Teller's Story*, *Ex Libris*, II (March 1925), 176-177.

Reprinted in the *Fitzgerald/Hemingway Annual: 1969*, pp. 72-74.

12 Play review. *Vorarlberger Landes-Zeitung* (Jan. 13, 1926). In German. Dateline: Schruns (Montafon), 12. Jänner.

Review of two Christmas performances, in Schruns, of Hans Sachs's *The Hot Iron* and Bernard Shaw's *How He Deceived Her Husband*. A facsimile appeared in the *Vorarlberg*, IV (Oct. 1965), 15. Reprinted, with a translation into English by James Franklin, in the *Fitzgerald/Hemingway Annual: 1971*, pp. 195-196.

NOTE: Hemingway referred to this review in *A Moveable Feast* (p. 203), "One Christmas there was a play by Hans Sachs that the school master directed. It was a good play and I wrote a review of it for the provincial paper that the hotel keeper translated."

13 Excerpt. *Golden Book Magazine*, VI (Dec. 1927), 864.

One-sentence excerpt from Chapter IV of *The Sun Also Rises*.

14 Short story. "Ein Tag Warten," *Die Sammlung*, I (July 1934), 638-641.

"A Day's Wait" translated into German by Annemarie Horschitz.

15 Short story. "Die Veränderung," *Die Sammlung*, II (Nov. 1934), 156-159.

"The Sea Change" translated into German by Annemarie Horschitz.

16 Short story reprinted. "The Tradesman's Return," *Fiction Parade*, II, v (March 1936), 567-574.
Reprinted from *Esquire*, v (Feb. 1936). See (C241).

17 NANA dispatch. "Shelling of Madrid." [Source not located.] Dateline: Madrid, April 11, 1937.
Reprinted in *By-Line* (edited by William White), pp. 259-261.

18 NANA dispatches reprinted. "The Spanish War," *Fact* (London), No. 16 (July 15, 1938), pp. 7-72.
Nineteen of Hemingway's North American Newspaper Alliance (NANA) dispatches are reprinted.
Part 1: "The Saving of Madrid." pp. 7-10: Dateline: On the Guadalajara Front, March 23, 1937. pp. 10-13: Madrid, March 29. pp. 13-17: Madrid, April 9th, 8.40 p.m. pp. 17-23: "The American Soldier" [Jay Raven]. Madrid, April (undated). pp. 23-25: "Madrid under Bombardment." Madrid, April 21st. pp. 25-33: ["The Chauffeurs of Madrid."] Paris, May 2nd.
Part 2: "The Aragon Front." pp. 34-36: Dateline: On the Aragon Front, September 14th, 1937. pp. 36-38: Teruel Front, September 24th. pp. 39-40: Madrid, September 30th.
Part 3: "Teruel." pp. 41-46: Dateline: Army Headquarters, Teruel Front, December 20th, 1937. pp. 46-51: Army Headquarters, Teruel Front, December 21st.
Part 4: "Franco Advancing." pp. 52-54: Dateline: Barcelona, April 3rd, 1938. pp. 54-57: Barcelona, April 5th. pp. 57-60: Tortosa, April 5th, *Evening*. pp. 60-62: Tortosa, April 10th. pp. 62-65: Tortosa, April 17th. pp. 65-67: Ebro Delta, April 18th.
Part 5: "Last Despatches." pp. 68-70: Dateline: Castellon, May 9th [1938]. pp. 70-72: Madrid, May 11th.
The introduction, on pp. 4-5, states that "No change has of course been made in anything that he wrote. Some abridgment alone has been necessary. The omitted matter consists chiefly of descriptions of events which in retrospect seem unimportant and speculations on the future course of the war which have no interest now. Only the titles of the chapters and a few cross-heads have been added by the editor." Note: This issue was bound with three others to form *Fact* (Second Series), published by Fact Publishing Company, London (no date). Bound in blue cloth with a white paper label, lettered in black, on the backstrip.

19 Short story reprinted. "A Story from Spain," *Lilliput*, v, iv (Oct. [1938?]), 369-370.

"Old Man at the Bridge" reprinted from *Ken,* I (May 19, 1938). See (C296).

20   Short story. "La Dénonciation," *Volontaires,* I, i (Dec. 1938), 25-37.
     "The Denunciation" translated into French by Roland Mairaux. See (C307).

21   Eulogy. "Eulogy To Gene Van Guilder," *Idaho Statesman* (Nov. 2, 1939), p. 4.
     Hemingway read this eulogy at the funeral of Gene Van Guilder, who was killed in a duck hunting accident in Sun Valley, Idaho. Quoted in "Hemingway's Idaho," *Venture,* V (Sept. 1968), 51; in Carlos Baker's *EH: A Life Story,* New York, 1969, p. 343. Note: The newspaper is erroneously listed as the *Boise Statesman* in Professor Baker's Notes, p. 628.

22   Short story reprinted. "The Killers," *Redbook,* LXXIV, vi (April 1940), 24-25, 80-82. See (C172).

23   Article reprinted. "Remembering Shooting-Flying: A Key West Letter," *American Rifleman,* XC, vi (June 1942), 11-12, 15.
     Reprinted from *Esquire,* III (Feb. 1935). See (C227).

24   Novel excerpt. *"Pour qui sonne le glas,"* Fontaine (Édition d'Alger), No. 27-28 (Aug. 1943), [35]-51.
     Chapter Two of *For Whom the Bell Tolls* translated into French by Robert Lebel. Note: This issue was bound in *Écrivains et poètes des États-Unis d'Amérique* edited by Max-Pol Fouchet and Jean Wahl, Paris: Fontaine, 1945, pp. [35]-51.

25   Novel excerpt. "Cinque sulla collina," *Il Mese,* No. 11 (Oct. 1944), pp. [630]-639. Illustrated by Ramón Gaya.
     Chapter 27 of *For Whom the Bell Tolls* (El Sordo's fight on the hilltop) translated into Italian. Introductory note on p. [629]. Note: This issue was bound in *Altri Sei Mesi: Il Mese,* Volume Two, Numbers 7-12, London: Fleet Street Press, (n.d.), pp. [629]-639.

26   Excerpts. "Man versus Bull," *Hulton's National Weekly Picture Post,* XXVI (Jan. 20, 1945), 21-23.
     Photographs of a bullfight in Mexico City with text from *Death in the Afternoon.*

27   Short story. "Une pêche à la truite," *U.S.A.* (U.S. Office of War Information), II, iv ([April?] 1945), 72-79.
     Part Two of "Big Two-Hearted River" translated into French. Editor's Note on pp. 70-72.

28   Short story reprinted. "Soldier's Home," *Encore,* VII (May 1945), 532-538. Special issue edited by the staff of *Yank, The Army Weekly.*

The prefatory note, on p. 532, explains that Hemingway's "short story of a returning soldier is as true of the veteran of World War II as it was of the World War I veteran about whom it was written."

29 Short story reprinted. "The Killers," *Ellery Queen's Mystery Magazine*, IX (June 1947), 54-61. See (C172).

30 Novel excerpt. "Ein spanischer Pfarrer," *Deutsche Universitätszeitung*, IV, vii (April 1949), 10-11.
   Excerpt from *For Whom the Bell Tolls* translated into German.

31 Novel excerpt, *Über den Fluss und in die Wälder, Christ und Welt* (Dec. 14, 1950), p. 12.
   Excerpts from *Across the River and Into the Trees* translated into German.

32 Short story. "Ein Tag Warten," *Welt und Wort*, VI (Feb. 1951), 60-61.
   "A Day's Wait" translated into German by Annemarie Horschitz-Horst. Reprinted from *49 Stories*, Hamburg: Rowohlt, 1950.

33 Novel excerpt. "Das letzte Abenteuer," *Welt und Wort*, VI (Aug. 1951), 316.
   Excerpt from *To Have and Have Not* translated into German by Annemarie Horschitz-Horst. Reprinted from *Haben und Nichthaben*, Hamburg: Rowohlt, 1951.

34 Novel. *Starik i more, Inostrannaya Literatura*, No. 3 (March 1955), 95-136.
   The Old Man and the Sea translated into Russian by E. Golysheva and B. Izakova.

35 Excerpt. "The True Writer," *N.Y. Times Book Review* (May 13, 1956), p. 2.
   Excerpt from Hemingway's Nobel pribe acceptance speech.

36 Article reprinted. "On the Blue Water," *Jack London's Adventure Magazine*, I, i (Oct. 1958), 34-40.
   Reprinted from *Esquire*, v (April 1936). See (C243).

37 Short story. "As neves do Kilimanjaro," *SR. Uma Revista para o Senhor*, I, i (March 1959), 66-83.
   "The Snows of Kilimanjaro" translated into Portuguese by Ivo Barroso.

38 Excerpts. *Zelenye kholmy Afriki, Inostrannaya Literatura*, No. 7 (July 1959), pp. 165-180.
   Excerpts from *Green Hills of Africa* translated into Russian by N. Volzhina. Introduction by Ivan Kashkin on pp. 164-165.

39 Article reprinted. "Who Murdered the Vets?" *Mainstream,* XIII (Jan. 1960), 24-30.
   Reprinted from the *New Masses,* XVI (Sept. 17, 1935). See (C236). Note: The cover title for this article is "Murder at Matecumbe."

40 Short story. "Mr. and Mrs. Elliot," *Senhor,* III, viii (Aug. 1961), 48-49.
   The short story and inter-chapter IX of *In Our Time* are translated into Portuguese by Olympio Monat.

41 Article reprinted. "Milan and the Mistletoe," *Topper* (Feb. 1962), pp. 8-10.
   Reprinted from the *Toronto Star Weekly* (Dec. 22, 1923), where it appeared under the title "A North of Italy Christmas." See (C151$_1$).

42 Excerpt. "Vară primejdioasă," *Secolul 20,* II (July 1962), 8-54.
   Excerpt from "The Dangerous Summer" translated into Rumanian by Eugen Barbu.

42$_1$ Short story. "Educația revoluționară," *ibid.,* pp. 55-66.
   "Nobody Ever Dies!" translated into Rumanian by Pop Simion.

42$_2$ Short story. "Fluturele și tancul," *ibid.,* pp. 67-73.
   "The Butterfly and the Tank" translated into Rumanian by Fănuș Neagu.

42$_3$ Short story. "Tabăra indiană," *ibid.,* pp. 74-77.
   "Indian Camp" translated into Rumanian by Petre Solomon.

42$_4$ Short story. "Ucigașii," *ibid.,* pp. 78-85.
   "The Killers" translated into Rumanian by Petre Solomon.

43 Excerpts from *A Moveable Feast, Argosy,* XXV [New series] (July 1964), 4-16; (Aug. 1964), 30-42; (Sept. 1964), 96-101; (Oct. 1964), 90-93. Illustrated by Edith Maclean. Introductory note on p. 4 of the first installment.

44 Excerpt. "Asi era Scott Fitzgerald," *Casa de las Américas,* IV (Dec. 1964), 81-85.
   "Scott Fitzgerald" [Chapter 17] of *A Moveable Feast* translated into Spanish by José Rodriguez Feo.

45 Excerpt. "Aus der Erzählung 'Schnee auf dem Kilimandscharo,'" *Vorarlberg,* IV (Oct. 1965), 10.
   Excerpt from "The Snows of Kilimanjaro" translated into German.

45$_1$ Excerpt. "'Wir liebten Vorarlberg,'" *ibid.,* pp. 11-19.
   The last chapter of *A Moveable Feast* translated into German. An English translation, "'We Loved the Vorarlberg,'" appears on pp. 21-30.

45₂ Play review reprinted. *Ibid.*, p. 15.

A facsimile of Hemingway's review of two plays is reproduced from the *Vorarlberger Landes-Zeitung* (Jan. 13, 1926). See (S-C12).

46 Excerpt. "Bei Sylvia Beach," *Welt und Wort*, xx (Nov. 1965), 372.

"Shakespeare and Company" [Chapter 4] of *A Moveable Feast* translated into German by Annemarie Horschitz-Horst.

47 Nonfiction. *Morte nel pomeriggio, Tempo*, xxviii, No. 3 (Jan. 19, 1966) *to* No. 13 (March 30, 1966). Illustrated by Pablo Picasso. Cover photograph of Hemingway on the first installment.

Death in the Afternoon translated into Italian by Fernanda Pivano. Serialized in eleven installments. For publication in book form, see (S-D62).

48 Short story reprinted. "Sepi Jingan," *Crest*, LXXIII, ii (Spring 1967), [12]-[13].

Reprinted from *Tabula*, xxiii (Nov. 1916). See (C10). Note: *Crest* is a literary magazine published by the students of Oak Park and River Forest High School.

48₁ Short story reprinted. "Judgment of Manitou," *ibid.*, p. [14].

Reprinted from *Tabula*, xxii (Feb. 1916). See (C3).

49 Article reprinted. "About Marlene Dietrich," *Playbill*, IV, x (Oct. 1967), [23]-[24].

Hemingway's tribute to Marlene Dietrich is reprinted from *Life*, xxxiii (Aug. 18, 1952). See (C367). Note: This issue of *Playbill* was the program for "Marlene Dietrich," which premiered Oct. 9, 1967, at the Lunt-Fontanne Theatre in New York.

50 Novel. *Fiesta, Soarele răsare soarele apune, Secolul 20*, No. 10 (Oct. 1967), pp. 133-188; No. 11 (Nov. 1967), pp. 95-177.

The Sun Also Rises translated into Rumanian by D. Mazilu.

51 Short story. "A borboleta e o tanque," *Livro de Cabeceira da Mulher*, ii, vii (1968), 145-158.

"The Butterfly and the Tank" translated into Portuguese.

52 NANA dispatches reprinted. *Daily Telegraph Magazine*, No. 172 (Jan. 19, 1968), pp. 32-34.

Three NANA dispatches reprinted from *By-Line*: "The Shelling of Madrid" (April 11, 1937), "The Chauffeurs of Madrid" (May 22, 1937), and "A Brush with Death" (Sept. 30, 1937).

53 Article reprinted. "Hemingway's 'Kerensky, the Fighting Flea,'" *Kansas City Star* (Jan. 28, 1968), p. 1 D. Drawing of Hemingway at 18.

Reprinted from the *K.C. Star* (Dec. 16, 1917). Introductory note by D. H. [Donald Hoffman], who identified the article through the recollections of Neil McDermott, who was an office boy at the *Kansas City Star* during the winter of 1917-1918 when Hemingway was a cub reporter on the paper. Reprinted in Mel Foor's article in the *K.C. Star* (July 21, 1968), see (S-C56); in *Ernest Hemingway, Cub Reporter* edited by Matthew J. Bruccoli, Pittsburgh, 1970, pp. 15-19. See (S-A16).

54 NANA dispatches. *Znamya*, No. 4 (April 1968), 98-104.

Hemingway's Spanish Civil War dispatches translated into Russian, by A. Startsev, from the *New Republic*. See (C263), (C276), (C290), and (C298). Foreword on p. 98.

55 Dispatches. ["From the legacy of Ernest Hemingway"], *Inostrannaya Literatura*, No. 6 (June 1968), pp. 232-248.

Four World War II dispatches translated into Russian from *Collier's*. See (C331), (C332), (C334), and (C336). Foreword, by B. Gribanov, on pp. 232-235.

56 Articles reprinted. "Remembering Hemingway's Kansas City Days" by Mel Foor, *Kansas City Star* (July 21, 1968), pp. 1 D, 2 D.

Four unsigned articles attributed to Hemingway by Mel Foor are reprinted from the *K.C. Star*. "Throng at Smallpox Case" (Feb. 18, 1918), "At the End of the Ambulance Run" (Jan. 20, 1918), "Kerensky, the Fighting Flea" (Dec. 16, 1917), and "Mix War, Art And Dancing" (April 21, 1918). They are reprinted in *Ernest Hemingway, Cub Reporter* edited by Matthew J. Bruccoli, Pittsburgh, 1970. See (S-A16).

57 Article reprinted. "Battle of Raid Squads" in "Ernest Hemingway as Cub Reporter," *Esquire*, LXX (Dec. 1968), 207, 265.

Reprinted from the *Kansas City Star* (Jan 6, 1918), with an introductory note by Matthew J. Bruccoli. Reprinted in *Ernest Hemingway, Cub Reporter* edited by Bruccoli, Pittsburgh, 1970, pp. 20-26. See (S-A16). See also Mel Foor's letter, regarding Hemingway's work in the *K.C. Star*, in *Esquire*, LXXI (Feb. 1969), 12.

58 Book review reprinted. "A Lost Book Review: *A Story-Teller's Story*," *Fitzgerald/Hemingway Annual: 1969*, pp. 71-75.

Hemingway's review of Sherwood Anderson's *A Story-Teller's Story* is reprinted, along with a review by Gertrude Stein, from *Ex Libris*, II (March 1925). Headnote by "M.J.B." [Matthew J. Bruccoli].

59 Article reprinted. "Will You Let These Kiddies Miss Santa Claus?" *Fitzgerald/Hemingway Annual: 1970*, pp. 105-107.

Reprinted from the *Co-operative Commonwealth*, II (Dec. 1920). See (C52). Note: A facsimile of this article and the front cover of the magazine were reproduced in a keepsake for the Friends of the *Fitzgerald/Hemingway Annual*. See (S-F171).

60 Short story. "Aconteceu em Michigan," *êle ela,* I, ii (March 1970), 99-105.

"Up in Michigan" translated into Portuguese by Mário Pontes.

61 Article reprinted. "At the End of the Ambulance Run," *University Times* (University of Pittsburgh) (May 28, 1970), p. 10.

Reprinted from *Ernest Hemingway, Cub Reporter* edited by Matthew J. Bruccoli, Pittsburgh, 1970, pp. 27-33. This article originally appeared in the *Kansas City Star* (Jan. 20, 1918).

62 NANA dispatch reprinted. "Die Einnahme von Teruel," *Welt und Wort,* XXV (July 1970), 214.

"The Fall of Teruel," NANA dispatch datelined December 23, 1937, translated into German by Ernst Schnabel and Elisabeth Plessen. Reprinted from *49 Depeschen (By-Line),* Hamburg: Rowohlt, 1969.

63 Article reprinted. "The Best Rainbow Trout Fishing," *Sports Afield,* CLXIV (Sept. 1970), 56-57, 138. Drawing of Hemingway by Bob Abbott.

Reprinted from the *Toronto Star Weekly* (Aug. 28, 1920). See (C47). Note: Heading on pp. 56-57: YOUNG HEMINGWAY—OUTDOOR WRITER Before he was Papa he was Ernie—and he wrote about fishing like no 21-year-old you ever read.

64 Novel excerpt. "Bimini," *Esquire,* LXXIV (Oct. 1970), 122-137, 190, 192, 194, 196, 198, 200, 202. Cover photograph of Hemingway, superimposed with seven lines from a page of the holograph manuscript.

First publication of a 34,000-word excerpt from Part One of *Islands in the Stream.* A note, on p. 122, explains that this excerpt "while reading as a continuous narrative, actually bridges various passages that will appear in their entirety in the book." See also the Publisher's Page, "Notes on Bimini," by "A. G." [Arnold Gingrich], pp. 6, 12; Backstage with *Esquire,* p. 30; and the Editor's Note, p. 121.

65 Novel excerpt. *Ostrova v okeane, Literaturnaya Gazeta* (Oct. 14, 1970), p. 13.

Excerpt from *Islands in the Stream* translated into Russian by N. Volzenova and E. Kalashnikova. Foreword by G. Borovik on p. 13.

66 Novel. *Ostrova v okeane, Inostrannaya Literatura,* No. 11 (Nov. 1970), pp. 120-178; No. 12 (Dec. 1970), pp. 90-220; No. 1 (Jan. 1971), pp. 89-167.

Islands in the Stream translated into Russian by N. Volzenova and E. Kalashnikova. Note by Mary Hemingway on p. 119 of the first installment. Foreword by G. Borovik on pp. 119-120 of the first installment.

67 Play review reprinted. "Lost Hemingway Review Found," *Fitzgerald/Hemingway Annual: 1971*, pp. 195-196.

Review of two Christmas performances, in Schruns, of Hans Sachs's *The Hot Iron* and Bernard Shaw's *How He Deceived Her Husband*. Reprinted in German from the *Vorarlberger Landes-Zeitung* (Jan. 13, 1926), with an English translation by James Franklin. See (S-C12).

67₁ Article reprinted. "'Buying Commission Would Cut Out Waste': A Newly Discovered Contribution to the *Toronto Daily Star*," *ibid.*, pp. 209-211.

A facsimile of Hemingway's unsigned article from the *Toronto Daily Star* (April 20, 1920) is reproduced on p. 211. The article is authenticated by C. E. Frazer Clark, Jr.

67₂ Poem reprinted. "Advice to a Son," *ibid.*, p. 246.

A facsimile of the poem and a photograph of Hemingway is reproduced from *Omnibus: Almanach auf das Jahr 1932*. See (C199).

68 Excerpt from *Islands in the Stream*, *Cosmopolitan*, CLXX (March 1971), 202-204, 206-216, 218-219, 222-223, 225-230. Illustrated by Wilson McLean.

A note, on p. 203, explains that this excerpt from "Cuba," the second section of the novel, "while reading as a continuous narrative, actually bridges various passages which appear in their entirety in the book."

69 Introduction partially reprinted. *Field & Stream*, LXXV (April 1971), 165-166.

Excerpts from Hemingway's Introduction to S. Kip Farrington's *Atlantic Game Fishing* (B27) are reprinted in an article excerpted from Farrington's *Fishing with Hemingway and Glassell*. See (S-B12).

70 Short story reprinted. "Sepi Jingan," *Chicago Daily News* (July 31–Aug. 1, 1971), Panorama section, p. 5.

Reprinted from *Tabula*, XXIII (Nov. 1916). See (C10).

71 Novel excerpt. "Ein Schwertfisch beisst an," *Welt und Wort*, XXVI (Oct. 1971), 524-526.

Excerpt from Chapter IX of Part One of *Islands in the Stream*, translated into German by Elisabeth Plessen and Ernst Schnabel. Reprinted from *Inseln im Strom*, Reinbek: Rowohlt, 1971. Introductory note on p. 524.

72 Short story reprinted. "Sepi Jingan," *NCR World,* v (Nov.–Dec. 1971), 22-23.

Reprinted from *Tabula,* XXIII (Nov. 1916). See (C10).

73 Journal. "African Journal," *Sports Illustrated,* XXXV (Dec. 20, 1971), 5, 40-52, 57-66; XXXVI (Jan. 3, 1972), 26-46; (Jan. 10, 1972), 22-30, 43-50. Illustrated by Jack Brusca.

Three-part serialization of excerpts from Hemingway's journal, written between 1954 and 1956, of his and Mary Hemingway's Kenya safari in 1953. Parts 1 and 2 are titled "Miss Mary's Lion," Part 3 is titled "Imperiled Flanks." The titles were chosen by the editor. See the "Introduction to An African Journal" by Ray Cave, on pp. 40-41 of the first installment, regarding the "stringent editing rules" which were followed in excerpting 55,000 words from the 200,000-word manuscript. See also Letter from the Publisher by Dick Munro in *SI,* XXXV (Dec. 6, 1971), 11; and in *SI,* XXXV (Dec. 20, 1971), 5. For facsimiles of portions of two pages of the holograph manuscript, see (S-F37) and (S-F38).

74 Poem. "The Ship," *Fitzgerald/Hemingway Annual: 1972,* p. 115.

Facsimile of the typescript of a thirty-line poem written aboard the *Chicago* en route to France in 1918. The poem is attributed to Hemingway by William Horne and Frederick W. Spiegel, who served with him in the Red Cross ambulance corps.

75 Excerpts. "Unpublished Hemingway: Secrets of Papa/Nick," *Detroit Free Press* (April 2, 1972), p. 5-B.

Excerpts from "On Writing," from *The Nick Adams Stories,* pp. 238-240.

76 Narration for the film *Adventures of a Young Man, WGAw News* (Writers Guild of America/West Newsletter) (June 1972), p. 21.

A section of the narration written by Hemingway to frame the action of the film is printed in William Nolan's review of *The Nick Adams Stories.*

77 Introduction quoted. The Last Word column, *N.Y. Times Book Review* (Dec. 3, 1972), p. 103.

A short excerpt, regarding New York literary reviews, from Hemingway's Introduction to Elio Vittorini's *In Sicily,* p. [8], serves as the epigraph to an essay by John Leonard.

78 Book review quoted. *N.Y. Times Book Review* (Jan. 28, 1973), p. 44.

Hemingway's review of *Batouala: A True Black Novel* by René Maran is quoted, from the *Toronto Star Weekly* (March 25, 1922), in a review, by Michael Olmert, of the Black Orpheus Press translation. See (C72).

79 Article reprinted. "On the Blue Water: A Gulf Stream Letter," *Esquire,* LXXX (Oct. 1973), 141-142, 380, 382. Fortieth Anniversary Issue.

Reprinted from *Esquire,* V (April 1936). See (C243). Brief note, on p. 141, regarding Hemingway's "Letters" in *Esquire.*

79₁ Short story reprinted. "The Snows of Kilimanjaro," *ibid.,* pp. 143-147, 366, 370, 372.

This story originally appeared in *Esquire,* VI (Aug. 1936). See (C249).

80 Tribute quoted. "Jimmy Cannon, Columnist, Dies; Sportswriter Ranged Far Afield" by Dave Anderson, *N.Y. Times* (Dec. 6, 1973), p. 50.

The obituary includes a quotation from Hemingway, which is described as "perhaps the finest tribute to Jimmy Cannon as a writer." The source of the quotation is not given.

SECTION D
TRANSLATIONS

This section was largely compiled from the *Index translationum* (the International Bibliography of Translations published annually in Paris by UNESCO), and supplemented by collectors' copies, library copies, and correspondence with Hemingway's foreign publishers. I am especially indebted to Frau Allo Becker-Berke of Rowohlt Verlag, Kirsten Jacobsen of Lademann, W. Hirsch of Bonniers, F. E. Breitenstein of A.J.G. Strengholt, and Mrs. Maria Barra of Mondadori.

AFRIKAANS

S-D1 *Vaarwel Wapens (FTA)*. Johannesburg: Afrikaanse Pers-Boekhandel, 1965. 273 pages. Translated by Chris Barnard.

ARABIC

2 *Liali baris (AMF)*. Damascus: Eds. Al Ayyam, 1965. 254 pages. Translated by Fath Allah Mouchaché.

BULGARIAN

3 *Bezkraen praznik (AMF)*. Plovdiv: Hr. G. Danov, 1967. 208 pages. Illustrated. Translated by Dimitri Ivanov.

4 *Sbogom na orǎžijata (FTA)*. Sofia: Nar. kultura, 1968. 280 pages. Translated by Živka Dragneva.

5 *Zelenite hǎlmove na Afrika (GHOA)*. Sofia: Zemizdat, 1969. 242 pages. Translated by Dimitri Ivanov.

BURMESE

6 *Ana-wa nhin. ahpō-o (OMATS)*. Rangoon, 1954. 162 pages. Translated by Nyan Wun.

7 *Thway Mye Ko Kyaw Khaing Ywal (FTA)*. Rangoon: Journal Kyaw Ma Ma Lay Sarpay, 1967. 474 pages. Translated by Khin Gyi Aung.

CHINESE

8 *Hai Ming Sei Hsiao shuo Hsüan* (short stories). Taipei: Chih Wen Pub. Ser., 1968. 228 pages. Translated by Hsü Wen Ta.

9 *Lao Jên Yü Hal (OMATS)*. Taichung: I Shan Pub. Ser., 1970. 149 pages.

10 *Tsai Wo Mên Ti Shih Tai Li (IOT)*. Taipei: Cactus Publishing Co., 1970. 175 pages. Translated by Kuo Chên T'ang.

CZECH

11 *Zelené pahorky Africké (GHOA)*. Prague: Státní Nakladatelství Krásné Literatury a Uměni, 1963. [Soudobá světová próza, 150.]

Translated by Luba Pellarovi and Rudolph Pellarovi. Afterword, by Josef Škvorecký, on pp. 217-223. Note: This is additional information, and an earlier date of publication, for D29.

12 *Pátá kolona (TFC)*. Prague: Orbis, 1964. [Divadlo, 71.] Translated by František Vrba. Afterword by the translator. Note: This is additional information on D28.

13 *Povídky* (short stories). Prague: Státní Nakladatelství Krásné Literatury a Uměni, 1965. 444 pages. Afterword by the editor, Josef Škvorecký, on pp. 434-444.

14 *I slunce vycházi (SAR)*. Prague: Mladá Fronta, 1966. [Kapka, No. 84.] 187 pages. Translated by František Vrba. Afterword by the translator on pp. 185-187.

15 *Pohyblivý svátek (AMF)*. Prague: Odeon, 1966. 205 pages. Translated by Stanislav Mareš. Afterword by Josef Škvorecký.

DANISH

16 *I vor tid (IOT)*. Copenhagen: J. H. Schultz, 1967. 248 pages. Translated by Sigvard Lund and Ole Restrup.

17 *Ingenting til vinderen (WTN)*. Copenhagen: J. H. Schultz, 1968. 155 pages. Translated by Sigvard Lund and Ole Restrup.

18 *Mænd uden kvinder (MWW)*. Copenhagen: J. H. Schultz, 1968. 160 pages. Translated by Sigvard Lund and Ole Restrup.

19 *Signeret: Ernest Hemingway (By-Line)*. Copenhagen: J. H. Schultz, 1968. 304 pages. Translated by Knud Holst.

20 *Øen og havet (Islands)*. Copenhagen: Lademann, 1971. 360 pages. Translated by Mogens Boisen.

DUTCH

21 *Mannen zonder vrouwen (MWW)*. Amsterdam: Uitgeverij Contact, 1965. 128 pages. Translated by Clara Eggink. Second edition.

22 *Wie wint krijgt niets (WTN)*. Amsterdam: Uitgeverij Contact, 1965. 132 pages. Translated by Jean A. Schalekamp.

23 *De oude man en de zee / Alsmede vijfentwintig korte verhalen (OMATS and 25 short stories)*. Hasselt: Heideland, 1965. 456 pages. Illustrated. Translated by E. Veegens-Latorf, J.W.F. Werumens Buning, et al.

24 *Hebben en niet hebben (THAHN)*. Amsterdam: Uitgeverij Contact, 1966. 187 pages. Translated by H.W.J. Schaap.

25 *De sneeuw van de Kilimandzaro, en andere verhalen* ("The Snows of Kilimanjaro" and five other short stories). Antwerp: Contact, 1967. 94 pages. Translated by Hans Edinga.

26 *In onze tijd (IOT)*. Amsterdam: Uitgeverij Contact, 1968. 111 pages. Translated by Clara Eggink.

27 *Kantlijn: Een keuze uit artikelen en berichten over een period van veertig jaar (By-Line)*. Amsterdam: Uitgeverij Contact N.V., 1970. 187 pages. Translated by Jean A. Schalekamp.

28 *Eilanden in de Golfstroom (Islands)*. Amsterdam: A.J.G. Strengholt, 1971. 442 pages. Translated by J. F. Kliphuis.

ESTONIAN

29 *Pidu sinus eneses (AMF)*. Tallinn: Periodika, 1965. 156 pages. Translated by Enn Soosair.

30 *Francis Macomberi üürike õnn* ("The Short Happy Life of Francis Macomber" and 34 other short stories). Tallinn: Eesti raamat, 1965. 384 pages. Translated by J. Lohk.

31 *(For Whom the Bell Tolls)*. Tallinn: Eesti raamat, 1970. 527 pages. Afterword by K. Simonov.

FINNISH

32 *Ernest Hemingway: Täyttä elämää (By-Line)*. Helsinki: Tammi, 1968. 260 pages. Translated by Veikko Polameri, Pentti Polameri, and Jouko Linturi.

33 *Saaret ja virta (Islands)*. Helsinki: Tammi, 1972. 408 pages. Translated by Juhani Jaskari.

FRENCH

34 *Oeuvres romanesques: Poèmes de guerre et d'après-guerre*. Tome I. Paris: Gallimard, 1966. [Bibliothèque de la Pléiade, v. 189.] 1,472 pages. Edited by Roger Asselineau. Foreword, preface, chronology, and notes by the editor. Contents: *TOS, FTA, SAR, AMF, DIA*, short stories and interchapters from the *First 49*, and poems from the *Collected Poems*. By various translators. Note: For a review of the first volume in the *Times Literary Supplement* (June 22, 1967), see (S-H342).

34₁ *Oeuvres romanesques: Reportages de guerre/poèmes à Mary*. Tome II. Paris: Gallimard, 1969. [Bibliothèque de la Pléiade, v. 207.] 1,760 pages. Edited by Roger Asselineau. Foreword, notes, and bibliography by the editor. Contents: *GHOA, THAHN, FWBT, TFC, ARIT, OMATS*, short stories from the *First 49*, articles from *By-*

Line, "A Man of the World," "Get a Seeing-Eyed Dog," "Two Poems to Mary," and Hemingway's Nobel prize acceptance speech. By various translators.

35 *En ligne: Choix d'articles et de dépêches de quarante années (By-Line).* Paris: Gallimard, 1970. 546 pages. Translated by Jean-René Major and Georges Magnane.

36 *Iles à la dérive (Islands).* Paris: Gallimard, 1971. 467 pages. Translated by Jean-René Major.

GERMAN

37 *Die fünfte Kolonne (TFC).* Reinbek bei Hamburg: Rowohlt, 1969. [Rororo, 1232.] Translated by Ernst Schnabel and Elisabeth Plessen.

38 *49 Depeschen: Ausgewählte Zeitungsberichte und Reportagen aus den Jahren 1920-1956 (By-Line).* Reinbek bei Hamburg: Rowohlt, 1969. 398 pages. Translated by Ernst Schnabel and Elisabeth Plessen. Preface, by Ernst Schnabel, on pp. 7-11. Note: This book contains 49 of the original 77 articles edited by William White. Reissued: 1972. [Rororo, 1533.] 317 pages. Preface, by Ernst Schnabel, on pp. 5-8.

39 *Inseln im Strom (Islands).* Reinbek bei Hamburg: Rowohlt, 1971. 441 pages. Translated by Elisabeth Plessen and Ernst Schnabel. Note by Mary Hemingway on p. [4].

40 *Die Nick Adams Stories (NAS).* Reinbek bei Hamburg: Rowohlt, 1973. Translated by Richard K. Flesch and Annemarie Horschitz-Horst.

GREEK

41 *Ta Chionia tou Kilimantzaro* ("The Snows of Kilimanjaro" and eleven other short stories). Athens: "Ho kosmos tes technes," [n.d.]. Translated by K.Ph.

42 *I prassini lofi tēs Afrikēs (GHOA).* Athens: Kampanas, 1970. 224 pages. Translated by Panagiōtēs Bernardos.

43 (*The Old Man and the Sea* and "The Snows of Kilimanjaro"). Athens: Angtra Publishing House, 1972. 129 pages. Translated by N. Kastrinaki.

HEBREW

44 *Šilge Kilimanjaro* ("The Snows of Kilimanjaro," "The Killers," and "The Short Happy Life of Francis Macomber"). Tel Aviv: Chief Education Officer, Ministry of Defense, 1965. 127 pages. Illustrated.

HUNGARIAN

45 *A folyón át, a fák közé (ARIT)*. Novi Sad: Forum Könyvkiadó, [1966]. 318 pages. Translated by Máthé Elek. Preface, by Sükösd Mihály, on pp. 5-40.

46 *Vándorünnep (AMF)*. Budapest: Európa Könyvkiadó, 1966. [Világrész Könyvei, 5.] 237 pages. Translated by Göncz Árpád. Preface by Hemingway on p. 5. Note by M.H. [Mary Hemingway] on p. 7.

47 *Halál délután (DIA)*. Budapest: Európa Könyvkiadó, 1969. 463 pages. Illustrated. Translated by Papp Zoltán.

48 *Francis Macomber rövid boldogsága / A Kilimandzáró hava* ("The Short Happy Life of Francis Macomber" and "The Snows of Kilimanjaro"). Budapest: Magyar Helikon, 1970. 72 pages. Translated by László András and Szász Imre.

49 *Művei: Elbeszélések* (short stories). Budapest: Magyar Helikon, 1970. 582 pages. Translated by László T. András et al.

50 *Szegények és gazdagok / A folyón át a fák közé / Az öreg halász és a tenger (THAHN, ARIT, and OMATS)*. Budapest: Magyar Helikon, 1971. 568 pages. *THAHN* translated by Szász Imre; *ARIT* translated by Göncz Árpád; *OMATS* translated by Ottlik Géza. Afterword, by Sükösd Mihály, on pp. 563-568.

ICELANDIC

51 *Veisla í farángrinum (AMF)*. Akureyri: Bókaforlag Odds Björnssonar, 1966. 240 pages. Translated by Halldór Laxness.

REGIONAL LANGUAGES OF INDIA

52 *Buddha te samundar (OMATS)*. Delhi: Navayug Press, 1965. 132 pages. Translated into Punjabi by Gurbakhaš Singh Sant.

53 *Eka koliyane (OMATS)*. Poona: Dešmukh, 1965. 154 pages. Illustrated. Translated into Marathi by Purushottam Lakshman Dešpande.

54 *Ghanaghanato ghantanda (FWBT)*. Bombay: Majestic Book Stall, 1965. 487 pages. Illustrated. Translated into Marathi by Digambar Balkrishma Mokaši.

55 *Deva-dundubhi baje kar babe (FWBT)*. Calcutta: Sribhumi Publishing Co., 1966. 614 pages. Translated into Assamese by Birendra Kumar Bhattacharya.

56 *Kahapaim ghanta baje (FWBT)*. Cuttack: Rashtrabhasa pustak bhandar, 1966. 553 pages. Translated into Oriya by Nagendrakumar Ray.

57 *Pagal* (eight short stories). Delhi: Hind Pocket Books, 1967. 111 pages. Translated into Hindi by Virendrakumar Gupta and Rameš Varma.

58 *Manimuzhangunnatu arkku venti (FWBT)*. Kottayam: Sahitya pravarthaka C.S., 1967. 643 pages. Translated into Malayalam by A. N. Nambiar.

59 *Manukh te sagar (OMATS)*. Ludhiana: Lahore Book Shop, 1969. 138 pages. Translated into Punjabi by S. S. Amol.

IRANIAN

60 *Vedā bā Aslahe (FTA)*. Tehran: Akhavan-e Golchin, 1970. 224 pages. Translated by R. Mar'ashi.

ITALIAN

61 *Il vecchio e il mare (OMATS.)* Milan: Mondadori, 1965. 248 pages. Illustrated. Translated by Domenico Manzella.

62 *Morte nel pomeriggio (DIA)*. Milan: Aldo Palazzi Editore, 1966. 171 pages. Illustrated by Pablo Picasso. Translated by Fernanda Pivano. Note: Reprinted in eleven installments in *Tempo,* xxviii (Jan. 19, 1966) to (March 30, 1966). See (S-C47).

63 *Dal nostro inviato Ernest Hemingway (By-Line)*. Milan: Mondadori, 1967. 456 pages. Illustrated. Translated by Ettore Capriolo and Giorgio Monicelli.

64 *Isole nella Corrente (Islands)*. Milan: Mondadori, 1970. 489 pages. Translated by Vincenzo Mantovani. Note by Mary Hemingway on p. [9].

65 *Storie della guerra di Spagna (TFC & 4 Stories)*. Milan: Mondadori, 1972. 235 pages. [Scrittori Italiani e stranieri.] *The Fifth Column* was translated by Giuseppe Trevisani. The four stories of the Spanish Civil War were translated by Vincenzo Mantovani.

66 *I racconti di Nick Adams (NAS)*. Milan: Mondadori, 1973. 274 pages. Translated by Giuseppe Trevisani.

JAPANESE

67 *Idô shuku saijitsu (AMF)*. Tokyo: Mikasa shobô, 1964. 318 pages. Translated by Fukuda Rikutarô.

68 *Gogo no shi (DIA)*. Tokyo: Mikasa shobô, 1966. 337 pages. Illustrated. Translated by Saeki Shôichi and Miyamoto Yôichi.

69 *Chôcho to sensha* ("The Butterfly and the Tank" and other short stories). Tokyo: Kawade shobô shinsha, 1966. 265 pages. Translated by Nakada Kôji.

KOREAN

70 *Jugeunjaneum Malieobda (Men at War).* Seoul: Jangmunsa, 1967. 200 pages. Translated by Chang-Ung Kim.

71 *(By-Line).* Seoul: Eul Yu Moon Wha Sa, 1967. 338 pages. Translated by Kuhn Sup Lee and Byong Chul Kim.

72 *Apeurikaeui pureun eondeog (GHOA).* Seoul: Hwimun, 1970. 635 pages. Translated by Jeong Byeong Jo.

73 *Haeryu sogeui seomdeul (Islands).* Seoul: Hyeonnam, 1970. 619 pages. Translated by Jo Sun Hwan.

LATVIAN

74 *Ardievas ieročiem (FTA).* Riga: Liesma, 1965. 397 pages. Translated by Tatjana Jarmolinska. Note: This is additional information for D229.

LEBANESE

75 *Wa lā Tazāl al-Shams Tushriq (SAR).* Beirut: Dār al-'Ilm Lilmalāyīn, 1965. 324 pages. Translated by Badi 'Haqqī.

76 *Wadā' li al-Silāh (FTA).* Beirut: Dār al-'Ilm Lilmalāyīn, 1965. 407 pages. Translated by Munīr Ba'albakī.

77 *Al-Shaykh wa al-Baḥr (OMATS).* Beirut: Dār al-'Ilm Lilmalāyīn, 1966. 184 pages. Translated by Munīr Ba'albakī.

78 *Liman tuqra'a al-Ajrās (FWBT).* Beirut: Dār Maktabat al'Haiāt, 1969. 576 pages. Translated by Kheiri Himād.

MALTESE

79 *Ix-xwejjah U L-Bahar (OMATS).* Malta: Progress Press, 1965. Translated by Fr. D. Mintoff.

MONGOLIAN

80 *Zer zevseg min' bayartaj (FTA).* Oulanbator: Ulsyn Hevlelijn gazar, 1970. 507 pages. Translated by M. Tsedendorj.

NORWEGIAN

81 *Med Hemingway på kryss og tvers: Artikler, reportasjer og reisebrev (By-Line).* Oslo: Gyldendal, 1968. 260 pages. Translated by Nils Lie.

82 *Øyer i havstrømmen (Islands).* Oslo: Gyldendal, 1971. 416 pages. Translated by Nils Lie. Note by Mary Hemingway on p. [6].

73

PAKISTANI

83 *Samudra sambhog (OMATS)*. Chittagong: Shahin Banoo, 1968. 97 pages. Translated into Bengali by Fateh Lohani.

POLISH

84 *Niepokonany* (short stories). Warsaw: Ksiażka i Wiedza, 1967. 82 pages. Translated by Jan Zakrzewski and Bronislaw Zieliński.

PORTUGUESE

85 *O velho e o mar (OMATS)*. Rio de Janeiro: Civilização Brasileira, 1955. [Obras Imortais, 2.] 150 pages. Translated by Fernando de Castro Ferro, see (D276); revised by José Baptista da Luz.

86 *As Torrentes da Primavera (TOS)*. Lisbon: Livros do Brasil, 1965. 142 pages. Translated by Maria Luísa Osório and Alexandre Pinheiro Torres.

87 *Contos de Hemingway* (27 short stories). Rio de Janeiro: Editôra Civilização Brasileira, 1965. [Biblioteca do Leitor Contemporaneo, 60.] 182 pages. Translated by A. Veiga Fialho.

88 *O sol também se levanta (SAR)*. Rio de Janeiro: Civilização Brasileira, 1966. [Biblioteca do Leitor Moderno, 73.] 227 pages. Translated by Berenice Xavier. Reissued: São Paulo: Abril S. A. Cultural e Industrial, 1971. [Os Imortais da Literatura Universal, 13.] 266 pages.

89 *Paris é una festa (AMF)*. Rio de Janeiro: Civilização Brasileira, 1967. [Biblioteca do Leitor Moderno, 84.] 204 pages. Translated by Énio Silveira.

90 *Ernest Hemingway, Repórter: Artigos e despachos selecionados ao longo de quatro décadas (By-Line)*. Rio de Janeiro: Civilização Brasileira, 1969. 2 volumes. [Biblioteca do Leitor Moderno, 99 and 99a.] Vol. I, subtitled *Tempo de viver*, 299 pages. Vol. II, subtitled *Tempo de morrer*, 254 pages. Translated by Álvaro Cabral.

RUMANIAN

91 *Cîştigătorul nu ia nimic* (22 short stories). Bucharest: Editura pentru Literatură, 1964. [Biblioteca pentru toţi, 221.] 310 pages. Translated by Radu Lupan. Preface by the translator on pp. III-XXII. Chronological table on pp. XXIII-XXIX.

92 *Pentru cine bat clopotele (FWBT)*. Bucharest: Editura pentru Literatură Universală, 1965. 602 pages. Translated by Dumitru Mazilu. Preface by Radu Lupan.

93 *O sărbătoare de neuitat (AMF)*. Bucharest: Editura pentru Literatură Universală, 1966. 232 pages. Translated by Emma Beniuc.

94 *Fiesta: Soarele răsare, soarele apune (SAR)*. Bucharest: Editura pentru Literatură Universală, 1968. [Colecția Meridiane.] 350 pages. Translated by Dumitru Mazilu.

95 *Adio, arme (FTA)*. Bucharest: Editura pentru Literatură, 1969. 357 pages. Translated by Radu Lupan.

96 *Pentru cine bat clopotele (FWBT)*. Bucharest: Editura Minerva, 1971. 2 volumes. 341 pages; 377 pages. Translated by Dumitru Mazilu. Preface, by Dan Grigorescu, on pp. v-ix. Chronology on pp. xi-xviii.

RUSSIAN AND OTHER SLAVIC TRANSLATIONS

97 *Garri Morgan | Rasskazy | Pjataja kolonna (THAHN*, short stories, and *TFC)*. Tbilisi: Literatura da helovneba, 1964. Translated into Georgian by V. Čelidze.

98 *Prazdnik, kotoryj vsegda s toboj (AMF)*. Moscow: Izd-vo Progress, 1965. 160 pages. Illustrated. Translated by M. Bruk, L. Petrov, and F. Rozental'.

99 *Sal men ten'iz (OMATS)*. Alma-Ata: Žazušy, 1966. 87 pages. Illustrated. Translated into Kazah by Nyğymet Gabdullin.

100 *Prazdnik, kotoryj vsegda s toboj (AMF)*. Erevan: Ajastan, 1966. 190 pages. Translated into Armenian by R. Avagjan.

101 *Snega Kilimandžaro* ("The Snows of Kilimanjaro"). Tbilisi: Nakaduli, 1967. 41 pages. Translated into Georgian by V. Čelidze.

102 *Senis ir jūra (OMATS)*. Vilna: Vaga, 1967. 103 pages. Illustrated. Translated into Lithuanian by R. Lankauskas.

103 *Fiesta (SAR)*. Vilna: Vaga, 1967. 291 pages. Translated into Lithuanian by P. Gasiulis.

104 *Sobranie sočinenij* (Hemingway's Collected Works). Moscow: Khudozhestvennaya literatura, 1968. 4 volumes. Translated by E. Golyševa et al. Afterword in Vol. 4 by A. Startsev. Note: Carl Proffer comments in *Soviet Criticism of American Literature in the Sixties*, Ann Arbor, Michigan, 1972, p. 116, "because of its sensitive subject matter *For Whom the Bell Tolls* was not published until 1968—and then in a four-volume set of Hemingway along with heavy cuts in the text, particularly Chapter Eighteen."

105 *Turéti ir neturéti (THAHN)*. Vilna: Vaga, 1968. 247 pages. Translated into Lithuanian by G. Zolubiene.

106 *Snigy Kilimandžaro ta inši noveli* ("The Snows of Kilimanjaro" and other short stories). Kiev: Veselka, 1968. 309 pages. Translated into Ukrainian by Volodymyr Mytrofanov.

107 *Reportaži* (53 dispatches from *By-Line*). Moscow: Izdatel'stvo Moskovskogo Universiteta, 1969. 204 pages. Edited by L. V. Kytykova. Translated by T. S. Tihmeneva and I. A. Kashkeen. Foreword by Ya. N. Zasurskii.

108 *Po komu b'je dzvin (FWBT)*. Kiev: Rad. pis'mennik, 1969. 507 pages. Illustrated. Translated into Ukrainian by Mar Pintevs'kyj.

109 *Atsisveikinimas su ginklais (FTA)*. Vilna: Vaga, 1970. 332 pages. Translated into Lithuanian by Gabrielė Berkerytė and Romualdas Lankauskas.

110 *Vesniani potoky (TOS)*. Kiev, 1970. 111 pages. Translated into Ukrainian.

111 *Ostrova v okeane (Islands)*. Moscow: "Progress," 1971. 445 pages. Translated by N. Volzenova and E. Kalashnikova. Preface, by Boris Izakova, on pp. 5-13. Note by Mary Hemingway on p. [15].

SLOVAK

112 *Slnko aj vychádza (SAR)*. Bratislava: Vydavatelstvo Slovensky spisovatel, 1968. [Spoločnosť priateľov krásnyoh kníh.] 215 pages. Translated by Jozef Kot. Glossary on p. 215.

113 *Snehy Kilimandžára* (ten short stories and *OMATS*). Bratislava: Tatran, 1970. [Čitanie Študujúcej mládeže, 23.] 270 pages. *Starec a more (OMATS)* translated by Peter Ždán. Short stories translated by Jozef Olexa. Afterword, "Kľúč k Hemingwayovej tvorbe" by Július Pašteka, on pp. 249-266. Glossary on pp. 267-270.

SPANISH

114 *El viejo y el mar (OMATS)*. Mexico City: Editorial Selecciones, 1955. 163 pages.

115 *Los asesinos* ("The Killers" and 16 other short stories). Mexico City: Editora "Zarco," 1956. 215 pages.

116 *Paris era una fiesta (AMF)*. Barcelona: Seix Barral, 1964. 218 pages. Translated by Gabriel Ferrater.

117 *Las verdes colinas de Africa (GHOA)*. Barcelona: Caralt, 1964. 310 pages.

118 *El vell i la mer (OMATS)*. Barcelona: Proa, 1966. 216 pages. Translated into Catalan by Ferran de Pol.

119 *Mes enlla del riu i entre els arbres (ARIT)*. Barcelona: Aymá, 1967.

120 *Enviado especial: Artículos seleccionados correspondientes a cuatro décadas (By-Line)*. Barcelona: Editorial Planeta, 1968. 506 pages. [Colección Omnibus, 61.] Translated by Agustín Puig.

121 *Por quien doblan las campañas (FWBT)*. Barcelona: Editorial Planeta, 1968. 556 pages. Translated by Lola de Aguado.

122 *En otro pais* ("In Another Country"). Buenos Aires: Editorial Estuario, 1968. 55 pages. Note: Also includes "Una entrevista con Ernest Hemingway," George Plimpton's interview in the *Paris Review*, v (Spring 1958), translated into Spanish by Susana de Hersch.

123 *Muerte en la tarde (DIA)*. Barcelona: Editorial Planeta, 1968. [Colección Infinito, 74.] 355 pages. Translated by Lola Aguado.

124 *Las nieves de Kilimanjaro / Los asesinos* ("The Snows of Kilimanjaro," "The Killers," and other stories). Barcelona: Ediciones G. P., [1969]. [Los clásicos del siglo xx, 22.] 319 pages.

125 *Obras selectas* (selected works). Barcelona: Editorial Planeta, 1969. 2 volumes. 1736 pages; 1584 pages. By various translators. Vol. i: *TOS, SAR, FTA, THAHN, FWBT, ARIT*, and *OMATS*. Vol. ii: Short stories, poems, *DIA, GHOA, AMF*, and *By-Line*. Introductory essay, "Ernest Hemingway: Su vida y su obra" by Carlos Pujol, on pp. 9-135.

126 *Per qui toquen les campanes (FWBT)*. Barcelona: Proa, 1971. 2 volumes. Translated into Catalan.

127 *Islas en el golfo (Islands)*. Buenos Aires: Emecé Editores, 1971. 478 pages. Translated by Marta Isabel Guastavino and Héctor Quesada Zapiola.

128 *Islas a la deriva (Islands)*. Madrid: Editorial Planeta, 1972. 453 pages. Translated by Mary Rowe.

SWEDISH

129 *I vår tid (IOT)*. Stockholm: Bonniers, 1967. 150 pages. Translated by Mårten Edlund and Thorsten Jonsson.

130 *Hemingway var där: Artiklar och reportage från fyra decennier (By-Line)*. Stockholm: Bonniers, 1968. 264 pages. Translated by Birgit Edlund and Mårten Edlund.

131 *Femte kolonnen och fyra noveller från spanska inbördeskriget (TFC and 4 stories)*. Stockholm: Bonniers, 1970. 214 pages. Translated by Birgit Edlund and Mårten Edlund.

132 *Öar i strömmen (Islands).* Stockholm: Bonniers, 1971. 342 pages. Translated by Birgit Edlund and Mårten Edlund.

THAI

133 *(The Snows of Kilimanjaro).* Bangkok, Thailand: Odeon Printer, 1972. Translated by Chua Prabhavivahhana.

TURKISH

134 *Yenilmez Adam* (short stories). Istanbul: Varlık Yayınevi, 1965. Translated by Tunç Yalman, Vahdet Gültekin, and Mustafa Yurdakul.

YUGOSLAV

135 *Bregovi kao beli slonovi (MWW).* Sarajevo: Svjetlost, 1965. 171 pages. Translated by Olivera Stefanović.

136 *U naše vreme: Doživljaji Nika Adamsa i druge priče (IOT).* Belgrade: Prosveta, 1965. 140 pages. Translated by Zorica Despić.

137 *Zeleni bregovi Afrike (GHOA).* Titograd: Grafički zavod, 1965. [Biblioteka "Bestseleri," No. 8.] 257 pages. Translated into Croatian by Aleksandar-Saša Petrović.

138 *Sabrana dela Ernesta Hemingveja u sest knjiga* (Works of Ernest Hemingway in six volumes). Novi Sad: Matica srpska, 1967. Translated into Croatian. Vol. I: *Sunce se ponovo rada (SAR).* 255 pages. Translated by Kaliopa B. Nikolajević. Preface, "Ernest Hemingvej" by Svetozar Brkić, on pp. 7-19. Vol. II: *Zbogom oružje (FTA).* 345 pages. Translated by Radojica V. Cirović. Hemingway's foreword, on pp. 7-11, is translated from the 1948 Scribner edition. Vol. III: *Imati i nemati / Starac i more (THAHN / OMATS).* 273 pages. *THAHN* translated by Ljubica Vuković and Jelena Stojanović; *OMATS* translated by Karlo Ostojić. Vol. IV: *Za kim zvono zvoni (FWBT).* [Not checked.] Vol. V: *Preko reke i u šumu (ARIT).* 261 pages. Translated by Predrag Milojević. Vol. VI: *Pripovetke (First 49* short stories). 516 pages. Translated by Vera Ilić.

139 *Čez reko in med drevje (ARIT).* Maribor: Založba Obzorja, 1967. 256 pages. Translated into Slovenian by Bruno Hartman.

140 *Sonceto odnovo izgreva (SAR).* Skoplje: Makedonska kniga, 1968. 260 pages. Translated into Macedonian by Save Cvetanovski.

SECTION E

ANTHOLOGIES

This section is listed chronologically, and is alphabetized within each year by the editor's name or, if no editor is given, by the title of the collection. With a few exceptions, new and revised editions have been listed only when there has been a change in the selection.

The index of short fiction anthologies by Landon C. Burns in *Studies in Short Fiction,* VII (Winter 1970), was a particularly helpful source for this listing. Other sources included Keneth Kinnamon's addenda to the bibliography in the *Journal of English and Germanic Philology,* LXVIII (July 1969), and George Monteiro's checklist of Portuguese anthologies in the *Papers of the Bibliographical Society of America,* LXV (Oct.-Dec. 1971). Correspondence with publishers and access to editorial libraries helped to expand this section.

S-E1 *These Our Moderns.* Edited by Robert E. Galbraith. New York: Thomas Nelson, 1933.

 p. 101: Excerpt from *FTA,* p. 196, under the general heading "Modern Soldiers Look at War." Biographical note on p. 393.

2 *Contemporary Trends: American Literature since 1914.* Edited by John Herbert Nelson. New York: Macmillan, 1933.

 pp. 439-445: "The Killers." Biographical note on p. 501.

3 *American Poetry and Prose.* Edited by Norman Foerster and Robert Morss Lovett. Boston: Houghton Mifflin, 1934.

 pp. 1450-1467: Excerpt from *FTA,* pp. 199-249, titled here "The Retreat from Caporetto." Introductory note on p. 1450. [Third edition, revised, 1947. Vol. II: pp. 1389-1394: "The Killers." pp. 1394-1405: "The Snows of Kilimanjaro." Introductory note on pp. 1388-1389. Shorter edition, 1952. "Complete" fourth edition 1962.]

4 *The Realm of Reading: The American Scene.* Vol. 5. Edited by Walter Barnes et al. New York: American Book, 1940.

 pp. 513-521: "Big Two-Hearted River." Questions and suggestions on pp. 521-522. Biographical note on p. 746.

5 *The Pocket Book of Short Stories.* Edited with an Introduction by M. E. Speare. New York: Pocket Books, 1941.

 pp. 1-13: "The Killers."

6 *This America.* Edited by John D. Kern and Irwin Griggs. New York: Macmillan, 1943.

 pp. 674-698: "Fifty Grand." Biographical note on p. 674.

7 *Os Melhores Contos Americanos.* First Series. Edited by João Gaspar Simões. Lisbon: Portugália Editora, 1943.

 pp. 317-331: "Os assassinos." "The Killers" translated into Portuguese by João de Oliveira.

8 *3 Novelas Norte-Americanas.* Edited with a preface by José de Barros Pinto. São Paulo: Editôra Flama, 1944. [Antologia de Novela Universal, II.]

pp. 110-155: "A vida curta e feliz de Francis Macomber." "The Short Happy Life of Francis Macomber" translated into Portuguese by the editor.

9 *Obras-Primas do Conto Moderno.* Edited by Almiro Rolmes Barbosa and Edgard Cavalheiro. São Paulo: Livraria Martins Editora, 1944. ["A Marcha do Espirito," 14.]

pp. 83-92: "Três dias de vento." "The Three-Day Blow" translated into Portuguese.

10 *The Avon Story Teller.* New York: Avon Book, 1945. [New Avon Library.]

pp. 11-23: "Che Ti Dice La Patria?"

11 *Two-Fisted Stories for Men.* Edited by R. M. Barrows. Chicago: Consolidated Book Publishers, 1945.

pp. 20-27: "The Killers."

12 *Os mais belos contos norteamericanos.* Vecchi, 1945.

Contains "Os matadores." "The Killers" translated into Portuguese by Alfredo Ferreira.

13 *The PL Book of Modern American Short Stories.* Edited by Nicholas Moore. London: Nicholson & Watson, 1945. [Editions Poetry London.]

pp. 81-87: "The Light of the World."

14 *Os Norte Americanos Antigos e Modernos.* Edited by Vinicius de Moraes. Introduction by Orígenes Lessa. Biographical notes by Tati de Melo Moraes. Preface by Morton Dauwen Zabel. Rio de Janeiro: Companhia Editôra Leitura, 1945. [Coleção Contos do Mundo, 3.]

pp. 382-389: "Os Bandidos." "The Killers" translated into Portuguese by Moacir Werneck de Castro.

15 *The Pocket Book of Adventure Stories.* Edited by Philip Van Doren Stern. New York: Pocket Books, 1945.

pp. 1-27: "Fifty Grand."

16 *15 Great Stories of Today: The Avon Annual, 1946.* New York: Avon Book, 1946.

pp. 172-186: "The Gambler, the Nun, and the Radio."

17 *Os Melhores Contos Americanos.* Second Series. Lisbon: Portugália Editora, 1946.

Contains "As neves de Kilimandjaro." "The Snows of Kilimanjaro" translated into Portuguese by Cabral do Nascimento.

18 *A New Collection of Great Stories*. New York: Avon Book, 1946. [Avon paperbacks, No. 33.]

    pp. 38-46: "The Three-Day Blow."

19 *As Melhores Histórias da Guerra*. Edited by Gil Sequeira and Valentim Garcia, with the collaboration of Erico Barreto. Lisbon: Edições Romera, [1946?].

    pp. 21-51: "Jornada para a vitoria." "Voyage to Victory" translated into Portuguese by Gil Sequeira and Valentim Garcia. See (C330).

20 *American Authors Today*. Edited by Whit Burnett and Charles Eli Slatkin. Boston: Ginn, 1947.

    Contains "On the Blue Water," reprinted from *Esquire*, v (April 1936). See (C243).

21 *Dos Siglos de Poesia Norteamericana: Poetas Blancos y Negros de los E. E. U. U.* Edited by Alfredo Casey. Buenos Aires: Editorial Claridad, 1947.

    pp. 160-161: "Montparnasse." Translated into Spanish by the editor.

22 *Midland Humor: A Harvest of Fun and Folklore*. Edited by Jack Conroy. New York: Current Books, 1947.

    pp. 237-244: "The Light of the World."

23 *11 Great Modern Stories: The Avon Annual, 1947*. New York: Avon Book, 1947.

    pp. 27-33: "Big Two-Hearted River: Part I."

24 *The Holiday Reader*. Edited by Bernard Smith and Philip Van Doren Stern. New York: Simon & Schuster, 1947.

    pp. 3-21: "Big Two-Hearted River."

25 *Living American Literature. Book 2: Masterpieces of American Literature*. Edited by W. Tasker Witham. New York: Stephen Daye Press, 1947.

    pp. 859-861: "The End of Something." pp. 861-868: Ch. 27 from *FWBT*, titled here "El Sordo on the Hilltop." Biographical note on pp. 918-919. For Book 1, see (G454).

26 *The Literature of Crime: Stories by World-Famous Authors*. Edited by Ellery Queen. London: Cassell, 1952.

    pp. 147-156: "The Killers." For the American edition, see (E169).

27 *New Problems in Reading & Writing*. Edited by Henry W. Sams and Waldo F. McNeir. New York: Prentice-Hall, 1953.

    pp. 173-177: "Indian Camp." Introductory note on pp. 172-173. Guide questions on p. 177. pp. 178-180: Excerpt from Ch. 1 of *DIA*, titled here "Why It Doesn't Matter About the Horses." Guide questions on p. 180. pp. 180-184: "A Clean, Well-Lighted Place." Guide questions on pp. 184-185. pp. 185-199: Excerpt from Ch. 43 of *FWBT*, titled here "The End of Robert Jordan." Guide questions on pp. 199-200. Writing and study aids on pp. 217-218. See also (S-G360).

28 *The Meaning in Reading.* Edited by J. Hooper Wise, J. E. Congleton, and Alton C. Morris. New York: Harcourt, Brace, 1953. Third edition.

    pp. 86-90: "On the Blue Water." Introductory note on p. 86. See also *Exercise Manual for The Meaning in Reading*, pp. 49-50.

29 *Champs and Bums.* Edited by Bucklin Moon. New York: Lion Books, 1954.

    pp. 69-78: "The Battler."

30 *The Damned.* Edited by Daniel Talbot. New York: Lion Books, 1954. [Lion Library Edition.]

    pp. 37-44: "Soldier's Home."

31 *The American Treasury: 1455-1955.* Edited by Clifton Fadiman. Assisted by Charles Van Doren. New York: Harper, 1955. pp. 206, 277, 408-409, 960-965.

32 Quotations and brief excerpts from Hemingway's fiction and non-fiction.

Esquire Cocktail. Edited by Arnold Gingrich. Vienna and Hamburg: Paul Zsolnay, 1955. [German translation of *The Esquire*
33 *Treasury*, New York, 1953. See (E184).]

    pp. 75-88: "Die Rückkehr des Schmugglers." "The Tradesman's Return," Part II of *THAHN*, translated into German by Luise Wasserthal-Zuccari.

Interpreting Literature. Edited by K. L. Knickerbocker and H. Willard Reninger. New York: Henry Holt, 1955.
34   pp. 132-137: "The Killers." Questions on p. 137.

Story, Poem, Essay: A University Reader. Edited by Benjamin B. Hoover and Donald S. Taylor. New York: Henry Holt, 1957.

    pp. 153-157: "In Another Country." Biographical note on pp. 598-599.

35 *Modern Rhetoric.* By Cleanth Brooks and Robert Penn Warren. New York: Harcourt, Brace, 1958.

    p. 221: Excerpt from *FWBT*, p. 35. p. 844: Excerpt from "My Old Man." [Third edition. Harcourt, Brace and World, 1970. pp. 301-302: Excerpt from *FWBT*. p. 612: Excerpt from "My Old Man."]

36 *College Reading: A Collection of Prose, Plays, and Poetry.* Edited by George Sanderlin. Lexington, Mass.: D.C. Heath, 1958.

pp. 523-531: "The Killers." Introductory note on p. 523.

37 *Story and Structure.* Edited by Laurence Perrine. New York: Harcourt, Brace, 1959.

pp. 244-248: "A Canary for One." Questions on p. 248.

38 *Short Stories for English Courses.* Edited by Rosa M. R. Mikels. Revision and Study Guides by Helen T. Munn. New York: Scribner's, 1960. Revised edition. See (E48).

pp. 397-401: "A Day's Wait." Questions to Stimulate Thoughtful Discussion on p. 402.

39 *Interpretation: Writer, Reader, Audience.* Edited by Wilma H. Grimes and Alethea Smith Mattingly. San Francisco: Wadsworth, 1961.

p. 265: Excerpt from *OMATS.*

40 *Themes from Experience: A Manual of Literature for Writers.* Edited by William E. Buckler. New York: W. W. Norton, 1962.

pp. 309-322: "My Old Man." Writing suggestions on pp. 322-323. See also *Themes from Experience: A Teacher's Classroom Manual,* p. 21.

41 *Idea & Image: Reading for College English.* Edited by Hans P. Guth. Belmont, Calif.: Wadsworth, 1962.

Part Two: Literature. pp. 109-115: "Soldier's Home." Headnote on p. 109. Discussion and writing questions on pp. 115-116.

42 *Contos norte-americanos.* Edited by Jacob Penteado. São Paulo: Gráfica e Editôra Edigraf, [1962?]. [Primores do Conto Universal, 7.]

pp. 249-257: "Os assassinos." "The Killers" translated into Portuguese.

43 *Literature for Writing: An Anthology of Major British and American Authors.* Edited by Martin Steinmann, Jr. and Gerald Willen. Belmont, Calif.: Wadsworth, 1962.

pp. 173-175: "In Another Country." Comment on pp. 175-176. Questions on p. 176. [Second edition, 1967.]

44 *Nuvela americană contemporană.* Bucharest: Editura pentru Literatură, 1963. ["Biblioteca pentru toți."]

Contains "Intr-o altă țară" ("In Another Country"). "In voia somnului" ("Now I Lay Me"). "Așa cum n-ai să fii niciodată" ("A Way You'll Never Be"). "Neînfrîntul" ("The Undefeated"). The stories were translated into Rumanian by Constantin Popescu.

45 *Contos Norte-americanos.* Preface by Enio Silveira. Rio de Janeiro: Biblioteca Universal Popular, 1963.

pp. 246-266: "Os bandidos." "The Killers" translated into Portuguese by Moacyr Werneck de Castro.

46 *24 izgalmas novella.* Budapest: Európa Könyvkiadó, 1963.

Contains "Bérgyilkosok." "The Killers" translated into Hungarian.

47 *The Rinehart Book of Short Stories.* Edited by C. L. Cline. New York: Holt, Rinehart and Winston, 1964. [Alternate edition.]

pp. 203-216: "Under the Ridge." Biographical note on pp. 202-203.

48 *American Short Stories: 1820 to the Present.* Edited by Eugene Current-García and Walton R. Patrick. Glenview, Ill.: Scott, Foresman, 1964. Revised edition.

pp. 476-480: "A Clean, Well-Lighted Place." Introductory note on pp. 475-476.

49 *Story: An Introduction to Prose Fiction.* Edited by Arthur Foff and Daniel Knapp. Belmont, Calif.: Wadsworth, 1964.

pp. 244-265: "Fifty Grand." [Second edition, 1971.]

50 *The Worlds of Fiction: Stories in Context.* Edited by T. Y. Greet, Charles E. Edge, and John M. Munro. Boston: Houghton Mifflin, 1964.

pp. 67-78: "My Old Man." Backgrounds on pp. 78-84.

51 *Modern Short Stories.* Edited by Jim Hunter. London: Faber and Faber, 1964. [New York: Transatlantic Arts, 1967.]

pp. 146-152: "Indian Camp." Introductory note on p. 146.

52 *Zigeunergeschichten.* Edited by Adalbert Keil. Munich: Kurt Desch, 1964.

pp. 268-278: Excerpt from *FWBT*, titled here "Finito," translated into German by Paul Baudisch.

53 *The Dimensions of the Short Story: A Critical Anthology.* Edited by James E. Miller, Jr. and Bernice Slote. New York: Dodd, Mead, 1964.

pp. 399-401: "Cat in the Rain." Biographical note on p. 559. See also (S-G300).

54 *American Literary Masters.* Vol. II. General Editor: Charles R. Anderson. New York: Holt, Rinehart and Winston, 1965.

pp. 1039-1052: "Big Two-Hearted River." pp. 1052-1065: Ch. XII from *GHOA*, titled here "Pursuit as Happiness." Introduction on pp. 1023-1039. Reading suggestions on pp. 1065-1066. Biography on pp. 1066-1068.

55 *Studies in Change: A Book of the Short Story*. Edited by Hugh Kenner. Englewood Cliffs, N.J.: Prentice-Hall, 1965.

pp. 175-179: "After the Storm." Analytical comments and questions on p. 175. See also Introduction, p. xii.

56 *Trio: A Book of Stories, Plays and Poems*. Edited by Harold P. Simonson. New York: Harper & Row, 1965. Second edition.

pp. 127-144: "Big Two-Hearted River." Biographical note on p. 651. [Third edition, 1970. pp. 189-204, 730-731.]

57 *Sources of the American Mind: A Collection of Documents and Texts in American Intellectual History*. Vol. II. Edited by Loren Baritz. New York: John Wiley, 1966.

pp. 230-234: Excerpts from *SAR*, pp. 173-174, 224-230. Introductory note on p. 229.

58 *Fitzgerald and the Jazz Age*. Edited by Malcolm Cowley and Robert Cowley. New York: Scribner's, 1966.

pp. 60-64: "Soldier's Home." Introductory note on p. 60. pp. 103-104: Excerpt from *DIA*, pp. 1-4, titled here "Commencing with the Simplest Things." Introductory note on p. 103.

59 *Image and Value: An Invitation to Literature*. Edited by Martha Heasley Cox. New York: Harcourt, Brace and World, 1966.

pp. 24-27: "A Day's Wait." Biographical note on p. 608.

60 *An Anthology of American Literature*. Edited by Thomas M. Davis and Willoughby Johnson. Indianapolis: Bobbs-Merrill, 1966.

pp. 815-826: "Big Two-Hearted River." Biographical chronology on p. 814.

61 *Seven Novellas*. Edited by Marsden V. Dillenbeck and John C. Schweitzer. New York: Scribner's, 1966.

pp. 70-104: "The Short Happy Life of Francis Macomber." Introductory note on p. 69. Discussion on pp. 105-107. Vocabulary on pp. 107-108. Glossary and suggestions on p. 108.

62 *Best Sports Stories*. Edited by Paul Edwards. London: Faber and Faber, 1966. pp. 11, 12.

pp. 171-180: "Big Two-Hearted River," Part I.

63 *Modern Choice: 2*. Edited by Eva Figes. London and Glasgow: Blackie, [1966].

pp. 20-61: "The Short Happy Life of Francis Macomber."

64 *The Short Story*. Edited by Willoughby Johnson and William C. Hamlin. New York: American Book, 1966.

pp. 244-248. "A Clean, Well-Lighted Place." Questions on pp. 248-249.

65 *The Short Story: Classic and Contemporary*. Edited by R. W. Lid. Philadelphia: J. B. Lippincott, 1966.

pp. 514-516: "Old Man at the Bridge." Introductory note on pp. 513-514. "A Student Discussion" on pp. 517-538.

66 *Los que fueron a España*. Buenos Aires: Editorial Jorge Alvarez, 1966. [Colección política concentrada, 13.]

pp. 33-42: "Los italianos en la guerra," translated into Spanish by S. Lugones. Reprinted from the *Revista Socialista*, Buenos Aires (Nov. 1938). Note: The source of the translation is not given; probably a NANA dispatch.

67 *The Experience of Literature: Anthology and Analysis*. Edited by Gene Montague and Marjorie Henshaw. Englewood Cliffs, N.J.: Prentice-Hall, 1966.

pp. 80-82: "A Clean, Well-Lighted Place." Questions for analysis on p. 82.

68 *Structure and Style: An Analytical Approach to Prose Writing*. By Harriet W. Sheridan. New York: Harcourt, Brace and World, 1966.

pp. 86-90: Excerpt from *SAR*, pp. 92-96, 111, titled here "From Bayonne to Pamplona." Analysis on pp. 90-92.

69 *The Rite of Becoming: Stories and Studies of Adolescence*. Edited by Arthur Waldhorn and Hilda K. Waldhorn. Cleveland: World, 1966.

pp. 159-166: "The Three-Day Blow." Introductory comments on pp. 157-158. See also (S-G416).

70 *Writer to Writer: Readings on the Craft of Writing*. Edited by Floyd C. Watkins and Karl F. Knight. Boston: Houghton Mifflin, 1966.

pp. 125-130: Excerpts from *DIA*, pp. 2-3, 54, 191-192, titled here "Write It as It Really Is." See also Introduction, pp. v, vii.

71 *The World in Literature: Science and Uncertainty*. Book Four. Edited by George K. Anderson and Robert Warnock. Glenview, Ill.: Scott, Foresman, 1967. Revised edition.

pp. 171-175: "The Killers." Introductory note on pp. 170-171.

72 *Heirlooms*. Edited by Margaret T. Applegarth. New York: Harper & Row, 1967.

p. 105: Excerpt from "A Natural History of the Dead," titled here "Assurance."

73 *Contos Norte-Americanos*. Edited by Aurélio Buarque de Hollanda and Paulo Rónai. Rio de Janeiro: Edição Copa de Ouro, 1967.

pp. 235-240: "O velho perto da ponte." "Old Man at the Bridge" translated into Portuguese by the editors.

74 *American Literature: Themes and Writers.* Edited by J. Robert Carlsen, Edgar H. Schuster, and Anthony Tovatt. New York: McGraw-Hill, 1967.

pp. 634-637: "In Another Country." Questions regarding implications and techniques on p. 637. Biographical note on p. 679. [Second edition, 1973.]

75 *The Shape of Fiction: Stories for Comparison.* Edited by Alan Casty. Boston: D. C. Heath, 1967.

pp. 300-304: "In Another Country." See also *Instructor's Manual.*

76 *The Art of Fiction: A Handbook and Anthology.* Edited by R. F. Dietrich and Roger H. Sundell. New York: Holt, Rinehart and Winston, 1967.

pp. 136-140: "A Clean, Well-Lighted Place." See also *Instructor's Manual.*

77 *Literary Reflections.* Edited by William R. Elkins, Jack L. Kendall, and John R. Willingham. New York: McGraw-Hill, 1967.

pp. 641-645: "A Clean, Well-Lighted Place." Questions and Topics for composition on p. 645. [Second edition, 1971.]

78 *Short Stories for Insight.* Edited by Teresa Ferster Glazier. New York: Harcourt, Brace and World, 1967.

pp. 95-104: "The Killers." Questions on pp. 104-105. Suggestions for questions on pp. 309-311. Biographical note on pp. 332-333. See also *Teacher's Manual.*

79 *An Introduction to Literature: Fiction.* Edited by Theodore L. Gross and Norman Kelvin. New York: Random House, 1967.

pp. 307-311: "In Another Country." Introduction and bibliography on pp. 299-306.

80 *The Shape of Fiction: British and American Short Stories.* Edited by Leo Hamalian and Frederick R. Karl. New York: McGraw-Hill, 1967.

pp. 133-143: "The Capital of the World." Study questions on mood, characterization, and theme on pp. 143-145. Biographical note on p. 530.

81 *Exposition: A Rhetoric and Reader with Literary Emphasis.* Edited by Earl Hilton and Darwin Shrell. Belmont, Calif.: Wadsworth, 1967.

pp. 279-286: "Big Two-Hearted River," Part II. Exercises on pp. 286-287. See also (S-G192).

82 *A College Treasury: Prose.* Edited by Paul A. Jorgensen and Frederick B. Shroyer. New York: Scribner's, 1967.

pp. 281-286: "Hunger Was Good Discipline," from *AMF*, pp. 69-77.

83 *Short Stories: Classic, Modern, Contemporary.* Edited by Marcus Klein and Robert Pack. Boston: Little, Brown, 1967.

pp. 396-418: "The Snows of Kilimanjaro." Introductory note on p. 393.

84 *The Short Story: An Inductive Approach.* Edited by Gerald Levin. New York: Harcourt, Brace and World, 1967.

pp. 135-138: "The Doctor and the Doctor's Wife." Suggestions for study on pp. 138-140.

85 *Perception and Pleasure: Stories for Analysis.* Edited by Fred H. Marcus. Boston: D. C. Heath, 1967.

pp. 70-77: "The Killers." Analysis on pp. 77-78.

86 *The Golden Shore: Great Short Stories Selected for Young Readers.* Edited by William Harwood Peden. New York: Platt & Munk, 1967.

pp. 16-22: "Ten Indians." Biographical note on pp. 22-23.

87 *Years of Protest: A Collection of American Writings of the 1930's.* Edited by Jack Salzman. New York: Pegasus, 1967.

pp. 191-195: "Dispatch from Spain," NANA dispatch reprinted from the *N.Y. Times* (April 25, 1937). See (C261). [Reprinted, 1970.]

88 *The Discovery of Fiction.* Edited by Thomas E. Sanders. Glenview, Ill.: Scott, Foresman, 1967.

pp. 304-316: "A Clean, Well-Lighted Place." Note: The story is interspersed with critical analysis. p. 453: Excerpt from *DIA*, pp. 191-192. See also (S-G361).

89 *Galaxy: Literary Modes and Genres.* Edited by Mark Schorer. New York: Harcourt, Brace and World, 1967.

pp. 175-181: "Soldier's Home." Biographical sketch on p. 601.

90 *The Art of Prose Fiction.* Edited by Ralph H. Singleton. Cleveland: World, 1967.

pp. 74-81: "The Killers." Biographical sketch on p. 91.

91 *The Experience of Literature: A Reader with Commentaries.* Edited by Lionel Trilling. Garden City, N.Y.: Doubleday, 1967.

pp. 726-729: "Hills Like White Elephants." Commentary on pp. 729-732. ["Briefer version," without the commentary, 1969.]

92 *Stories from the Quarto.* Edited by Leonard Brown. New York: Scribner's 1968.

pp. 85-98: "The Short Happy Life of Francis Macomber." Biographical note on p. 85. See (E45).

93 *A Preface to Our Times: Contemporary Thought in Traditional Rhetorical Forms.* Edited by William E. Buckler. New York: American Book, 1968.

pp. 881-886: "After the Storm." Biographical note, on p. 881.

94 *American Composition and Rhetoric.* Edited by Donald Davidson. New York: Scribner's 1968. Fifth edition.

pp. 348-351: Excerpt from Ch. xxx of *FTA*, titled here "The Lieutenant Escapes." Introductory note on p. 347. pp. 375-383: "The Killers." Suggestions for study on pp. 383-385. For earlier edition, see (G336).

95 *Controversy in Literature: Fiction, Drama and Poetry with Related Criticism.* Edited by Morris Freedman and Paul B. Davis. New York: Scribner's 1968.

pp. 122-125: "A Clean, Well-Lighted Place." Comment on pp. 121-122. See also (S-G136).

96 *Ten Modern American Short Stories.* Edited by David Galloway and John Whitley. London: Methuen, 1968.

pp. 33-43: "The Killers." Introductory essay on pp. 29-32.

97 *Literature in Critical Perspectives: An Anthology.* Edited by Walter K. Gordon. New York: Appleton-Century-Crofts, 1968.

pp. 242-253: "The Snows of Kilimanjaro." Suggestions for discussion on p. 253.

98 *The Modern Stylists: Writers on the Art of Writing.* Edited by Donald Hall. New York: Free Press/London: Collier-Macmillan, 1968.

pp. 31-32, 59: Excerpts from *DIA*. Discussion on p. 29.

99 *Modern Essays: A Rhetorical Approach.* Edited by James G. Hepburn and Robert A. Greenberg. New York: Macmillan, 1968. Second edition.

pp. 148-155: Excerpt from *DIA*. Introductory note on p. 148. Questions on pp. 155-156.

100 *The Art of the Story: An Introduction.* Edited by Robert Hollander and Sidney E. Lind. New York: American Book, 1968.

pp. 336-341: "Ten Indians." Introductory note on the "Hemingway style" on pp. 333-335. Biographical note on pp. 335-336. Questions for discussion and writing on p. 341.

101 *The Modern Tradition: An Anthology of Short Stories.* Edited by Daniel F. Howard. Boston: Little, Brown, 1968.

pp. 409-427: "Big Two-Hearted River." Biographical sketch on pp. 537-538. [Second edition, 1972. See also *Instructor's Manual*.]

102 *Studies in the Short Story.* Edited by Adrian H. Jaffe and Virgil Scott. New York: Holt, Rinehart and Winston, 1968. Third edition.

pp. 326-350: "The Short Happy Life of Francis Macomber." Questions on p. 351. For earlier editions, see (E154).

103 *Contemporary American Thought.* Edited by E. W. Johnson. New York: Free Press, 1968.

pp. 3-10: "Soldier's Home."

104   *The Best of Both Worlds*: *An Anthology of Stories for All Ages.*
Edited by Georgess McHargue. Garden City, N.Y.: Doubleday,
1968.
  pp. 118-122: "Indian Camp." Biographical note on p. 767.

105   *An Editor's Treasury*: *A Continuing Anthology of Prose, Verse,*
and Literary Curiosa. Part I, Volume II. Edited by Herbert R.
Mayes. New York: Antheneum, 1968.
  p. 1209: Excerpt from *FWBT*, p. 35, titled here "Before the Blow-
Up." pp. 1864-1865: Excerpt from *SAR*, pp. 173-174, titled here
"Maximum of Exposure."

106   *The Lonely Voice*: *A Study of the Short Story.* By Frank O'Connor.
New York: Bantam, 1968. [Special Anthology Edition.]
  pp. 318-322: "Hills Like White Elephants." Essay, "A Clean Well-
Lighted Place," on pp. 307-317. See (G301).

107   *An Introduction to Literature.* Edited by Mary Rohrberger, Samuel
H. Woods, Jr., and Bernard F. Dukore. New York: Random House,
1968.
  pp. 227-251: "The Short Happy Life of Francis Macomber." Biographical note on p. 227. Comments on pp. 251-252.

108   *Winners and Losers*: *An Anthology of Great Sports Fiction.* Edited
by L. M. Schulman. New York: Macmillan, 1968.
  pp. 207-224: "My Old Man."

109   *Discovering Short Stories.* Edited by John C. Schweitzer. New
York: Scribner's, 1968. [Also Scribner School Paperbacks, 13.]
  pp. 166-170: "The Doctor and the Doctor's Wife." Introductory
note on p. 166. Questions for discussion and writing on pp. 170-171.

110   *A Variety of Short Stories.* Edited by John C. Schweitzer. New
York: Scribner's 1968 [Also Scribner School Paperback, 14.]
  pp. 176-205: "The Undefeated." Biographical note on p. 176.
Questions for discussion and writing on p. 205. Glossaries on
pp. 206-207.

111   *Reading for Understanding*: *Fiction, Drama, Poetry.* Edited by
Caroline Shrodes, Justine Van Gundy, and Joel Dorius. New York:
Macmillan, 1968.
  pp. 182-186: "In Another Country." Biographical note on p. 701.

112   *Thirty-Eight Short Stories*: *An Introductory Anthology.* Edited by
Michael Timko and Clinton F. Oliver. New York: Knopf, 1968.
  pp. 605-615: "The Killers." Introductory note on pp. 605-606. See
also (S-G404).

113   *Classics in the Kitchen*: *An Edible Anthology for the Literary Gour-*

met. By Jean Aaberg and Judith Homme Bolduc. Los Angeles: Ward Ritchie Press, 1969.

    pp. 87-92: "October: Ernest Hemingway and Viands of Valencia." Includes a short excerpt from *FWBT*, p. 85.

114 *The Art of the Short Story: An Introductory Anthology*. Edited by J. Leeds Barroll, III and Austin M. Wright. Boston: Allyn and Bacon, 1969.

    pp. 89-93: "Hills Like White Elephants." Questions on pp. 93-94. Analysis of the story on pp. 102-104.

115 *Detail and Pattern: Essays for Composition*. Edited by Robert A. Baylor. New York: McGraw-Hill, 1969.

    p. 11: Excerpt from *FTA*, p. 196, titled here "I was always embarrassed. . . ." Discussion and application on p. 11. Biographical data on pp. 246-247. See also *Instructor's Manual*. [Second edition, 1972.]

116 *The Bitter Years: The Thirties in Literature*. Edited by Max Bogart. New York: Scribner's, 1969. [Scribner School Paperbacks, 29.]

    pp. 74-79: Ch. 26 from *FWBT*. Introductory note on p. 74. Questions on p. 138.

117 *The Jazz Age*. Edited by Max Bogart. New York: Scribner's, 1969. [Scribner School Paperbacks, 18.]

    pp. 56-65: "Soldier's Home." Biographical note on p. 56.

118 *Short Stories of the Western World*. Edited by Eugene Current-García and Walton R. Patrick. Glenview, Ill.: Scott, Foresman, 1969.

    pp. 562-566: "Hills Like White Elephants." Biographical note on p. 624.

119 *Microcosm: An Anthology of the Short Story*. Edited by Donna Gerstenberger and Frederick Garber. San Francisco: Chandler, 1969.

    pp. 166-184: "Big Two-Hearted River." Introductory note on p. 166. Questions and analyses on pp. 395-398.

120 *Americans Today*. Edited by Roger B. Goodman. New York: Scribner's, 1969. [Scribner School Paperbacks, 22.]

    pp. 17-29: "Big Two-Hearted River, Part II." Introductory note on p. 17.

121 *War: An Anthology*. Edited by Edward Huberman and Elizabeth Huberman. New York: Washington Square Press, 1969.

    pp. 111-115: "Jay Raven from Pittsburgh," NANA dispatch reprinted from the *N.Y. Times* (April 25, 1937). See (C261).

122 *Short Stories International*. Edited by Edward Warren Johnson Boston: Houghton Mifflin, 1969.

pp. 358-362: "Hills Like White Elephants." Biographical note on p. 358.

123 *Fiction: Form and Experience.* Edited by William McKendrey Jones. Lexington, Mass.: D. C. Heath, 1969.

pp. 68-71: "Indian Camp." Commentary by G. Thomas Tanselle on pp. 362-363; by Kenneth Bernard on p. 364.

124 *Symposium.* Edited by Arthur F. Kinney, Kenneth W. Kuiper, and Lynn Z. Bloom. Boston: Houghton Mifflin, 1969.

pp. 777-780: "Indian Camp."

125 *Twelve Short Stories.* Second Series. Edited by Marvin Magalaner and Edmond L. Volpe. New York: Macmillan, 1969.

pp. 106-110: "Indian Camp." Introduction on pp. 101-105.

126 *As Melhores Histórias Americanas.* Rio de Janeiro: Editôra Saga, 1969. [Ficção Estrangeira Contemporãnea, 4.]

pp. 133-157: "As neves do Kilimanjaro." "The Snows of Kilimanjaro" translated into Portuguese by Francisco Rocha Filho.

127 *American Literature: Tradition & Innovation.* Vol. 2. Edited by Harrison T. Meserole, Walter Sutton, and Brom Weber. Lexington, Mass.: D. C. Heath, 1969.

pp. 3084-3098: "Big Two-Hearted River." Bio-bibliographical headnote on pp. 3082-3084.

128 *Stylists on Style: A Handbook with Selections for Analysis.* Edited by Louis T. Milic. New York: Scribner's, 1969.

pp. 285-287: Excerpt from *DIA*, pp. 190-192. Annotated on pp. 478-484. See also (S-G299).

129 *Short Stories: An Anthology.* Edited by Norman Nathan. Indianapolis: Bobbs-Merrill, 1969.

pp. 93-97: "A Clean, Well-Lighted Place." Questions on pp. 97-98. Biographical note on p. 338.

130 *The College Writer: Essays for Composition.* Edited by William Pratt. New York: Scribner's, 1969.

pp. 252-255: "People of the Seine," from *AMF*, pp. 41-45. Exercises on pp. 255-256.

131 *The Short Story: An Introductory Anthology.* Edited by Robert Rees and Barry Menikoff. Boston: Little, Brown, 1969.

pp. 382-387: "Hills Like White Elephants."

132 *The Short Story: Fiction in Transition.* Edited by J. Chesley Taylor. New York: Scribner's, 1969.

pp. 404-433: "The Short Happy Life of Francis Macomber." Headnote on p. 404.

133 *Fifty Years of the American Short Story: From the O. Henry Awards, 1919-1970.* Vol. I. Edited by William Abrahams. Garden City, N.Y.: Doubleday, 1970.

pp. 381-389: "The Killers."

134 *The Culture of The Twenties.* Edited by Loren Baritz. Indianapolis: Bobbs-Merrill, 1970. [American Heritage Series.]

pp. 20-28: "Soldier's Home." Biographical note on pp. 19-20. pp. 297-300: "American Bohemians in Paris," reprinted from the *Toronto Star Weekly* (March 25, 1922). See (C72₁). See also (S-G22).

135 *Facing Some Problems: Paintings, Drawings, Short Stories, Poetry, Fables, Drama.* Edited by John H. Bens. New York: Holt, Rinehart and Winston, 1970.

pp. 5-7: "A Day's Wait." Questions on pp. 7-8.

136 *Icarus: An Anthology of Literature.* Edited by John H. Bens and Douglas R. Baugh, New York: Macmillan, 1970.

pp. 332-337: "The Killers."

137 *American Short Fiction: Readings and Criticism.* Edited by James K. Bowen and Richard Van der Beets. Indianapolis: Bobbs-Merrill, 1970.

pp. 215-223: "The Killers." Biographical note on p. 451. See also (S-G41).

138 *About Language: Contexts for College Writers.* Edited by Marden J. Clark, Soren F. Cox, and Marshall R. Craig. New York: Scribner's, 1970.

pp. 600-608: "The Killers." Brief introductory note on p. 600. Questions on pp. 608-609. Suggestions for Writing on p. 609.

139 *Modern English Reader.* Edited by Robert M. Gorrell, Charlton Laird, and Ronald E. Freeman. Englewood Cliffs, N.J.: Prentice-Hall, 1970.

pp. 372-373: "How to be Popular in Peace Though a Slacker in War," reprinted from the *Toronto Star Weekly* (March 13, 1920). See (C35₁). pp. 374-381: "Pamplona: World Series of Bullfighting," reprinted from the *Toronto Star Weekly* (Oct. 27, 1923). See (C144). Study guides on pp. 381-382. See also (S-G160).

140 *A Thousand Afternoons.* Edited by Peter Haining. New York: Cowles, 1970.

pp. 202-233: "The Undefeated." See also (S-G175).

141 *The Responsible Man: Essays, Short Stories, Poems.* Edited by C. Jeriel Howard and Richard Francis Tracz. San Francisco: Canfield Press, 1970.

pp. 168-171: "A Clean, Well-Lighted Place." Suggestions for discussion on pp. 171-172.

142 *The Curious Eye.* Edited by Walden A. Leecing and James L. Armstrong. New York: McGraw-Hill, 1970.

pp. 156-159: "Old Man at the Bridge." Questions and Suggestions on pp. 159-160. See also the Instructor's Manual for this book.

143 *Fisherman's Bounty: A Treasury of Fascinating Lore and the Finest Stories from the World of Angling.* Edited by Nick Lyons. New York: Crown, 1970.

pp. 176-180: "Marlin Off the Morro: A Cuban Letter," reprinted from *Esquire,* 1 (Autumn 1933). See (C209).

144 *The Theory of the American Novel.* Edited by George Perkins. New York: Holt, Rinehart and Winston, 1970.

pp. 347-353: "Ernest Hemingway: Digressions on Writing," excerpts from *DIA*, pp. 1-4, 52-54, 173, 191-192, 278.

145 *Literature: Structure, Sound, and Sense.* Edited by Laurence Perrine. New York: Harcourt, Brace and World, 1970. Third edition.

pp. 221-225: "Hills Like White Elephants." Questions on pp. 225-226.

146 *American Literature.* Vol. II. Edited by Richard Poirier and William L. Vance. Boston: Little, Brown, 1970.

pp. 807-830: "The Short Happy Life of Francis Macomber." pp. 830-834: "A New Kind of War," NANA dispatch, dated April 14, 1937. See (C260). Note: Items C260 and C261 in the bibliography are the same dispatch. Introductory chronology on p. 807.

147 *Alienation and Belonging: A Search for Values.* Edited by Audrey J. Roth and Helen P. Scroggins. New York: Holt, Rinehart and Winston, 1970.

pp. 155-159: "Indian Camp." Introductory note on p. 155. Exercises on pp. 373-376. Biographical note on p. 414.

148 *The Literature of America: Twentieth Century.* Edited by Mark Schorer. New York: McGraw-Hill, 1970.

pp. 583-597: "Big Two-Hearted River." Biographical note and Further Reading list on pp. 581-583.

149 *The Loners: Short Stories About the Young and Alienated.* Edited by L. M. Schulman. New York: Macmillan, 1970.

pp. 203-212: "Soldier's Home." Biographical note on p. 278.

150 *Narrative Experience: The Private Voice.* Edited by John L. Somer. Glenview, Ill.: Scott, Foresman, 1970.

pp. 57-62: "Soldier's Home."

151 *Affinities*: *A Short Story Anthology*. Edited by John Tytell and Harold Jaffe. New York: Crowell, 1970.

  pp. 164-175: "My Old Man."

152 *Exposition*. Edited by Jerome W. Archer and Joseph Schwartz. New York: McGraw-Hill, 1971. Second edition.

  pp. 149-151: "Camping Out." Reprinted from the *Toronto Star Weekly* (June 26, 1920). See (C45).

153 *A Reader for Writers*: *A Critical Anthology of Prose Readings*. Edited by Jerome W. Archer and Joseph Schwartz. New York: McGraw-Hill, 1971. Third edition.

  pp. 185-187: "Camping Out." Reprinted from the *Toronto Star Weekly* (June 26, 1920). See (C45).

154 *An Introduction to Literature*: *Fiction, Poetry, Drama*. Edited by Sylvan Barnet, Morton Berman, and William Burto. Boston: Little, Brown, 1971. Fourth edition, p. 22.

  pp. 202-228: "The Short Happy Life of Francis Macomber." For earlier edition, see (E281).

155 *Western Literature III*: *The Modern World*. Edited by Peter Brooks. New York: Harcourt Brace Jovanovich, 1971.

  pp. 487-490: "A Clean, Well-Lighted Place." Introductory note on p. 486.

156 *The Rebel*: *His Moment and His Motives*. Edited by John O. Cole and F. L. Schepman. Englewood Cliffs, N.J.: Prentice-Hall, 1971.

  pp. 86-92: "Soldier's Home."

157 *The Lesson of the Masters*: *An Anthology of the Novel from Cervantes to Hemingway*. Edited by Malcolm Cowley and Howard E. Hugo. New York: Scribner's, 1971.

  pp. 496-511: Chapter 27 of *FWBT*, here titled "El Sordo on the Hilltop." Biographical note on pp. 491-494. Synopsis of *FWBT* on pp. 494-496. Afterword on pp. 511-514.

158 *The Art of Narration*: *The Short Story*. Edited by A. Grove Day. New York: Webster Division, McGraw-Hill, 1971.

  pp. 321-332: "My Old Man." "Purely What Really Happened," biographical note on p. 320.

159 *The Realities of Literature*. Edited by Richard F. Dietrich. Waltham, Mass.: Xerox College Publishing, 1971.

  pp. 265-268: "A Clean, Well-Lighted Place."

160 *The World of the Short Story*: *Archetypes in Action*. Edited by Oliver Evans and Harry Finestone. New York: Knopf, 1971.

  pp. 53-56: "A Canary for One."

161 *The Shapes of Fiction: Open and Closed.* Edited by Beverly Gross and Richard Giannone. New York: Holt, Rinehart and Winston, 1971.

   pp. 216-222: "The Light of the World."

162 *The World of Short Fiction: An International Collection.* Edited by Thomas A. Gullason and Leonard Casper. New York: Harper & Row, 1971. Second edition.

   pp. 304-308: "Hills Like White Elephants." Introduction by Thomas Gullason on pp. 300-303. Selected Bibliography on pp. 647-650.

163 *The Literature of America.* Vol. II. Edited by Irving Howe, Mark Schorer, and Larzer Ziff. New York: McGraw-Hill, 1971.

   pp. 822-836: "Big Two-Hearted River." Headnote on pp. 820-822.

164 *Statement and Craft: Means and Ends in Writing.* Edited by Tom E. Kakonis and David Allan Evans. Englewood Cliffs, N.J.: Prentice-Hall, 1971.

   pp. 284-288: Excerpts from *DIA*, pp. 1-4, 190-192. pp. 288-297: "The Killers." Biographical introduction on p. 283. Questions on pp. 297-298.

165 *The Tunnel and the Light: Readings in Modern Fiction.* Edited by Robert Lambert. Boston: Houghton Mifflin, 1971. [Houghton Books in Literature series.]

   pp. 39-43: "A Clean, Well-Lighted Place." Interpretation on p. 43.

166 *Nobel Prize Library: Ernest Hemingway/Knut Hamsun/Hermann Hesse.* Published under the sponsorship of the Nobel Foundation and the Swedish Academy. New York: Alexis Gregory/Del Mar, Calif.: CRM Publishing, 1971.

   pp. 9-11: "A Clean, Well-Lighted Place." pp. 13-30: Excerpt from *OMATS*, pp. 44-101. pp. 31-66: Chapters xv-xviii of *SAR*. pp. 67-102: Book I of *FTA*. See also (S-G315).

167 *Short Fiction: Shape and Substance.* By William Peden. Boston: Houghton Mifflin, 1971. pp. 13, 15, 31-32, 43.

   pp. 277-280: "Today is Friday."

168 *Synthesis: Responses to Literature.* Edited by Charles Sanders, Robert R. Rice, and Watt J. Cantillon. New York: Knopf, 1971.

   pp. 173-178: "A Natural History of the Dead."

169 *Patterns of Exposition.* Edited by Randall E. Decker. Boston: Little, Brown, 1972. Second edition.

   pp. 127-129: "The Bull Fight as Symbolism," reprinted from the *Toronto Star Weekly* (Oct. 20, 1923). See (C143). Note: Editor's title. Biographical note on p. 127. Questions on pp. 129-130.

170 *Killing Time*: *A Guide to Life in the Happy Valley*. Edited by Robert Disch and Barry Schwartz. Englewood Cliffs, N.J.: Prentice-Hall, 1972.

　　p. 230: "The Revolutionist."

171 *Best Racing and Chasing Stories*. Edited by Dick Francis and John Welcome. London: Faber and Faber, 1972.

　　pp. 151-164: "My Old Man."

172 *The Forms of Imagination*: *An Anthology of Poetry, Fiction, and Drama*. Edited by O. B. Hardison, Jr. and Jerry Leath Mills. Englewood Cliffs, N.J.: Prentice-Hall, 1972.

　　pp. 314-321: "The Killers." Biographical note on p. 610.

173 *Interpretation*: *An Approach to the Study of Literature*. Edited by Joanna H. Maclay and Thomas O. Sloan. New York: Random House, 1972.

　　pp. 264-272: "The Killers." Study Questions on pp. 272-273, 279.

174 *Collection*: *Literature for the Seventies*. Edited by Gerald Messner and Nancy S. Messner. Lexington, Mass.: D. C. Heath, 1972.

　　pp. 246-249: "A Clean, Well-Lighted Place."

175 *Comparisons*: *A Short Story Anthology*. Edited by Nicolaus Mills. New York: McGraw-Hill, 1972.

　　pp. 270-283: "Big Two-Hearted River."

176 *Harbrace College Reader*. Edited by Mark Schorer, Philip Durham, and Everett L. Jones. New York: Harcourt Brace Jovanovich, 1972. Fourth edition.

　　pp. 14-33: "Scott Fitzgerald," from *AMF*, pp. 149-176. Exercises on pp. 34-35. Suggestions for Discussion on p. 35. Biographical note on pp. 600-601.

177 *Travellers*: *Stories of Americans Abroad*. Edited by L. M. Schulman. New York: Macmillan, 1972.

　　pp. 197-203: "In Another Country." Biographical note on p. 284.

178 *Three Love Stories*. Edited by Shoh Yamamoto. Tokyo: Kinseido, 1972. In English.

　　pp. 49-113: "The Short Happy Life of Francis Macomber." Notes on pp. 121-128. Note: This study text includes stories by William Faulkner and John Steinbeck.

179 *American Literature*: *The Makers and the Making*. Vol. ii. Edited by Cleanth Brooks, R.W.B. Lewis, and Robert Penn Warren. New York: St. Martin's Press, 1973.

　　pp. 2271-2281: "The Snows of Kilimanjaro." Introductory essay on pp. 2250-2270. Biographical Chart on p. 2270. Further Readings on pp. 2270-2271.

180 *Amerika forteller: Amerikanske noveller.* Edited by Gordon Hølme-
bakk. Oslo: Norske Bokklubben, 1973.

pp. 9-32: "Kilimanjaros Sne." "The Snows of Kilimanjaro" translated into Norwegian by Peter Magnus. Biographical note on
pp. 7-8.

181 *Shake the Kaleidoscope: A New Anthology of Modern Poetry.*
Edited by Milton Klonsky. New York: Pocket Books, 1973. Drawing
of Hemingway on the cover by Wilson McLean.

pp. 23-24: "Oklahoma," "Mitraigliatrice," and "The Age De-
manded." The three poems are reprinted from the *Collected Poems*,
Pirated edition, San Francisco, 1960. See (A26c). Brief biographical
note on p. 311.

182 *Order and Diversity: The Craft of Prose.* Edited by Robert Brown
Parker and Peter Lars Sandberg. New York: John Wiley, 1973.

pp. 93-95: Excerpt from *DIA*, pp. 1-4.

SECTION F
LIBRARY HOLDINGS
OF MANUSCRIPTS
AND LETTERS;
FACSIMILES
OF MANUSCRIPTS;
PUBLISHED LETTERS
AND EPHEMERA

The first part of this section is mainly comprised of library holdings of Hemingway manuscripts and letters. The libraries who had reported Hemingway holdings in the bibliography were again contacted regarding new acquisitions. Letters were also sent to libraries reporting Hemingway material in the *National Union Catalogue for Manuscripts*. For additional libraries with Hemingway holdings, the bibliographer is indebted to J. Albert Robbins, Chairman of the Committee on Manuscript Holdings for the revision of *American Literary Manuscripts*.

The collection of Hemingway papers which Mary Hemingway has deposited in the John F. Kennedy Library are now available with Mrs. Hemingway's permission for research use at the Library, which is temporarily located in Waltham, Massachusetts. The collection was inventoried by Philip Young and Charles W. Mann in *The Hemingway Manuscripts*, University Park, Pennsylvania, 1969.

The bibliographer is grateful for the cooperation of all the librarians who responded to her inquiries.

LIBRARY HOLDINGS OF MANUSCRIPTS

S-F1   The Bancroft Library, University of California at Berkeley.

A. Typescript of a statement on the problems of writing during wartime. 5 pages. Presumably prepared in 1939 for the Congress of the League of American Writers. In the Archives of the League of American Writers.

2   The Beinecke Rare Book and Manuscript Library, Yale University, New Haven, Conn.

A. Typescript of original ending of "Big Two-Hearted River." 11 pages (numbered 172 to 182). Published as "On Writing" in *The Nick Adams Stories*.

3   The John Hay Library, Brown University, Providence, Rhode Island.

A. *The Fifth Column.* Carbon of typescript of the play. 115 pages.

4   The Houghton Library, Harvard University, Cambridge, Mass.

A. *A Farewell to Arms.* Holograph manuscript, signed. 672 pages. The complete working draft, heavily revised throughout. (On deposit.)

B. *For Whom the Bell Tolls.* Holograph manuscript and typescript, signed. 1,165 pages. Heavily revised throughout. The complete working draft, with Chapter 32 in two slightly variant versions. (On deposit.)

c. Fragments from "Ernst von Hemingstein's Journal." Typescript. 5 pages. Copy by Harvey Breit, ca. May 30, 1952.

5 McKeldin Library, University of Maryland, College Park.

A. *Green Hills of Africa.* Typescript, with corrections, of two chapters for the fifth installment in *Scribner's Magazine* (Sept. 1935). Ca. 42 pages.

B. "Cat in the Rain." Typescript with holograph corrections. 5 pages.

6 Humanities Research Center, University of Texas, Austin.

A. [Untitled poem]. Begins: "There was cat named crazy christian. . . ." Carbon copy of typescript. 1 page. No date.

B. Acceptance speech for the Gold Medal of the Cuban Tourist Institute. Composite holograph and typewritten manuscript, signed. 1 page. In Spanish.

c. "Across the Board." Poem. Carbon copy of typescript. No date.

D. Autobiographical sketch for Georges Schreiber's *Portraits and Self-Portraits,* 1936. See (B21). Typescript. 1 page.

E. "Country Poem with Little Country." Carbon copy of typescript. 1 page. December 22, 1949.

F. "First Poem to Mary in London." See (C426). Carbon copy of typescript. 3 pages. [May 1944.]

G. "Poem to Mary" (second poem). See (C426). Carbon copy of typescript. 7 pages. September 1944.

H. "Ford Madox Ford and the Devil's Disciple." (*AMF*, pp. 79-88.) Carbon copy of typescript. 11 pages.

I. "Indian Country and the White Army." Carbon copy of typescript. 19 pages. No date.

J. Introduction to *Kiki's Memoirs,* 1930. See (B7). Typescript, with holograph emendations and additions, signed. 3 pages. Also page proofs with holograph corrections.

K. "My Grandmother." Holograph manuscript. 3 pages. Translation of Chapter 12 of *Kiki's Memoirs.* See (S-F167).

L. "The Monument." Carbon copy of typescript. 14 pages. No date.

M. 28 NANA (North American Newspaper Alliance) dispatches on the Spanish Civil War. Typescripts of releases. March 17, 1937 to May 11, 1939.

N. 9 news dispatches. Typescripts, various incomplete dates.

O. Preface to Luis Quintanilla's *All the Brave,* 1939. See (B34). Typescript. 3 pages. April 23, 1938.

P. "A Room on the Garden Side." Typescript. 11 pages. No date.

Q. *To Have and Have Not.* Galley proofs. 67 pages. ANS to Lee Samuels on first page. No date.

7. The University of Wisconsin Library, Milwaukee.

    A. "Valentine." Poem. Typescript. 1 page. Written for the final number of the *Little Review*, XII (May 1929). See (C187).

    B. "In Our Time." Typescript. 3 pages. Six chapters of *iot*. See (C124).

    C. "They All Made Peace—What Is Peace?" Poem. Typescript. 2 pages. See (C124₁).

    D. "Banal Story." Holograph manuscript. 5 pages. See (C170).

    E. "Mr. and Mrs. Elliot." Typescript. 5 pages. See (C159). The typescript shows that the original title was "Mr. and Mrs. Smith." Since "Smith" was the real name of the people in the story, the title was changed to "Elliot" when the story appeared in the *Little Review* (Autumn-Winter 1924-1925), see Carlos Baker's *EH: A Life Story*, p. 585.

LIBRARY HOLDINGS OF LETTERS

8. The Bancroft Library, University of California at Berkeley.

    A. TLS and a telegram to Franklin Folsom. April 9, 1939 and June 23, 1939. Havana. Regarding the Congress of the League of American Writers. In the Archives of the League of American Writers.

    B. TL with facsimile signature. 1 page. Form letter, dated February 13, 1940. Written on behalf of the Fourth Annual Conference of the American Committee for Protection of the Foreign Born. In the Peter Gulbrandsen Papers.

9. The Beinecke Rare Book and Manuscript Library, Yale University, New Haven, Conn.

    A. 2 TLS, with holograph notes, and TL (dictated) to Donald Ogden Stewart. November 3, 1924, December 28 [1930], February 7, 1931. Piggott, Arkansas, and Key West. The first regarding the ending of "Big Two-Hearted River," and the other two regarding a misunderstanding with Archibald MacLeish. In the Donald Ogden Stewart Papers.

    B. TLS, with holograph note, to Lawrence Langner. [Received March 19, 1940.] Camaguey, Cuba. 2 pages. Regarding *The Fifth Column*. In the Theatre Guild Archive.

10. Butler Library, Columbia University, New York.

    A. 2 TLS and 1 ALS to John N. Wheeler. 1949-1950.

    B. ANS to Louis L. Snyder. [April 1949.] San Francisco de Paula, Cuba.

    C. 6 TLS, 4 ALS, and 1 cablegram to Daniel Longwell. July 6, 1952 to May 5, 1953. San Francisco de Paula, Cuba. Regarding the publication of *The Old Man and the Sea* in *Life* magazine.

11 The Charles Patterson Van Pelt Library, University of Pennsylvania, Philadelphia.

    A. Telegram and TLS to James T. Farrell. December 25, 1936, Key West, and January 15, 1937, n.p., 1 page.

    B. Cable to Burton Rascoe. 1 page. Paris. January 8, 1938.

12 Clark Library, Brigham Young University, Provo, Utah.

    A. Letter to "Dear Mac." May 13, 1926. Regarding Morley Callaghan's manuscript entitled "Backwater."

13 The Library of Congress, Washington, D.C.

    A. Letter to "Bill." July 17, 1923. Photocopy. In the papers of Huntington Cairns. (Restricted.)

    B. 11 letters and 1 telegram to Owen Wister. 1928-1933.

    C. Letter to Frank R. McCoy. May 4, 1931. (Restricted.)

    D. 5 letters and 2 telegrams to Irita Van Doren. 1940-1952.

    E. Letters to MacKinley Kantor. (Restricted.)

    F. Additional letters to Archibald MacLeish. See (F16A). (Restricted.)

14 The Firestone Library, Princeton University, Princeton, N.J.

    A. 189 letters and related pieces to Charles Scribner. 1939-1952. Personal correspondence. (Restricted.)

    B. 317 letters and related pieces to Charles Scribner's Sons. [Presumably 1926 to 1961.] (On deposit. Restricted.)

    C. 13 letters to Mr. and Mrs. Milford J. Baker. February 12, 1930 to October 2, 1930. Key West, Florida. In the Milford J. Baker Collection.

    D. 18 letters to William B. Smith. December 1918 to July 28, 1927.

    E. 9 letters to Isabel Simmons Godolphin. December 1922 to Fall 1929.

    F. 3 letters to Solita Solano. 1933-1942.

    G. Letter to "Jan" [Janet Flanner]. 2 pages. April 8 [1933]. Key West, Florida.

    H. Letter to Dale Wilson. 6 pages. May 19, 1918. From the Hotel Earle, New York City. Regarding his stopover in New York en route to Europe as a Red Cross ambulance driver.

    I. Letter to Paul A. Bartlett. August 11, 1939. From Hotel Ambos Mundos, Havana.

    J. Letter to Whit Burnett. September 9, 1954. Finca Vigia, San Francisco de Paula, Cuba. In the Story Magazine Collection.

    Note: The letters are in the Ernest Hemingway Collection unless otherwise noted.

15 The Houghton Library, Harvard University, Cambridge, Mass.

    A. 93 letters to Harvey Breit. 1950-1961.

16 Humanities Research Center, University of Texas, Austin.

    A. 3 ALS and 1 TLS to James Donald Adams. April 16, 1953 to January 20, 1958.

    B. 8 ALS, 6 TLS, and 1 telegram to Rupert Belleville. 1953-1959.

    C. ALS to David Garnett. Dec. 10 (n.y.).

    D. TLS to Stephen Graham. July 14 (n.y.).

    E. TL/copy to "Grandfather" [Anson Tyler Hemingway]. March 14, 1923.

    F. PCI (with note by Grace Hall Hemingway) and telegram to Clarence Edmonds Hemingway. September 4, 1904 and April 10, 1928.

    G. 10 ALS, 1 TLS, 2 telegrams, and a Christmas card to Grace Hall Hemingway (and family). January 19, 1904 to December 19, 1938.

    H. 4 ALS and 3 TLS to Leicester "Baron" Hemingway. 1937-1947.

    I. 4 ALS to John Herrmann. The dated one being September 28 [1930].

    J. ANS to La Casa Belga in Havana. See (F105). 1948.

    K. ALS to Edward Verrall Lucas. December 10, 1929.

    L. Telegram to Karl Pfeiffer. No date.

    M. 2 telegrams to Paul M. Pfeiffer. November 20, 1931 and November 25, 1931.

    N. ALS to Mr. Rider. July 29, 1956. Regarding William Faulkner. See (F137).

    O. ALS to Edward W. Titus. January 4 (n.y.).

    P. TLS to Irita Van Doren. November 15, 1951.

    Q. 4 TL/copies to Hugh Walpole. The dated ones being April 14, 1927 and October 16, 1929.

    R. 1 ALS, 2 TLS, and 1 TLS/photostat to Jerome Weidman. 1941-1955.

    S. 65 ALS to Adriana Ivancich. 1949-1955.

17 Iowa State Education Association, Salisbury House, Des Moines.

    A. APC to Carl Weeks. May 31 [1936]. Key West, Florida.

18 The John Hay Library, Brown University, Providence, Rhode Island.

    A. TLS to Miss Buss. 1 page. May 12, 1922. Montreux, Switzerland.

    B. TNS, with holograph addition, to "Bob" [Robert R. Edge]. 1 page. December 31, 1954. San Francisco de Paula, Cuba.

19 McKeldin Library, University of Maryland, College Park.

    A. AL unsigned to Maxwell Perkins. July 13 [1933?]. Regarding the order of the stories in *Winner Take Nothing*.

    B. 9 TLS, with holograph notations, to Arthur Mizener. July 1949 to January 1951. San Francisco de Paula, Cuba. Regarding F. Scott Fitzgerald.

c. 4 ALS and 4 TLS to Edward O'Brien. May 21, 1923 to September 7, 1927. Paris, Hendaye, Toronto, and Spain. The early letters "detail the struggle and hopes of young Hemingway trying to get his work published."

20 Maxim Gorky Institute of World Literature, Moscow.
A. 2 letters to Sergei Dinamov. July 24, 1937 and August 7, 1937. Note: Reported in "American Literary Manuscripts in Continental Libraries" by George Hendrick, *Bulletin of Bibliography*, xxv (May-Aug. 1967), 54.

21 Morris Library, Southern Illinois University, Carbondale.
A. ALS to Col. N. N. Wallack. 1 page. May 19 (n.y.). Havana.

22 Mugar Memorial Library, Boston University, Boston, Mass.
A. TLS, with holograph additions, to Meyer Levin. No date. [probably January 1940]. Regarding Levin's novel *Citizens*. See (S-F178).
B. ALS to Lambert Davis. May 7, 1940.
C. ANS to Judson Jerome. November 31, 1956.
D. Hemingway material in the Martha Gellhorn Collection. Gift of Miss Gellhorn in 1965. (Restricted for twenty-five years.)

23 The Newberry Library, Chicago, Ill.
A. Photostat of ALS to Edwin L. Peterson. 4 pages. March 30 [1926]. Paris. Regarding *The Torrents of Spring*.

24 The Ohio State University Libraries, Columbus.
A. ALS to Louis Bromfield. 2 pages. No date.
B. TLS to Louis and Mary Bromfield. 1 page. December 6, 1926.

25 University of Oregon Library, Eugene.
A. TLS, with holograph marginal notes, to Robert Cantwell. 3 pages. August 28, 1950. Finca Vigia, San Francisco de Paula, Cuba. Apparently in response to a request for information on his writing methods and certain biographical data.

25-A Seymour Library, Knox College, Galesburg, Illinois.
A. 2 TLS, with holograph additions, to James Gamble, Hemingway's commanding officer during World War I. March 3, [1919], from Oak Park, Illinois, and Dec. 12, 1923.
B. ALS to George Horace Lorimer, editor of the *Saturday Evening Post*, regarding "The Undefeated." Jan. 21, 1925. Austria.
C. TLS to John M. Stahl. July 26, 1926. Paris.
D. ALS to Miss Langstreth (?). January 17, 1928. Gstaad, Switzerland.

E. ALS to [George Frederich] Wilson, thanking him for his appreciation of *A Farewell to Arms*. Oct. 28, 1929. Paris.

F. ALS to Mr. Schoenfeld, regarding *The Sun Also Rises* as a play. Nov. 5, 1929. Paris.

G. ALS to Everett R. Perry, Librarian at the Los Angeles Public Library, concerning the use of "dirty" words in his writings. Feb. [7] 1933. Key West. Florida.

H. TLS, with holograph addition, to [Paul] Jones, discussing bull fights. March 10, 1933. Key West, Florida.

I. TLS to Patrick Hemingway, with a holograph addition to Gregory Hemingway. June 30, [1940]. Havana.

J. TLS to [Mike] Murphy. July 28, 1957. San Francisco de Paula, Cuba.

K. ALS to Peter Briggs. August 24, 1958. San Francisco de Paula, Cuba.

L. 4 ALS to Monique [de Beaumont]. Sept. 20, 1959 to March 6, 1960. Málaga, Spain, Tallahassee, Florida, Ketchum, Idaho, and San Francisco de Paula, Cuba.

M. AN to Marshall E. Bean. Oct. 1, 1960. Madrid.

N. TLS to Mrs. Vera Hill, regarding his health. January 15, 1961. Rochester, Minnesota.

Note: All letters are in the James H. Hughes Collection of Ernest Hemingway and the Lost Generation.

26 University of Virginia Libraries, Charlottesville.

A. TLS to Patrick and Gregory Hemingway. 1 page. July 14 [1939].

B. 6 ALS and 4 TLS to Bronislaw Zieliński. 1958-1961.

Note: A and B are in the Ernest Hemingway Collection in the Clifton Waller Barrett Library.

C. APCS to William B. Smith, Jr. July 26 (n.y.).

D. 12 ALS, 4 AL, 9 TLS, 2 TL, and a TLS/photostat to John Dos Passos. April 22, 1925 to October 30, 1951.

E. TLS, with holograph addition, to Katy and John Dos Passos. 2 pages. January 13, 1936.

F. TLS to Katharine Foster Smith (later Mrs. John Dos Passos). 3 pages. February 16, 1922.

Note: C to F are in the John Dos Passos Collection. On deposit by Mrs. Elizabeth Holdridge Dos Passos in the Alderman Library.

27 Eugene P. Watson Memorial Library, Northwestern State University of Louisiana, Natchitoches.

A. ALS to [James] Aswell. 1 page. October 21, 1929. Paris. Expressing his pleasure over a review by Aswell. [Presumably of *A Farewell to Arms* in the *Richmond Times-Dispatch* (Oct. 6, 1929).]

28 The University of Wisconsin Library, Milwaukee.

A. 5 ALS and 1 TLS to Jane Heap, editor of the *Little Review*. Not dated. [Probably 1921-1929.]

PUBLISHED FACSIMILES OF HEMINGWAY'S MANUSCRIPTS

29 *Texas Quarterly*, IX (Winter 1966), p [69]. See (S-H279). Facsimile of page 24 of the typescript of "The Snows of Kilimanjaro," with holograph corrections. This page mentions "poor Scott Fitzgerald." From the Ernest Hemingway Collection at the University of Texas.

29₁ *Ibid.*, p. [73]. Facsimile of page 28, the last page, of the typescript of "The Snows of Kilimanjaro," with holograph corrections. From the Ernest Hemingway Collection at the University of Texas.

29₂ *Ibid.*, p. [97]. Facsimile of page 12 of the typescript, with holograph corrections, of "The Snows of Kilimanjaro." This page shows that the name "Henry Walden" was originally considered for the main character. From the Ernest Hemingway Collection at the University of Texas. Also reproduced as the frontispiece of *Hemingway's African Stories* by John M. Howell, New York: Scribner's, 1969. See (S-B9).

30 *Ernest Hemingway: A Comprehensive Bibliography* by Audre Hanneman. Princeton: Princeton University Press, 1967. Opposite p. 51. Facsimile of page four of the holograph manuscript of *A Moveable Feast* (published in chapter two, "Miss Stein Instructs," pp. 12-13).

31 *Charles Hamilton Galleries* catalogue for Auction No. 19 (May 24, 1967), item 316. Facsimile of page seven of the typescript, with holograph corrections, of an unpublished 26-page manuscript titled "Black Ass at the Cross Roads." Reproduced in *Hemingway at Auction*, p. 129. See (S-B18).

32 *Empreintes* by Suzanne Bresard. Paris: Delachaux et Niestlé, 1968. pp. 22, 23, and 25. Facsimiles of a holograph manuscript page of "The Battler." Used for an analysis of Hemingway's handwriting. See (S-G47). This page was reproduced in the *Paris Review*, No. 18 (Spring 1958). See (F34).

33 *The Hemingway Manuscripts: An Inventory* by Philip Young and Charles W. Mann. University Park: Pennsylvania State University Press, 1969. Following p. 18. Facsimile of the last page of the holograph notebook draft of *The Sun Also Rises*. This page shows the name "Duff" [Twysden] in place of "Brett" [Ashley]. Note: Also reproduced on the front cover of the dust jacket.

33₁ *Ibid.*, following p. 18. Facsimile of the first page of the holograph manuscript of "Summer People," probably the first Nick Adams story. This page shows the names "Nick," "Wemedge," and "Allan" deleted, and the name "Nick" again inserted. Also reproduced in the *N.Y. Times* (Sept. 22, 1969), p. 36.

33₂ *Ibid.*, following p. 18. Facsimile of the first page of the typescript of "The Killers," with marginal notations. The page shows the original title, "The Matadors," changed to "The Killers." Also reproduced in *Research in the College of Liberal Arts* (Pennsylvania State University) (Jan. 1970), p. 10.

33₃ *Ibid.*, following p. 18. Facsimile of the first page of the typescript, with holograph corrections, of the discarded opening of "Fifty Grand." Note: Facsimiles of pages two and three of the discarded opening are reproduced in the limited edition of this book. See (S-B11).

34 *Fitzgerald/Hemingway Annual: 1970*, p. 221. See (S-H651). Facsimile of the first page of the original typescript of "The Short Happy Life of Francis Macomber." From the holdings of the Morris Library, Southern Illinois University. Also reproduced in *Proof*, II (1972), see (S-F39).

34₁ *Ibid.*, p. 222. Facsimile of page 37 of the original typescript of "The Short Happy Life of Francis Macomber." From the holdings of the Morris Library, Southern Illinois University.

35 *Texas Quarterly*, XIII (Summer 1970), [83]. See (S-H705). Facsimile of page one of the typescript of "The Snows of Kilimanjaro." From the Ernest Hemingway Collection at the University of Texas.

35₁ *Ibid.*, p. [121]. Facsimile of page 19 of the typescript of "The Snows of Kilimanjaro," with holograph corrections. From the Ernest Hemingway Collection at the University of Texas.

35₂ *Ibid.*, p. [139]. Facsimile of page 26b of the typescript of "The Snows of Kilimanjaro," with holograph corrections. From the Ernest Hemingway Collection at the University of Texas.

36 *Esquire*, LXXIV (Oct. 1970), cover. Facsimile of seven lines of the holograph manuscript of "Bimini," the first part of *Islands in the Stream*, superimposed on a photograph of Hemingway. See (S-C64).

37 *Sports Illustrated*, XXXV (Dec. 6, 1971), 11. Facsimile of a portion of a holograph manuscript page of the "African Journal." See (S-C73).

38 *Sports Illustrated*, XXXV (Dec. 20, 1971), 41. Facsimile of a portion of a holograph manuscript page of the "African Journal." See

(S-C73). Note: This is a different portion than the one listed in the above entry.

39 *Proof: The Yearbook of American Bibliographical and Textual Studies,* II (1972), p. 216. See (S-H877). Facsimile of page [1], the title page, of the typescript of "The Short Happy Life of Francis Macomber." From the holdings of Morris Library, Southern Illinois University. Also reproduced in the *Fitzgerald/Hemingway Annual: 1970.* See (S-F34).

39₁ *Ibid.,* p. 220. Facsimile of page 19 of the typescript, with holograph corrections, of "The Short Happy Life of Francis Macomber." From the holdings of Morris Library, Southern Illinois University. Also reproduced in *ICarbS,* I (Fall-Winter 1973). See (S-F41₂).

39₂ *Ibid.,* p. 222. Facsimile of page 34 of the typescript, with holograph corrections, of "The Short Happy Life of Francis Macomber." From the holdings of Morris Library, Southern Illinois University.

39₃ *Ibid.,* p. 234. Facsimile of page 16 of the typescript, with holograph corrections, of "The Short Happy Life of Francis Macomber." From the holdings of Morris Library, Southern Illinois University.

40 *Hemingway at Auction: 1930-1973* compiled by Matthew J. Bruccoli and C. E. Frazer Clark, Jr. Detroit: Gale Research Co., 1973. See (S-B18). Frontispiece. Facsimile of the first page of the typescript of *Death in the Afternoon,* with holograph corrections. Reproduced from the Parke-Bernet Galleries catalogue of the sale of the library of Dr. Don Carlos Guffey, October 14, 1958. See (F35).

40₁ *Ibid.,* p. 35. Facsimile of a holograph manuscript page from chapter three of *DIA.* Reproduced from the Parke-Bernet Galleries catalogue of the sale of the library of Dr. Don Carlos Guffey, October 14, 1958. See (F35₁).

40₂ *Ibid.,* p. 129. Facsimile of page seven of the typescript, with holograph corrections, of an unpublished story titled "Black Ass at the Cross Roads." Reproduced from the catalogue of Charles Hamilton Galleries, Auction No. 19 (May 24, 1967). See (S-F31).

41 *ICarbS,* I (Fall-Winter 1973), [40]. See (S-H1047). Facsimile of page three of the typescript of "After the Storm," with holograph corrections. From the collection at Morris Library, Southern Illinois University at Carbondale.

41₁ *Ibid.,* p. [44]. Facsimile of page two of the holograph manuscript of "a.d. in Africa." This article, originally published in *Esquire,* I (April 1934), was the first of three "Tanganyika Letters." From the collection at Morris Library, Southern Illinois University at Carbondale.

4$_{12}$ *Ibid.*, p. [46]. Facsimile of p. 19 of the typescript of "The Short Happy Life of Francis Macomber," with holograph corrections. From the collection of Morris Library, Southern Illinois University at Carbondale. This page was also reproduced in *Proof*, II (1972), see (S-F39$_1$).

SECTION F: PART II

Although Hemingway specifically stated that it was his wish that none of his letters be published (quoted in the bibliography, p. 256), the list of Hemingway letters published in full or partially quoted has continued to grow. Most of them have been quoted, or reproduced in facsimile, in auction and dealers' catalogues. Many of these catalogues are reproduced in *Hemingway at Auction: 1930-1973* compiled by Matthew J. Bruccoli and C. E. Frazer Clark, Jr., Detroit, 1973.

Where a letter has been reprinted from a source reported in the bibliography, a cross reference is given.

PUBLISHED LETTERS

42 May 11, 1913. To his father, regarding his conduct at church. Quoted in Carlos Baker's *EH: A Life Story*, p. 16.

43 [Sept. 1918]. To his parents, from the American Red Cross Hospital in Italy. Excerpted in Carlos Baker's *EH: A Life Story*, p. 48. For earlier reprints of the full letter, see (F43).

44 October 18, 1918. To his father, on the subject of dying young versus growing old. Published in the *Oak Parker* (Nov. 16, 1918), pp. 6-7. Briefly quoted in Carlos Baker's *EH: A Life Story*, pp. 52, 552.

45 May 21, 1923 to Sept. 7, 1927. Eight letters to Edward O'Brien, from Paris, Toronto, Hendaye, and Spain, are quoted in the catalogue of Sotheby Parke Bernet, New York, Sale No. 3476 (Feb. 20, 1973), item 211. Reproduced in *Hemingway at Auction*, pp. 241-243. See (F45).

46 [1925?]. From Paris, to Ethel Moorhead and Ernest Walsh. Regarding his plans for spending a check received for a short story. Quoted in the catalogue of the Gotham Book Mart, New York, No. 39 (Winter 1938). Reproduced in *Hemingway at Auction*, p. 191.

47 Jan. 29, 1925. From Austria, to Ernest Walsh and Ethel Moorhead. Autobiographical sketch. Reproduced from the catalogue of the Ulysses Book Shop, London, No. 1 (March 1930), in *Hemingway at Auction*, p. 235. Also reproduced in the *Fitzgerald/Hemingway Annual: 1970*, p. 188. Note: In the bibliography, the annotations under

this letter (F57) and the letter dated February 28, 1925 (F59) were reversed.

48 Feb. 28, 1925. From Austria, to Ernest Walsh and Ethel Moorhead. Regarding Boni and Liveright's acceptance of *IOT*. Extracts reproduced from the catalogue of the Ulysses Book Shop, London, No. 1 (March 1930), in *Hemingway at Auction*, p. 235. Also reproduced in the *Fitzgerald/Hemingway Annual: 1970*, p. 188. See note under above entry.

49 May 11, 1925. From Paris, to Horace Liveright. Regarding a new story for *IOT* to replace ["Up in Michigan"], which the publisher considered censorable. Quoted in the catalogue of the American Art Association Anderson Galleries, New York, Sale No. 4228 (Jan. 30, 1936), item 314. Reproduced in *Hemingway at Auction*, p. 7.

50 June 21, 1925. From Paris, to Horace Liveright. Regarding *IOT*. Briefly quoted in the catalogue of the American Art Association Anderson Galleries, New York, Sale No. 4228 (Jan. 30, 1936), item 314. Reproduced in *Hemingway at Auction*, p. 7.

51 July 20, 1925. From Madrid, to Ernest Walsh and Ethel Moorhead. Regarding his trip to Spain. Extract reproduced from the catalogue of the Ulysses Book Shop, London, No. 1 (March 1930), in *Hemingway at Auction*, p. 235. See (F61). Also reproduced in the *Fitzgerald/Hemingway Annual: 1970*, p. 188.

52 [1926?]. From [Paris?], to Ernest Walsh. Regarding *IOT*. Quoted in the catalogue of the American Art Association Anderson Galleries, New York (1936), item 251. Reproduced in *Hemingway at Auction*, p. 8.

53 Jan. 2, 1926. From Madrid, to Ernest Walsh and Ethel Moorhead. Regarding his work and Catholicism. Extracts reproduced from the catalogue of the Ulysses Book Shop, London, No. 1 (March 1930), in *Hemingway at Auction*, p. 235. See (F64). Also reproduced in the *Fitzgerald/Hemingway Annual: 1970*, p. 188.

54 Feb. 1, 1926. From Paris, to Ernest Walsh. Regarding Robert Mac-Almon and dying. Quoted in the catalogue of *The American Writer in England: An Exhibition Arranged in Honor of the Sesquicentennial of the University of Virginia,* Charlottesville: University Press of Virginia, 1969, p. 131. Reprinted in the *Fitzgerald/Hemingway Annual: 1972*, p. 355.

55 March 23, [1926]. From Schruns (Vorarlberg), Austria, to Isidor Schneider. Regarding Waldo Frank's *Virgin Spain*. Quoted in the catalogue of the Parke-Bernet Galleries, New York, Sale No. 2474

(Nov. 9, 1966), item 134. Reproduced in *Hemingway at Auction*, p. 114.

56 May 4, 1926. From Paris, to Isidor Schneider. Regarding his plans for going to Madrid. Quoted in the catalogue of the Parke-Bernet Galleries, New York, Sale No. 2474 (Nov. 9, 1966), item 135. Reproduced in *Hemingway at Auction*, p. 114.

57 June 29, [1926]. From Juan les Pins [France], to Isidor Schneider. Regarding *SAR*. Quoted in the catalogue of the Parke-Bernet Galleries, New York, Sale No. 2474 (Nov. 9, 1966), item 136. Reproduced in *Hemingway at Auction*, p. 116.

58 [Early Oct. 1926]. To Isidor Schneider. Regarding suicide. Quoted in the catalogue of the Parke-Bernet Galleries, New York, Sale No. 2474 (Nov. 9, 1966), item 137. Reproduced in *Hemingway at Auction*, p. 116.

59 Jan. 18-19-20 [1927]. From Gstaad, Switzerland, to Isidor Schneider. Regarding *SAR*. Quoted in the catalogue of the Parke-Bernet Galleries, New York, Sale No. 2474 (Nov. 9, 1966), item 138. Reproduced in *Hemingway at Auction*, p. 117.

60 Feb. 14, 1927. From Gstaad, Switzerland, to Isidor Schneider. Regarding his work. Briefly quoted in the catalogue of the Parke-Bernet Galleries, New York, Sale No. 2474 (Nov. 9, 1966), item 139. Reproduced in *Hemingway at Auction*, p. 117.

61 [ca. March 22, 1927]. From Rimini, Italy, to Isidor Schneider. Regarding his trip to Italy with Guy Hickok. Quoted in the catalogue of the Parke-Bernet Galleries, New York, Sale No. 2474 (Nov. 9, 1966), item 140. Reproduced in *Hemingway at Auction*, p. 117.

62 [Spring 1927]. Facsimile of a bibliographical note issued by the Walden Book Shop, Chicago, 1930, reproduced in the catalogue of J&S Fine Books, Chicago, No. 5 (April 1970), item 251. See (F69) and (H433). Reproduced in *Hemingway at Auction*, p. 213.

63 May 18, [1927]. From [Paris?], to Isidor Schneider. Quoted in the catalogue of the Parke-Bernet Galleries, New York, Sale No. 2474 (Nov. 9, 1966), item 141. Reproduced in *Hemingway at Auction*, p. 118.

64 Jan. 28, 1928. From Hotel Rossli, Gstaad, Switzerland, to [Glen Walton] Blodgett. Reply to a request for his autograph. Hemingway inaccurately quoted the opening lines of the first "chapter" of *iot*. Quoted, with facsimile of *iot* quotation and signature, in the catalogue of Paul C. Richards, Autographs, Brookline, Massachusetts, No. 50 (March 1970), item 74. Reproduced in *Hemingway at Auc-*

tion, p. 226. A facsimile of the complete letter appears in *Ernest Hemingway as Recalled by His High School Contemporaries* edited by Ina Mae Schleden and Marion Rawls Herzog, Oak Park, 1973, p. [46]. See (S-G367).

65 Aug. 15, [1928?]. From Hendaye, France, to "Mr. Shelton." A facsimile of the letter is reproduced in the catalogue of Charles Hamilton, New York, Auction No. 51 (Aug. 5, 1971), item 191. Reproduced in *Hemingway at Auction*, p. 163.

66 Jan. 23, 1929. From Key West, Florida, to Russell Spencer. Briefly quoted in the catalogue of the Parke-Bernet Galleries, New York, Sale No. 627 (Jan. 23-24, 1945), item 248. Reproduced in *Hemingway at Auction*, p. 23.

67 Nov. 21, [1929]. From Paris, to [Lawrence] Drake. Regarding *FTA*. Quoted in the catalogue of Paul C. Richards, Brookline, Massachusetts, No. 24 (n.d.), item 333. Reproduced in *Hemingway at Auction*, p. 225.

68 Feb. 18, 1930. From Key West, to Ernst Rowohlt. Regarding the title for the German translation of *FTA*. Translated into German in *Die Zeit*, xvi (July 14, 1961), 9. Printed in English in H. M. Ledig-Rowohlt's *Meeting Two American Giants*, Reinbek, 1962, pp. 31-33.

69 Oct. 10, 1930. From the L-T Ranch, Cooke, Montana, to "Dear Mathew." Regarding literary and financial matters. Quoted, with a facsimile of part of page two, in the catalogue of the Charles Hamilton Galleries, New York, Auction No. 71 (Sept. 20, 1973), item 152.

70 Nov. 30, 1930. From Montana, to Ernst Rowohlt, his German publisher. Translated into German in *Die Zeit*, xvi (July 14, 1961), 9. Printed in English in H. M. Ledig-Rowohlt's *Meeting Two American Giants*, Reinbek, 1962, pp. 30-31.

71 [1931]. To Louis Henry Cohn. Stating his reasons for not wishing any of his work prior to *In Our Time* being listed in Captain Cohn's *A Bibliography of the Work of Ernest Hemingway*. See (F77). Quoted in *Ernest Hemingway, Cub Reporter* edited by Matthew J. Bruccoli, Pittsburgh, 1970, p. [vii].

72 April 12, 1931. From Key West, Florida, to Dr. Don Carlos Guffey. Regarding *Three Stories & Ten Poems*. Extract reproduced from the catalogue of the Parke-Bernet Galleries, New York, Sale No. 1843 (Oct. 14, 1958), item 147, in *Hemingway at Auction*, p. 36. See (F78). Also quoted in the catalogue of John F. Fleming, New York (Jan. 1961), item 381. Reproduced in *Hemingway at Auction*, p. 188.

73 April 27, 1931. From Key West, Florida, to Dr. Don Carlos Guffey. Extract reproduced from the catalogue of the Parke-Bernet Gal-

leries, New York, Sale No. 1843 (Oct. 14, 1958), item 147, in *Hemingway at Auction*, p. 36. See (F79). Also quoted in the catalogue of John F. Fleming, New York (Jan. 1961), item 381. Reproduced in *Hemingway at Auction*, p. 188.

74 [May 1931?]. From [Paris?], to Dr. Don Carlos Guffey. Full page inscription, in letter form, regarding the publication of *in our time*. See (F80). Facsimile reproduced from the catalogue of the Parke-Bernet Galleries, New York, Sale No. 1843 (Oct. 14, 1958), item 152, in *Hemingway at Auction*, p. 40.

75 [Jan. 15, 1932]. From Key West, Florida, to Paul Romaine. Regarding William Faulkner and *Salmagundi*. See (B11). Quoted in the catalogue of the Parke-Bernet Galleries, New York, Sale No. 2350 (May 4, 1965), item 154. Reproduced in *Hemingway at Auction*, p. 86.

76 July 6, 1932. From Piggott, Arkansas, to Paul Romaine. Regarding politics in literature. Quoted in the catalogue of the Parke-Bernet Galleries, New York, Sale No. 2350 (May 4, 1965), item 154. Reproduced in *Hemingway at Auction*, p. 86.

77 Aug. 9, [1932]. From Cooke, Montana, to Paul Romaine. Regarding writing on "the Lost Generation and bulls." Quoted in the catalogue of the Parke-Bernet Galleries, New York, Sale No. 2350 (May 4, 1965), item 154. Reproduced in *Hemingway at Auction*, p. 86.

78 Feb. 12, 1935. From Key West, Florida, to "Mr. Meyers." Reply to a request from a book collector. Quoted in the catalogue of J&S Fine Books, Chicago, No. 5 (April 1970), item 69. Reproduced in *Hemingway at Auction*, pp. 214, 215, 225.

79 Aug. 19, 1935. From Key West, Florida, to Ivan Kashkin. Translated into Russian in Kashkin's *Ernest Khemingueĭ*, Moscow, 1966, pp. 276-282. Printed in English in Kashkin's "Letters of Ernest Hemingway to Soviet Writers," see (F90); reprinted in the *Fitzgerald/Hemingway Annual: 1971*, pp. 200-203. This letter is quoted in Carlos Baker's *EH: A Life Story*, p. 277.

80 Dec. 6, 1935. From Key West, Florida, to Joseph M. Hopkins, a young American writer. Regarding his own work. Quoted in the catalogue of John Howell—Books, San Francisco, No. 40 (1970), item 45. Reproduced in *Hemingway at Auction*, p. 211.

81 Dec. 15, 1935. From Key West, Florida, to Joseph M. Hopkins. Regarding Hopkins's work. Quoted in the catalogue of John Howell—Books, San Francisco, No. 40 (1970), item 45. Reproduced in *Hemingway at Auction*, p. 211.

82 Dec. 24, 1935. From Key West, Florida, to Joseph M. Hopkins. Regarding Hopkins's work. Quoted in the catalogue of John Howell—Books, San Francisco, No. 40 (1970), item 45. Reproduced in *Hemingway at Auction*, p. 212.

83 Dec. 31, 1935. From Key West, Florida, to Joseph M. Hopkins. On writing. Quoted in the catalogue of John Howell—Books, San Francisco, No. 40 (1970), item 45. Reproduced in *Hemingway at Auction*, p. 212.

84 Feb. 6, 1936. From Key West, to Joseph M. Hopkins. Regarding "The Tradesman's Return," later Part II of *THAHN*. Quoted in the catalogue of John Howell—Books, San Francisco, No. 40 (1970), item 45. Reproduced in *Hemingway at Auction*, p. 212.

85 March 7, 1936. From Key West, to "Mr. Reed." Regarding C. S. Forester's *The African Queen*. Quoted in the catalogue of J&S Fine Books, Chicago, No. 11 (1971), item 1417. Reproduced in *Hemingway at Auction*, pp. 214, 217. A longer excerpt appears in the catalogue of Paul C. Richards, Autographs, Brookline, Mass., No. 24 (n.d.), item 334. Reproduced in *Hemingway at Auction*, p. 225.

86 March 17, 1936. From Key West, to T. [Thomas] Aitken. Regarding fishing off Cuba. An extract and a partial facsimile are reproduced from the catalogue of Charles Hamilton, New York, Auction No. 4 (May 21, 1964), item 87, in *Hemingway at Auction*, p. 81. See (F93).

87 March 31, 1936. From Key West, to Joseph M. Hopkins. Regarding his own work. Quoted in the catalogue of John Howell—Books, San Francisco, No. 40 (1970), item 45. Reproduced in *Hemingway at Auction*, p. 212.

88 July 24, 1937. From Key West, Florida, to S. Dinamov. Regarding Ivan Kashkin's articles on Hemingway. Quoted in Kashkin's "Letters of Ernest Hemingway to Soviet Writers," *Soviet Literature*, No. 11 (Nov. 1962). Reprinted in the *Fitzgerald/Hemingway Annual: 1971*, p. 198.

89 Feb. 1, 1938. From Key West, to Paul Drus, an artist. Regarding his role as editor of *Ken* magazine. Quoted in the catalogue of Sotheby Parke Bernet, New York, Sale No. 3428 (Oct. 31, 1972), item 204. Reproduced in *Hemingway at Auction*, p. 175.

90 July 28, 1938. From Key West, to Paul Drus. Regarding manuscripts submitted to *Ken* magazine. Quoted in the catalogue of Sotheby Parke Bernet, New York, Sale No. 3428 (Oct. 31, 1972), item 204. Reproduced in *Hemingway at Auction*, p. 175.

91 March 23, 1939. From Key West, Florida, to Ivan Kashkin. Translated into Russian in Kashkin's *Ernest Khemingueĭ*, Moscow, 1966,

pp. 283-287. Printed in English in Kashkin's "Letters of Ernest Hemingway to Soviet Writers," see (F95). Reprinted in the *Fitzgerald/Hemingway Annual: 1971*, pp. 203-205.

92 July 14, [1939?]. From Havana, Cuba, to Patrick and Gregory Hemingway. Regarding plans for a trip to the ranch in Wyoming. Quoted in the catalogue of Kenneth W. Rendell, Newton, Mass., No. 60 (1971), item 75. Reproduced in *Hemingway at Auction*, pp. 222-224.

93 [Jan. 1941]. To Milton Wolff. Regarding *FWBT*. Quoted in Carlos Baker's *EH: A Life Story*, p. 357, from *American Dialog*, 1 (Oct.-Nov. 1964). See (C424₁). Also quoted in the serialization of Professor Baker's biography in the *Atlantic*, ccxxiii (Jan. 1969), p. 67.

94 Aug. 21, 1941. From Finca Vigia, San Francisco de Paula, Cuba, to "Bumby" [John Hemingway]. Regarding plans for a trip to the ranch. Quoted in the catalogue of Charles Hamilton, New York, Auction No. 19 (May 24, 1967), item 295. Reproduced in *Hemingway at Auction*, p. 120.

95 Sept. 3, 1945. To Malcolm Cowley. Regarding William Faulkner. Briefly quoted in *The Faulkner-Cowley File*, New York, 1966, p. 29. Reprinted in Carlos Baker's *EH: A Life Story*, p. 656.

96 June 20, 1946. From Finca Vigia, to Konstantin Simonov. See (F102). A facsimile of the portion regarding Ivan Kashkeen is reproduced in *Sputnik*, No. 7 (July 1967), pp. 40-41. The letter is reprinted in the *Fitzgerald/Hemingway Annual: 1971*, pp. 206-208.

97 Dec. 18, 1946. To Ernst Rowohlt, his German publisher. See (F104). An excerpt is translated into German in *Die Zeit*, xvi (July 14, 1961), 9; in *Der Spiegel*, xv (July 12, 1961), 45. Quoted in English in H. M. Ledig-Rowohlt's *Meeting Two American Giants*, Reinbek, 1962, pp. 33-34. An excerpt, in English, appears in Wayne Kvam's *Hemingway in Germany*, Athens, Ohio, 1973, p. 33.

98 July 29, 1948. From Finca Vigia, San Francisco de Paula, Cuba, to [W. G.] Rogers. Regarding Gertrude Stein. Facsimile reproduced in the prospectus of the Gotham Book Mart, 1973. See (S-F173).

99 Jan. 18, 1949. From Villa Aprile, Cortina D'Ampezzo, Italy, to W. J. Weatherby. Regarding the vision of bulls and their ability to distinguish color. Quoted in the catalogue of Charles Hamilton, New York, Auction No. 6 (Jan. 14, 1965), item 85. See (F106). Reproduced in *Hemingway at Auction*, p. 84. Quoted in the catalogue of Paul C. Richards, Autographs, Brookline, Mass., No. 15 (March 1965), item 116. Reproduced in *Hemingway at Auction*, p. 225. A facsimile of the letter is reproduced in *Ernest Hemingway as Re-*

called by His High School Contemporaries edited by Ina Mae Schleden and Marion Rawls Herzog, Oak Park, 1973, p. 47. See (S-G367).

100 March 7, 1949. From Villa Aprile, Cortina D'Ampezzo, Italy, to "Dear Jack." Refuses to let an article be reprinted without remuneration, unless it is for charity. Facsimile reproduced in the catalogue of the Parke-Bernet Galleries, New York, Sale No. 2676 (April 2 and 3, 1968), item 333. Reproduced in *Hemingway at Auction*, p. 141.

101 July 6, 1949. From Finca Vigia, to Arthur Mizener. Regarding F. Scott Fitzgerald. Quoted in the catalogue of Sotheby Parke Bernet, New York, Sale No. 3428 (Oct. 31, 1972), item 203. Reproduced in *Hemingway at Auction*, p. 174. Also quoted in the *N.Y. Times* (Oct. 25, 1972), p. 38.

102 Aug. 4, [19]49. From Finca Vigia, to Charles Poore. Regarding the Battle of Huertgen in World War II. Quoted in the catalogue of Charles Hamilton, New York, Auction No. 56 (March 9, 1972), item 144. Reproduced in *Hemingway at Auction*, p. 166.

103 Sept. 7, 1949. From Finca Vigia, to John Austin Parker of Syracuse, New York. Regarding critics, especially Malcolm Cowley and Edmund Wilson. Quoted in the catalogue of Charles Hamilton, New York, Auction No. 37 (Nov. 6, 1969), item 179. Reproduced in *Hemingway at Auction*, p. 151. Quoted in *Escapade* (March 1970), p. 36.

104 Sept. 9, 1949. From Finca Vigia, to the Literary Editor of the *Chicago Daily News*. Regarding his inability to send a contribution to the Christmas Book Section due to his working on a novel. Quoted in the catalogue of J&S Fine Books, Chicago, No. 11 (Oct. 1971), item 1396. Reproduced in *Hemingway at Auction*, p. 217. Reprinted in the *Fitzgerald/Hemingway Annual: 1972*, p. 357.

105 [1950-1955]. To Adriana Ivancich. Hemingway's letters were quoted in the *Times*, London (Oct. 21, 1967), p. 17. For background on these letters, see the catalogue of Christie, Manson & Woods, London (Nov. 29, 1967), item 158, reproduced in *Hemingway at Auction*, pp. 132-135; and the catalogue of the House of El Dieff, New York, No. 70 (1970), item 42, reproduced in *Hemingway at Auction*, p. 208.

106 April 4, 1950. From Finca Vigia, to Arthur Mizener. Regarding F. Scott Fitzgerald. Quoted in the catalogue of Sotheby Parke Bernet, New York, Sale No. 3428 (Oct. 31, 1972), item 203. Reproduced in *Hemingway at Auction*, p. 174. Quoted in the *N.Y. Times* (Oct. 25, 1972), p. 38 (dated April 5, 1950).

107 May 12, 1950. From Finca Vigía, to Arthur Mizener. Regarding writing, F. Scott Fitzgerald, and Edmund Wilson. Quoted in the catalogue of Sotheby Parke Bernet, New York, Sale No. 3428 (Oct. 31, 1972), item 203. Reproduced in *Hemingway at Auction*, p. 174.

108 June 1, 1950. From Finca Vigía, to Arthur Mizener. Regarding James Joyce. Quoted in the catalogue of Sotheby Parke Bernet, New York, Sale No. 3428 (Oct. 31, 1972), item 203. Reproduced in *Hemingway at Auction*, pp. 174-175.

109 June 2, 1950. From Finca Vigía, to Arthur Mizener. Regarding *ARIT*, Edmund Wilson's remark about "hidden wounds," and his sister Ursula. A facsimile of the first page of the typewritten letter (dated: 2/6/50, with a holograph note dated: 29/8/50) is reproduced in the *Washington Post* (Oct. 30, 1972), p. B 1. Quoted, with other letters, all undated, on p. B 2. Also quoted in the catalogue of Sotheby Parke Bernet, New York, Sale No. 3428 (Oct. 31, 1972), item 203 (dated June 6, 1950). Reproduced in *Hemingway at Auction*, p. 175.

110 June 18, 1950. To Clara H. Franklin, about fishing. Quoted in the catalogue of Charles Hamilton, New York, Auction No. 37 (Nov. 6, 1969), item 178. Reproduced in *Hemingway at Auction*, p. 151. See also *Hemingway at Auction*, p. 89, for (F111).

111 July 22, 1950. To Russ Burton. Regarding Lillian Ross's profile of Hemingway in the *New Yorker*. See (H627). Quoted in the *Los Angeles Mirror* [Home edition] (July 5, 1961), p. 1. A longer excerpt, not dated, appeared in the *Los Angeles Herald-Examiner* (Dec. 1, 1968), *California Living* section, p. 10.

112 Aug. 4, 1950. From Finca Vigía, to Russ Burton. Refers to Lillian Ross's profile of Hemingway in the *New Yorker*. See (H627). Quoted in the *Los Angeles Herald-Examiner* (Dec. 1, 1968), *California Living* section, pp. 10-11.

113 Jan. 2, 1951. From Finca Vigía, to Arthur Mizener. Regarding F. Scott Fitzgerald's suggestions for *FTA*. Quoted in the catalogue of Sotheby Parke Bernet, New York, Sale No. 3428 (Oct. 31, 1972), item 203. Reproduced in *Hemingway at Auction*, p. 175.

114 Jan. 4, 1951. From Finca Vigía, to Arthur Mizener. Regarding F. Scott Fitzgerald and "The Snows of Kilimanjaro." Quoted in the catalogue of Sotheby Parke Bernet, New York, Sale No. 3428 (Oct. 31, 1972), item 203. Reproduced in *Hemingway at Auction*, p. 175. Also quoted in the *N.Y. Times* (Oct. 25, 1972), p. 38 (last quotation, undated).

115 April 1, 1951. To Carlos Baker. On his liberal stand during the Spanish Civil War. See (F119). Quoted in Frederick R. Benson's *Writers in Arms*, New York, 1967, p. 63.

116 [ca. July 15, 1951]. From Finca Vigia, to C. L. Sulzberger. Regarding "Michel Dupont," Hemingway's driver in France and Germany during World War II. Quoted in Sulzberger's *The Resistentialists*, New York, 1962, pp. 18-21.

117 Aug. 10, 1951. From Finca Vigia, to C. L. Sulzberger. Regarding "Michel Dupont." Quoted in Sulzberger's *The Resistentialists*, New York, 1962, pp. 21-24.

118 [ca. Sept. 5, 1951]. From Finca Vigia, to C. L. Sulzberger. Regarding "Michel Dupont's" bravery. Quoted in Sulzberger's *The Resistentialists*, New York, 1962, pp. 24-25.

119 Sept. 23, 1951. To Charles A. Fenton. Briefly quoted in *The Apprenticeship of Ernest Hemingway*, New York, 1954, p. 170.

120 [1952]. Letters to Sidney James, from Finca Vigia. Regarding publication of *The Old Man and the Sea* in *Life* magazine. See (C370). Quoted in *Life*, LI (July 14, 1961), 2. Reprinted in *Ernest Hemingway/William Faulkner*, *Life* Educational Reprint, [1968], p. 24. See (S-G259).

121 Jan. 19, 1952. To Charles A. Fenton. Quoted in *New World Writing*, Second Number (Nov. 1952), p. 316 and *passim*.

122 [April 1952]. To Leonard Lyons. Regarding Sidney Franklin's autobiography in *Town & Country*. See (H716). Two paragraphs are quoted in the Lyons Den column, *N.Y. Post* (April 20, 1952), p. 8-M.

123 May 4, 1952. From Finca Vigia, to "Dear Bob" [Robert J. Carino]. Regarding writing and his luck with *OMATS*. Quoted in the catalogue of the Charles Hamilton Galleries, New York, Auction No. 67 (May 3, 1973), item 133.

124 July 29, 1952. To Charles A. Fenton. Briefly quoted in *The Apprenticeship of Ernest Hemingway*, New York, 1954, p. 198 (note 24).

125 Sept. 11, 1952. From Finca Vigia, to Russ Burton. Regarding his tiredness after finishing *OMATS*. Facsimile reproduced in the *Los Angeles Herald-Examiner* (Dec. 1, 1968), *California Living* section, p. 11. Quoted in the *Los Angeles Mirror* [Home edition] (July 5, 1961), p. 8.

126 Jan. 14, 1953. From Finca Vigia, to Charles Poore. Regarding poetry he wrote during World War II. Quoted in the catalogue of Charles Hamilton, New York, Auction No. 56 (March 9, 1972), item 145. Reproduced in *Hemingway at Auction*, p. 166.

127 Jan. 23, 1953. From Finca Vigia, to Charles Poore. Regarding his writing and *The Hemingway Reader*, which Poore was editing. See (A25). Quoted, with a facsimile of page six, in the catalogue of Charles Hamilton, New York, Auction No. 56 (March 9, 1972), item 146. Reproduced in *Hemingway at Auction*, pp 167, 169. Also quoted in *Ernest M. Hemingway: The Paris Years . . . And Before*, catalogue of an exhibition from the collection of C. E. Frazer Clark, Jr., at Farmington, Michigan, 1973, item 28. See (S-G79).

128 Jan. 30, 1953. From Finca Vigia, to Charles Poore. Regarding Philip Young. Quoted in the catalogue of Charles Hamilton, New York, Auction No. 56 (March 9, 1972), item 147. Reproduced in *Hemingway at Auction*, pp. 167-168.

129 Feb. 7, [19]53. From Finca Vigia, to Charles Poore. Regarding his masculinity and his ancestors. Quoted in the catalogue of Charles Hamilton, New York, Auction No. 56 (March 9, 1972), item 148. Reproduced in *Hemingway at Auction*, p. 168.

130 Feb. 23 and 28, 1953. From Finca Vigia, to Charles Poore. Relates an experience in the hospital in Milan during World War I. Quoted in the catalogue of Charles Hamilton, New York, Auction No. 56 (March 9, 1972), item 149. Reproduced in *Hemingway at Auction*, pp. 168, 170.

131 March 16, 1953. From Finca Vigia, to Charles Poore. Regarding the 4th Infantry Division during World War II, and F. Scott Fitzgerald. Quoted in the catalogue of Charles Hamilton, New York, Auction No. 56 (March 9, 1972), item 150. Reproduced in *Hemingway at Auction*, p. 170. Briefly quoted in *Ernest M. Hemingway: The Paris Years . . . And Before*, catalogue of an exhibition from the collection of C. E. Frazer Clark, Jr., at Farmington, Michigan, 1973, item 29. See (S-G79).

132 April 3, 1953. From Finca Vigia, to Charles Poore. Regarding his experiences in World War II. Quoted in the catalogue of Charles Hamilton, New York, Auction No. 56 (March 9, 1972), item 151. Reproduced in *Hemingway at Auction*, pp. 170-171.

133 May 21, 1953. From Finca Vigia, to Charles Poore. Regarding his Pulitzer prize for *OMATS*. Quoted in the catalogue of Charles Hamilton, New York, Auction No. 56 (March 9, 1972), item 152. Reproduced in *Hemingway at Auction*, p. 171.

134 [1954]. From Cuba, to Peter Viertel. Regarding Luis Miguel Dominguín's visit to Finca Vigia. Quoted in *Gentlemen's Quarterly*, XXXIV (April 1965), 128.

135 Dec. 17, 1954. From on board *Pilar*, to Jed Kiley. Regarding "un-

truths, mis-statements and falsehoods" in Kiley's manuscript for *Hemingway: An Old Friend Remembers*. Quoted, with a facsimile of the last page, in the catalogue of David Battam Autographs, Fresno, California, No. 12 (n.d.), item 70. Reproduced in *Hemingway at Auction*, pp. 181-182. Also quoted, with a facsimile of the first page, in the catalogue of Charles Hamilton, New York, Auction No. 39 (Jan. 29, 1970), item 189A. Reproduced in *Hemingway at Auction*, pp. 153-154. The letter was also quoted in the *Fitzgerald/Hemingway Annual: 1972*, p. 354.

136 April 13, 1956. From Finca Vigía, to B. G. Rudd, of Billings, Montana. Granting permission to use an extract from *GHOA*. Quoted in the catalogue of Doris Wilson, No. 15 (n.d.). Reprinted in *Hemingway notes*, III (Spring 1973), 25.

137 July 29, 1956. From Finca Vigía, to "Mr. Rider." Regarding William Faulkner's work. A facsimile of the holograph letter is reproduced from the catalogue of Charles Hamilton, New York, Auction No. 5 (Oct. 8, 1964), item 113, in *Hemingway at Auction*, p. 83. See (F137).

138 Aug. 24, 1958. From Finca Vigía, to Peter Briggs. About wine. Extracts reproduced from the catalogue of Charles Hamilton, New York, Auction No. IX (Sept. 30, 1965), item 83, in *Hemingway at Auction*, p. 89. See (F139).

139 Feb. 22, 1959. From Ketchum, Idaho, to "Dear Bill" [Nathan Davis]. Regarding Antonio Ordóñez's forthcoming visit. Quoted in the catalogue of Charles Hamilton, New York, Auction No. 19 (May 24, 1967), item 296. Reproduced in *Hemingway at Auction*, p. 120. Also quoted, with a facsimile of the first page of the holograph letter, in the catalogue of Charles Hamilton, Auction No. 44 (Sept. 17, 1970), item 162. Reproduced in *Hemingway at Auction*, p. 155. Also quoted, with a facsimile of the first page, in the catalogue of Kenneth W. Rendell, Somerville, Mass., No. 54 (1970), item 30. Reproduced in *Hemingway at Auction*, p. 220.

140 April 11, 1959. From S. F. de Paula, Cuba, to Frank Crowther. Quoted, with a facsimile, in the catalogue of Charles Hamilton, New York, Auction No. 49 (May 6, 1971), item 181. Reproduced in *Hemingway at Auction*, p. 161.

141 April 12, 1959. From Finca Vigía, to José Luis Castillo-Puche. In Spanish. Regarding plans for a trip to Spain. Facsimile reproduced in Castillo-Puche's *Hemingway, entre la vida y la muerte*, Barcelona, 1968, following p. 376.

142 April 12, 1959. From Finca Vigía, to "Dear Bill" [Nathan Davis]. Regarding his health. Quoted in the catalogue of Charles Hamilton,

New York, Auction No. 19 (May 24, 1967), item 297. Reproduced in *Hemingway at Auction*, p. 121. Also quoted in the catalogue of Charles Hamilton, Auction No. 44 (Sept. 17, 1970), item 163. Reproduced in *Hemingway at Auction*, p. 155.

143 [May ? 1959]. Draft of a telegram, in Spanish, to Antonio Ordóñez. Quoted in the catalogue of Charles Hamilton, New York, Auction No. 19 (May 24, 1967), item 298. Reproduced in *Hemingway at Auction*, p. 121.

144 Aug. 31, 1959. From Hotel Suecia, Madrid, to "Dear Monique" [Monique de Beaumont]. In English, French, and Spanish. Regarding the bullfights and his travels through Spain. Quoted in the catalogue of Paul C. Richards, Autographs, Brookline, Mass., No. 69 (Sept. 1971), item 232. Reproduced in *Hemingway at Auction*, p. 227.

145 [Oct. ? 1959]. From "La Cónsula," near Málaga, to Juanito Quintana. In Spanish. Regarding Antonio Ordóñez being injured in a bullfight. A facsimile of a portion of the letter is reproduced in J. L. Castillo-Puche's *Hemingway, entre la vida y la muerte*, Barcelona, 1968, following p. 184. Quoted on p. 219.

146 Oct. 21, 1959. From Hotel Suecia [Madrid], to "Dear John." Denying his rumored visit to Moscow with President Eisenhower. Quoted in the catalogue of Charles Hamilton, New York, Auction No. 19 (May 24, 1967), item 299. Reproduced in *Hemingway at Auction*, p. 121. Also quoted in the catalogue of Charles Hamilton, Auction No. 68 (June 7, 1973), item 131.

147 Oct. 28, 1959. From on board *Liberté*, to "Dear Miss Annie" [Annie Davis]. Quoted in the catalogue of Charles Hamilton, New York, Auction No. 19 (May 24, 1967), item 301. Reproduced in *Hemingway at Auction*, p. 122.

148 Oct. 28, 1959. From on board *Liberté*, to "Dear Negro" [Nathan (Bill) Davis]. Regarding the sea voyage. Quoted in the catalogue of Charles Hamilton, New York, Auction No. 19 (May 24, 1967), item 300. Reproduced in *Hemingway at Auction*, p. 121.

149 Oct. 31, 1959. From on board *Liberté*, to "Negro" [Nathan (Bill) Davis]. Regarding the sea voyage. Quoted in the catalogue of Charles Hamilton, New York, Auction No. 19 (May 24, 1967), item 302. Reproduced in *Hemingway at Auction*, p. 122.

150 Oct. 31, 1959. From on board *Liberté*, to "Ma chère et Belle Annie" [Annie Davis]. Regarding his plans for his stay in New York. Quoted in the catalogue of Charles Hamilton, New York, Auction No. 19 (May 24, 1967), item 303. Reproduced in *Hemingway at Auction*, p. 122.

151 Nov. 8, 1959. From Finca Vigia, to "Negro" [Nathan (Bill) Davis]. Refers to "the Paris book." Quoted, with a facsimile of the first page, in the catalogue of Charles Hamilton, New York, Auction No. 19 (May 24, 1967), item 304. Reproduced in *Hemingway at Auction*, pp. 122-124.

152 Nov. 28, 1959. From Ketchum, Idaho, to "Dear Negro" [Nathan (Bill) Davis]. Regarding a trip through the Southwest, with Antonio and Carmen Ordóñez, and Mary Hemingway's broken arm. Quoted in the catalogue of Charles Hamilton, New York, Auction No. 19 (May 24, 1967), item 305. Reproduced in *Hemingway at Auction*, p. 124. Also quoted, with a partial facsimile, in the catalogue of Charles Hamilton, Auction No. 46 (Dec. 10, 1970), item 163. Reproduced in *Hemingway at Auction*, p. 158. Also quoted, with a facsimile of the first page and four partially hidden pages, in the catalogue of J&S Fine Books, Chicago, No. 11 (October 1971), item 1345. Reproduced in *Hemingway at Auction*, p. 215.

153 Jan. 7, 1960. From Ketchum, Idaho, to "Dear Negro" [Nathan (Bill) Davis]. Regarding Mary Hemingway's broken arm and trap shooting with A. E. Hotchner. Quoted in the catalogue of Charles Hamilton, New York, Auction No. 19 (May 24, 1967), item 306. Reproduced in *Hemingway at Auction*, p. 124. Also quoted in the catalogue of Paul C. Richards, Autographs, Brookline, Mass., No. 59 (Nov. 1970), item 25. Reproduced in *Hemingway at Auction*, pp. 226-227.

154 Jan. 13, 1960. From "La Barata," Ketchum, Idaho, to "Dear Negro" [Nathan (Bill) Davis]. Regarding the weather and trap shooting. Quoted in the catalogue of Charles Hamilton, New York, Auction No. 19 (May 24, 1967), item 307. Reproduced in *Hemingway at Auction*, p. 125. Also quoted in the catalogue of Paul C. Richards, Autographs, Brookline, Mass., No. 63 (March 1971), item 157. Reproduced in *Hemingway at Auction*, p. 227. Also reproduced in the catalogue of Sotheby & Co., London (Dec. 4, 1973), item 187A.

155 Feb. 8, 1960. From Finca Vigia, to "Dear Negro" [Nathan (Bill) Davis]. Regarding books and television rights. Quoted in the cata-logue of Charles Hamilton, New York, Auction No. 19 (May 24, 1967), item 308. Reproduced in *Hemingway at Auction*, p. 125. Also quoted in the catalogue of Charles Hamilton, Auction No. 46 (Dec. 10, 1970), item 166. Reproduced in *Hemingway at Auction*, p. 159. Also quoted in the catalogue of Robert K. Black, Upper Montclair, N.J., No. 127 (Spring 1971), item 81. Reproduced in *Hemingway at Auction*, p. 183.

156 Feb. 25, 1960. From Finca Vigia, to "Dear Negro" [Nathan (Bill)

Davis]. Regarding copies of *Ruedo*, which he needed for research on the bullfights in 1959. Quoted in the catalogue of Charles Hamilton, New York, Auction No. 19 (May 24, 1967), item 309. Reproduced in *Hemingway at Auction*, p. 125.

157 March 12, 1960. From Finca Vigia, to "Dear Negro" [Nathan (Bill) Davis]. Regarding his bull-fighting manuscript. Quoted in the catalogue of Charles Hamilton, New York, Auction No. 19 (May 24, 1967), item 310. Reproduced in *Hemingway at Auction*, pp. 125-126.

158 April 1, 1960. From Finca Vigia, to "Dear Negro" [Nathan (Bill) Davis]. Regarding his bull-fighting manuscript. Quoted in the catalogue of Charles Hamilton, New York, Auction No. 19 (May 24, 1967), item 311. Reproduced in *Hemingway at Auction*, p. 126.

159 May 9, 1960. From Finca Vigia, to "Dear Negro" [Nathan (Bill) Davis]. Regarding his contracts with Rowohlt and *Life* magazine. Quoted in the catalogue of Charles Hamilton, New York, Auction No. 19 (May 24, 1967), item 312. Reproduced in *Hemingway at Auction*, p. 127.

160 June 1, 1960. From Finca Vigia, to "Muy Monique mia" [Monique de Beaumont]. Quoted, with a facsimile of the last page, in the catalogue of Charles Hamilton, New York, Auction No. 51 (Aug. 5, 1971), item 192. Reproduced in *Hemingway at Auction*, pp. 163-164.

161 [Aug. 1960]. From Finca Vigia, to Juanito Quintana. In Spanish. A facsimile of the last page is reproduced in J. L. Castillo-Puche's *Hemingway, entre la vida y la muerte*, Barcelona, 1968, following p. 320.

162 Jan. 13, 1961. From Rochester, Minnesota, to Mel Evans, Jr. See (F144). A facsimile of a portion of the letter is reproduced from the catalogue of Charles Hamilton, New York, Auction No. 2 (Oct. 17, 1963), item 117, in *Hemingway at Auction*, p. 76.

163 Jan. 19, 1961. From Rochester, Minnesota, to Peter Briggs. Regarding his health. See (F146). Reproduced from the catalogue of Charles Hamilton, New York, Auction No. IX (Sept. 30, 1965), item 83, in *Hemingway at Auction*, p. 89.

164 June 15, 1961. From St. Mary's Hospital, Rochester, Minnesota, to Fritz [Saviers]. See (F147). Facsimile of holograph letter reproduced in Billie Pesin Rosen's *The Science of Handwriting Analysis*, New York, 1965, pp. 217-218. Facsimiles of the two-page letter, to the ten-year-old son of his doctor, are also reproduced in the *Valley Sun*, XXIX (Aug. 1966), [6].

EPHEMERA

165 *Hemingway's First Picture Story.* A 16-page feature on an African Safari reprinted from *Look*, XVIII (Jan. 26, 1954). See (C379). 13 1/4 x 10 3/8. Published in February 1954, by *Look* magazine, Des Moines, Iowa. Photographs by Earl Theisen.

166 "The Way I See It: The Badge of Courage" "by Ernest Hemingway," *Hi-Life* (New York), VI, iv (July 1965), 24-26. Photographs of Hemingway. This article consists solely of quotations from General Karl von Clausewitz, reprinted from *Men at War*, p. [120].

167 Translation. "Hemingway as Translator: Kiki's Grandmother" by William White, *English Language Notes*, IV (Dec. 1966), 128-132. Hemingway's translation of Chapter 12 of *Kiki's Memoirs*, Paris, 1930, is printed in parallel columns, on pp. 130-132, with Samuel Putnam's translation. See (B7). The three-page holograph manuscript is in the collection of the University of Texas.

168 Keepsake. Facsimile of *Ciao* (June 1918), the monthly newspaper published by the American Red Cross ambulance unit, Section IV, in Vicenza, Italy. 12 1/4 x 8 5/8. 4 pages. Issued in beige paper covers, slightly larger than the pages, printed in brown on the front cover: 11 November 1918 | 11 November 1968 | [enclosed in decorative brackets:] THE GREAT WAR | *a collection of books presented in memory of* | JOSEPH M. BRUCCOLI.
Hemingway's article, "Al Receives Another Letter," is on p. [2]. See (C32). Hemingway is mentioned on p. [1] and p. [3].
NOTE: The colophon, on the inside of the back cover, states: 200 Copies Of This Facsimile | Printed To Commemorate The First | Exhibition From The | Joseph M. Bruccoli Great War Collection, | Alderman Library, | The University of Virginia.
NOTE: Issued by Matthew J. Bruccoli.

169 Microfilm. *Ernest Hemingway in High School: Writings About and By Ernest Hemingway as They Appeared in the Publications of Oak Park and River Forest High School, 1916-1919.* There are over 130 items from *Trapeze*, the student newspaper, and *Tabula*, the student literary magazine, on the microfilm. Compiled and edited by Daniel P. Reichard, Oak Park and River Forest High School, Oak Park, Illinois, 1969. $25.00. Accompanied by a nine-page index.

170 HEMINGWAY: A portrait in sound, broadcast May 26, 1970, on CBC radio. Written and prepared by Patrick Hynan. Produced by Howard Engel. Two long-playing 33 1/3 r.p.m. records. Released by the Canadian Broadcasting Corporation, in Toronto, in 1970, at $7.50. Photograph of Hemingway by Yousuf Karsh on the cover of

the album. Introduction to the recording by Malcolm Cowley on the inside of the album.

Readings from *In Our Time*, including "Big Two-Hearted River," *AMF*, *GHOA*, *FWBT*, "Fathers and Sons," and "The Snows of Kilimanjaro."

NOTE: This record is "an attempt to unravel some of the complexities in Hemingway's personality." It is a condensation of many hours of recordings made during interviews with Sylvia Beach, Toby Bruce, Morley Callaghan, Malcolm Cowley, Ben Finney, Mary Hemingway, A. E. Hotchner, Major-General Charles T. (Buck) Lanham, Harold Loeb, Archibald MacLeish, Hadley Mowrer, Marcelline Hemingway Sanford, Bill Smith, Air Marshal Sir Peter Wykeham, and Philip Young.

171 Keepsake. Facsimile of three pages of the *Co-operative Commonwealth*, II, iv (Dec. 1920). See (C52). 9 x 6. 4 pages. Issued by Matthew J. Bruccoli and C. E. Frazer Clark, Jr., in December 1970. Issued in light brown paper covers, slightly larger than the pages, printed in dark brown on the front cover: Will You Let These Kiddies Miss | Santa Claus? | ERNEST M. HEMINGWAY.

CONTENTS: p. [1]: Facsimile of the cover of the magazine; pp. [2]-[3]: Facsimile of Hemingway's article "Will You Let These Kiddies Miss Santa Claus?"; p. [3] note by "M.J.B./C.E.F.C."; p. [4]: Colophon: *125 Copies Printed | For Friends of The | Fitzgerald/Hemingway | Annual In 1970. | This Is Copy* ____.

NOTE: This facsimile was made from the copy of the *Co-operative Commonwealth* in the collection of Waring Jones, of Wayzata, Minnesota. This was the copy described in C52, and is the only issue that has been located for the period of December 1920 to the fall of 1921 when Hemingway worked on the magazine.

172 Keepsake. Facsimile of page one of the *Trapeze*, VI (Nov. 3, 1916). See (C11). 9 1/2 x 6 1/4. Reproduced on a single sheet folded once; gray paper with a cream-colored paper label, printed in gray, pasted onto the front cover. The label reads: *150 Copies Printed | for Distribution at the | Chicago Hemingway Conference, | 28 December 1971, | to Friends of the | Fitzgerald/Hemingway Annual | This is copy* ____.

Hemingway's article, "Athletic Association to Organize Next Week," is partially included in the facsimile, which is reproduced on pp. [2]-[3]. Note: Also reproduced on the back endpapers of *Ernest Hemingway's Apprenticeship* edited by Matthew J. Bruccoli, Washington, D.C., 1971.

NOTE: A transcription of the panel discussion at this conference, moderated by Charles W. Mann, is printed in the *Fitzgerald/Hemingway Annual: 1972*, pp. 113-144.

173 Prospectus. *We are pleased to offer an* | Ernest Hemingway Letter | *of exceptional literary* | *importance*. 11 x 8 1/2. Issued by Gotham Book Mart & Gallery, Inc., New York, in January 1973. Printed on a single sheet folded once; pale gray paper, printed in black.

A facsimile of Hemingway's typewritten letter to W. G. Rogers, from Finca Vigia, San Francisco de Paula, Cuba, July 29, 1948, regarding Gertrude Stein, is on pp. [2]-[3]. The envelope, partially hidden by the letter, is reproduced on p. [2].

NOTE: The colophon, on p. [4], states: One-hundred numbered copies of | this prospectus have been printed. Note: According to Andreas Brown, the owner of Gotham Book Mart, there could be some duplication in the numbering due to "secretarial confusion."

174 Facsimile of a twelve-line statement which Hemingway had printed in a girl's memory book, November 23, 1919. Reproduced in the catalogue of Carry Back Books, Franconia, New Hampshire, No. 6 (Winter 1974), p. 21. The item was not offered for sale, it was published "solely out of proprietary whimsy" by Ruth and Donald St. John. Note: The girl, who is not identified in the catalogue, was Georgianna Bump (Marjorie Bump's younger sister).

BOOK BLURBS BY HEMINGWAY

175 Book band. *Nothing is Sacred* by Josephine Herbst. New York: Coward-McCann, 1928. White paper band, printed in black. 2 3/16 x 20. Reads: ERNEST HEMINGWAY—"A fine book by an | honest writer." Note: Blurbs by Ring Lardner and Ford Madox Ford also appear on the band.

176 Dust jacket. *Two Wars and More to Come* by Herbert L. Matthews. New York: Carrick & Evans, 1938. Hemingway's cablegram from Paris, January 8, 1938, is quoted on the dust jacket and included in the publisher's ad in the *N.Y. Times* (Jan. 24, 1938), p. 21. The cablegram, including the original last sentence, which was "discreetly omitted" from the dust jacket and the ad, is quoted in Matthews's *A World in Revolution*. See (S-G289). Note: For a later appearance of the ad and facsimiles of Hemingway's cablegram, see (F161).

177 Dust jacket. *The Lincoln Battalion: The Story of the Americans who Fought in Spain in the International Brigades* by Edwin Rolfe. New York: Random House, 1939. Blurb on back cover reads: *From a letter to the author.* | "The galleys came. I think you did a fine, fine job, Ed. It is a book to have. | Good luck and congratulations." | ERNEST HEMINGWAY. See also (S-G353).

178   Advertisement. *Citizens* by Meyer Levin. New York: Viking
       Press, 1940. The publisher's full-page ad in the *N.Y. Times Book Re-*
       view (March 31, 1940), p. 13, includes the following quotation: "A
       fine and exciting American novel . . . One of | the best I have ever
       read." | —Ernest Hemingway. Note: Hemingway's letter to Meyer
       Levin from which this quotation was taken is among the holdings
       of Mugar Memorial Library, Boston University. See (S-F22A).

179   Paperback book cover. *The Enemy* by Wirt Williams. New York:
       New American Library, 1957. Paperback edition. [No. S1292.] In
       a letter in 1956, Hemingway offered the following quotation, which
       appears on the cover, specifically for the NAL edition: "A first-rate
       novel of the way it really was." Note: In an earlier letter to the au-
       thor, in 1952, he wrote: "I think [Wirt Williams] writes as well as
       anybody writing." Hemingway authorized this quotation for use in
       1957, and it has appeared on all of Williams's books since 1963.

180   Paperback book cover. *The Professional* by W. C. Heinz. New
       York: Berkley, 1959. [Berkley Books, paperback edition.] Blurb on
       front cover reads: ". . . the only good novel I've ever | read about a
       fighter and an excel- | lent first novel in its own right." | —ERNEST
       HEMINGWAY.

181   Dust jacket. *To the Bullfight Again* by John Marks. New York:
       Alfred A. Knopf, 1967. [Enlarged and revised edition.] Hemingway
       is quoted on the front flap: "The best book on the subject—after
       mine," | Ernest Hemingway assured the author of *To the* | *Bullfight*
       (1953) in Pamplona when he, "Papa" | —beaming, grizzled—re-
       turned with nostalgia to | Spain, the wars over. He confirmed this
       hand- | some compliment later to a mutual friend, but | phrased it
       still more generously, saying "by a | foreigner" instead of "after
       mine." Note: Also quoted in the publisher's ad in the *N.Y. Times*
       Book Review (March 12, 1967), p. 18.

182   Dust jacket. *The Perishing Republic* by Jerome Bahr. Washing-
       ton, D.C.: Trempealeau Press, 1971. Blurb on back cover, under the
       heading What the Critics Say [about] *All Good Americans*, reads:
       ". . . a fine honest writer with a talent which is both sturdy | and del-
       icate." | —Ernest Hemingway (from his Preface). Note: Heming-
       way's preface appeared in the opening volume of Bahr's short
       stories series. See (B23). This is the concluding volume.

PART TWO

BIOGRAPHICAL

AND CRITICAL

MATERIAL ON

ERNEST HEMINGWAY

SECTION G

BOOKS ON OR

SIGNIFICANTLY

MENTIONING

HEMINGWAY

CHRONOLOGICAL LIST OF SOME
RECENT PRINCIPAL BOOKS ON HEMINGWAY

1966. *Hemingway.* John Brown et al. (S-G54).

1966. *Ernest Kheminguei.* Ivan Kashkin. (S-G221).

1967. *Ernest Hemingway: An Introduction and Interpretation.* Sheridan Baker. (S-G17).

1967. *Ernest Hemingway: A Comprehensive Bibliography.* Audre Hanneman. (S-G178).

1968. *High on the Wild with Hemingway.* Lloyd R. Arnold. (S-G9).

1968. *Hemingway, entre la vida y la muerte.* J. L. Castillo-Puche. (S-B6).

1968. *Ernest Hemingway and the Pursuit of Heroism.* Leo Gurko. (S-G170).

1968. *Hemingway: The Inward Terrain.* Richard B. Hovey. (S-G199).

1968. *Ernest Hemingway and the Little Magazines: The Paris Years.* Nicholas Joost. (S-G212).

1968. *Hemingway's Nonfiction.* Robert O. Stephens. (S-G388).

1969. *Ernest Hemingway: A Life Story.* Carlos Baker. (S-B10).

1969. *Hemingway: The Writer's Art of Self-Defense.* Jackson J. Benson. (S-G30).

1969. *Hemingway's African Stories.* John M. Howell. (S-B9).

1969. *Hemingway: Direct and Oblique.* Richard K. Peterson. (S-G329).

1969. *Hemingway's Heroes.* Delbert E. Wylder. (S-G444).

1969. *The Hemingway Manuscripts: An Inventory.* Philip Young and Charles W. Mann. (S-B11).

1971. *The Narrative Pattern in Ernest Hemingway's Fiction.* Chaman Nahal. (S-G313).

1971. *Ernest Hemingway and the Arts.* Emily Stipes Watts. (S-G424).

1972. *Papa: Hemingway in Key West.* James McLendon. (S-G277).

1972. *Hemingway and The Sun Set.* Bertram D. Sarason. (S-G363).

1972. *A Reader's Guide to Ernest Hemingway.* Arthur Waldhorn. (S-G417).

1973. *Hemingway at Auction: 1930-1973.* Compiled by Matthew J. Bruccoli and C. E. Frazer Clark, Jr. (S-B18).

1973. *Hemingway's Craft.* Sheldon Norman Grebstein. (S-B16).

1973. *Hemingway in Germany.* Wayne E. Kvam. (S-G242).

1974. *Hemingway in Our Time.* Edited by Richard Astro and Jackson J. Benson. (S-G12).

S-G1 Adams, J. Donald. *Copey of Harvard: A Biography of Charles Townsend Copeland*. Boston: Houghton Mifflin, 1960. pp. 142, 256, 257.

p. 142: Brief reference to a visit to Professor Copeland by Hemingway, Waldo Peirce, and Archibald MacLeish following a Harvard-Dartmouth football game. p. 257: Quotes a letter from Maxwell Perkins regarding Hemingway in New York revising the manuscript of *FWBT*.

2 Alberto, Giovanni. *E. Hemingway: Il poeta dell'avventura*. Milan: U. Mursia, 1971. 153 pages. Illustrated by Giuseppe Laganà.

3 Aldridge, John W. *The Devil in the Fire: Retrospective Essays on American Literature and Culture, 1951-1971*. New York: Harper & Row, 1972. [A Harper's Magazine Press Book.] pp. 4-6, 78, 83-100, 112, 136, 142, 145-146, 163, 172-173, 181, 209, 248.

pp. 83-85: "Homage to Hemingway," reprinted from *After the Lost Generation*, New York, 1951, pp. 23-26. pp. 86-90: "A Last Look at the Old Man," reprinted from the *N.Y. Herald Tribune Book Week* (June 20, 1965); *Time to Murder and Create*, New York, 1966, pp. 185-191. pp. 91-100: "*Islands in the Stream*," reprinted from the *Saturday Review*, LIII (Oct. 10, 1970).

4 Altick, Richard D. *Preface to Critical Reading*. New York: Henry Holt, 1946. [Revised, 1951.] pp. 236-237.

Examines metaphors in an excerpt from a NANA dispatch by Hemingway on the Spanish Civil War.

5 Amory, Cleveland, and Frederic Bradlee, eds. *Vanity Fair: Selections from America's Most Memorable Magazine: A Cavalcade of the 1920s and 1930s*. New York: Viking Press, 1960. p. 157.

"Nominated for the Hall of Fame: 1928." Photograph of Hemingway by Helen Breaker.

6 Arlen, Michael J. *Exiles*. New York: Farrar, Straus & Giroux, 1970. pp. 117, 224-226.

pp. 224-226: The author describes the last meeting between his father, Michael Arlen, and Hemingway in the early 1950s.

7 Armour, Richard. *American Lit Relit*. New York: McGraw-Hill, 1964. pp. 150-154.

"Ernest Hemingway." Biographical satire.

8 Armstrong, Hamilton Fish. *Peace and Counterpeace: From Wilson to Hitler*. New York: Harper & Row, 1971. [A Cass Canfield Book.] pp. 471-476.

"Hemingway in Madrid." Reminiscences by the editor of *Foreign Affairs* of Hemingway in Madrid, in August of 1931. p. 476: Regarding Hemingway's "grudge" against Louis Bromfield.

9 Arnold, Lloyd R. *High on the Wild with Hemingway*. Caldwell, Idaho: Caxton Printers, 1968. xvi + 344 pages. 11 x 8 ½. 160 photographs. Foreword by John H. Hemingway on p. [vii].

A friend's account of the nine seasons, between 1939 and 1961, that Hemingway spent in Idaho.

10 Asselineau, Roger. *Ernest Hemingway*. Paris: Seghers, 1972. [Collection Écrivains d'hier et d'aujourd'hui, No. 41.] 167 pages. Tableau synoptíque on pp. 5-23. Bibliographie on pp. 159-163. Filmographie on pp. 165-166.

11 Astre, G.-A. [Georges-Albert]. *Hemingway por ele próprio*. Lisbon: Portugália Editora, 1968. [Escritores de Sempre, 6.] 189 pages. *Hemingway par lui-même*, see (G21), translated into Portuguese by João Gaspar Simões. Includes a section on translations of Hemingway's work into Portuguese.

12 Astro, Richard, and Jackson J. Benson, eds. *Hemingway in Our Time*. Corvallis: Oregon State University Press, 1974. viii + 214 pages. Preface by Richard Astro.

These essays were originally delivered at a conference devoted to the study of Hemingway's work at Oregon State University on April 26-27, 1973.

Contents: pp. 1-12: Introduction by Jackson J. Benson.

pp. 13-23: "Posthumous Hemingway, and Nicholas Adams" by Philip Young. Includes comments on the critical reception of *NAS*.

pp. 25-38: "Sketches of the Author's Life in Paris in the Twenties" by George Wickes. On *AMF*.

pp. 39-51: "Hemingway's Islands and Streams: Minor Tactics for Heavy Pressure" by Joseph M. DeFalco. On *Islands*.

pp. 53-65: "Internal Treachery in the Last Published Short Stories of Ernest Hemingway" by Delbert E. Wylder. On "A Man of the World" and "Get a Seeing-Eyed Dog."

pp. 67-86: "*To Have and Have Not* as Classical Tragedy: Reconsidering Hemingway's Neglected Novel" by Gerry Brenner.

pp. 87-97: "Hemingway and Fitzgerald" by Peter L. Hays. Examines the structural and situational similarities in *SAR* and *The Great Gatsby*, Fitzgerald's influence on Hemingway, and the influence of T. S. Eliot's *The Waste Land* on both writers.

pp. 99-111: "*A Moveable Feast* and *Remembrance of Things Past*: Two Quests for Lost Time" by Faith G. Norris. Discusses the "illuminating parallels" between the works of Hemingway and Marcel Proust.

pp. 113-143: "Hemingway's Sense of Place" by Robert W. Lewis. Discusses how "*terribly* important" landscape and terrain were to Hemingway.

pp. 145-157: "A Sometimes Great Notion: Ernest Hemingway's Roman Catholicism" by John Clark Pratt.

pp. 159-173: "Rectitude in Hemingway's Fiction: How Rite Makes Right" by John Griffith.

pp. 175-189: "Hemingway and the Modern Metaphysical Tradition" by Michael Friedberg.

pp. 191-212: "Hemingway Among the Moderns" by Richard Lehan.

13 Atkinson, Brooks. *Brief Chronicles*. New York: Coward-McCann, 1966. pp. 176-178.
"Code of the Cad." Regarding Hemingway's recollections of Gertrude Stein and F. Scott Fitzgerald in *AMF*. Reprinted from the *N.Y. Times* (July 7, 1964).

14 Bab, Julius. *Amerikas Dichter der Gegenwart*. Berlin and Hamburg: Christian-Verlag, 1951. pp. 15-22, 26, 27, 45, 46, 49.

15 Baker, Carlos. *Ernest Hemingway: A Life Story*. New York: Scribner's, 1969. xviii + 697 pages. Photographs. Sources and Notes on pp. 567-668. [(a) Book-of-the-Month Club edition, 1969. (b) Literary Guild edition, 1969. (c) Paperback edition: New York: Bantam Books, 1970. (Bantam, No. Y5554.) 978 pages. Photographs. (d) English edition: London: Collins, 1969. 702 pages. (e) English paperback edition: Middlesex, England: Penguin Books, 1972. (Pelican Biography.) 907 pages. (f) Translated into Italian by Ettore Capriolo, *Hemingway: Storia di una vita*. Milan: Mondadori, 1970. 1076 pages. (g) Translated into Norwegian by Helge Simonsen, *Ernest Hemingway: Historien om hans liv*. Oslo: Gyldendal, 1970. 578 pages. (h) Translated into Finnish by Inkeri Hämäläinen, *Ernest Hemingway: Elämäkerta*. Helsinki: Tammi, 1971. 587 pages. (i) Translated into French by Claude Noël and Andrée R. Picard, *Hemingway: Histoire d'une vie*. Two volumes. Paris: Éditions Robert Laffont, 1971. 496 pages; 477 pages. (j) Translated into German by Christian Herburg, *Hemingway: Die Geschichte Eines Abenteuerlichen Lebens*. Munich/Vienna/Zurich: Edition Praeger, 1971. 678 pages. (k) Translated into Portuguese by Alvaro Cabral, *Ernest Hemingway: O Romance de uma vida*. Rio de Janeiro: Editora Civilização Brasileira, 1971. 639 pages.]
A full-length biography "undertaken at the invitation of Charles Scribner, Jr. . . . with the full knowledge and cooperation of Mary Welsh Hemingway" (p. xi). Parts of this book first appeared in the *Atlantic Monthly*, CCXXIII (Jan. and Feb. 1969). For previously unpublished work by Hemingway and a description of this book, see (S-B10).

16 Baker, Carlos. *Hemingway: The Writer as Artist*. Princeton: Princeton University Press, 1972. Fourth revised edition. 438 pages. A Working Check-List of Hemingway's Prose, Poetry, and Journalism —With Notes on pp. 409-426. [Paperback edition: Princeton University Press, 1972. (Princeton Paperbacks, No. 86.)]

The first two chapters, on Hemingway's early career, have been revised; two new chapters, on *AMF* and *Islands*, have been added. For earlier editions, see (G26).

17 Baker, Sheridan. *Ernest Hemingway: An Introduction and Interpretation*. New York: Holt, Rinehart and Winston, 1967. [American Authors and Critics Series.] x + 150 pages. Photographs. Selected bibliography on pp. 137-142.

A study of Hemingway and the "undefeated loser" who emerges in his work.

18 Bakewell, Charles M. *The Story of the American Red Cross in Italy*. New York: Macmillan, 1920. p. 224.

"Hemingway, Ernest M.*" appears in Appendix IX under Ambulance Service—Section IV. The asterisk indicates that he received the Silver Medal, an Italian decoration.

19 Bakker, J. *Ernest Hemingway as a Man of Action*. Assen, The Netherlands: Van Gorcum, 1972. [Van Gorcum's Literaire Bibliotheek.] viii + 294 pages. In English.

20 Baragwanath, John. *A Good Time Was Had*. New York: Appleton-Century-Crofts, 1962. p. 211.

The author recalls visits with Hemingway and Martha Gellhorn at San Francisco de Paula, Cuba, in the early 1940s.

21 Barbosa, A. Rolmes. *Escritores Norte Americanos e outros*. Porto Alegre: Edição da Livraria do Globo, 1943. pp. 69-77.

Surveys Hemingway's career through the publication of *FWBT*.

22 Baritz, Loren, ed. *The Culture of The Twenties*. Indianapolis: Bobbs-Merrill, 1970. [American Heritage Series.] pp. xlviii, l-liii, 19-20, 297, 307, 309-310, 315-316.

pp. 19-20: Biographical note. pp. 309-310: Letter to Hemingway from F. Scott Fitzgerald, written in December 1927. See also (S-E134).

23 Barrett, William. *Time of Need: Forms of Imagination in the Twentieth Century*. New York: Harper & Row, 1972. pp. 20, 37, 54, 55, 57, 62, 64-95, 97, 98, 101-102, 108, 111, 112, 134, 136, 137, 155, 225, 261.

pp. 64-95: Ch. 3: "Winner Take Nothing: A nothing that he knew too well." A study of Hemingway's novels and short stories, especially "A Clean, Well-Lighted Place" and "The Gambler, the Nun, and the Radio."

24 Bassan, Maurice, ed. *Stephen Crane: A Collection of Critical Essays.* Englewood Cliffs, N.J.: Prentice-Hall, 1967. pp. 52-56.
"Crane and Hemingway" by Philip Young, excerpt from *Ernest Hemingway*, New York, 1952, pp. 161-166.

25 Beachcroft, T. O. *The Modest Art: A Survey of the Short Story in English.* London: Oxford University Press, 1968. pp. 124, 234-235, 240-248, 252.

26 Beatty, Clyde, with Edward Anthony. *Facing the Big Cats: My World of Lions and Tigers.* Garden City, N.Y.: Doubleday, 1965. pp. 15-19, 161.
Relates a visit with Hemingway in Beatty's dressing room in Madison Square Garden, in New York, in the 1930s. Recalls Hemingway's interest in the circus and in bullfighting.

27 Beebe, Maurice. *Ivory Towers and Sacred Founts: The Artist as Hero in Fiction from Goethe to Joyce.* New York: New York University Press, 1964. pp. 66, 78, 101, 306-307.

28 Behlmer, Rudy, ed. *Memo from David O. Selznick.* New York: Viking Press, 1972. pp. 307, 333, 443-462.
Regarding the filming of *FWBT* and the second version of *FTA.* pp. 457-461: A long letter from Selznick to Hemingway, dated August 14, 1957, and marked NOT SENT, is quoted.

29 Benson, Frederick R. *Writers in Arms: The Literary Impact of the Spanish Civil War.* New York: New York University Press, 1967. pp. 35, 42-44, 60-63, 112-115, 123-129, 142, 143, 147, 153, 156, 174-175, 177-178, 180, 190, 216, 219-220, 225-227, 237-240, 246-248, 262-266, 273, 274, 292-296.
pp. 124-126: On *The Spanish Earth.* pp. 125-127: On *The Fifth Column. FWBT* is quoted and discussed *passim.* See also (S-F115).

30 Benson, Jackson J. *Hemingway: The Writer's Art of Self-Defense.* Minneapolis: University of Minnesota Press, 1969. x + 202 pages. [Paperback edition: Minneapolis Paperbacks Series, 1970. No. 22.]
Reinterpretations of Hemingway's major novels and short stories, with separate chapters devoted to *SAR, FTA, FWBT, ARIT,* and *OMATS.*

31 Berry, Thomas Elliott. *The Newspaper in the American Novel, 1900-1969.* Metuchen, N.J.: Scarecrow Press, 1970. pp. 61, 75, 78-79, 135.
Regarding Jake Barnes, in *SAR,* and Karkov, the Russian correspondent in *FWBT.*

32 Berryman, John. *His Toy, His Dream, His Rest: 308 Dream Songs.* New York: Farrar, Straus & Giroux, 1968. p. 164.
[Number] 235: "Tears Henry shed for poor old Hemingway . . ."

33 Bieńkowski, Zbigniew. *Piekła i Orfeusze*. Warsaw, 1960.
"Zjawisko 'Hemingway,'" reprinted in Leszek Elektorowicz's *Hemingway w oczach krytyki światowej*, Warsaw, 1968, pp. 501-511.

34 Biles, J. I. *The Aristotelian Structure of A Farewell to Arms*. Atlanta: Georgia State College, 1965. [School of Arts and Sciences Research Papers, No. 9.] 23 pages.

35 Birmingham, Stephen. *The Late John Marquand: A Biography*. Philadelphia: J. B. Lippincott, 1972. pp. 116, 172, 217-218, 241, 258.
pp. 217-218: John P. Marquand's version of Gene Tunney's account of a visit to Hemingway in Cuba.

36 Blanck, Jacob, ed. *Merle Johnson's American First Editions*. Waltham, Mass.: Mark Press, 1965. Fourth edition, revised and enlarged. pp. 235-237.

37 Bluefarb, Sam. *The Escape Motif in the American Novel: Mark Twain to Richard Wright*. Columbus: Ohio State University Press, 1972. pp. 67, 71, 75-92, 156, 160.
pp. 75-92: Ch. 6: "Frederic Henry: The Run for Life."

38 Borges, Jorge Luis. In collaboration with Esther Zemborain de Torres. *An Introduction to American Literature*. Lexington: University Press of Kentucky, 1971. pp. ix, 36, 50-51, 56, 95. Translated and edited by L. Clark Keating and Robert O. Evans from *Introduccion a la literatura norteamericana*, Buenos Aires: Editorial Columba, 1967.
pp. 50-51: A concise biography of Hemingway.

39 Borovik, G. A. *Vash spetsial'nyĭ korrespondent vstretilsya . . .* Moscow, 1967. pp. 16-32, 38-40.
pp. 16-32: "Vash korrespondent vstretilsya s Ernestom Khemingueem" [Your correspondent met Ernest Hemingway]. pp. 38-40: "Vash korrespondent vstretilsya s Meri Kheminguei" [Your correspondent met Mary Hemingway].

40 Bourjaily, Vance. *The Unnatural Enemy*. New York: Dial Press, 1963. pp. 18-23, 166-168.
Discusses "Big Two-Hearted River" and the fishing and hunting passages in *GHOA*.

41 Bowen, James K., and Richard Van der Beets, eds. *American Short Fiction: Readings and Criticism*. Indianapolis: Bobbs-Merrill, 1970. pp. 224-228.
pp. 224-225: "Hemingway and His Heroes" by Robert Daniel, abstracted from *Queen's Quarterly*, LIV (Winter 1947-1948). pp. 225-226: "Time and the Contagion of Flight in 'The Killers'" by

Charles A. Owen, Jr., abstracted from *Forum*, III (Fall-Winter 1960). pp. 226-227: "The Protagonist of Hemingway's 'The Killers' " by Oliver Evans, abstracted from *Modern Language Notes*, LXXIII (Dec. 1958). pp. 227-228: "Some Questions About Hemingway's 'The Killers' " by Edward Stone, abstracted from *Studies in Short Fiction*, V (Fall 1967). See also (S-E137).

42 Brack, O M, Jr., and Warner Barnes, eds. *Bibliography and Textual Criticism: English and American Literature, 1700 to the Present.* Chicago: University of Chicago Press, 1969. [Patterns of Literary Criticism, 8.] pp. 247-249, 314-333.

pp. 314-333: "The Text of Ernest Hemingway" by James B. Meriwether, reprinted with revisions from the *Papers of the Bibliographical Society of America*, LVII (Oct.-Dec. 1963).

43 Bradbury, Malcolm, Eric Mottram, and Jean Franco, eds. *The Penguin Companion to American Literature.* New York: McGraw-Hill, 1971. pp. 120-121, 158-159.

pp. 120-121: Biographical sketch of Hemingway by "B.W." [Brian Way]. pp. 158-159: "Lost Generation" by "M.B." [Malcolm Bradbury].

44 Bradbury, Ray. *I Sing the Body Electric!* New York: Knopf, 1969. pp. 3-14.

"The Kilimanjaro Device," reprinted from *Life*, LVIII (Jan. 22, 1965). Note: The original title was "The Kilimanjaro Machine."

45 Braden, Spruille. *Diplomats and Demagogues: The Memoirs of Spruille Braden.* New Rochelle: Arlington House, 1971. pp. 283-286, 311, 312.

Reminiscences by the former U.S. Ambassador to Cuba of Hemingway in the early 1940s. p. 286: Hemingway's inscription in a copy of *OMATS* is quoted.

46 Brashers, Howard C. *An Introduction to American Literature: For European Students.* Stockholm: Svenska Bokförlaget (Bonniers), 1964. pp. 132-142, 144, 147, 166, 215.

pp. 132-142: Ch. 11: "Hemingway and the 'Lost Generation.' "

47 Bresard, Suzanne. *Empreintes.* Paris: Delachaux et Niestlé, 1968. [Collection "L'homme et ses problemes."] pp. 21-26.

Analysis of Hemingway's handwriting. For facsimiles of the manuscript of "The Battler," see (S-F32).

48 Brian, Denis. *Murderers and Other Friendly People: The Public and Private Worlds of Interviewers.* New York: McGraw-Hill, 1973. pp. ix, x, 1-81, 107-109, 117, 146, 194-195, 231, 232.

pp. 1-81: Part One: "The Hemingway Hunters." Interviews with A. E. Hotchner, Malcolm Cowley, Barnaby Conrad, George Plimpton, Arnold Gingrich, William Seward, Mary Hemingway, and John Hemingway. pp. 107-109: Interview with Truman Capote. All of the interviews, except Barnaby Conrad and Arnold Gingrich, were excerpted in *Esquire*, LXXVII (Feb. 1972), under the title "The Importance of Knowing Ernest." See (S-H882).

49 Bridgman, Richard. *The Colloquial Style in America.* New York: Oxford University Press, 1966. pp. 4, 5, 11, 12, 31, 62, 129-130, 137, 188, 195-230.

pp. 195-230: Ch. Six: "Ernest Hemingway."

50 Brooks, Cleanth, ed. *Tragic Themes in Western Literature.* New Haven: Yale University Press, 1955. pp. 5, 151-154, 157, 176.

pp. 150-177: "The Saint as Tragic Hero" by Louis L. Martz. Includes references to Catherine Barkley and Frederic Henry in *FTA*. Partially reprinted in *Twentieth Century Interpretations of A Farewell to Arms* edited by Jay Gellens, Englewood Cliffs, N.J., 1970, pp. 55-56.

51 Brooks, Cleanth. *A Shaping Joy: Studies in the Writer's Craft.* New York: Harcourt Brace Jovanovich, 1971. pp. 30-31, 57, 292-295, 299, 308.

pp. 292-295: Draws an analogy between A. E. Housman's themes of courage and stoic endurance and those in Hemingway's works.

52 Brophy, Brigid, Michael Levey, and Charles Osborne. *Fifty Works of English [and American] Literature We Could Do Without.* London: Rapp & Carroll, 1967. [New York: Stein & Day, 1968.] pp. 149-150.

"Ernest Hemingway: *A Farewell to Arms.*"

53 Brown, [Ernest] Francis, ed. *Page 2: The Best of 'Speaking of Books' from The New York Times Book Review.* New York: Holt, Rinehart & Winston, 1969. [A New York Times Book.] pp. 197-201, 217-221, 245-251.

pp. 197-201: "Hemingway's Italia" by Carlos Baker, reprinted from the *N.Y. Times Book Review* (Jan. 23, 1966). pp. 217-221: "The Relevance of a Writer's Life" by Carlos Baker, reprinted from the *N.Y. Times Book Review* (Aug. 20, 1967). pp. 245-251: "Perkins's Three Generals" by Andrew Turnbull, regarding Maxwell Perkins, Hemingway, F. Scott Fitzgerald, and Thomas Wolfe, reprinted from the *N.Y. Times Book Review* (July 16, 1967).

54 Brown, John, et al. *Hemingway.* Paris: Hachette, 1966. [Collection Génies et Réalités, 28.] 292 pages. Photographs in color and black and white. Photograph of Hemingway by Karsh on the endpapers.

pp. 7-35: "Une vie légendaire" by John Brown. pp. 57-75: "Paradis perdu" by Marc Saporta. pp. 77-101: "Un Américain à Paris" by

Georges-Albert Astre. pp. 121-131: "La fascination du néant" by Michel Mohrt. pp. 133-149: "Solitaire et solidaire" by Michel del Castillo. pp. 169-187: "Hommes sans femmes" by Roger Grenier. pp. 189-201: " 'Il était un fois un vieil homme . . .' " by Jorge Semprun. pp. 221-237: "Le style et l'homme" by Jean-Louis Curtis. pp. 259-283: "Cours, cours chère légende" by Alain Bosquet.

55 Bruccoli, Matthew J., and Jackson R. Bryer, eds. *F. Scott Fitzgerald in His Own Time: A Miscellany.* Kent, Ohio: Kent State University Press, 1971. pp. 145-149.
   "How to Waste Material: A Note on My Generation," reprinted from the *Bookman,* LXIII (May 1926). Includes a review of *IOT.*

56 Bruccoli, Matthew J., ed. With the assistance of Jennifer McCabe Atkinson. *As Ever, Scott Fitz—: Letters Between F. Scott Fitzgerald and His Literary Agent Harold Ober, 1919-1940.* Philadelphia: J. B. Lippincott, 1972. pp. 77, 86n., 92, 125-126, 142-143, 146, 149, 153, 154, 157-158, 163, 206n., 291.

57 [Bruccoli, Matthew J., and C. E. Frazer Clark, Jr.]. *F. Scott Fitzgerald and Ernest M. Hemingway in Paris.* Catalogue of an exhibition at the Bibliothèque Benjamin Franklin in Paris, June 23-24, 1972, in conjunction with a conference at the Institut d'Études Américaines. 18 pages. 6 x 9. Facsimiles.
   Eighteen Hemingway items, including inscribed presentation copies, galley proofs, periodicals containing first appearances, and letters. Introduction by MJB/CEFC. Note: 650 copies of the exhibit catalogue were printed.

58 Bruccoli, Matthew J., and C. E. Frazer Clark, Jr., compilers. *Hemingway at Auction: 1930-1973.* Detroit: Gale Research Co., 1973. Introduction by Charles W. Mann. xxii + 286 pages. Indexed. Facsimiles of title pages, inscriptions, manuscript pages, and letters.
   Reproductions of pages from sixty auction sale catalogues and fifty-five dealer catalogues issued from 1930 to 1973. Prices of all items bringing over $5.00 have been added in the margins. For previously unpublished work by Hemingway and a description of this book, see (S-B18). For facsimiles of manuscript pages, see (S-F40). See also entries under published letters in Section F.

59 Bruttini, Adriano. *Nick Hemingway.* Siena: Libreria Ticci, 1967. 96 pages. Selected bibliography on p. 96.

60 Bryer, Jackson R., ed. *Fifteen Modern American Authors: A Survey of Research and Criticism.* Durham, N.C.: Duke University Press, 1969. pp. 201, 219, 223, 226, 229, 235, 275-300, 379, 450.
   pp. 275-300: "Ernest Hemingway" by Frederick J. Hoffman. Part I: Bibliography and texts. Includes a long description of Audre Han-

neman's *EH: A Comprehensive Bibliography*. Part II: Biography and criticism. Includes an overview of the critical reception of Hemingway's novels, from *IOT* to *OMATS*.

61 Buchloh, Paul G., ed. *Amerikanische Erzählungen von Hawthorne bis Salinger: Interpretationen*. Neumünster: Karl Wachholtz Verlag, 1968. [Kieler Beiträge zur Anglistik und Amerikanistik, VI.] pp. 112-154, 187-241.

pp. 112-154: "Die Darstellung des Kampfes bei Stephen Crane, Hemingway, Faulkner, und Britting" by Dietrich Jäger. pp. 187-223: "Hemingways 'My Old Man' und Faulkners 'Barn Burning': Ein Vergleich" by Peter Nicolaisen. pp. 224-241: "Bedeutungsschichten in Ernest Hemingways *The Old Man and the Sea*" by Paul G. Buchloh.

62 Burgess, Anthony. *Urgent Copy: Literary Studies*. New York: W. W. Norton, 1968. pp. 121-126.

"He Wrote Good," review of A. E. Hotchner's *Papa Hemingway* and recent Penguin paperback editions of Hemingway's work, reprinted from the *Spectator*, CCXVII (July 8, 1966).

63 Butcher, Fanny. *Many Lives—One Love*. New York: Harper & Row, 1972. pp. 17, 78, 133, 233, 238, 335-336, 426-438.

pp. 335-336: Hemingway's poem "Ultimately" is quoted. pp. 426-438: Ch. 22: "Ernest Hemingway." Reminiscences of Hemingway, in Paris in the 1920s and later at Finca Vigia, by the book reviewer for the *Chicago Tribune*.

64 Cabau, Jacques. *La Prairie perdue: histoire du roman américain*. Paris: Éditions du Seuil, 1966. pp. 256-275.

Part Two [Ch. 11]: "Ernest Hemingway: *Pour qui sonne le glas*."

65 Canning, John, ed. *100 Great Modern Lives: Makers of the World To-day from Faraday to Kennedy*. London: Odhams Books, 1965. pp. 589-593. [New York: Hawthorn, 1965.]

"Ernest Hemingway, 1898-1961."

66 Carey, Gary. *The Sun Also Rises: Notes*. Lincoln, Nebr.: Cliff's Notes, 1968. [New edition.] 77 pages.

67 Carlisle, Harry, ed. *The Legacy of Abner Green: A Memorial Journal*. New York: American Committee for the Protection of the Foreign Born, 1959. pp. 2-3.

Regarding Abner Green's open letter to Hemingway, under the pseudonym Paul Harris, which appeared in the *American Criterion*, I (Dec. 1935). See (H271). The letter led to a correspondence with Hemingway, who became the Co-Chairman of the Committee of Sponsors of the American Committee for the Protection of the Foreign Born. A letter from Hemingway to Abner Green is briefly quoted on p. 3.

68 Carlucci, Carlo. *Ernest Hemingway dieci anni dopo.* Lugano: Casa Editrice, Cenobio, 1970. 38 pages.
    This essay first appeared in *Cenobio,* xix (July-Aug. 1970).

69 Carpeaux, Otto Maria. *Hemingway, tempo, vida e obra.* Rio de Janeiro: Bruguera, 1971. [Coleçao Tempo, vida e obra, 2.] 160 pages.

70 Carroll, Gordon, ed. *Famous Writers Annual: Book One.* Westport, Conn.: Famous Writers School, 1970. pp. 49-56. Photograph of Hemingway during World War II on p. 178.
    "Lieutenant Hemingway, 1918" by Carlos Baker, excerpt from *EH: A Life Story,* pp. 38-56.

71 Caruthers, Clifford M., ed. *Ring Around Max: The Correspondence of Ring Lardner and Maxwell Perkins.* DeKalb: Northern Illinois University Press, 1973. pp. xvi, 1, 33, 73, 111, 116, 127, 135, 142, 147, 162-164.

72 Casteel, Homer. *The Running of the Bulls: A Description of the Bullfight.* New York: Dodd, Mead, 1953. pp. 15, 67, 83, 121, 143. [London: Faber & Faber, 1954.]

73 Castillo-Puche, José Luis. *América de cabo a rabo.* Madrid: Ediciones Cid, 1959. pp. 486-495.
    An account of a visit with the Hemingways at "La Vigia" in Cuba. Note: This book is dedicated: A Mary y Ernesto Hemingway.

74 Castillo-Puche, José Luis. *Hemingway, entre la vida y la muerte.* Barcelona: Ediciones Destino, 1968. 467 pages. Photographs. Biographical chronology on pp. 447-465, with special emphasis on Hemingway's trips to Spain. Chronological list of Hemingway's work on pp. 466-467. For work by Hemingway, see (S-B6). For facsimiles of letters, see (S-F141), (S-F145), and (S-F161).

75 Cecil, David. *Max, A Biography.* Boston: Houghton Mifflin, 1965. p. 484.
    Regarding Max Beerbohm's response to *OMATS.*

76 Cerf, Bennett. *Try and Stop Me: A Collection of Anecdotes and Stories, Mostly Humorous.* New York: Simon & Schuster, 1944. pp. 74, 85, 95-96, 106, 208, 245. Drawing of Hemingway and Max Eastman by Carl Rose on p. 95.
    pp. 95-96: On the Hemingway-Eastman encounter in 1937.

77 Christensen, Francis. *Notes Toward a New Rhetoric: Six Essays for Teachers.* New York: Harper & Row, 1967. pp. 23-38.
    "A Lesson from Hemingway," an analysis of "The Undefeated," reprinted from *College English,* xxv (Oct. 1963). Reprinted in *Modern English Reader* edited by Robert M. Gorrell et al., Englewood Cliffs, N.J., 1970. pp. 367-372.

78 Churchill, Allen. *The Literary Decade*. Englewood Cliffs, N.J.: Prentice-Hall, 1971. pp. 80, 188, 212, 236-246, 310-311, 316-317. Facsimile of dust jacket of *SAR* and photograph of Hemingway following p. 78.

A popular view of the American literary scene from 1920 to 1930. pp. 236-255: Ch. 15: "The Champs: EH . . . Lewis . . . Fitzgerald."

79 [Clark, C. E. Frazer, Jr.]. *Ernest M. Hemingway: The Paris Years . . . And Before*. Catalogue of an exhibition from the collection of C. E. Frazer Clark, Jr., on May 2, 1973, at Oakland Community College, Farmington, Michigan. Single sheet folded once. 8 1/2 x 11. Introduction, on p. [2], by Frazer Clark.

Thirty-two items, including inscribed presentation copies, galley proofs, periodicals containing first appearances, and letters. See (S-F127) and (S-F131). Note: 250 copies of the exhibit catalogue were printed.

80 Cohen, Henning, ed. *Landmarks of American Writing*. New York: Basic Books, 1969. pp. 83, 137, 303-314, 336, 341, 352, 384-385.

pp. 303-314: "Ernest Hemingway: *The Sun Also Rises*" by Earl H. Rovit. Note: The essays in this book were originally prepared for the Voice of America.

81 [Coles]. *Hemingway's A Farewell to Arms and For Whom the Bell Tolls*. London: Pan Books Ltd., 1968. [Coles Notes Series, No. D8.96.] Study guide. Other guides for *OMATS*, 1968, No. D8.88; *SAR*, 1968, No. D8.120.

82 Collins, Larry, and Dominique Lapierre. *Is Paris Burning?* London: Victor Gollancz, 1965. [New York: Simon & Schuster, 1965.] pp. 170-171, 196, 215, 233, 304, 326.

Regarding Hemingway's intelligence efforts at Rambouillet preceding the Liberation of Paris, in August 1944.

83 Connolly, Cyril. *The Modern Movement: One Hundred Key Books from England, France and America, 1880-1950*. London: Hamish Hamilton, 1966. [New York: Atheneum, 1966.] pp. 53, 60, 123-124, 129.

p. 53: *In Our Time* is No. 49; *The Sun Also Rises* is No. 50. p. 60: *A Farewell to Arms* is No. 60. Note: *FTA* was omitted in (G97).

84 Connolly, Cyril. *The Evening Colonnade*. London: David Bruce & Watson, 1973. pp. 303-310.

pp. 303-306: Ch. 15: "Ernest Hemingway: 1," review of *AMF*, reprinted from the *Sunday Times*, London (May 24, 1964). pp. 307-310: Ch. 16: "Ernest Hemingway: 2," review of Carlos Baker's *EH: A Life Story*, reprinted from the *Sunday Times*, London (Aug. 10, 1969).

85 Conrad, Barnaby. *Gates of Fear*. New York: Thomas Y. Crowell, 1957. [Bonanza Books.] pp. 7, 23, 46, 71, 85*n.*, 110, 127, 218, 233*n.*, 245, 252-255, 282, 284, 294.

pp. 252-259: "The Only Beast: Reflections on Not Attending the Bullfights" by Lysander Kemp, reprinted from *Discovery 4*, New York: Pocket Books, 1954.

86 Considine, Bob. *Toots*. New York: Meredith Press, 1969. pp. 169-171.

Regarding Hemingway's inscriptions in books presented to Toots Shor, the restaurateur.

87 Cook, Albert. *The Meaning of Fiction*. Detroit: Wayne State University Press, 1960. pp. 121-122, 177-179, 239, 268, 278, 304.

88 Cooperman, Stanley. Revised and edited by Ingrid Wiegand. *The Major Novels of Hemingway*. New York: Monarch Press, 1965. [Monarch Notes and Study Guide, No. 621-3.] 68 pages.

Includes critical commentary on *FTA, SAR, FWBT*, and *OMATS*.

89 Cooperman, Stanley. *Ernest Hemingway's The Old Man and the Sea: A Critical Commentary*. New York: Monarch Press, 1965. [Monarch Notes and Study Guide, No. 673.] 66 pages.

90 Cooperman, Stanley. *Hemingway's For Whom the Bell Tolls: A Critical Commentary*. New York: Barrister, 1966. [Bar-Notes: Literature Study and Examination Guide.] 64 pages. Bibliography on pp. 62-64.

91 Cooperman, Stanley, and Murray H. Cohen. *Hemingway's The Old Man and the Sea: A Critical Commentary*. New York: Barrister, 1966. [Bar-Notes: Literature Study and Examination Guide.] 72 pages. Bibliography on pp. 69-72.

92 Cooperman, Stanley. *World War I and the American Novel*. Baltimore: Johns Hopkins Press, 1967. pp. 8-9, 127, 181-190, 197*n.*, 199, 210.

pp. 8-9: Hemingway's poem "Champs d'Honneur" is quoted. pp. 181-190: "Death and Cojones: Frederic Henry (Ernest Hemingway)."

93 Cowley, Malcolm. *The Faulkner-Cowley File: Letters and Memories, 1944-1962*. New York: Viking Press, 1966. pp. 10-11, 21, 29, 32, 87, 100-101, 104, 112, 122-125, 127, 159-160, 173.

p. 21: Regarding the Viking Portable *Hemingway*. p. 29: A Hemingway letter regarding Faulkner is quoted. See (S-F95).

94 Cowley, Malcolm. *Think Back On Us . . . : A Contemporary Chronicle of the 1930's*. Edited by Henry Dan Piper. Carbondale and Ed-

wardsville: Southern Illinois University Press, 1967. pp. 219-225, 310-314, 361-364.

pp. 219-225: "A Farewell to Spain," review of *DIA*, reprinted from the *New Republic*, LXXIII (Nov. 30, 1932). pp. 310-314: "Hemingway: Work in Progress," review of *THAHN*, reprinted from the *New Republic*, XCII (Oct. 20, 1937). pp. 361-364: "Hemingway's 'Nevertheless,' " review of *FWBT*, reprinted from the *New Republic*, CIV (Jan. 20, 1941), where it appeared under the title "Death of a Hero."

95 Cowley, Malcolm. *A Second Flowering*: *Works and Days of the Lost Generation*. New York: Viking Press, 1973. pp. viii, ix, 3, 10-11, 13, 16-18, 34, 48-73, 85, 106, 168, 216-232, 236, 237, 239, 242, 247-255. Photographs.

pp. 48-73: Ch. III: "Hemingway in Paris." pp. 216-232: Ch. x: "Hemingway The Old Lion." p. 228: A poem, "Ernest," which the author wrote after reading *GHOA*, is quoted.

96 Crane, R. S. *The Idea of the Humanities and Other Essays Critical and Historical*. Vol. II. Chicago: University of Chicago Press, 1967. pp. 303-326.

pp. 303-314: "Ernest Hemingway: 'The Killers.' " Written in 1956 and previously unpublished. pp. 315-326: "Ernest Hemingway: 'The Short Happy Life of Francis Macomber.' " This essay originally appeared in *English "A" Analyst*, No. 16 (Nov. 1, 1949); reprinted here from *Readings for Liberal Education* edited by Louis G. Locke et al., New York, 1957, see (E143); reprinted in John M. Howell's *Hemingway's African Stories*, New York, 1969, pp. 128-136.

97 Craven, Thomas. *Modern Art: The Men, The Movements, The Meaning*. New York: Simon & Schuster, 1934. pp. 30, 40.

98 Crichton, Kyle. *Total Recoil*. Garden City, N.Y.: Doubleday, 1960. pp. 157-161.

p. 159: Letter from Hemingway, regarding anti-fascism in America, is quoted. pp. 159-161: Letter from Hemingway, regarding the author's criticism of him in *Redder Than the Rose* (G150) and his writing habits, is quoted.

99 Crothers, George Dunlap, ed. *Invitation to Learning*. New York: Basic Books, 1966. pp. 329-336.

"*A Farewell to Arms*." Transcription of a discussion by Carlos Baker, Philip Young, and George D. Crothers.

100 Cunard, Nancy. *These Were the Hours: Memories of My Hours Press, Réauville and Paris 1928-1931*. Carbondale and Edwardsville: Southern Illinois University Press, 1969. pp. 127-128.

101 Curley, Dorothy Nyren, Maurice Kramer, and Elaine Fialka Kramer, eds. *A Library of Literary Criticism: Modern American Literature.* Vol. II. New York: Frederick Ungar, 1969. Fourth enlarged edition. pp. 65-76.

Thirty short excerpts from critical studies of Hemingway's works. Note: For earlier edition, see (G299).

102 Davenport, Marcia. *Too Strong for Fantasy.* New York: Scribner's, 1967. pp. 138, 175, 214, 298.

p. 298: The novelist recalls Hemingway's rudeness when Maxwell Perkins tried to introduce them.

103 Davidson, Marshall B., and the Editors of American Heritage. *The American Heritage History of The Writers' America.* New York: American Heritage, 1973. pp. 285, 286, 319, 326, 328, 331-335, 373, 374, 376. Photographs.

pp. 331-335: Biographical sketch of Hemingway. p. 332: Facsimile of Sherwood Anderson's letter, in 1921, introducing the Hemingways to Gertrude Stein.

104 Desnoes, Edmundo. *Inconsolable Memories.* New York: New American Library, 1967. pp. 55-73.

A long scene in this novel takes place in the Hemingway Museum in San Francisco de Paula, Cuba.

105 Dickinson, Asa Don *The World's Best Books: Homer to Hemingway. 3000 Books of 3000 Years, 1050 B.C. to 1950 A.D.* New York: H. W. Wilson, 1953. p. 158.

SAR, FTA, DIA, First 49, and *FWBT* are included in this list, which was selected on the basis of a consensus of expert opinion.

106 Doležel, Lubomír, and Richard W. Bailey, eds. *Statistics and Style.* New York: American Elsevier, 1969. pp. 80-91.

"A Study in Prose Styles: Edward Gibbon and Ernest Hemingway" by Curtis W. Hayes, reprinted from *Texas Studies in Literature and Language,* VII (Winter 1966).

107 Dos Passos, John. *The Fourteenth Chronicle: Letters and Diaries of John Dos Passos.* Edited by Townsend Ludington. Boston: Gambit, 1973. pp. 337-339, 419-434, *et passim.* Photographs.

p. 337: Regarding Dos Passos meeting Hemingway in Paris in 1924. Twenty-eight letters from Dos Passos to Hemingway, written between March 27, 1927 and October 23, 1951, are included. Note: Also published in a limited edition of 300 numbered copies.

108 Dow, M. J. *A Visit to the Hemingway Museum in Key West.* [Key West, Fla.: Ernest Hemingway Home and Museum], 1972. Booklet. 24 pages. Color photographs. Drawings by R. C. Parker. Biographical chronology on inside back cover.

109 DuBose, LaRocque. *For Whom the Bell Tolls*: *Notes*. Lincoln, Nebr.: Cliff's Notes, 1967. Revised edition. 55 pages.

110 Durant, Will, and Ariel Durant. *Interpretations of Life*: *A Survey of Contemporary Literature*. New York: Simon and Schuster, 1970. pp. 28-42.

    Ch. II: "Ernest Hemingway."

111 Earnest, Ernest. *Expatriates and Patriots*: *American Artists, Scholars, and Writers in Europe*. Durham, N.C.: Duke University Press, 1968. pp. 258-260, 266-268, 274, 277, 280.

    Regarding Hemingway's early years in Paris as "roving correspondent" for the *Toronto Daily Star*, and his early creative writing.

112 Earnest, Ernest. *The Single Vision*: *The Alienation of American Intellectuals*. New York: New York University Press/London: University of London Press, 1970. pp. 144-150, 189, 196, 218, 220.

    pp. 144-150: Discusses Hemingway's characters as dramatization of Hemingway.

113 Eby, Cecil D. *Between the Bullet and the Lie*: *American Volunteers in the Spanish Civil War*. New York: Holt, Rinehart and Winston, 1969. pp. 31, 55, 78-80, 84-89, 144, 165, 192, 228, 247, 267, 279, 310.

    p. 31: Regarding Hemingway's use of Robert Hale Merriman as a model for "Robert Jordan" in *FWBT*.

114 Egri, Péter. *Hemingway*. Budapest: Gondolat, 1967. 107 pages.

115 Eisenstaedt, Alfred. *People*. New York: Viking, 1973. [A Studio Book.] pp. 132-133.

    p. 132: Three Eisenstaedt photographs of Hemingway in Cuba in the early 1950s. p. 133: Photograph of "Santiago."

116 Eisinger, Chester E. *Fiction of the Forties*. Chicago: University of Chicago Press, 1963. pp. 21-23, 25-26, 28, 41, 59, 115-116, 190, 205, 331, 333, 345, 372.

    pp. 21-23, 25-26: Discussion of Hemingway's influence on the "war novel." pp. 115-116: On the politics of *FWBT*.

117 Elektorowicz, Leszek, ed. *Hemingway w oczach krytyki światowej*. Warsaw: Państwowy Instytut Wydawniczy, 1968. 538 pages.

    pp. 5-7: Foreword by "H. K." [Henryka Krzeczkowskiego].

    pp. 9-26: "Hemingway: Krótki opis kariery" [Synopsis of a career] by Alfred Kazin. Translated by Michał Sprusiński from *On Native Grounds*, New York, 1942. See (G211).

    pp. 27-59: "Hemingway" by Robert Penn Warren. Translated by Leszek Elektorowicz from *Kenyon Review,* IX (Winter 1947). See (H566).

pp. 61-99: "Ernest Hemingway: Tragedia mistrzostwa" [A tragedy of craftsmanship] by Ivan Kashkin. Translated by Ewa Krasnowolska from *International Literature*, No. 5 (May 1935). See (H250).

pp. 101-116: "Hemingway i jego krytycy" [Hemingway and his critics] by Lionel Trilling. Translated by Ewa Krasnowolska from *Partisan Review*, VI (Winter 1939). See (H385).

pp. 117-148: "Ernest Hemingway: "Tępy wół' " [The dumb ox] by Wyndham Lewis. Translated by Ewa Krasnowolska from *Men Without Art*, London, 1934. See (G235).

pp. 149-164: "Ernest Hemingway" by Dwight Macdonald. Translated by Henryka Krzeczkowskiego from *Encounter*, XVIII (Jan. 1962). See (H1328).

pp. 165-177: "Byk po poludniu" [Bull in the afternoon] by Max Eastman. Translated by Ewa Krasnowolska from the *New Republic*, LXXV (June 7, 1933). See (H212).

pp. 179-203: "Ernest Hemingway i psychologia 'straconego pokolenia' " [Ernest Hemingway and the psychology of the 'lost generation'] by Edwin Berry Burgum. Translated by Maria Skroczyńska from *The Novel and the World's Dilemma*, New York, 1947. See (G72).

pp. 205-238: "Uwagi o stylu Ernesta Hemingwaya" [Observations on the style of Ernest Hemingway] by Harry Levin. Translated by Leszek Elektorowicz from *Contexts of Criticism*, Cambridge, 1957. See (G233).

pp. 239-258: "Koszmar i rytuał u Hemingwaya" [Nightmare and ritual in Hemingway] by Malcolm Cowley. Translated by Ewa Krasnowolska from the Introduction to the Viking Portable *Hemingway*, pp. vii-xxiv. See (A22a).

pp. 259-279: "Hemingway w świetle Hegla" [Hemingway à la lumière de Hegel] by Georges Bataille. Translated by Ewa Krasnowolska from *Critique*, IX (March 1953). See (H802).

pp. 281-299: "Hemingwayowska perspektywa narracyjna" [Hemingway's narrative perspective] by E. M. Halliday. Translated by Michał Sprusiński from the *Sewanee Review*, LX (April-June 1952). See (H720).

pp. 301-314: "Opowiadania Hemingwaya" [Hemingway's short stories] by H. E. Bates. Translated by Michał Sprusiński from *Baker anthology*. See (G27).

pp. 315-334: "Hemingway w swoich głównych dziełach" [Hemingway of the major works] by Pier Francesco Paolini. Translated by Henryka Krzeczkowskiego from *Baker anthology*. See (G27).

pp. 335-354: "Śmierć miłości w 'Słońce tez wschodzi' " [The death of love in *SAR*] by Mark Spilka. Translated by Ewa Krasnowolska from *Baker anthology*. See (G27).

pp. 355-403: "Sędziwy marynarz" [The ancient mariner] by Carlos Baker. Translated by Jerzy Strzetelski from *Hemingway: The Writer as Artist*, Second edition, Princeton, 1956. See (G26).

pp. 405-416: "Marlin i rekin: Parę słów o książce 'Stary człowiek i morze' " [The marlin and the shark: a note on *OMATS*] by Keiichi Harada. Translated by Maria Skroczyńska from *Baker anthology*. See (G27).

pp. 417-436: "Hemingwaya 'Za rzekę w cień drzew' " [Hemingway's *ARIT*] by Horst Oppel. Translated by Henryka Krzeczkowskiego from *Baker anthology*. See (G27).

pp. 437-455: "Ernest Hemingway: Gdy zawiodła wrażliwość [The failure of sensibility] by Ray B. West. Translated by Maria Skroczyńska from the *Sewanee Review*, LIII (Jan.-March 1945). See (H531).

pp. 457-499: "Ernest Hemingway" by Philip Young. Translated by Henryka Krzeczkowskiego from William Van O'Connor's *Seven Modern American Novelists*, Minneapolis, 1964. See (G304).

pp. 501-511: "Zjawisko 'Hemingway' " by Zbigniew Bieńkowski, reprinted from *Piekła i Orfeusze*, Moscow, 1960.

pp. 512-522: Biographical chronology by Leszek Elektorowicz.

pp. 523-524: Checklist of Polish translations of Hemingway's works.

118 Ellmann, Mary. *Thinking About Women*. New York: Harcourt, Brace & World, 1968. pp. 47, 52, 54, 76, 77.

p. 76: The "soliloquy forced upon the woman named Doris Hollis" in *THAHN* is quoted.

119 Fallaci, Oriana. *The Egotists: Sixteen Surprising Interviews*. Chicago: Henry Regnery, 1968. pp. 3, 141-158, 184, 208.

p. 3: Norman Mailer "admits to have been influenced by Hemingway, although, he claims, only on a literary level: 'His style was so magnetic, an adult style. I write differently, but I've learned so much from him. The man was a great cobbler, he taught everybody how to make shoes.' " pp. 141-158: "Mary Hemingway: My Husband Hemingway." Interview reprinted, with slight revisions, from *Look*, XXX (Sept. 6, 1966). See (S-H196). Reprinted in *Limelighters*, London: Michael Joseph, 1968.

120 Farr, Finis. *O'Hara: A Biography*. Boston: Little, Brown, 1973. pp. 19, 77, 147, 156, 198-199, 203, 209, 251, 277, 278. Photograph of Hemingway, Sherman Billingsley, and John O'Hara following p. 146.

121 Farrington, S. Kip, Jr. *Fishing with Hemingway and Glassell*. New York: David McKay, 1971. 118 pages. Photographs.

pp. 3-5: The author recalls his first meeting with Hemingway in Bimini in 1935. p. 38: A postscript by Hemingway, to a letter of Mary Hemingway's to Chisie Farrington, the author's wife, from Finca Vigia, April 22, 1951, is quoted. pp. 64-68: Regarding the filming of *OMATS* in April 1955, off Cabo Blanco, Peru. Excerpts from this book appeared in *Field & Stream*, LXXV (April 1971). Note: Hemingway's introduction to Farrington's *Atlantic Game Fishing* is reprinted on pp. 9-14. See (S-B12).

122 [Feldman, Lew David]. *Seventy One: The World of Books, Arts and Letters, circa 1170-1970.* New York: House of El Dieff, 1971. Catalogue. Photograph.

Number 30: A Portrait Bust of Ernest Hemingway by Luis Sanguino [Madrid, 1968]. One of two casts made by the Spanish sculptor. The other cast was unveiled by Mary Hemingway on July 7, 1968, as a memorial in Pamplona.

123 [Feldman, Lew David]. *Seventy Two: American/British/Continental First Editions, Manuscripts, Autograph Letters and Works of Art.* New York: House of El Dieff, 1972. Catalogue. Photograph on back cover.

Number 233: A Portrait Bust of Ernest Hemingway by Robert Berks [1959]. The bronze bust served as the visual symbol for a television series of Hemingway adaptations in 1959.

124 Fenton, Charles A., ed. *The Best Short Stories of World War II: An American Anthology.* New York: Viking, 1957. pp. vii, x-xii, xviii.

Discusses Hemingway's influence on the younger war writers.

125 Fiedler, Leslie A. *An End to Innocence: Essays on Culture and Politics.* Boston: Beacon Press, 1955. pp. 101, 105, 134, 181, 185, 193-195, 198-200.

pp. 193-195: Discusses Hemingway's "failure to achieve maturity."

126 Fiedler, Leslie A. *The Return of the Vanishing American.* New York: Stein and Day, 1968. pp. 21, 143-147, 149, 172-174.

Discusses Hemingway's writings about Indians, especially the Indian sections of *TOS*.

127 Fiedler, Leslie. *The Collected Essays of Leslie Fiedler.* Vol. II. New York: Stein and Day, 1971. pp. 66, 105, 196, 238, 247, 343-354, 391, 446-447, 454, 457.

pp. 343-354: "An Almost Imaginary Interview: Hemingway in Ketchum," reprinted from the *Partisan Review*, XXIX (Summer 1962).

128 Finney, Ben. *Feet First.* New York: Crown, 1971. Foreword by John O'Hara. pp. ix, 13, 19, 25-26, 67, 145-146, 187-199, 208, 210. Photographs.

pp. 187-199: Ch. 18: "The Ernest Hemingway I Knew." Recollections of Hemingway in the early 1920s, in France, in the 1930s, in Bimini, and in the 1940s and 1950s, in Cuba.

129 Fitzgerald, F. Scott. *Afternoon of an Author: A Selection of Uncollected Stories and Essays*. Introduction and notes by Arthur Mizener. Princeton: Princeton University Library, 1957. pp. 117-122.

"How to Waste Material: A Note on My Generation," reprinted from the *Bookman*, LXIII (May 1926). Includes a review of *IOT*.

130 Flanner, Janet (Genêt). *Paris Journal, 1944-1965*. New York: Atheneum, 1965. pp. 193, 414, 492.

p. 193: Regarding the French reception of *OMATS*.

131 Flanner, Janet (Genêt). *Paris Was Yesterday, 1925-1939*. Edited by Irving Drutman. New York: Viking Press, 1972. pp. vii-viii, xvi-xvii, 12, 56, 90.

pp. vii-viii: Recalls a discussion with Hemingway regarding suicide. Reprinted in *Life*, LXXIII (July 28, 1972).

132 Ford, Corey. *The Time of Laughter*. Boston: Little, Brown, 1967. pp. 83-85, 197.

pp. 83-85: A parody interview with Hemingway, reprinted from *Vanity Fair*, XXIX (Jan. 1928). See (H90). p. 85: An anecdote about F. Scott Fitzgerald reading Ford's parody to Hemingway.

133 Ford, Ford Madox. *Letters of Ford Madox Ford*. Edited by Richard M. Ludwig. Princeton: Princeton University Press, 1965. pp. 162, 191, 195, 198, 212, 216, 293-294.

p. 216: Letter to Hemingway, written November 6, 1932, requesting a testimonial for Ezra Pound. See (B12).

134 Ford, Hugh, ed. *The Left Bank Revisited: Selections from the Paris Tribune 1917-1934*. Foreword by Matthew Josephson. University Park and London: Pennsylvania State University Press, 1972. Drawing of Hemingway by Don Brown on p. 262. pp. xxi, xxiii, 68, 92, 99-100, 107-109, 121, 126, 129-130, 241-242, 257, 259, 262-263, 268, 274-277, 279, 288-289.

pp. 99-100: "Open Letter to Ernest Hemingway" by Eugène Jolas, criticizing Hemingway's poems in *Der Querschnitt*, reprinted from the *Paris Tribune* (Nov. 16, 1924). pp. 108-109: "Mrs. Ernest Hemingway, Author's Wife, Gets Divorce in Paris," reprinted from the *Paris Tribune* (March 11, 1927). pp. 129-130: "Hemingway Back in Paris; Sails for New York" by Don Brown, reprinted from the *Paris Tribune* (Sept. 20, 1931). p. 257: Review of *TSTP* by Gertrude Stein, reprinted from the *Paris Tribune* (Nov. 27, 1923). pp. 262-263: "Hemingway's New Novel," review of *SAR* by Fanny Butcher, reprinted from the *Paris Tribune* (Dec. 19, 1926).

135 Fowler, Austin. *Ernest Hemingway's The Snows of Kilimanjaro.*
New York: Monarch Press, 1966. [Monarch Notes and Study
Guides, No. 839.] 78 pages.

136 Freedman, Morris, and Paul B. Davis, eds. *Controversy in Litera-*
ture: Fiction, Drama and Poetry with Related Criticism. New York:
Scribner's, 1968. pp. 121-141.
   Section Seven: "The Dark Corners in Hemingway's Well-Lighted
Place." pp. 121-122: Introductory comment. pp. 126-135: "The
Logic of Confusion in Hemingway's 'A Clean, Well-Lighted Place' "
by Joseph F. Gabriel, reprinted from *College English*, XXII (May
1961). pp. 135-141: "Tidying Up Hemingway's 'Clean, Well-Lighted
Place' " by John V. Hagopian, reprinted from *Studies in Short Fic-*
tion, I (Winter 1964). p. 141*n*.: Note reprinted from *Studies in Short*
Fiction, I (Summer 1964), ii, regarding Scribner's decision to emend
the text of "A Clean, Well-Lighted Place" as suggested by Dr.
Hagopian in the above essay. See (S-A7F). See also (S-E95).

137 Freeman, Donald C., ed. *Linguistics and Literary Style.* New York:
Holt, Rinehart & Winston, 1970. pp. 271-273, 279-296.
   pp. 271-273: Discussion of the conclusion of "Soldier's Home" by
Richard Ohmann. pp. 279-296: Ch. 16: "A Study in Prose Styles:
Edward Gibbon and Ernest Hemingway" by Curtis W. Hayes, reprinted from *Texas Studies in Literature and Language*, VII (Winter 1966).

138 [Freeman, Elsie T.] *Books and Manuscripts from A. E. Hotchner's*
Recent Gift to the Rare Book Department. Catalogue of an exhibi-
tion at the John M. Olin Library, Washington University, St. Louis,
Missouri, March 5, 1968–April 5, 1968. Single sheet folded twice.
Photograph of Hotchner and Hemingway on the reverse side. Intro-
duction by Elsie T. Freeman.
   The exhibition included Hotchner's adaptations of Hemingway's
work and items relating to *Papa Hemingway.*

139 French, Warren. *The Social Novel at the End of an Era.* Carbondale and Edwardsville: Southern Illinois University Press, 1966.
pp. 9, 15, 87-124, 158, 160-167, 170.
   pp. 87-124: "A Troubled World." Partially reprinted in Sheldon
Norman Grebstein's *The Merrill Studies in For Whom the Bell*
Tolls, Columbus, Ohio, 1971, pp. 56-70.

140 French, Warren, ed. *The Thirties: Fiction, Poetry, Drama.* Deland,
Fla.: Everett/Edwards, 1967. pp. 6, 21-30, 64.
   pp. 21-30: "Hemingway's Dark and Bloody Capital" by Sheldon
Norman Grebstein. On "The Capital of the World."

141 French, Warren, ed. *The Forties: Fiction, Poetry, Drama.* Deland,
Fla.: Everett/Edwards, 1969. pp. 8, 9, 19-20, 27, 46, 156, 262.

142 French, Warren, ed. *The Fifties: Fiction, Poetry, Drama.* Deland, Fla.: Everett/Edwards, 1970. pp. 41-50.
"Hemingway's Craft in *The Old Man and the Sea*" by Sheldon Norman Grebstein.

143 French, Warren G., and Walter E. Kidd, eds. *American Winners of the Nobel Literary Prize.* Norman: University of Oklahoma Press, 1968. pp. 158-192.
"Ernest Hemingway" by Ken Moritz. Includes Hemingway's Nobel prize acceptance speech on pp. 161-162.

144 Frenz, Horst, ed. *Nobel Lectures: Literature, 1901-1967.* Amsterdam/London/New York: Elsevier, 1969. pp. 282, 283, 288, 496-503, 574.
pp. 497-500: Presentation speech by Anders Österling. p. 501: Hemingway's acceptance speech, which was read by John C. Cabot, U.S. Ambassador. p. 502: Comment by H. S. Nyberg. Regarding Hemingway's absence from the presentation ceremonies and his work. p. 503: Brief biography.

145 Friedman, Melvin J., and John B. Vickery, eds. *The Shaken Realist: Essays in Modern Literature in Honor of Frederick J. Hoffman.* Baton Rouge: Louisana State University Press, 1970. pp. 5-20.
"The Silence of Ernest Hemingway" by Ihab Hassan. A study of silence as metaphor.

146 Gadda Conti, Giuseppe. *Hemingway e la Pace dei Nostri Giorni: Saggio.* Milan: Edikon, 1969. 40 pages. Essays.

147 Galinsky, Hans, Leo Marx, and Calvin Rus, eds. *Amerikanische Dichtung in der höheren Schule.* Berlin: Diesterweg, 1961. pp. 5-45, 55, 56.
pp. 5-45: "Beharrende Strukturzüge im Wandel eines Jahrhunderts amerikanischer Kurzgeschichte (Dargelegt an E. A. Poes 'The Masque of the Red Death' und Ernest Hemingways 'The Killers')" by Hans Galinsky.

148 Gellens, Jay, ed. *Twentieth Century Interpretations of A Farewell to Arms: A Collection of Critical Essays.* Englewood Cliffs, N.J.: Prentice-Hall, 1970. [Spectrum Books, S-863.] 121 pages. Note: A number of the essays have been retitled by the editor.
Contents: pp. 1-14: Introduction by Jay Gellens.

Part One: Interpretations
pp. 15-27: "The Unadulterated Sensibility" by Ray B. West, Jr., reprinted from *The Art of Modern Fiction*, New York, 1949, pp. 622-634.

pp. 28-32: "Loser Take Nothing" by Philip Young, reprinted from *EH: A Reconsideration*, University Park, Penn., 1966, pp. 89-95.

pp. 33-40: "Learning to Care" by Earl Rovit, reprinted from *Ernest Hemingway*, New York, 1963, pp. 98-106.

pp. 41-53: "The Tough Romance" by Robert W. Lewis, Jr., reprinted from *Hemingway on Love*, Austin, 1965, pp. 39-54.

pp. 54-71: Symposium on Sensibility and/or Symbol in *FTA*

pp. 54-55: "Rain as Disaster" by Malcolm Cowley, reprinted from the Introduction to the Viking Portable *Hemingway*, p. 16.

pp. 55-56: "The Unreferable Rain" by Louis L. Martz, reprinted from *Tragic Themes in Western Literature* edited by Cleanth Brooks, New Haven, 1955, pp. 153-154.

pp. 56-64: "The Mountain and the Plain" by Carlos Baker, reprinted from *Hemingway: The Writer as Artist*, Third edition, Princeton, 1963, pp. 94-96, 101-108.

pp. 64-71: "Hemingway's Ambiguity: Symbolism and Irony" by E. M. Halliday, reprinted from *American Literature*, xxvii (March 1956).

pp. 72-90: "The 'Dumb Ox' in Love and War" by Wyndham Lewis, reprinted from *Men Without Art*, New York, 1964, pp. 17-41.

pp. 91-102: "Ciphers at the Front" by D. S. Savage, reprinted from *The Withered Branch*, London, 1950, pp. 23-36.

Part Two: View Points

pp. 103-105: "The Existential Hero" by John Killinger, reprinted from *Hemingway and the Dead Gods*, Lexington, Ky., 1960, pp. 46-48.

pp. 105-107: "Small Hips, Not War" by Norman Friedman, reprinted from "Criticism and the Novel," *Antioch Review*, xviii (Fall 1958), pp. 352-355.

pp. 108-111: "The Secret Wound" by Frederick J. Hoffman, reprinted from *The Twenties*, New York, 1955, pp. 67-72.

pp. 111-112: "Love and Death" by Leslie Fiedler, reprinted from *Love and Death in the American Novel*, New York, 1966, pp. 317-318.

pp. 112-114: "Farewell the Separate Peace" by Edgar Johnson, reprinted from the *Sewanee Review*, xlviii (July-Sept. 1940).

pp. 114-115: "The Human Will" by Maxwell Geismar, reprinted from *Writers in Crisis*, Boston, 1942, pp. 46-47.

pp. 116-118: Chronology of Important Dates.

149 Gibson, Walker. *Tough, Sweet, and Stuffy: An Essay on Modern American Prose Styles*. Bloomington: Indiana University Press, 1966. pp. 28-42.
"Tough Talk: The Rhetoric of Frederic Henry."

150 Gil'dina, Z. M., R. E. Gotkharde, and Z. P. Dorofeeva, eds. *Problemy lingvistiki i zarubeznoi literatury*. Riga: Zinatne, 1968. pp. 205-222. In English.

"Hemingway's New Epic Genre in His Spanish Novel" by R. E. Gotkharde. On *FWBT*.

151 Gilmer, Walker. *Horace Liveright: Publisher of the Twenties*. New York: David Lewis, 1970. pp. 120-125.

Regarding the publication of *IOT* by Liveright, in 1925, and Hemingway's break with his first American publisher, later in the same year, over publication of *TOS*.

152 Gingrich, Arnold. *Nothing But People: The Early Days at Esquire, A Personal History, 1928-1958*. New York: Crown, 1971. pp. 84-87, 111, 145, 147, 243, 246-248, 267-268, 270-286, 307-308.

pp. 85-86: Gingrich tells of his first meeting with Hemingway, in the Spring of 1933, and Hemingway's agreement to write for *Esquire* at "twice whatever anybody else gets." pp. 277-280: Regarding "libelous" sections in the manuscript of *THAHN*, which Hemingway cut before publication. pp. 307-308: Regarding the excerpt from *Islands* that appeared in *Esquire*, LXXIV (Oct. 1970).

153 Glassco, John. *Memoirs of Montparnasse*. Toronto and New York: Oxford University Press, 1970. pp. ix, 48-49, 52-53, 56, 58, 72, 88-90, 130, 154.

Reminiscences of Hemingway in Paris, in the late 1920s, by a young Canadian writer.

154 Glicksberg, Charles I. *The Sexual Revolution in Modern American Literature*. The Hague: Nijhoff, 1971. pp. 20, 46, 58, 82-95, 98, 125, 130, 133, 145, 146.

pp. 82-95: Ch. VIII: "The Hemingway Cult of Love."

155 Goethals, Thomas. *For Whom the Bell Tolls: A Critical Commentary*. New York: American R.D.M. Corporation, 1963. [Study Master Publication, No. 436.] 59 pages.

156 Goethals, Thomas. *The Old Man and the Sea: A Critical Commentary*. New York: American R.D.M. Corporation, 1965. [Study Master Publication, No. 425.] 56 pages.

157 Gohdes, Clarence, ed. *Essays on American Literature in Honor of Jay B. Hubbell*. Durham, N.C.: Duke University Press, 1967. pp. 19, 299-301, 306.

pp. 299-301: Comparison of Dashiell Hammett's work with Hemingway's by Walter Blair.

158 Golden, Herbert H., ed. *Studies in Honor of Samuel Montefiore Waxman*. Boston: Boston University Press, 1969. pp. 158-176.

"Gironella and Hemingway: Novelists of the Spanish Civil War" by Robert L. Sheehan. A study of "two of the great human documents of twentieth-century Spanish history," *FWBT* and José María Gironella's *Un millón de muertos.*

159 Goodman, Paul. *Speaking and Language: Defense of Poetry.* New York: Random House, 1971. pp. 181-190.

Part 4 of "Literary Style as Hypothesis." A version of this essay appeared in the *New York Review of Books*, XVII (Dec. 30, 1971), under the title "The Sweet Style of Ernest Hemingway."

160 Gorrell, Robert M., Charlton Laird, and Ronald E. Freeman, eds. *Modern English Reader.* Englewood Cliffs, N.J.: Prentice-Hall, 1970. pp. v, 366-372.

pp. 367-372: "A Lesson from Hemingway" by Francis Christensen, reprinted from *College English*, XXV (Oct. 1963). See also (S-E139).

161 Graham, John, ed. *The Merrill Studies in A Farewell to Arms.* Columbus, Ohio: Merrill, 1971. [Charles E. Merrill Studies.] 105 pages.

Contents: pp. iii-iv: Preface by John Graham.

Part I: Contemporary Reviews

pp. 3-8: Review of *FTA* by Malcolm Cowley, reprinted from the *N.Y. Herald Tribune* (Oct. 6, 1929).

pp. 9-13: "Nothing Ever Happens to the Brave," review of *FTA* by T. S. Matthews, reprinted from the *New Republic*, LX (Oct. 9, 1929).

pp. 14-19: Review of *FTA* by Henry Seidel Canby, reprinted from the *Saturday Review of Literature,* VI (Oct. 12, 1929).

pp. 20-22: Review of *FTA* by Clifton P. Fadiman, reprinted from the *Nation,* CXXIX (Oct. 30, 1929).

pp. 23-24: Review of *FTA* by B. E. Todd, reprinted from the *Spectator,* CXLIII (Nov. 16, 1929).

Part II: Studies

pp. 27-38: "Ernest Hemingway: *A Farewell to Arms*" by Carlos Baker, reprinted from *The American Novel* edited by Wallace Stegner, New York, 1965, pp. 192-205.

pp. 39-45: "The Religion of Death in *A Farewell to Arms*" by James F. Light, reprinted from *Modern Fiction Studies*, VII (Summer 1961). Note: Revised by the author for this collection.

pp. 46-54: "Ernest Hemingway: Joy Through Strength" by Otto Friedrich, excerpt reprinted from *American Scholar*, XXVI (Autumn 1957).

pp. 55-65: "The Stopped Worlds of Frederic Henry" by Charles Vandersee. Not previously published.

pp. 66-82: "Hemingway's *A Farewell to Arms*: The Novel as Pure Poetry" by Daniel J. Schneider, reprinted from *Modern Fiction Studies,* XIV (Autumn 1968).

pp. 83-87: "Language as a Moral Code in *A Farewell to Arms*" by Blanche Gelfant, reprinted from *Modern Fiction Studies,* IX (Summer 1963).

pp. 88-105: "Ernest Hemingway: The Meaning of Style" by John Graham, reprinted from *Modern Fiction Studies,* VI (Winter 1960-1961). Note: This essay was revised in 1970.

162 Graham, Sheilah. *The Garden of Allah.* New York: Crown, 1970. pp. 176-180, 212. Photographs.

pp. 176-178: Regarding Hemingway's visit to Hollywood for fundraising showings of the film *The Spanish Earth,* in 1937. pp. 179-180: Regarding the filming of *OMATS* and other movies made from Hemingway's books.

163 Granatstein, J. L., and R. D. Cuff, eds. *War and Society in North America.* Toronto: Thomas Nelson, 1971. pp. 135-152.
"Hemingway's Unpublished Remarks on War and Warriors" by Bickford Sylvester.

164 Gray, Ronald, ed. *Kafka: A Collection of Critical Essays.* Englewood Cliffs, N.J.: Prentice-Hall, 1962. pp. 75-83.
"Notes on Hemingway and Kafka" by Caroline Gordon, reprinted from the *Sewanee Review,* LVII (April-June 1949).

165 Grebstein, Sheldon Norman, ed. *The Merrill Studies in For Whom the Bell Tolls.* Columbus, Ohio: Merrill, 1971. [Charles E. Merrill Studies.] 122 pages.
Contents: pp. iii-v: Preface by Sheldon Norman Grebstein.

Part One: Contemporary Reviews
pp. 2-5: "The Soul of Spain," review of *FWBT* by Howard Mumford Jones, reprinted from the *Saturday Review of Literature,* XXIII (Oct. 26, 1940).

pp. 6-15: "Review of *For Whom the Bell Tolls*" by Alvah C. Bessie, reprinted from *New Masses,* XXXVII (Nov. 5, 1940). A "postscript" by Bessie, dated 13 April 1970, appears on pp. 12-15.

pp. 16-17: "Books of the Week," review of *FWBT* by J. N. Vaughan, reprinted from *Commonweal,* XXXIII (Dec. 13, 1940).

pp. 18-20: "Thou Tellest Me, Comrade," review of *FWBT* by Gilbert Highet, reprinted from the *Nation,* CLII (March 1, 1941).

pp. 21-23: "Mr. Hemingway's New Novel," review of *FWBT* by Graham Greene, reprinted from the *Spectator,* CLXVI (March 7, 1941).

pp. 24-29: "Current Literature," review of *FWBT* by V. S. Pritchett, reprinted from the *New Statesman & Nation*, XXI (March 15, 1941).

Part Two: Scholarship and Criticism

pp. 32-42: "Ernest Hemingway's Spanish Civil War Experiences" by David Sanders, reprinted from *American Quarterly*, XII (Summer 1960).

pp. 43-49: "The Real Robert Jordan" by Cecil D. Eby, reprinted from *American Literature*, XXXVIII (Nov. 1966).

pp. 50-55: "*For Whom the Bell Tolls*: The Origin of General Golz" by Jerzy R. Krzyżanowski, reprinted from the *Polish Review*, VII (Autumn 1962).

pp. 56-70: Excerpt from *The Social Novel at the End of an Era* by Warren French, Carbondale, Illinois, 1966, pp. 87-91, 109-124.

pp. 71-79: "Mechanized Doom: Ernest Hemingway and the Spanish Civil War" by Allen Guttmann, reprinted from the *Massachusetts Review*, I (May 1960).

pp. 80-90: "Not Spain but Hemingway" by Arturo Barea, reprinted from *Horizon*, III (May 1941).

pp. 91-93: "The English of Hemingway's Spaniards" by John J. Allen, reprinted from the *South Atlantic Bulletin*, XXVII (Nov. 1961).

pp. 94-101: "The Martyrdom of Robert Jordan" by William T. Moynihan, reprinted from *College English*, XXI (Dec. 1959).

pp. 102-106: "The Power of the Tacit in Crane and Hemingway" by Robert P. Weeks, reprinted from *Modern Fiction Studies*, VII (Winter 1962-1963).

pp. 107-112: "Hemingway's Tyrannous Plot" by Thornton H. Parsons, reprinted from the *University of Kansas City Review*, XXVII (Summer 1961).

pp. 113-122: Excerpt from *Ernest Hemingway* by Earl Rovit, New York, 1963, pp. 136-146.

166 Grebstein, Sheldon Norman. *Hemingway's Craft*. Carbondale and Edwardsville: Southern Illinois University Press/London and Amsterdam: Feffer & Simons, 1973. xvii + 245 pages. Preface by Harry T. Moore.

The author notes that his special concern is with "those aspects of structure, language, and narrative technique which distinguish [Hemingway's] writing from all other." pp. 202-218: Appendix: "The Manuscripts of *A Farewell to Arms* and *For Whom the Bell Tolls*." See (S-B16).

167 Gribanov, Boris Timofeevich. *Khemingueĭ*. Moscow: "Molodaya Gvardiya," 1970. 446 pages. Photographs. Biographical chronology on pp. 442-444. Bibliography on p. 445.

168 Gross, Theodore L. *The Heroic Ideal in American Literature*. New York: Free Press/London: Collier-Macmillan, 1971. pp. xi-xii, 83, 193-194, 198-221, 294.

pp. 198-220: (From Part 4: "The Disenchanted Hero") "Ernest Hemingway: The Renunciation of America."

169 Guernsey, Otis L., Jr. *The Best Plays of 1966-1967*. New York: Dodd, Mead, 1967. [The Burns Mantle Year Book.] pp. 59, 397.

Data on A. E. Hotchner's play "The Hemingway Hero," which opened Feb. 21, 1967, in New Haven, and closed March 4, 1967, in Boston.

170 Gurko, Leo. *Ernest Hemingway and the Pursuit of Heroism*. New York: Crowell, 1968. [Twentieth Century American Writers Series.] viii + 248 pages. [Paperback edition: New York, Apollo Editions, 1969. (No. A-211).]

A study of Hemingway's "search for a relevant and sustainable heroism." Selected bibliography on pp. 240-242.

171 Gussow, Mel. *Don't Say Yes Until I Finish Talking*: *A Biography of Darryl F. Zanuck*. Garden City, N.Y.: Doubleday, 1971. pp. 190-193, 231-232.

pp. 189-196: Part III, Ch. 1: "The Sun Also Rises." Includes reminiscences of Hemingway in Sun Valley. Zanuck produced the films *SAR* and *The Snows of Kilimanjaro*.

172 Guth, Hans P. *English for a New Generation*. New York: McGraw-Hill, 1973. pp. 11, 64, 153, 201-203.

pp. 201-202: Discusses Hemingway's "attempt to establish new values untainted by the hypocrisies of conventional language."

173 Hackett, Alice Payne. *70 Years of Best Sellers: 1895-1965*. New York: R. R. Bowker, 1967. pp. 6, 8, 19, 26, 38, 53, 54, 161-164, 184, 185, 190, 224, 226.

Lists best sellers by years and gives number of copies sold. pp. 38, 161-164: On *FWBT*. pp. 53, 54: Paperback editions of *SAR* and *FTA*. pp. 184, 185: On *ARIT*. p. 190: On *OMATS*. pp. 224, 226: On *AMF*.

174 Hagopian, John V., and Martin Dolch, eds. *Insight I: Analyses of American Literature*. Frankfurt am Main: Hirschgraben, 1962. pp. 91-122. [Third enlarged edition, 1967.]

Critical interpretations of Hemingway's work, as follows: pp. 91-96: "Cat in the Rain." pp. 96-99: "A Canary for One." pp. 99-103: "The Killers." pp. 103-105: "A Day's Wait." pp. 105-111: "A Clean, Well-Lighted Place." pp. 111-112: *OMATS*.

175 Haining, Peter, ed. *A Thousand Afternoons*. New York: Cowles, 1970. pp. ix, xvi, xvii, 18-29, 68-69, 75, 93, 95, 105, 202-233.

pp. 18-29: "A Man Called Hemingway" by Sidney Franklin, reprinted from *Bullfighter from Brooklyn*, New York, 1958, pp. 169-181. See also (S-E140).

176 Handy, William J. *Kant and the Southern New Critics*. Austin: University of Texas Press, 1963. pp. 86-88.

177 Handy, William J. *Modern Fiction*: *A Formalist Approach*. Carbondale and Edwardsville: Southern Illinois University Press/London and Amsterdam: Feffer & Simons, 1971. [Crosscurrents/Modern Critiques.] pp. xi, 9, 17-23, 94-118.

pp. 17-19: Examines the opening scene of "The Short Happy Life of Francis Macomber." pp. 20-23: Examines the opening scene of *FTA*. pp. 94-118: Ch. 5: "Hemingway's *The Old Man and the Sea*."

178 Hanneman, Audre. *Ernest Hemingway*: *A Comprehensive Bibliography*. Princeton, N.J.: Princeton University Press, 1967. xiv + 568 pages. Facsimiles. See (S-F30).

Contents: p. [vii]: Foreword by Charles Scribner, Jr.

pp. ix-xi: Preface by the bibliographer.

Part One: The Works of Ernest Hemingway

pp. [3]-88: Section A: Books and pamphlets. (English editions on pp. 79-88.)

pp. 91-122: Section B: Contributions and first appearances in books and pamphlets.

pp. 125-172: Section C: Contributions to newspapers and periodicals.

pp. 175-205: Section D: Translations.

pp. 209-246: Section E: Anthologies.

pp. 249-270: Section F: Library holdings of manuscripts and letters, published facsimiles of manuscripts, published letters, and ephemera (including book blurbs).

Part Two: Biographical and Critical Material on Hemingway

pp. 275-339: Section G: Books on or significantly mentioning Hemingway.

pp. 343-527: Section H: Newspaper and periodical material (1918-1965).

Note: First printing, in December 1967, of 2500 copies. Second printing, with minor corrections, in April 1969.

179 Hapgood, Hutchins. *A Victorian in the Modern World*. New York: Harcourt, Brace, 1939. pp. 451, 452, 533-536, 551, 552, 554.

Reminiscences of Hemingway in Lausanne, Switzerland, in 1922, and in Key West. pp. 534-536: A letter from the author to Hemingway, regarding Gertrude Stein's objection to "Robert Cohn" in *SAR*, is quoted.

180 Hardy, John Edward. *Man in the Modern Novel*. Seattle: University of Washington Press, 1964. pp. 123-141, 197.

pp. 123-136: Ch. 7: "*A Farewell to Arms*: The Death of Tragedy."

181 Harkness, Ross. *J. E. Atkinson of the Star*. Toronto: University of Toronto Press, 1963. pp. 155, 163-166, 276.

Regarding Hemingway's work on the *Toronto Star Weekly* and the *Toronto Daily Star*.

182 Harrison, Gilbert A., ed. *The Critic as Artist*: *Essays on Books 1920-1970*. New York: Liveright, 1972. pp. 257-262.

Review of *FTA* by T. S. Matthews, reprinted from the *New Republic*, LX (Oct. 9, 1929).

183 Hassan, Ihab Habib. *The Dismemberment of Orpheus*: *Toward a Postmodern Literature*. New York: Oxford University Press, 1971. pp. 23, 80-109, 253, 256.

pp. 80-109: "Hemingway: Valor Against the Void."

184 Hauck, Richard Boyd. *A Cheerful Nihilism*: *Confidence and "The Absurd" in American Humorous Fiction*. Bloomington: Indiana University Press, 1971. p. 241.

Comments that Hemingway "displayed an absurd sense without humor. . . . Santiago's story, while containing little intentional humor, is a parable of absurd confidence. . . ."

185 Hays, Peter L. *The Limping Hero*: *Grotesques in Literature*. New York: New York University Press, 1971. pp. 4, 68-77, 84, 155-162, 189, 206, 213.

pp. 68-70, 155-158: On Jake Barnes in *SAR*. pp. 70-72: On "Indian Camp." pp. 72-76: On "God Rest You Merry, Gentlemen." pp. 76-77: On Harry in "The Snows of Kilimanjaro." pp. 158-160: On Nick Adams.

186 Hayward, Max, and Leopold Labedz, eds. *Literature and Revolution in Soviet Russia, 1917-1962*. London: Oxford University Press, 1963. pp. 78, 185, 186.

p. 185: Evgeny Evtushenko's poem "Encounter," which was dedicated to Hemingway, is partially reprinted. See (G459). p. 186: Short analysis of Hemingway's style and its influence on young Soviet writers.

187 Hefner, Hugh M., ed. *The Twelfth Anniversary Playboy Reader*. Chicago: Playboy Press, 1965. pp. ix, 726-734.

pp. 726-732: "Papa and the Playwright" by Kenneth Tynan, an account of the meeting between Hemingway and Tennessee Williams in 1959, reprinted from *Playboy*, XI (May 1964). pp. 733-734: "Meeting with Hemingway" poem by Evgeny Evtushenko, reprinted from *Playboy*, X (Jan. 1963). For description of this book, see (S-B1).

SECTION G · Books on Hemingway

188 Heiney, Donald W. *Essentials of Contemporary Literature.* Woodbury, N.J.: Barron's Educational Series, 1954. pp. 35, 66, 67, 70-83, 126, 134, 187.

    pp. 70-83: "Ernest Hemingway."

189 Heiney, Donald. *Recent American Literature.* Great Neck, N.Y.: Barron's Educational Series, 1958. pp. 52, 103, 121, 148-165, 580.

    pp. 148-165: "Ernest Hemingway." Biographical commentary and a discussion of Hemingway's chief works.

190 Hellman, Lillian. *An Unfinished Woman—A Memoir.* Boston: Little, Brown, 1969. pp. 68-73, 77-81, 84, 102-104, 181. [Paperback edition: New York: Bantam Books, 1970. (No. T5458).]

    Reminiscences of Hemingway in Paris and Madrid, in 1937, and in Hollywood for the fund-raising showings of the film *The Spanish Earth.*

191 Hemingway, Leicester. *My Brother, Ernest Hemingway.* Cleveland: World, 1962. See (G188). Additional translations: (l) Translated into Portuguese by Correia Lobo. *Meu irmão Ernest Hemingway.* Lisbon: Editora Ulisseia, 1966. [Documentos do Tempo Presente, 37.] 327 pages. (m) Translated into Ukrainian by Volodymyr Brjuggen. *Mij brat, Ernest Heminguej.* Kiev: Dnipro, 1968, 163 pages. (n) Translated into Korean by Kim Byeong Cheol. *Naeui hyeong Hemingwei.* Seoul: Eulyu, 1969. 281 pages.

192 Hilton, Earl, and Darwin Shrell, eds. *Exposition: A Rhetoric and Reader with Literary Emphasis.* Belmont, Calif.: Wadsworth, 1967. pp. 91, 127, 206, 299-309.

    pp. 299-307: "Hemingway's 'Two-Hearted River' " by Sheridan Baker, reprinted from the *Michigan Alumnus Quarterly Review,* LXV (Winter 1959). See also (S-E81).

193 Himelstein, Morgan Y. *Drama Was a Weapon: The Left-Wing Theatre in New York, 1929-1941.* New Brunswick, N.J.: Rutgers University Press, 1963. pp. 146-147, 220-221.

    On the Theatre Guild's production of *The Fifth Column* in 1940.

194 Hoffman, Frederick J. *The Mortal No: Death and the Modern Imagination.* Princeton: Princeton University Press, 1964. pp. 8, 12, 150, 152-154, 162, 165-169, 171, 177, 207-209, 212, 215-219, 228-231, 234, 250, 254-256, 260, 289, 361, 363, 453, 457.

    pp. 215-219: Discussion of the quality of "abject factuality" in passages from *IOT* and *FTA.* pp. 228-231: Regarding the influence of the Spanish Civil War on Hemingway's work. p. 361: On Hemingway's style.

195 Holmes, Charles S. *The Clocks of Columbus: The Literary Career*

167

of James Thurber. New York: Atheneum, 1972. pp. 92, 95, 102-103, 129, 148, 156, 174, 194, 281-282, 287.

pp. 102-103: "A Visit from Saint Nicholas," Thurber's parody of Hemingway's style, is partially reprinted from the *New Yorker*, III (Dec. 24, 1927). p. 129: Thurber's fable of Hemingway and the "which-clause" is quoted. p. 148: Hemingway's blurb on the dust jacket of Thurber's *My Life and Hard Times* is quoted. See (F159).

196 Hoopes, Ned E., and Richard Peck, eds. *Edge of Awareness: 25 Contemporary Essays*. New York: Delacorte Press, 1966. pp. 41-47.

"Portrait of Hemingway—Preface, 1961" by Lillian Ross, reprinted from *Portrait of Hemingway*, New York, 1961, pp. 11-19.

197 Hopper, J. L., Jr. *The Sun Also Rises: Review Notes*. Boston: Ivy Notes, 1966. 55 pages.

198 Hotchner, A. E. *Papa Hemingway: A Personal Memoir*. New York: Random House, 1966. See (G198). Additional editions and translations: (b) Paperback edition: New York: Bantam Books, 1967. [No. Q-3366.] 335 pages. (c) London: Weidenfeld and Nicolson, 1966, xiv + 299 pages. (d) London: Mayflower, 1968. [A Mayflower paperback, No. 113370.] 253 pages. (e) Translated into French by Jean-René Major. Paris: Mercure de France, 1966. 381 pages. (f) Translated into Finnish by Aira Aalto. Helsinki: Weilin & Göös, 1966. 323 pages. (g) Translated into German by Paul Baudisch. Munich: R. Piper, 1966. 367 pages. (h) Translated into Danish by Knud Søgaard and Birthe Søgaard. Copenhagen: Gyldendal, 1967. 286 pages. (i) Translated into Dutch by G. Messelaar. Utrecht: Bruna, 1967. 315 pages. (j) Translated into Japanese by Nakada Kôji. Tokyo: Hayakawa shobô, 1967. 317 pages. (k) Translated into Lebanese by M. Batouti. *Bābā Hamıngway*. Beirut: Dār al-'Ādab, 1967. 384 pages. (l) Translated into Norwegian by Per Wollebaek. Oslo: Cappelen, 1967. 371 pages. (m) Translated into Swedish by Olov Jonason. Stockholm: Norstedt, 1967. 327 pages. (n) Translated into Portuguese by Carlos Barbosa de Carvalho. Lisbon: Bertrand, 1968. 411 pages. (o) Translated into Spanish by Domenec Guansé. Barcelona: Grijalbo, 1968. 319 pages. (p) Translated into Slovenian by Jože Fistrovič. Maribor: Obzorja, 1968. 308 pages.

199 Hovey, Richard B. *Hemingway: The Inward Terrain*. Foreword by Frederick C. Crews. Seattle and London: University of Washington Press, 1968. xxiv + 248 pages.

A study of Hemingway and his writings from a partly psychological viewpoint. Bibliographical Note, with a Checklist of Selected Readings, on pp. 239-241.

200 Howard, Leon. *Literature and the American Tradition*. Garden City, N.Y.: Doubleday, 1960. pp. 266, 318, 323-327, 329.

201 Howard, Michael S. *Jonathan Cape, Publisher*. London: Jonathan Cape, 1971. pp. 78-80, 110, 195, 210, 240, 244, 269, 304-305. Photograph of Hemingway opposite p. 88.

pp. 78-80: Regarding the publication of the English editions of Hemingway's books by Jonathan Cape, and Hemingway's friendship with H. Jonathan Cape from 1926 until Cape's death in 1960.

202 Howe, Irving. *Decline of the New*. New York: Harcourt, Brace and World, 1970. pp. 152, 153, 155-161, 164-166.

On Hemingway's writing and influence in "The Quest for Moral Style," reprinted from *A World More Attractive*, New York, 1963, pp. 59-76.

203 Howell, John M. *Hemingway's African Stories: The Stories, Their Sources, Their Critics*. New York: Scribner's, 1969. [Scribner Research Anthologies.] x + 169 + ix pages. For facsimile, see (S-F29₂). For work by Hemingway, see (S-B9).

pp. 1-2: Introduction by John M. Howell.

Part Three: Experience
pp. 55-59: "The Slopes of Kilimanjaro" by Carlos Baker, reprinted from *American Heritage*, xix (Aug. 1968).

pp. 60-62: "Asia Minor" by Charles A. Fenton, reprinted from *The Apprenticeship of Ernest Hemingway*, New York, 1954, pp. 178-184.

Part Four: Context
pp. 93-94: "Hemingway's Riddle of Kilimanjaro: Idea and Image" by Robert O. Stephens, reprinted from *American Literature*, xxxii (March 1960).

pp. 95-96: Excerpt from *Across East African Glaciers: An Account of the First Ascent of Kilimanjaro* by Hans Meyer, London: George Philip & Son, 1891, pp. 182-184, 273, 297.

pp. 97-98: Excerpt from *Snows on the Equator* by H. W. Tilman, New York: Macmillan, 1938, pp. 42, 171-173, 176-177.

pp. 99-100: "The Leopard of Kilimanjaro: Dr. Richard Reusch's Letter to the Editor." Reprinted in John M. Howell's "Hemingway's Riddle and Kilimanjaro's Reusch," *Studies in Short Fiction*, viii (Summer 1971).

pp. 101-109: "Vivienne de Watteville, Hemingway's Companion on Kilimanjaro" by Robert W. Lewis, Jr., reprinted from *Texas Quarterly*, ix (Winter 1966).

Part Five: Criticism
pp. 113-115: "Dangerous Game" by Carlos Baker, reprinted from *Hemingway: The Writer as Artist*, Third edition, Princeton, 1963, pp. 186-191.

pp. 116-118: "The Hero and the Code" by Philip Young, reprinted from *EH: A Reconsideration*, University Park, Pennsylvania, 1966, pp. 69-74.

pp. 119-128: "The Shorter Happy Life of Mrs. Macomber" by Warren Beck, reprinted from *Modern Fiction Studies*, I (Nov. 1955).

pp. 129-136: "Ernest Hemingway: 'The Short Happy Life of Francis Macomber' " by R. S. Crane, reprinted from *The Idea of the Humanities and Other Essays Critical and Historical*, Chicago, 1967, pp. 315-326.

pp. 137-141: "Macomber and the Critics" by Robert B. Holland, reprinted from *Studies in Short Fiction*, v (Winter 1967).

pp. 142-144: " 'The Snows of Kilimanjaro': Commentary" by Caroline Gordon and Allen Tate, reprinted from *The House of Fiction*, New York, 1950, pp. 419-423.

pp. 145-149: "The Leopard and the Hyena: Symbol and Meaning in 'The Snows of Kilimanjaro' " by Marion Montgomery, reprinted from the *University of Kansas City Review*, xxvii (Summer 1961).

pp. 150-157: " 'The Snows of Kilimanjaro': A Revaluation" by Oliver Evans, reprinted from *PMLA*, lxxvi (Dec. 1961).

pp. 158-161: " 'The Snows of Kilimanjaro': Harry's Second Chance" by Gloria R. Dussinger, reprinted from *Studies in Short Fiction*, v (Fall 1967).

pp. 162-164: "Suggested Topics for Controlled Research."

pp. 165-169: "Suggested Topics for Library Research."

204 Hyman, Stanley Edgar. *Standards: A Chronicle of Books for Our Time*. New York: Horizon Press, 1966. [A New Leader Book.] pp. 28-32, 209-213.

pp. 28-32: "The Best of Hemingway," reprinted from the *New Leader*, xliv (Aug. 14-21, 1961). pp. 209-213: "Ernest Hemingway with a Knife," review of *AMF*, reprinted from the *New Leader*, xlvii (May 11, 1964).

205 Ingersoll, R. Sturgis. *Recollections of a Philadelphian at Eighty*. Philadelphia: National Publishing Co., 1972. pp. 80-86.

"Ernest Hemingway." Reminiscences of a brief friendship with Hemingway at Sun Valley in late 1939. Note: Reviewed in *Hemingway notes*, ii (Fall 1972), p. 21.

206 Iribarren, José María. *Hemingway y los Sanfermines*. Pamplona: Editorial Gómez, 1970. [Colección Ipar, 34.] 215 pages. Photographs. Bibliography on pp. 213-215.

207 Ishi, Ichirō. *Heminguwei no Sekai*. Tokyo: Kochi Shuppansha, 1970. 295 pages.

A study of Hemingway.

208 Izzo, Carlo. *La letteratura nord-americana.* Milan: Sansoni, 1967. pp. 553, 555, 562-564, 573-576, 581, 584, 605.

    pp. 573-576: "Ernest Hemingway."

209 Jacobbi, Ruggero, ed. *Ernest Hemingway: Premio Nobel per la letteratura 1954.* Milan: Fabbri, 1968.

210 Janssens, G.A.M. *The American Literary Review: A Critical History, 1920-1950.* The Hague and Paris: Mouton, 1968. pp. 80-81, 85, 166-167, 244, 302.

211 Jobes, Katharine T., ed. *Twentieth Century Interpretations of The Old Man and the Sea: A Collection of Critical Essays.* Englewood Cliffs, N.J.: Prentice-Hall, 1968. [Spectrum Books, S-831.] vi + 120 pages.

    Contents: pp. 1-17: Introduction by Katharine T. Jobes.

    Part One: Interpretations

    pp. 18-26: "*The Old Man and the Sea*: Vision/Revision" by Philip Young, reprinted from *EH: A Reconsideration*, University Park, Pennsylvania, 1966, pp. 123-133, 274-275. Note: Title by the author.

    pp. 27-33: "The Boy and the Lions" by Carlos Baker, reprinted from *Hemingway: The Writer as Artist*, Third edition, Princeton, 1963, pp. 304-311.

    pp. 34-40: "Fakery in *The Old Man and the Sea*" by Robert P. Weeks, reprinted from *College English*, xxiv (Dec. 1962).

    pp. 41-55: "New World, Old Myths" by Claire Rosenfield. Not previously published.

    pp. 56-63: "A Ritual of Transfiguration: *The Old Man and the Sea*" by Arvin R. Wells, reprinted from the *University Review*, xxx (Winter 1963).

    pp. 64-71: "The Heroic Impulse in *The Old Man and the Sea*" by Leo Gurko, reprinted from *English Journal*, xliv (Oct. 1955).

    pp. 72-80: "*The Old Man and the Sea*: Hemingway's Tragic Vision of Man" by Clinton S. Burhans, Jr., reprinted from *American Literature,* xxxi (Jan. 1960).

    pp. 81-96: "Hemingway's Extended Vision: *The Old Man and the Sea*" by Bickford Sylvester, reprinted from *PMLA*, lxxxi (March 1966).

    pp. 97-102: "*The Old Man and the Sea* and the American Dream" by Delmore Schwartz, reprinted from *Perspectives USA*, No. 13 (Autumn 1955). Note: Editor's title.

    Part Two: View Points

    p. 103: Excerpt from " 'The American Myth': Paradise (To Be) Regained" by Frederick I. Carpenter, reprinted from *PMLA*, lxxiv (Dec. 1959), 606.

pp. 103-106: Excerpt from *Ernest Hemingway* by Earl Rovit, New York, 1963, pp. 87-90.

pp. 106-108: Excerpt from review of *OMATS* by Malcolm Cowley, reprinted from the *N.Y. Herald Tribune Book Review* (Sept. 7, 1952).

p. 108: Excerpt from *An End to Innocence* by Leslie A. Fiedler, Boston, 1955, p. 194.

pp. 108-109: Excerpt from "The Later Hemingway" by Nemi D'Agostino, reprinted from the *Sewanee Review*, LXVIII (Summer 1960).

pp. 109-110: Excerpt from review of *OMATS* by Robert Gorham Davis, reprinted from the *N.Y. Times Book Review* (Sept. 7, 1952).

pp. 110-112: Excerpt from *Image and Idea* by Philip Rahv, New York, 1957, pp. 192-195.

p. 112: Excerpt from "Hemingway" by Philip Toynbee, reprinted from *Encounter,* XVII (Oct. 1961).

pp. 112-113: Hemingway is quoted from George Plimpton's interview in the *Paris Review*, No. 18 (Spring 1958).

pp. 114-116: Chronology of Important Dates.

pp. 119-120: Selected Bibliography.

212 Joost, Nicholas. *Ernest Hemingway and the Little Magazines: The Paris Years.* Barre, Massachusetts: Barre Publishers, 1968. 186 pages.

A study of Hemingway's contributions during 1922-1925 in the *Double Dealer, Little Review, Poetry: A Magazine of Verse, Der Querschnitt, This Quarter,* and *Transatlantic Review.*

213 Josephson, Matthew. *Life Among the Surrealists: A Memoir.* New York: Holt, Rinehart and Winston, 1962. pp. 7-9, 89-90, 241, 312, 315, 317-321.

pp. 317-321: Regarding the real-life counterparts of characters in *SAR.*

214 Josephson, Matthew. *Infidel in the Temple: A Memoir of the Nineteen-Thirties.* New York: Knopf, 1967. pp. 414, 416-435, 477.

pp. 416-435: Ch. Twenty: "Hemingway Goes to Spain." Reminiscences of Hemingway in Key West during the winter of 1936-1937.

215 Kane, Thomas S., and Leonard J. Peters, eds. *Expository Prose.* London: Oxford University Press, 1966. pp. 122, 257-261, 274, 326, 338, 505.

p. 122: On *AMF.* pp. 257-261, 505: On *FTA.*

216 Kanin, Garson. *Tracy and Hepburn: An Intimate Memoir.* New York: Viking Press, 1971. pp. 32, 224-226.

On the lack of rapport between Spencer Tracy and Hemingway during the filming of *OMATS,* in 1957.

217 Kann, Hans-Joachim. *Übersetzungsprobleme in den deutschen Übersetzungen von drei anglo-amerikanischen Kurzgeschichten*: *Aldous Huxleys "Green Tunnels," Ernest Hemingways "The Killers" und "A Clean, Well-Lighted Place."* Munich: Max Hueber Verlag, 1968. [Mainzer amerikanistische Beiträge, X.] 143 pages.

218 Kaplan, Harold. *The Passive Voice: An Approach to Modern Fiction.* Athens: Ohio University Press, 1966. pp. 17, 93-110, 120, 133*n.*, 173.

    pp. 93-110: "Hemingway and the Passive Hero."

219 Kaplan, Martin, ed. *The Harvard Lampoon Centennial Celebration, 1876-1973.* Boston and Toronto: Little, Brown, 1973. [An Atlantic Monthly Press Book.] p. 121.

    "Winner Take Headache-Powders by Ernest Hemingway."

220 Karsh, Yousuf. *Karsh Portfolio.* London: Thomas Nelson, 1967. pp. 81-83. Photograph.

    Regarding the frequently reproduced photograph of Hemingway taken by Karsh in 1957.

221 Kashkin, Ivan. *Ernest Khemingueĭ: kritiko-biograficeskij ocherk.* Moscow: Khudozhestvennaya Literatura Publishing House, 1966. 295 pages. Photographs. Preface by E. Golyseva, on pp. 3-6. For letters from Hemingway to the author, see (S-F79) and (S-F91).

222 Kawin, Bruce F. *Telling It Again and Again: Repetition in Literature and Film.* Ithaca and London: Cornell University Press, 1972. pp. 23-26, 31, 32.

    On Hemingway's constructive use of repetition.

223 Kazin, Alfred. *Bright Book of Life: American Novelists and Storytellers from Hemingway to Mailer.* Boston: Atlantic-Little, Brown, 1973. pp. 3-20, 23, 25, 71, 74, 75, 93, 105, 149, 151, 297, 302.

    pp. 3-20: Ch. 1: "A Dream of Order: Hemingway."

224 Keats, John. *You Might As Well Live: The Life and Times of Dorothy Parker.* New York: Simon and Schuster, 1970. pp. 80, 97-98, 113-114, 129, 142, 150-151, 220, 222, 296, 304. Photograph.

    p. 109: Regarding Dorothy Parker's first meeting with Hemingway, in New York in February 1926. pp. 113-114: Regarding the poem about Dorothy Parker that Hemingway read at a party in Paris, in October 1926. Donald Ogden Stewart found the poem objectionable.

225 Kenchoshvili, I. A. *Novella Khemingueia.* Tbilisi, USSR, 1965. [Tbilisskii gosudarstvennyĭ universitet.] 21 pages. Bibliography on p. 21.

226 Kenner, Hugh. *The Pound Era.* Berkeley and Los Angeles: University of California Press, 1971. pp. 20, 363, 387-388, 527-528.

227 Kermode, Frank. *Continuities.* London: Routledge & Kegan Paul, 1968. [New York: Random House, 1969.] pp. 161-167.
"Hemingway's Last Novel," review of *AMF*, reprinted from the *New York Review of Books*, II (June 11, 1964).

228 Kim, Pyŏng-ch'ŏl. *Hemingwei nunhak ŭi yŏn'gu.* Seoul, 1968. 533 pages.

229 Kim, Pyŏng-ch'ŏl. *Hemingwei chŏn'gi.* Seoul, 1970. 383 pages. Photographs.

230 Klibbe, Lawrence. *Ernest Hemingway's A Farewell to Arms: A Critical Commentary.* New York: Monarch Press, 1964. [Monarch Notes and Study Guide, No. 671.] 58 pages.

231 Klibbe, Lawrence. *Ernest Hemingway's For Whom the Bell Tolls: A Critical Commentary.* New York: Monarch Press, 1965. [Monarch Notes and Study Guide, No. 672.] 48 pages.

232 Klibbe, Lawrence. *Ernest Hemingway's The Sun Also Rises: A Critical Commentary.* New York: Monarch Press, 1965. [Monarch Notes and Study Guide, No. 674.] 76 pages.

233 Klimo, Vernon (Jake), and Will Oursler. *Hemingway and Jake: An Extraordinary Friendship.* Garden City, N.Y.: Doubleday, 1972. xiii + 245 pages. [Paperback edition: New York: Popular Library, 1972. 223 pages.]
Recollections of Hemingway (Stein) in Key West and Cuba, in the 1930s, by a friend of Hemingway's brother, Leicester (Hank).

234 Köpeczi, Béla, and Péter Juhász, eds. *Littérature et réalité.* Budapest: Akadémiai Könyvkiadó, 1966. pp. 246-263.
"Hemingway and the New Realism" by György Bodnár.

235 Kopelev, Lev Zalmanovich. *Serdtse vsegda sleva.* Moscow, 1960. pp. 200-239.
"Naperekor otchaianiiu i smerti (Ernest Kheminguei)" [In opposition to disillusionment and death (Ernest Hemingway)].

236 Kopp, Richard. *Der Alte Mann und das Meer: Versuch einer Analyse.* Munich, 1964.

237 Kristensen, Sven Møller, ed. *Fremmede digtere i det 20. ärhundrede.* Vol. II. Copenhagen: G.E.C. Gads Forlag, 1968. pp. 257-278, 624-625. Photographs.
pp. 257-278: "Ernest Hemingway" by Klaus Rifbjerg. pp. 624-625: List of translations of Hemingway's works into Danish.

238 Kronenberger, Louis, and Emily Morison Beck, eds. *Atlantic Brief Lives: A Biographical Companion to the Arts.* Boston: Little, Brown, 1971. pp. 359-361.

   p. 359: Biographical note. pp. 359-361: "Ernest Hemingway" by Robert Manning.

239 Kuehl, John, and Jackson R. Bryer, eds. *Dear Scott | Dear Max: The Fitzgerald-Perkins Correspondence.* New York: Scribner's, 1971. pp. 9-10, 78, 95, 104-106, 126-137, 139, 142, 144, 145, 147, 148, 157-161, 165, 167-170, 172-178, 180, 194, 213, 217-219, 223-226, 231, 232, 236-245, 247, 248, 252-253, 255, 261-268.

   p. 78: F. Scott Fitzgerald's letter [ca. October 10, 1924] telling Maxwell Perkins about "a young man named Ernest Hemmingway, who lives in Paris." pp. 126-137: Letters regarding Hemingway's contract with Liveright and his subsequent arrangements with Scribner's. p. 231: Fitzgerald's letter, of September 19, 1936, regarding Hemingway's use of "poor old Scott" in "The Snows of Kilimanjaro." pp. 238-240: Maxwell Perkins's description of the Hemingway-Eastman "altercation," in a letter dated August 24, 1937.

240 Kumar, Shiv K., and Keith F. McKean. *Critical Approaches to Fiction.* New York: McGraw-Hill, 1968. pp. 9, 39-41, 118, 148, 171, 173, 186, 197, 204-207, 262-263, 281-283, 320.

241 Kunzweiler, Diana. *Ernest Hemingway's A Farewell to Arms: A Critical Commentary.* New York: American R.D.M. Corporation, 1967. [A Study Master Publication.] 55 pages.

242 Kvam, Wayne E. *Hemingway in Germany: The Fiction, the Legend, and the Critics.* Athens: Ohio University Press, 1973. x + 214 pages.

   A study of the German critical reaction to Hemingway's books, with excerpts (translated into English) from articles and reviews. An Epilogue covers the reassessment of the Hemingway legend between 1965 and 1971. The Selected Bibliography, on pp. 185-208, includes a list of German dissertations on Hemingway, on pp. 204-205.

243 Landis, Arthur H. *The Abraham Lincoln Brigade.* New York: Citadel Press, 1967. Photograph. pp. xvi, 306, 327-329, 376, 440, 496-497, 500-574.

   p. xvi: Hemingway is quoted regarding the 11th Brigade.

244 Laney, Al. *Paris Herald: The Incredible Newspaper.* New York and London: Appleton-Century, 1947. pp. 4, 152, 159-160, 163-164.

   On Hemingway in Paris in the 1920s.

245 Lanzinger, Klaus, ed. *Americana-Austriaca: Festschrift des Amerika-Instituts der Universität Innsbruck anlasslich seines zehnjahrigen Bestehens.* Vol. 1. Vienna and Stuttgart: Wilhelm Braumüller, 1966. pp. 229-246.

"Aspects of American Fiction: A Whale, a Bear, and a Marlin" by Herbert Wilner. Examines Herman Melville's *Moby Dick*, William Faulkner's "The Bear," and *OMATS*.

246 Lanzinger, Klaus, ed. *Americana-Austriaca: Beiträge zur Amerika-kunde*. Vol. II. Vienna: Wilhelm Braumüller, 1970. pp. 3-14, 30-44.

pp. 3-14: "Hemingway's 'Moment of Truth' " by John R. Dunbar. Examines Hemingway's novels "as love stories on a primitive level." pp. 30-44: "Responses of German Men of Letters to American Literature, 1945-1955" by Joseph J. Keviat and Gerhard Weiss. General article. Discusses Hemingway's influence on the postwar German short story.

247 Lash, Joseph P. *Eleanor and Franklin*. New York: W. W. Norton, 1971. pp. 431, 482, 567.

pp. 482, 567: References to Eleanor Roosevelt's encouragement of the romance between her friend Martha Gellhorn and Hemingway. p. 567: Regarding the showing of *The Spanish Earth* at the White House, in July 1937. The Roosevelts "wanted the film to be made stronger." See (H311).

248 Latham, Aaron. *Crazy Sundays: F. Scott Fitzgerald in Hollywood*. New York: Viking Press, 1970. pp. 19-21, 177-179, 201.

pp. 177-179: Charles M. Warren's account of a visit Hemingway made to Fitzgerald, in Hollywood, during the time he was writing *FWBT*. Note: For Sheilah Graham's denial that Hemingway visited Fitzgerald in Hollywood, see "Scott Fitzgerald Legend a Bonanza for Literary Set," *Variety* (Jan. 3, 1972), pp. 5, 62.

249 Leavis, F. R., ed. *A Selection from Scrutiny*. Vol. II. Cambridge: Cambridge University Press, 1968. pp. 89-97.

"Hollywooden Hero" by W. H. Mellers, review of the *First 49*, reprinted from *Scrutiny*, VIII (Dec. 1939).

250 Ledig-Rowohlt, H. M. *Meeting Two American Giants: Marginal Notes*. Reinbek: Rowohlt, 1962. pp. 29-35.

"Death in the Morning." Regarding the friendship between Hemingway and his German publisher, Ernst Rowohlt, and reminiscences of the two occasions when the author met Hemingway, in the thirties and in Paris in November 1959. Originally published in German in *Die Zeit*, XVI (July 14, 1961). Three letters to Ernst Rowohlt are quoted, see (S-F68), (S-F70), and (S-F97). Note: This booklet also contains an essay on Thomas Wolfe.

251 Lehan, Richard D. *F. Scott Fitzgerald and the Craft of Fiction*. Carbondale and Edwardsville: Southern Illinois University Press/London and Amsterdam: Feffer & Simons, 1966. [Crosscurrents/Modern Critiques.] pp. 36, 39-45, 48, 52, 151, 168.

pp. 39-45, 48: Comparison of the Fitzgerald hero, who is a hopeless Romantic, and the Hemingway hero, who "pits his will against an indifferent universe."

252 Lehan, Richard. *A Dangerous Crossing: French Literary Existentialism and the Modern American Novel.* Carbondale and Edwardsville: Southern Illinois University Press/London and Amsterdam: Feffer & Simons, 1973. [Crosscurrents/Modern Critiques.] pp. xiv, xvi, 35-38, 46-56, 60-61, 68.

pp. 35-79: Ch. 3: "French and American Literary Existentialism: Dos Passos, Hemingway, Faulkner." Discusses *FTA, SAR, THAHN, FWBT,* and *Islands,* on pp. 46-56.

253 Leipold, L. E. *Famous American Fiction Writers.* Minneapolis: T. S. Denison, 1972. pp. 69-75.
"Ernest Hemingway: Nobel Prize Winner."

254 Levidova, Nina Mikhailovna, and B. M. Parchevskaia. *Ernest Kheminguei̇̆: Bio-bibliograficeskij ukazatel.* Moscow: Kniga, 1970. [Vsesoiuznaia gosudarstvennaia biblioteka inostrannoĭ literatury.] 144 pages. Preface by N. M. Levidova on pp. 5-23. Bibliography on pp. 24-120.

255 Levin, Martin, ed. *The Saturday Review Sampler of Wit and Wisdom.* New York: Simon and Schuster, 1966. pp. 288-294.
"Havana" by Mary Hemingway, reprinted from the *Saturday Review,* XLVIII (Jan. 2, 1965).

256 Levin, Meyer. *In Search: An Autobiography.* Paris: Author's Press, 1950. pp. 39, 112, 114, 116, 125-126.
pp. 125-126: Regarding Hemingway's writing for *Ken* (called here *Inside*).

257 Levine, David. *Pens and Needles.* Literary caricatures by David Levine. Selected and Introduced by John Updike. Boston: Gambit, 1969. pp. 16, 17. [Paperback edition: New York: Liveright, 1973. p. (12).]
p. 16: Caricature of Hemingway and F. Scott Fitzgerald. p. 17: Caricature of Hemingway standing, with gun, over a second Hemingway. Note: Also published in a limited, signed edition of 300 copies.

258 Libman, Valentina A. *Russian Studies of American Literature: A Bibliography.* Chapel Hill: University of North Carolina Press, 1969. Edited by Clarence Gohdes. Translated by Robert V. Allen. pp. 30, 33, 37, 38, 95-102.
pp. 95-102: Checklist of 115 items on Hemingway between 1929 and 1963. Note: No items are listed between 1939 and 1955.

259 [*Life*]. *Ernest Hemingway* / *William Faulkner*. New York: *Life* Educational Reprint Program, [1968]. [*Life* Educational Reprint, 6.] pp. 15-24. 13 3/4 x 10 1/2. Photographs.

    pp. 15-21: "Hemingway: Driving Force of a Great Artist," photographic essay reprinted from *Life*, LI (July 14, 1961). pp. 22-23: "His Mirror Was Danger" by Archibald MacLeish, reprinted from *Life*, LI (July 14, 1961). p. 23: "How Hemingway works" by Malcolm Cowley, excerpt from "A Portrait of Mister Papa," reprinted from *Life*, XXV (Jan. 10, 1949). p. 24: "Our Warmest Memories of Hemingway," editor's note reprinted from *Life*, LI (July 14, 1961). Several letters from Hemingway to Sidney James, in 1952, are quoted regarding publication of *OMATS* in *Life*.

260 Linn, James Weber, and Houghton Wells Taylor. *A Foreword to Fiction*. New York and London: Appleton-Century, 1935. pp. 25, 36-37, 89, 90, 109, 110, 112-113.

    pp. 112-113; Discussion on Hemingway's style.

261 Lins, Álvaro. *O Relógio e o Quadrante: Obras, Autores e Problemas de Literatura Estrangeira*. Rio de Janeiro: Editôra Civilização Brasileira, 1964. pp. 67-74.

    Ch. 5: "Aventura Pessoal e Ordenação Literária." Essay on Hemingway, dated June 1942.

262 Liptzin, Sol. *The Jew in American Literature*. New York: Bloch, 1966. pp. 153-156.

    Robert Cohn in *SAR* is described as "an unpleasant, ridiculous figure." Hutchins Hapgood's letter to Hemingway, regarding Cohn, is quoted from *A Victorian in the Modern World*, New York, 1939, p. 535.

263 Lodge, David. *The Novelist at the Crossroads and Other Essays on Fiction and Criticism*. Ithaca, N.Y.: Cornell University Press, 1971. pp. 184-202, 288-289.

    pp. 184-202: Ch. 10: "Hemingway's Clean, Well-lighted, Puzzling Place," reprinted from *Essays in Criticism*, XXI (Jan. 1971).

264 Longstreet, Stephen. *We All Went to Paris: Americans in the City of Light: 1776-1971*. New York: Macmillan, 1972. pp. 15, 18, 242, 243, 250, 252, 253, 274, 307-316, 320-321, 347, 353, 372, 374, 377.

    pp. 307-314: Ch. 38: "Hem."

265 Longyear, Christopher Rudston. *Linguistically Determined Categories of Meanings: A Comparative Analysis of Meaning in "The Snows of Kilimanjaro."* The Hague and Paris: Mouton, 1971. [Janua linguarum. Series practica, 92.] 138 pages. [New York: Humanities Press, 1971.]

266 Lupan, Radu. *Hemingway, Scriitorul*. Bucharest: Editura Pentru Literatură Universală, 1966. 397 pages. Selected Bibliography on pp. 371-378. Chronology on pp. 379-384. An excerpt, in English, appeared in *Literary Review*, x (Winter 1966-1967).

267 Lutwack, Leonard. *Heroic Fiction: The Epic Tradition and American Novels of the Twentieth Century*. Carbondale and Edwardsville: Southern Illinois University Press/London and Amsterdam: Feffer & Simons, 1971. [Crosscurrents/Modern Critiques.] pp. 22, 26, 64-87, 111, 142, 143, 145, 154.
   pp. 64-87: *"For Whom the Bell Tolls."*

268 Lynen, John F. *The Design of the Present: Essays on Time and Form in American Literature*. New Haven and London: Yale University Press, 1969. pp. 40, 153, 169, 188, 192, 196, 289.

269 Lytle, Andrew. *The Hero with the Private Parts: Essays*. Baton Rouge: Louisiana State University Press, 1966. pp. 95-99.
   "A Moveable Feast: The Going To and Fro," reprinted from the *Sewanee Review*, LXXIII (Spring 1965).

270 McAlmon, Robert. *Being Geniuses Together: 1920-1930*. Revised and with supplementary chapters by Kay Boyle. New York: Doubleday, 1968. pp. 175-182, 249, 273-277, 346. Photograph. Kay Boyle's reminiscences of Hemingway on pp. 114-115, 201, 204-205, 351-352. See (G253).

271 McBratnie, Betty. *Hemingway for the Young*. [Key West, Fla.: Florida Keys Star, 1969.] 28 pages. Sketches by John H. Hooton. Juvenile biography.

272 McCaffery, John K. M., ed. *Ernest Hemingway: The Man and His Work*. New York: Cooper Square Publishers, 1969. Reissued. 352 pages. For contents, see 1950 edition (G255).

273 McCormick, John, and Mario Sevilla Mascareñas. *The Complete Aficionado*. Cleveland: World, 1967. pp. 31, 50, 78, 231, 232, 235-246, 251, 257.
   p. 31 *et passim*: References to *DIA*. pp. 235-246: On Hemingway's influence on the fiction of toreo (bullfighting), including a discussion of *SAR* and "The Undefeated."

274 McCormick, John. *The Middle Distance: A Comparative History of American Imaginative Literature: 1919-1932*. New York: Free Press, 1971. pp. 1-5, 42-74, 105, 123, 180, 196, 204, 208, 210, 212-213.
   pp. 42-60: "The Useable Present." Essay on the "critical fury" over Hemingway. pp. 61-74: "The Romantic Warriors." On the parallels between Hemingway and Henry de Montherlant.

275 MacLeish, Archibald. *A Continuing Journey.* Boston: Houghton Mifflin, 1968. pp. 307-312.

"Ernest Hemingway, 1961." This essay originally appeared in *Life,* LI (July 14, 1961), under the title "His Mirror Was Danger."

276 MacLeish, Archibald. *The Human Season: Selected Poems, 1926-1972.* Boston: Houghton Mifflin, 1972. p. 42.

"Hemingway" ["In some inexplicable way an accident." *Mary Hemingway*], reprinted from the *Atlantic,* ccviii (Nov. 1961), where it appeared under the title "The Gunshot."

277 McLendon, James. *Papa: Hemingway in Key West.* Miami, Fla.: E. A. Seemann, 1972. 222 pages. Photographs. [Paperback edition: New York: Popular Library, 1972. 222 pages. Photographs.]

An account of the years 1928 to 1940 when Hemingway lived in Key West. Includes reminiscences of Hemingway by Charles and Lorine Thompson and Toby Bruce. pp. 155, 174: Regarding the real-life models for the characters in *THAHN.*

278 MacLennan, Hugh. *Thirty & Three.* Edited by Dorothy Duncan. Toronto: Macmillan, 1954. pp. 85-96.

Ch. Eleven: "Homage to Hemingway." Not previously published.

279 MacShane, Frank. *The Life and Work of Ford Madox Ford.* London: Routledge & Kegan Paul, 1965. [New York: Horizon Press, 1965.] pp. 152, 155, 157-161, 163, 164, 179, 192, 196, 215.

157-161: Regarding Hemingway's role in the editing of the *Transatlantic Review.*

280 Madden, Charles F., ed. *Talks With Authors.* Carbondale and Edwardsville: Southern Illinois University Press/London and Amsterdam: Feffer & Simons, 1968. pp. xv, 73-88.

pp. 73-88: "Carlos Baker on Hemingway." Dated: March 9, 1964. A short talk on *FTA*, followed by questions and answers.

281 Madden, David, ed. *Tough Guy Writers of the Thirties.* With a Preface by Harry T. Moore. Carbondale and Edwardsville: Southern Illinois University Press/London and Amsterdam: Feffer & Simons, 1968. [Crosscurrents/Modern Critiques.] pp. xxi-xxiii, xxxii, 18-50, 89, 90, 102, 129-131, 227, 239*n.*, 240*n.*

pp. 18-41: "The Tough Hemingway and His Hard-Boiled Children" by Sheldon Norman Grebstein. pp. 42-50: "Focus on *To Have and Have Not*: To Have Not: Tough Luck" by Philip Young.

282 Madden, David, ed. *American Dreams, American Nightmares.* Carbondale and Edwardsville: Southern Illinois University Press/London and Amsterdam: Feffer & Simons, 1970. [Crosscurrents/Modern Critiques.] pp. 24, 26-27, 45, 49-51, 73-75, 197.

pp. 73-75: Discussion of the Hemingway code, "as a *show* of physical and occasional mental endurance . . . a compulsive dream of health," in Irving Malin's essay "The Compulsive Design."

283 *Maekawa Shun'ichi Kyōju Kanreki Kinen rombun shū.* [Essays and Studies in Commemoration of Professor Shun'ichi Maekawa's Sixty-first Birthday.] Tokyo: Eihōsha, 1968. pp. 165-176, 229-239. In Japanese.

pp. 165-176: "Macomber and Lion and Theme" by Muneyoshi Kato. pp. 229-239: "The Style of Hemingway's Short Stories" by Tadashi Watanabe.

284 Magny, Claude-Edmonde. *The Age of the American Novel: The Film Aesthetic of Fiction Between the Two Wars.* New York: Frederick Ungar, 1972. pp. 3, 26n., 40, 48, 65, 110, 142, 144-160, 162. Translated from the French by Eleanor Hochman. See (G269).

pp. 144-160: Ch. 7: "Hemingway, or the Exaltation of the Moment."

285 Maiants, Zil'ma. *Chelovek odin ne mozhet . . . Ernest Kheminguei: Zhizn' e tvorchestvo.* Moscow, 1966. 309 pages.

On the life and works of Hemingway.

286 Mailer, Norman. *Cannibals and Christians.* New York: Dial Press, 1966. pp. xi, 99, 156-159, 270-271.

pp. 156-159: "Punching Papa: A Review of *That Summer in Paris.*" Discusses Morley Callaghan's account of his boxing match with Hemingway, in Paris in June of 1929, when F. Scott Fitzgerald let one round go for four minutes.

287 Maini, Darshan Singh, ed. *Variations on American Literature.* New Delhi: U.S. Educational Foundation in India, 1968. pp. 76-92.

pp. 76-85: "The World and Experience of the Hemingway Hero" by S. P. Das. pp. 86-88: "The Style of Ernest Hemingway" by Vishaw M. Kapoor. pp. 89-92: "*The Old Man and the Sea*: A Reading" by Jai S. Gahlot.

288 Mantle, Burns, ed. *The Best Plays of 1939-40: And the Year Book of the Drama in America.* New York: Dodd, Mead, 1949. pp. 9, 442.

p. 442: Production details, cast, and synopsis of *The Fifth Column.*

289 Matthews, Herbert L. *A World in Revolution: A Newspaperman's Memoir.* New York: Scribner's, 1971. pp. 11, 23-25, 28-30, 34, 35, 41, 69, 320-321, 432-433.

pp. 23-25: Regarding his friendship with Hemingway, whom he met in Madrid in March 1937. pp. 432-433: Hemingway's blurb for the dust jacket of Matthews' *Two Wars and More to Come,* New York, 1938, is quoted; including the original last sentence: "I hope his office will keep some uncut copies of his despatches in case he dies." See (S-F176).

290 Matthews, Herbert L. *Half of Spain Died: A Reappraisal of the Spanish Civil War.* New York: Scribner's, 1973. pp. 12, 14, 120-121, 195, 202, 207-208, 211, 216. Photograph (No. 18) of Herbert Matthews and Hemingway in Madrid, in 1937.

291 Maxwell, D.E.S. *American Fiction: The Intellectual Background.* New York: Columbia University Press/London: Routledge & Kegan Paul, 1963. pp. 268-269.

292 Mayfield, Sara. *Exiles from Paradise: Zelda and Scott Fitzgerald.* New York: Delacorte Press, 1971. pp. 90-94, 105-110, 112-114, 119, 133, 135-137, 140-143, 149, 155-156, 160, 162, 164, 186, 200, 203-204, 209, 217-218, 236, 250, 276-277.

p. 133: Regarding the Hemingways' visit to Ellerslie, the Fitzgeralds' home in Maryland.

293 Meacham, Harry M. *The Caged Panther: Ezra Pound at Saint Elizabeths.* New York: Twayne, 1967. pp. 39, 53, 55-56, 61-62, 65, 94, 96, 113, 117-120, 122-123, 131, 158.

pp. 118-119: Regarding the Frost-Eliot-Hemingway letter, dated January 14, 1957, which was drafted by Archibald MacLeish and sent to the Attorney General of the United States, urging Ezra Pound's release from Saint Elizabeths Hospital. p. 53: A Hemingway letter to Dorothy Pound is quoted regarding his comment on Pound in *Time*, LXIV (Dec. 13, 1954).

294 Mendel'son, Moris Osipovich. *Sovremennaia amerikanskaia literatura.* Moscow, 1962. pp. 111-156.
"Tragediia Khemingueia."

295 Meriwether, James B., and Michael Millgate, eds. *Lion in the Garden: Interviews with William Faulkner, 1926-1962.* New York: Random House, 1968. pp. 21, 58, 78, 81, 88-89, 91, 101, 104, 107, 121-122, 137-138, 179, 225.

p. 58: During an interview in 1947, Faulkner rated Hemingway last in a list of his five most important contemporaries. pp. 137-138: During an interview in Japan, in 1955, Faulkner discussed Hemingway's style.

296 [Methuen]. *Notes on Hemingway's The Old Man and the Sea.* London: Methuen, 1967. [Study-Aid Series.] iv + 36 pages. "Test-yourself" Questions (with answers) on pp. 17-21.

297 Michener, James A. *Iberia: Spanish Travels and Reflections.* New York: Random House, 1968. pp. 51, 285, 289, 490-502, 570, 642.

pp. 490-502: "Colloquium on Hemingway." Regarding A. E. Hotchner's *Papa Hemingway*.

298 Milford, Nancy. *Zelda: A Biography*. New York: Harper & Row, 1970. pp. xiii, 113-117, 119, 121-122, 139, 148-149, 153-156, 287, 347.

pp. 113-117: Regarding the Fitzgeralds' meeting with Ernest and Hadley Hemingway in Paris in 1925. p. 119: Regarding the Hemingways' joining the Fitzgeralds on the Riviera, in May 1926.

299 Milic, Louis T. *Stylists on Style: A Handbook with Selections for Analysis*. New York: Scribner's, 1969. pp. 15, 41, 230, 259, 285-287, 341, 379, 382, 454, 468, 476, 478-486, 498.

pp. 478-484: "Hemingway." Annotation of the selection from *DIA*, see (S-E128).

300 Miller, James E., Jr., and Bernice Slote, eds. *The Dimensions of the Short Story: A Critical Anthology*. New York: Dodd, Mead, 1964. pp. 531-533.

"Symmetry in 'Cat in the Rain' " by John V. Hagopian, reprinted from *College English*, xxiv (Dec. 1962). See also (S-E53).

301 Mizener, Arthur. *Twelve Great American Novels*. New York: New American Library, 1967. pp. 8, 21, 120-141.

pp. 120-141: [Ch. 9]: "Ernest Hemingway: *The Sun Also Rises*."

302 Mizener, Arthur. *The Saddest Story: A Biography of Ford Madox Ford*. New York and Cleveland: World, 1971. pp. 208, 330-335, 339-344, 347, 355-356, 416, 417, 519.

pp. 330-335, 339-344: Regarding Hemingway's sub-editorship on the *Transatlantic Review*. p. 333: Regarding Ford and Stella Bowen as "Braddocks" and "Mrs. Braddocks" in *SAR*.

303 Mizener, Arthur. *Scott Fitzgerald and His World*. New York: G. P. Putnam's, 1972. Photograph of Hemingway on p. 77.

pp. 45, 62, 68, 73, 77-78, 109, 114, 115.

304 Montgomery, Marion. *The Reflective Journey Toward Order: Essays on Dante, Wordsworth, Eliot, and Others*. Athens, Ga.: University of Georgia Press, 1973. pp. 283-295.

"Emotion Recollected in Tranquility," reprinted from the *Southern Review*, vi (July 1970). Examines *A Moveable Feast*.

305 Moore, Harry T. *Age of the Modern and Other Literary Essays*. Carbondale and Edwardsville: Southern Illinois University Press/ London and Amsterdam: Feffer & Simons, 1971. [Crosscurrents/ Modern Critiques.] pp. x, xvii-xix, 23-27, 47, 78, 86, 89-91, 124, 129.

pp. 23-27: Ch. 7: "An Ernest Hemingwaiad," an essay in verse form, reprinted from *Encounter*, x (June 1958). Note: The spelling has been changed from "Earnest" to "Ernest." pp. 89-91: Ch. 19:

"Hemingway and a Chronology without Characterization," review of Carlos Baker's *EH: A Life Story*, reprinted from the *Chicago Daily News* (April 5, 1969).

306 Morehead, Albert H., Harold J. Blum, et al. *100 Great American Novels*. New York: New American Library, 1966. [A Signet Book.] pp. 53, 269, 284-296, 448, 628-630, 640.

pp. 284-296: "Ernest Hemingway." Biographical note on pp. 284-285. Plot summary of *SAR* on pp. 285-288. Plot summary of *FTA* on pp. 288-291. Plot summary of *FWBT* on pp. 292-296.

307 Mudrick, Marvin. *On Culture and Literature*. New York: Horizon Press, 1970. pp. 9, 117-127, 178, 180, 199.

pp. 117-127: "Hemingway," revised essay on *AMF*; originally published in *Hudson Review,* XVII (Winter 1964-1965).

308 Murphy, Geraldine. *The Study of Literature in High School*. Waltham, Mass.: Blaisdell, 1968. pp. 324, 380, 388, 393, 402, 404.

p. 324: On "My Old Man." p. 380: On "Soldier's Home." p. 388: On ,"The Killers." p. 393: On "A Clean, Well-Lighted Place." pp. 402, 404: On "In Another Country."

309 Murray, Edward. *The Cinematic Imagination: Writers and the Motion Pictures*. New York: Frederick Ungar, 1972. pp. 113, 115, 165n., 218-243, 254, 263, 291, 292.

pp. 218-243: Ch. 16: "Ernest Hemingway—Cinematic Structure in Fiction and Problems in Adaptation."

310 Muste, John M. *Say That We Saw Spain Die: Literary Consequences of the Spanish Civil War*. Seattle: University of Washington Press, 1966. pp. 18, 28, 31, 44-46, 60-68, 90-119, 134, 142, 153, 161-163, 188.

pp. 60-68: Regarding *The Fifth Column*. pp. 90-119: Regarding *FWBT*. pp. 161-163: Discusses "Hemingway's one truly successful work about the Spanish Civil War," "Old Man at the Bridge."

311 Nabuco, Carolina. *Panorama da literatura estrangeira contemporanea*. Rio de Janeiro: Academia Brasileira de Letras, 1943. pp. 399-413.

"Literatura dos Estados Unidos." Includes discussion of *FWBT*.

312 Nabuco, Carolina. *Retrato dos Estados Unidos à luz da sua literatura*. Rio de Janeiro: Livraria José Olympio Editôra, 1967. pp. 76, 132, 136, 188-192, 194.

313 Nahal, Chaman. *The Narrative Pattern in Ernest Hemingway's Fiction*. Rutherford, N.J.: Fairleigh Dickinson University Press, 1971. 245 pages. Appendix on *Islands*, on pp. 211-223. Selected Bibliography on pp. 235-242.

314 Nelson, Gerald B. *Ten Versions of America*. New York: Knopf, 1972. pp. 23-42.
"Jake Barnes."

315 [Nobel Foundation and the Swedish Academy, published under the sponsorship of.] *Nobel Prize Library: Ernest Hemingway | Knut Hamsun | Hermann Hesse*. New York: Alexis Gregory/Del Mar, Calif.: CRM Publishing, 1971. pp. 3-115. Frontispiece: Etching of Hemingway. *OMATS* and *FTA* illustrated by Robert Shore. *SAR* illustrated by John Groth.

pp. 3-6: Presentation Address by Anders Österling. p. 7: Acceptance Speech by Hemingway. pp. 103-111: "The Life and Works of Ernest Hemingway" by John Brown. pp. 113-115: "The 1954 Prize" by Kjell Strömberg. Translated by Dale McAdoo. See also (S-E166).

316 Noble, David W. *The Eternal Adam and the New World Garden: The Central Myth in the American Novel Since 1830*. New York: George Braziller, 1968. pp. 145-153, 163, 164.

pp. 145-153: A discussion of the Nick Adams stories in *IOT* as related to the central myth: the transcendence of time.

317 North, Joseph, ed. *New Masses: An Anthology of the Rebel Thirties*. New York: International Publishers, 1969. Introduction by Maxwell Geismar. pp. 9, 10, 21, 28-29, 213, 231, 248-254, 308.

pp. 248-254: "Hemingway's Development," review of the *First 49* by Edwin Berry Burgum, reprinted from the *New Masses*, XXIX (Nov. 22, 1938). See (H382). For work by Hemingway, see (S-B7).

318 Oag, Shay. *In the Presence of Death: Antonio Ordóñez*. New York: Coward-McCann, 1969. pp. 15, 66, 74, 120, 129, 152, 155-156, 158, 159, 162, 169, 171-173, 183, 235-236. Photographs.

p. 66: Regarding Ordóñez's father, the bullfighter Niño de la Palma, who was the model for "Pedro Romero" in *SAR*. p. 74: Regarding Niño de la Palma in *DIA*. p. 120: Regarding Hemingway's first meeting with Ordóñez in July 1953. pp. 172-173: On Hemingway's "unjust" treatment of Luis Miguel Dominguín in "The Dangerous Summer."

319 O'Connor, Richard. *Ernest Hemingway*. New York: McGraw-Hill, 1972. [American Writers Series.] 144 pages. Foreword by Carlos Baker. Frontispiece drawing of Hemingway by George Sottung. Juvenile biography.

320 O'Connor, William Van, ed. *Modern Prose: Form and Style*. New York: Crowell, 1959. pp. 124-126.

Review of *FTA*, reprinted from the *Times Literary Supplement* (Nov. 28, 1929). Exercises on p. 126.

321 Orlova, Raisa. [*The Work of Ernest Hemingway.*] Novosibirsk, 1968. In Russian. An English translation appears in Carl R. Proffer's *Soviet Criticism of American Literature in the Sixties*, Ann Arbor, Michigan, 1972, pp. 117-148, under the title *"For Whom the Bell Tolls."*

322 Parker, Dorothy. *Constant Reader.* New York: Viking Press, 1970. pp. 14-17, 37, 56, 66-68, 78, 114, 135.

   pp. 14-17: "A Book of Great Short Stories," review of *MWW*, reprinted from the *New Yorker*, III (Oct. 29, 1927). Note: The reviewer is not identified under (H81). pp. 66-68: "Excuse It, Please," reprinted from the *New Yorker*, III (Feb. 18, 1928). Regarding her statement in the review of *MWW* that Hemingway was "the greatest living writer of short stories." See (S-H10).

323 Parker, Dorothy. *The Portable Dorothy Parker.* New York: Viking Press, 1973. Revised and enlarged edition. Introduction by Brendan Gill. pp. viii, ix, 458-461, 495-496, 582-588.

   pp. 458-461: "A Book of Great Short Stories," review of *MWW*, reprinted from the *New Yorker*, III (Oct. 29, 1927). Note: The reviewer is not identified under (H81). pp. 495-496: "Excuse It, Please," reprinted from the *New Yorker*, III (Feb. 18, 1928). See (S-H10). pp. 582-588: "The Artist's Reward," profile of Hemingway, reprinted from the *New Yorker*, V (Nov. 30, 1929).

324 Patmore, Derek, ed. *My Friends When Young: The Memoirs of Brigit Patmore.* London: Heinemann, 1968. pp. 9, 75, 99-100, 150. Photograph.

   pp. 99-100: Recalls the occasion when Ezra Pound took her and her son, Derek, to the Hemingways' apartment in Paris, in 1925.

325 Pearsall, Robert Brainard. *The Life and Writings of Ernest Hemingway.* Amsterdam: Rodopi N.V., 1973. [Melville Studies in American Culture, Vol. 2.] 282 pages.

326 Pepper, Dennis. *A Hemingway Selection.* London: Longman, 1972. [Longman Imprint Books.] 211 pages. For work by Hemingway, see (S-B13).

   Contents: [Part One: Introduction]
   pp. 162-167: "The Early Years: 1899-1930."
   pp. 167-179: "Fact and Fiction: the creative process at work."

   [Part Two:] What the Critics Thought
   p. 181: Excerpt from Edmund Wilson's review of *iot, Dial,* LXXVII (Oct. 1924).
   p. 181: Excerpt from Marjorie Reid's review of *iot, Transatlantic Review,* I (April 1924).

pp. 181-182: Excerpt from D. H. Lawrence's review of *IOT, Calendar of Modern Letters,* IV (April 1927).

p. 182: Excerpt from Edward J. O'Brien's review of *IOT, Now & Then,* No. 21 (Autumn 1926).

pp. 182-183: Excerpt from Paul Rosenfeld's review of *IOT, New Republic,* XLV (Nov. 25, 1925).

p. 183: Excerpt from Robert Wolf's review of *IOT, N.Y. Herald Tribune Books* (Feb. 14, 1926).

pp. 183-184: Excerpt from an unsigned review of *IOT, N.Y. Times Book Review* (Oct. 18, 1925).

p. 184: Excerpt from Cyril Connolly's review of *MWW, New Statesman,* XXX (Nov. 26, 1927).

pp. 185-186: Excerpt from Percy Hutchison's review of *MWW, N.Y. Times Book Review* (Oct. 16, 1927).

pp. 186-187: Excerpt from Lee Wilson Dodd's review of *MWW, Saturday Review of Literature,* IV (Nov. 19, 1927).

pp. 188-190: Excerpt from Virginia Woolf's essay-review of *MWW* and *SAR, N.Y. Herald Tribune Books* (Oct. 9, 1927).

pp. 190-191: Excerpt from Louis Kronenberger's review of *WTN, N.Y. Times Book Review* (Nov. 5, 1933).

p. 191: Excerpt from Peter Monro Jack's review of the *First 49, N.Y. Times Book Review* (Oct. 23, 1938).

pp. 191-192: Excerpt from "The Hero of the Code," *Time,* LXXVIII (July 14, 1961).

p. 192: Excerpt from Cyril Connolly's "Death of a Titan," *Sunday Times,* London (July 9, 1961).

[Part Three:] Hemingway on Writing

pp. 194-196: Excerpts from George Plimpton's interview in the *Paris Review,* V (Spring 1958).

p. 195: Excerpt from Carlos Baker's *EH: A Life Story.*

p. 195: Excerpt from Christopher Lucas's "Ernest Hemingway's temper also rises," *Sunday Dispatch,* London (Oct. 27, 1957).

pp. 195-196: Excerpts from A. E. Hotchner's *Papa Hemingway.*

[Part Four: Appendices:]

pp. 197-207: "Suggestions for Discussion and Writing" for each short story in this collection.

pp. 208-209: "Dates of First Publication" of each short story in this collection.

pp. 210-211: "Further Reading."

327 Perelman, S. J. *The Rising Gorge.* New York: Simon and Schuster, 1961. pp. 153-161.

Ch. VII: "The Importance of Healing Ernest." Parody regarding Hemingway's recuperation in Africa following the plane crashes in January 1954.

328 [Perfection Form]. *Essay Literature Test for A Farewell to Arms.* Logan, Iowa: Perfection Form Company, 1966. Part of a teaching packet which contains a teacher edition of the "Essay Literature Test," a "50-Question Series Literature Test," and "Literary Prints" (10-by-13 photographs of scenes from the movie version of the novel). Other teaching packets for *SAR*, 1966; *OMATS*, 1967; and *FWBT*, 1967.

329 Peterson, Richard K. *Hemingway: Direct and Oblique.* The Hague and Paris: Mouton, 1969. 231 pages. Selected bibliography on pp. 217-223. [New York: Humanities Press, 1970. (Studies in American Literature, 14).]

A critical study of Hemingway's earlier and later styles.

330 Phelps, Robert, and Peter Deane. *The Literary Life: A Scrapbook Almanac of the Anglo-American Literary Scene from 1900-1950.* New York: Farrar, Straus and Giroux, 1968. pp. 75, 86, 91, 93, 102, 105, 107, 108, 114, 124, 126, 131, 140, 143, 145, 153, 163, 166, 170, 180, 190, 192, 198, 201, 210, 226. Photographs of Hemingway on pp. 73, 109, 167, 225. Hemingway is quoted on pp. 101 and 154.

331 Phillips, Cabell. *From the Crash to the Blitz: 1929-1939.* New York: Macmillan, 1969. pp. 95, 402, 465. Photographs. Facsimiles of the dust jacket of *GHOA*, on p. 397, and *THAHN*, on p. 400. Facsimile of the title page of *DIA* (Collier edition, 1942) on p. 401.

p. 95: Regarding the first film version of *FTA*.

332 Poli, Bernard J. *Ford Madox Ford and The Transatlantic Review.* Syracuse, N.Y.: Syracuse University Press, 1967. pp. 12, 14, 15, 17, 58-59, 71, 72, 74-75, 102-115, 119-120, 142, 143, 157-158, 161-162.

pp. 102-111: Regarding Hemingway's editorship of the *Transatlantic Review* during Ford's absence on a trip to the United States.

333 Pontes, Joel. *O Aprendiz de Crítica.* Rio de Janeiro: Instituto Nacional do Livro, 1960. [Biblioteca de Divulgação Cultural. Série A. Vol. 26.] pp. 223-234.

"Hemingway e Santiago," review of *OMATS*, reprinted from *Diário de Pernambuco* (Jan. 27, 1956).

334 Porter, Katherine Anne. *The Collected Essays and Occasional Writings of Katherine Anne Porter.* New York: Delacorte Press, 1970. [A Seymour Lawrence Book.] pp. 102-106.

"A Little Incident in the Rue de l'Odéon," regarding her meeting with Hemingway in Sylvia Beach's bookshop in Paris, around 1934, reprinted from the *Ladies' Home Journal*, LXXXI (Aug. 1964).

335 Prescott, Peter S. *Soundings: Encounters with Contemporary Books.* New York: Coward, McCann & Geoghegan, 1972. pp. 21, 74-76, 241-244, 272.

pp. 74-76: "Hemingway: The Last Wheeze," review of *Islands*, reprinted from *Look*, xxxiv (Oct. 20, 1970). pp. 241-244: "Hemingway: The Whole Truth and Nothing But," review of Carlos Baker's *EH: A Life Story*, reprinted from *Look*, xxxiii (April 29, 1969).

336 Price, Lawrence Marsden. *The Reception of United States Literature in Germany*. Chapel Hill: University of North Carolina Press, 1966. [University of North Carolina Studies in Comparative Literature, No. 39.] pp. 121, 124, 144, 147-150, 153, 186, 218-220.

pp. 147-150: Discussion of the critical reception to Hemingway's work translated into German. pp. 218-220: Checklist of reviews and articles on Hemingway's work in German periodicals.

337 Price, Reynolds. *Things Themselves: Essays and Scenes*. New York: Atheneum, 1972. pp. 176-213.

"For Ernest Hemingway," essay reprinted from the *New American Review*, No. 14 (June 1972).

338 Priestley, J. B. *Literature and Western Man*. London: Heinemann, 1960. pp. 373, 432, 435-436.

pp. 435-436: A short analysis of Hemingway's style.

339 Proffer, Carl R., edited and translated by. *Soviet Criticism of American Literature in the Sixties: An Anthology*. Ann Arbor, Michigan: Ardis, 1972. pp. 12, 13, 58, 59, 67, 76, 97, 99, 113-114, 116-148, 164, 181-189.

p. 116: "Orlova on Hemingway." pp. 117-148: *"For Whom the Bell Tolls"* by R. [Raisa] Orlova. This essay was originally published in Russian, under the title *The Work of Ernest Hemingway*, Novosibirsk, 1968. pp. 181-189: "What Is Hemingway's Style" by Ivan Kashkin. Translated by Ralph Parker.

340 [Putnam, Samuel]. *We Moderns, 1920-1940*. New York: Gotham Book Mart, [1940]. Catalogue No. 42. pp. 35-36.

p. 35: "Ernest Hemingway" by Samuel Putnam. Introduction to books by Hemingway, items No. 431-440. Reprinted in *Hemingway at Auction*, p. 192. See (S-B18).

341 Rahv, Philip. *Literature and the Sixth Sense*. Boston: Houghton Mifflin. 1969. pp. 351-357.

"Hemingway in the 1950s." pp. 351-355: Review of *ARIT*, reprinted from *Commentary*, x (Oct. 1950). pp. 355-357: Review of *OMATS*, reprinted from *Commentary*, xiv (Oct. 1952). For reprints of these reviews, see (G328).

342 Raines, Charles A. *Ernest Hemingway's The Sun Also Rises: A Critical Commentary*. New York: American R.D.M. Corporation, 1967. [Study Master Publication, No. 424.] 64 pages. Bibliography on pp. 63-64.

343 Randall, David A. *Dukedom Large Enough.* New York: Random House, 1969. pp. 39, 165, 235-241, 243, 256, 257, 259.

   pp. 235-241: "Hemingway and the Printed Word," reprinted from the *Papers of the Bibliographical Society of America,* LVI (July-Sept. 1962).

344 Ray, Cyril, ed. *The Compleat Imbiber 8.* London: Collins, 1965. pp. 81-85. Photographs.

   "Defeat of a Drinking Man" by Alan Brien, regarding a meeting with Hemingway on a transatlantic crossing in 1956, reprinted from the *Spectator,* CCXII (June 5, 1964).

345 Reiger, George. *Profiles in Saltwater Angling: A History of the Sport—Its People and Places, Tackle and Techniques.* Englewood Cliffs, N.J.: Prentice-Hall, 1973. pp. 11, 127, 185-186, 250-264, 284, 288, 303, 311, 328-329. Photographs.

   pp. 250-264: Ch. 16: "The Literary Naturalist." On Hemingway's years in Key West, Bimini, and Cuba. p. 303: Hemingway's inscription to Tommy Gifford, in a copy of *American Big Game Angling,* is quoted.

346 Reynolds, Paul R. *The Middle Man: The Adventures of a Literary Agent.* New York: William Morrow, 1972. pp. 36-39.

   Regarding Laurence Stallings' dramatization of *FTA* and the sale of the film rights to Paramount.

347 Richards, Norman. *Ernest Hemingway.* Chicago: Childrens Press, 1968. [People of Destiny: A Humanities Series.] 96 pages. 11 x 8 3/8. Photographs and drawings. Bibliography on pp. 90-91. Juvenile biography.

348 Roberts, James L. *The Snows of Kilimanjaro and Other Stories: Notes.* Lincoln, Nebr.: Cliff's Notes, 1964. 56 pages.

349 Roberts, James L. *A Farewell to Arms: Notes.* Lincoln, Nebr.: Cliff's Notes, 1966. Revised edition. 61 pages.

350 Rogers, Katharine M. *The Troublesome Helpmate: A History of Misogyny in Literature.* Seattle and London: University of Washington Press, 1966. pp. 229, 237, 247-251, 257, 261, 263.

   pp. 247-251: Discussion of Hemingway's portrayals of women in the Nick Adams stories, *FWBT, TFC, SAR,* and "The Short Happy Life of Francis Macomber."

351 Rogers, W. G. *When This You See Remember Me: Gertrude Stein in Person.* New York: Rinehart, 1948. pp. 56, 99, 123, 198, 226, 236-237, 244, 256.

p. 56: An early letter from Hemingway to Gertrude Stein is quoted regarding writing. p. 237: Regarding Hemingway's indebtedness to Gertrude Stein.

352 Rogers, W. G. *Gertrude Stein Is Gertrude Stein Is Gertrude Stein: Her Life and Work.* New York: Crowell, 1973. [Women of America series.] pp. 35, 45, 105-110, 172, 173.

pp. 105-110: Regarding references to each other in the works of Gertrude Stein and Hemingway.

353 Rolfe, Edwin. *The Lincoln Battalion: The Story of the Americans who Fought in Spain in the International Brigades.* New York: Random House, 1939. pp. 70, 111, 130, 236. Photograph of Hemingway opposite p. 212. For Hemingway's blurb on the dust jacket, see (S-F177).

354 Rosen, Billie Pesin. *The Science of Handwriting Analysis: A Guide to Character and Personality.* New York: Crown, 1965. pp. 216-221.

Analysis of two specimens of Hemingway's handwriting. Facsimile of Hemingway's Last Will and Testament, written in 1955, on p. 216. See (H1317). Facsimile of Hemingway's letter to Fritz Saviers, dated June 15, 1961, on pp. 217-218. See (F147).

355 Ross, Ishbel. *The Expatriates.* New York: Crowell, 1970. pp. 223-224, 236-238, 241, 244, 246, 248, 255-262, 265, 287-288. Photograph.

pp. 255-266: Ch. 16: "Hemingway and Fitzgerald."

356 Roth, Philip. *The Great American Novel.* New York: Holt, Rinehart and Winston, 1973. pp. 1, 25-37.

pp. 25-37: A fictional account, in the Prologue, of a fishing trip with Hemingway off the coast of Florida, in March 1936, during which the Great American Novel is the main topic of conversation.

357 Rovit, Earl. *Hemingway.* New York: Twayne, 1963. See (G345). Translated into Italian by R. Angial. Florence: La Nuova Italia, 1967. [Il Castoro, 7.] 190 pages.

358 Rühle, Jürgen. *Literature and Revolution: A Critical Study of the Writer and Communism in the Twentieth Century.* New York: Praeger, 1969. [First published in German, *Literatur und Revolution,* Kieppenheuer and Witsch, 1960.] Translated and edited by Jean Steinberg. pp. 56, 430-432, 465, 471, 473.

p. 432: Regarding André Marty in *FWBT.*

359 Russell, Leonard, ed. *Parody Party.* London: Hutchinson, 1936. pp. 17-35.

"Week-End at the Hoppers (Please, Mr. H*m*ngway)" by Rose Macaulay.

360 Sams, Henry W., and Waldo F. McNeir, eds. *New Problems in Reading & Writing.* New York: Prentice-Hall, 1953. pp. 172-173, 200-216. See also (S-E27).

pp. 172-173: "An Author and His Critics." pp. 200-204: Excerpt from "Hemingway: Gauge of Morale" by Edmund Wilson, reprinted from *The Wound and the Bow*, New York, 1947. Guide questions on pp. 204-205. pp. 205-207: Excerpt from "Bull in the Afternoon" by Max Eastman, reprinted from *Art and the Life of Action*, New York, 1934. Guide questions on p. 207. pp. 207-210: "Hemingway's Discipline," excerpt from *The Novel of Violence in America* by Wilbur M. Frohock, Dallas, 1950. Guide questions on p. 211. pp. 211-213: "Tenderly Tolls the Bell," excerpt from *On Second Thought* by James Gray, Minneapolis, 1946. Guide questions on p. 213. pp. 214-216: "Hemingway in Spain" by Leo Gurko, reprinted from *The Angry Decade*, New York, 1947, pp. 187-190. Guide questions on p. 216.

361 Sanders, Thomas E. *The Discovery of Fiction.* Glenview, Ill.: Scott, Foresman, 1967. pp. 203, 238, 290-293, 296-298, 303-316, 331, 333, 340, 359, 452-453.

pp. 290-293: Examines the opening paragraph of "A Clean, Well-Lighted Place" as an example of Hemingway's style. See also (S-E88).

362 San Juan, José María. *Acción, periodismo y literatura en Ernest Hemingway.* Madrid: Ediciones Punta Europa, 1958.

363 Sarason, Bertram D. *Hemingway and The Sun Set.* Washington, D.C.: NCR/Microcard Editions, 1972. xiv + 279 pages. Photographs.

Contents: pp. ix-xii: Preface by Bertram D. Sarason.

Part I: The Background
pp. 3-107: "Hemingway and *The Sun* Set" by Bertram D. Sarason.

Part II: From the Characters Themselves
pp. 111-135: "Hemingway's Bitterness" by Harold Loeb, reprinted from the *Connecticut Review*, I (Oct. 1967). "Robert Cohn" is portrayed after Loeb.

pp. 136-144: "With Duff at Ascain" by Harold Loeb, reprinted from *The Way It Was*, New York, 1959, pp. 267-278. Regarding Lady Duff Twysden, the model for "Brett Ashley."

pp. 145-150: "Scenes with a Hero" by Kathleen Cannell, reprinted from the *Connecticut Review*, II (Oct. 1968). Regarding "Frances Clyne."

pp. 151-188: "Interview with Hemingway's 'Bill Gorton' " by Donald St. John, reprinted from the *Connecticut Review*, I (April 1968);

III (Oct. 1969). Interview with Bill Smith, one of the models for "Bill Gorton."

pp. 189-206: "Interview with Donald Ogden Stewart" by Donald St. John. Stewart was another model for "Bill Gorton."

pp. 207-211: " 'Montoya' Remembers *The Sun Also Rises*" by Leah Rice Koontz. Regarding Juanito Quintana, the model for "Montoya."

pp. 212-221: "The Sun Also Sets" by Sam Adams, reprinted from *Sports Illustrated*, XXXII (June 29, 1970). Regarding Cayetano Ordóñez, the bullfighter Niño de la Palma, who was the model for "Pedro Romero."

Part III: Friends and Experts

pp. 225-227: "On the Characters in *The Sun Also Rises*." A letter from Robert McAlmon to Norman Holmes Pearson, dated March 31, 1951.

pp. 228-240: "Lady Brett Ashley and Lady Duff Twysden" by Bertram D. Sarason, reprinted from the *Connecticut Review*, II (April 1969).

pp. 241-246: "Pat and Duff, Some Memories" by James Charters, reprinted from the *Connecticut Review*, III (April 1970). Regarding Pat Guthrie, who was the model for "Mike Campbell," and Lady Duff Twysden.

pp. 247-255: "Fitzgerald's *Sun Also Rises*: Notes and Comment" by Philip Young and Charles W. Mann, reprinted from the *Fitzgerald/Hemingway Annual: 1970*, pp. 1-9. See next entry.

pp. 256-259: "Letter to Ernest Hemingway" from F. Scott Fitzgerald, written in 1926, criticizing *SAR*, reprinted from the *Fitzgerald/Hemingway Annual: 1970*, pp. 10-13.

pp. 260-264: "Two Essays on Ford Madox Ford" by Kathleen Cannell, reprinted from the *Christian Science Monitor* (Dec. 23, 1965) and the *Providence Sunday Journal* (Sept. 20, 1964). Ford was portrayed as "Braddocks."

pp. 265-270: "*The Sun Also Rises* Revisited" by Morrill Cody, reprinted from the *Connecticut Review*, IV (April 1971).

pp. 271-274: "Duke Zizi" by James Charters.

pp. 275-279: "Cavalier and Cowboy: Goodbye to all that, Mr. Ford Braddocks Ford!" by Bernard Poli.

364 Saroyan, William. *I Used to Believe I Had Forever Now I'm Not So Sure*. New York: Cowles, 1968. pp. 85-90.

"The Adventures of American Writers in Paris in 1929," review of Morley Callaghan's *That Summer in Paris*, reprinted from the *New Republic*, CXLVIII (Feb. 9, 1963).

365 Scavone, Rubens Teixeira. *Ensaios Norte-americanos*. São Paulo: EdArt, Livraria Editôra, 1963. pp. 45-57.

pp. 45-52: "Hemingway e a Morte." Surveys Hemingway's themes through *OMATS*. pp. 53-57: "Réquiem para Hemingway." A recapitulating obituary.

366 Scherman, David E., ed. *The Best of Life*. New York: Time-Life Books, 1973. p. 247. Photograph of Hemingway in Idaho, in 1959, by John Bryson.

367 Schleden, Ina Mae, and Marion Rawls Herzog, eds. *Ernest Hemingway as Recalled by His High School Contemporaries*. Oak Park, Ill.: The Historical Society of Oak Park and River Forest, 1973. [Monograph No. 1.] 47 pages. Photographs. Facsimiles of two Hemingway letters, see (S-F64) and (S-F99).

Contents: p. 5: Foreword by Charles Bolles Gale. pp. 7-8: Preface by the editors.

Transcriptions of four talks given at the Historical Society's program, "The Hemingways in Retrospect," on October 29, 1971:

pp. 9-14: "The Early Years of Ernest Hemingway" by Frank J. Platt, who taught Ernest in freshman English.

pp. 19-28: "The High School Years" by Susan Lowrey Kesler, a classmate.

pp. 31-37: "Ernest Hemingway As I Knew Him, 1911 to 1918" by Lewis Clarahan, a boyhood friend.

pp. 39-42: "Hemingway the Writer" by Nina Grace Smith.

p. [43]: A letter from Charles Scribner, Jr., regarding Hemingway's loyalty to his publishers.

Note: John Gehlmann was moderator of the panel and Hemingway's sister, Madelaine (Sunny) Miller, was the guest of honor. A photograph of Mrs. Clarence Hemingway with her painting of Ernest as a young man is on p. 38. This monograph was also published in a limited edition of 100 numbered copies.

368 Schorer, Mark. *The World We Imagine: Selected Essays*. New York: Farrar, Straus and Giroux, 1968. pp. 20-22, 316-325, 330-337, 339-355, 358-361, 363-382.

pp. 299-402: Part Six: "Some Relationships: Gertrude Stein, Sherwood Anderson, F. Scott Fitzgerald, and Ernest Hemingway."

369 Schulberg, Budd. *The Four Seasons of Success*. Garden City, N.Y.: Doubleday, 1972. pp. 3-4, 12-18, 20-21, 72, 77, 79, 92-95, 100, 102, 103, 106, 114, 130-131, 149.

pp. 12-18: Discusses the effect of Hemingway's success on F. Scott Fitzgerald.

370 Schulz, Franz. *Der nordamerikanische Indianer und seine Welt in den Werken von Ernest Hemingway und Oliver LaFarge*. Munich: Max Hueber, 1964. [Mainzer Amerikanistische Beiträge, VII.] 192 pages.

371 Schwartz, Delmore. *Selected Essays of Delmore Schwartz*. Edited by Donald A. Dike and David H. Zucker. Chicago: University of Chicago Press, 1970. pp. 40, 103, 235, 255-273, 288, 368n., 414.

pp. 255-273: "The Fiction of Ernest Hemingway: Moral Historian of the American Dream," reprinted from *Perspectives U.S.A.*, No. 13 (Autumn 1955).

372 Schwerner, Armand, ed. *A Farewell to Arms: A Critical Commentary*. New York: American R.D.M. Corporation, 1963. [Study Master Publication, No. 442.] 42 pages. Bibliography on pp. 41-42.

373 Scott, Nathan A., Jr. *Ernest Hemingway: A Critical Essay*. Grand Rapids, Mich.: William B. Eerdmans, 1966. [Contemporary Writers in Christian Perspective series.] 46 pages. Selected Bibliography on pp. 45-46.

An examination of the Christian values to be found in Hemingway's novels.

374 Seldes, George. *World Panorama, 1918-1933*. Boston: Little, Brown, 1933. pp. 173, 199, 247, 283, 333, 349.

375 Seward, William W., Jr. *Contrasts in Modern Writers: Some Aspects of British and American Fiction Since Mid-Century*. New York: Frederick Fell, 1963. pp. 62-80.

"Ernest Hemingway." pp. 62-66: "Prophetic Genius of War," review of *ARIT*, reprinted from the *Norfolk Virginian-Pilot* (Sept. 10, 1950). pp. 66-68: Review of *OMATS*, reprinted from the *Norfolk Virginian-Pilot* (Sept. 7, 1952). pp. 68-69: Discussion of "A Man of the World" and "Get a Seeing-Eyed Dog," transcribed from a radio broadcast (Nov. 14, 1957). pp. 69-80: Reviews of six books on Hemingway.

376 Seward, William. *My Friend Ernest Hemingway: An Affectionate Reminiscence*. South Brunswick and New York: A. S. Barnes/London: Thomas Yoseloff, 1969. 69 pages. Photographs.

Reminiscences by a professor of English of his friendship with Hemingway, which began through correspondence in 1940 and continued until Hemingway's death. pp. 42-43: Excerpt from a review of *ARIT*, reprinted from the *Norfolk Virginian-Pilot* (Sept. 10, 1950). pp. 66-68: The original version of a review of *AMF*, which appeared in abbreviated form in the *Virginian-Pilot* (May 17, 1964).

377 Sharma, D. R. *Ernest Hemingway: His Consciousness of Human Predicament*. Chandigarh, India: Panjab University, 1968. [The Research Bulletin (Arts), No. 72.] 30 pages.

378 Shaw, Samuel. *Ernest Hemingway*. New York: Frederick Ungar, 1973. [Modern Literature Monographs.] 136 pages. Bibliography on pp. 127-129.

A study of the humanistic core beneath the nihilistic surface of Hemingway's fiction.

379 Shiga, Masaru. *Heminguwei kenkyū.* Tokyo, 1966. 284 pages.

380 Shvedov, S. S. *Ernest Kheminguei.* Moscow, 1969. 35 pages. See also (S-B8).

381 Škvorecký, Josef. [*Ernest Hemingway.*] Prague: Presfoto, 1965. Collection of photographs of Hemingway, with the text in Czech.

382 Smetana, Josette. *La Philosophie de l'action chez Hemingway et Saint-Exupéry.* Paris: La Marjolaine, 1965. 181 pages. Preface, by Edouard Morot-Sir, on pp. 1-6.
     Recounts the similarities and divergencies in the two writers.

383 Smith, Godfrey, ed. *1000 Makers of the Twentieth Century.* Newton Abbott: David & Charles, 1971. p. [72].
     "Ernest Hemingway" by G. M. MacB. [George M. MacBeth].

384 Sokoloff, Alice Hunt. *Hadley: The First Mrs. Hemingway.* New York: Dodd, Mead, 1973. 111 pages. Photographs.
     A biography of Elizabeth Hadley Richardson, who met Hemingway in Chicago in October 1920. They were married in September 1921, in Michigan, and divorced in January 1927, in Paris. A number of her letters to Hemingway are quoted; however, his letters to her of the same period have been lost.

385 Spivey, Ted R. *Religious Themes in Two Modern Novelists.* Atlanta: Georgia State College, 1965. [School of Arts and Sciences Research Papers, No. 12.] 31 pages.
     A study of Hemingway and Romain Gary.

386 Stearns, Harold E., ed. *America Now: An Inquiry Into Civilization in the United States.* New York: Scribner's, 1938, pp. 36, 37, 39-42, 44, 375.
     pp. 36-47: "Literature" by John Chamberlain. Includes a discussion, on pp. 39-42, on what Hemingway failed to say in *THAHN*, and how he thereby spoiled a good book.

387 Steen, Mike. *A Look at Tennessee Williams.* New York: Hawthorn Books, 1969. pp. 132, 187-189, 219.
     pp. 187-189: Peter Viertel discusses the films made from Hemingway's work. p. 219: Regarding Hemingway's meeting with Tennessee Williams in Cuba, in 1959. See (H1509).

388 Stephens, Robert O. *Hemingway's Nonfiction: The Public Voice.* Chapel Hill: University of North Carolina Press, 1968. xiv + 391 pages.

A study of Hemingway's nonfictional writing from his early articles in the *Toronto Star* to the posthumously published *AMF*. pp. 347-361: Appendix A: "A Chronological List of Hemingway's Nonfiction" (According to Date of Publication). pp. 362-377: Appendix B: "More Sources, Analogues, and Echoes."

389 Stevick, Philip. *The Theory of the Novel.* New York: Free Press, 1967. pp. 81-82, 92, 120, 130, 134, 146, 162, 186, 211-213, 217, 219.

pp. 211-213: Discusses *FTA*.

390 Stevick, Philip. *The Chapter in Fiction: Theories of Narrative Division.* Syracuse, N.Y.: Syracuse University Press, 1970. pp. 127-128.

On the "controlled and considered artistic structure" of the interchapters of *IOT*.

391 Stewart, Randall. *American Literature and Christian Doctrine.* Baton Rouge: Louisiana State University Press, 1958. pp. 120*n.*, 123, 134-137.

pp. 134-137: Regarding the "virtue of ritualistic discipline" in "A Clean, Well-Lighted Place" and "Big Two-Hearted River."

392 Stirling, Nora. *Who Wrote the Modern Classics?* New York: John Day, 1970. pp. 235-283.

"Ernest Hemingway (1899-1961)." Note: This book also includes biographical studies of W. Somerset Maugham, Sinclair Lewis, Willa Cather, Eugene O'Neill, Thomas Wolfe, and F. Scott Fitzgerald.

393 Stuckey, W. J. *The Pulitzer Prize Novels: A Critical Backward Look.* Norman: University of Oklahoma Press, 1966. pp. 70, 82-84, 117, 122-124, 165-170.

pp. 122-124: Regarding the Pulitzer prize Advisory Board's recommendation of *FWBT* for the fiction prize in 1941 and Nicholas Murray Butler's "unyielding opposition" to their selection. pp. 165-170: Regarding the Pulitzer prize awarded in 1953 to *OMATS*.

394 Sükösd, Mihály. *Hemingway világa.* Budapest: Európa Könyvkiadó, 1969. 185 pages. Bibliography on pp. 179-182.

395 Sulzberger, Cyrus. *The Resistentialists.* New York: Harper, 1962. pp. 6-7, 18-25.

pp. 5-68: Ch. 2: "The Bravest Collaborator." The story of Hemingway's "jeep driver and self-constituted bodyguard" in France and Germany during World War II. He is called here "Michel Dupont." (Cf. Carlos Baker's *EH: A Life Story*, p. 654, third note.) pp. 18-25: Three letters from Hemingway to the author, from Finca Vigia in 1951, are extensively quoted. See (S-F116) to (S-F118).

Note: This book was withdrawn before publication day. The number of copies distributed as review copies and to libraries is not known. See Sulzberger's *Unconquered Souls*, pp. 13-14, regarding his explanation of the revision of this book. (See entry below.)

396 Sulzberger, C. L. *Unconquered Souls: The Resistentialists.* Woodstock, N.Y.: Overlook Press, 1973. pp. 10, 13-14, 82-83, 86-90, 93-105, 121, 124, 133-135, 212, 213.

pp. 81-144: Ch. 2: "The Bravest Collaborator." Note: This revision of *The Resistentialists* (see entry above) has no direct quotations from Hemingway's letters. See the author's explanation on pp. 13-14. See also "Story Behind Two Books *The Tooth Merchant* and *Unconquered Souls*" by Barbara A. Bannon, *Publishers Weekly,* CCIII (Feb. 19, 1973), 54-55.

397 Sulzberger, C. L. *A Long Row of Candles: Memoirs and Diaries, 1934-1954.* New York: Macmillan, 1969. pp. 4, 611-612, 641, 646, 665, 670.

Regarding the author's correspondence with Hemingway about "Michel Dupont." See the previous two entries.

398 Sutherland, Fraser. *The Style of Innocence: A Study of Hemingway and Callaghan.* London: Clarke, Irwin, 1973. 120 pages.

A comparison study of the work of Hemingway and Morley Callaghan.

399 Sutton, Walter. *Modern American Criticism.* Englewood Cliffs, N.J.: Prentice-Hall, 1963. [The Princeton Studies: Humanistic Scholarship in America.] pp. 71, 88, 196, 212, 214, 279.

400 Takigawa, Motoo. *Hemingway Saiko* [Second thoughts on Hemingway]. Tokyo: Nan-un-do, 1967.

401 Taniguchi, Rikuo. [*Ernest Hemingway: A Critical Study.*] Tokyo: Mikasa-Shobo, 1965. 326 pages. In Japanese. Note: This book is Volume 9 of the collected works of Hemingway. See (D214) and (S-H306).

402 Thurber, James. *The Years with Ross.* Boston: Little, Brown, 1959. [An Atlantic Monthly Press Book.] pp. 157-158.

Biography of Harold Ross. Thurber mentions Hemingway's blurb for the dust jacket of *My Life and Hard Times.* See (F159).

403 *T.L.S.: Essays and Reviews from The Times Literary Supplement, 1964.* No. 3. London: Oxford University Press, 1965. pp. 55-63.

pp. 55-61: "The Bruiser and the Poet: Hemingway's Paris," review of *AMF* [by Douglas Grant], reprinted from *TLS* (May 21, 1964). p. 61: Letter from Malcolm Foster, reprinted from *TLS* (June 11, 1964). pp. 61-62: Letter from John Guenther, reprinted from *TLS* (July 9, 1964). p. 63: Letter from Archibald MacLeish, reprinted from *TLS* (Sept. 3, 1964).

404 Timko, Michael, and Clinton F. Oliver, eds. *Thirty-Eight Short Stories: An Introductory Anthology*. New York: Knopf, 1968, pp. 69-86.

"Hemingway's 'The Killers' and Mann's 'Disorder and Early Sorrow' " by Clinton F. Oliver. See also (S-E112).

405 Tomkins, Calvin. *Living Well Is the Best Revenge*. New York: Viking Press, 1971. pp. 4, 27, 98-100, 102, 112, 114, 120, 136. Photographs.

A biography of Gerald and Sara Murphy, which originally appeared as a profile in the *New Yorker,* xxxviii (July 28, 1962), 31-69. pp. 98-100: Regarding the Hemingways and the Murphys at Schruns, at Antibes, and in Pamplona, in 1926.

406 Trilling, Lionel. *The Liberal Imagination: Essays on Literature and Society*. New York: Viking Press, 1950. pp. 117, 214, 247, 250, 296-300.

pp. 296-300: On Hemingway and Faulkner from the essay "The Meaning of a Literary Idea," reprinted from the *American Quarterly,* i (Fall 1949).

407 Turnbull, Andrew. *Thomas Wolfe*. New York: Scribner's 1968. pp. 133-134, 192-194, 242-243, 272, 273, 277.

pp. 133-134: Regarding Maxwell Perkins and publication of *SAR*. p. 194: An unpublished review by Wolfe of *FTA* is quoted.

408 Tynan, Kenneth. *Tynan Right and Left*. New York: Atheneum, 1967. pp. 285, 287, 330-336, 374, 378-380.

pp. 330-336: "Papa and the Playwright," regarding the meeting between Hemingway and Tennessee Williams in Havana, in 1959, reprinted from *Playboy,* xi (May 1964). pp. 378-380: Regarding the Hemingways as guests of Bill and Annie Davis in Málaga, Spain, in the late 1950s.

409 Ulanov, Barry. *The Two Worlds of American Art: The Private and the Popular*. New York: Macmillan, 1965. pp. 194-196, 226, 258-264.

pp. 194-196: Discussion of Hemingway's short stories, particularly "The Capital of the World." pp. 258-264: Discussion of Hemingway's novels.

410 [USIA]. *Ernest Hemingway: A Bibliography*. Bonn: United States Information Agency, Office of the U.S. High Commissioner for Germany, 1954. 18 pages.

p. 5: Brief biography. pp. 6-18: Checklist of Hemingway's novels and short stories, with the latest German translations; anthologies containing his work; and biographical material and criticism in books and periodicals.

411 [USIS]. *The Literature of America.* Printed by the United States Information Service, 1970.

pp. 10-11: "Ernest Hemingway."

412 Van Nostrand, Albert. *The Denatured Novel.* Indianapolis: Bobbs-Merrill, 1960. pp. 123-125, 142-143, 180, 181, 188, 208-213.

p. 188: Regarding Hemingway's blurb for Wirt Williams' novel *The Enemy.* See (S-F179). pp. 208-213: Discussion of Hemingway's style and its influence.

413 Volpe, Edmond L. *A Reader's Guide to William Faulkner.* New York: Farrar, Straus & Giroux, 1964. pp. 214-215, 227, 230, 409.

Regarding the parallels between Charlotte and Harry's love affair in Faulkner's "The Wild Palms" and Catherine and Frederic Henry's in *FTA.*

414 Wager, Willis. *American Literature: A World View.* New York: New York University Press/London: University of London Press, 1968. pp. 174, 231, 238-241.

pp. 238-241: Brief analyses of *SAR, FTA, FWBT,* and *OMATS.*

415 Walcutt, Charles Child. *Man's Changing Mask: Modes and Methods of Characterization in Fiction.* Minneapolis: University of Minnesota Press, 1966. pp. 141, 154, 242-243, 302, 305-314, 316-317, 338.

pp. 305-314: "Hemingway's Naked Eyeballs." "The Killers" is analyzed on pp. 305-306. *SAR* is analyzed on pp. 309-313.

416 Waldhorn, Arthur, and Hilda K. Waldhorn, eds. *The Rite of Becoming: Stories and Studies of Adolescence.* Cleveland: World, 1966. pp. 167-169.

Excerpt from Joseph DeFalco's *The Hero in Hemingway's Short Stories,* Pittsburgh, 1963. See also (S-E69).

417 Waldhorn, Arthur. *A Reader's Guide to Ernest Hemingway.* New York: Farrar, Straus & Giroux, 1972. xiv + 284 pages. [Paperback edition: New York: Noonday Press, 1972. (Reader's Guide Series, N 427.)]

A study of Hemingway's life and writing style, and an analysis, in chronological order, of his work through *Islands.* pp. 259-261: Appendix A: *"In Our Time."* Regarding the placement of the interchapters. pp. 262-264: Appendix B: "Nick Adams." Chronology of the Nick Adams stories. pp. 265-266: Appendix C: Filmography. Covering the years 1932 to 1962. pp. 267-278: Selected Bibliography. Chapter one, "Life," is reprinted in Arthur Waldhorn's *EH: A Collection of Criticism,* New York, 1973, pp. 1-17.

418 Waldhorn, Arthur, ed. *Ernest Hemingway: A Collection of Criticism*. New York: McGraw-Hill, 1973. [Contemporary Studies in Literature series.] x + 149 pages.

Contents: pp. vii-viii: Preface by Arthur Waldhorn.

pp. 1-17: "Artist and Adventurer: A Biographical Sketch" by Arthur Waldhorn, reprinted from *A Reader's Guide to Ernest Hemingway*, New York, 1972, pp. 3-20.

pp. 18-34: "Ernest Hemingway: The Meaning of Style" by John Graham, reprinted from *Modern Fiction Studies*, VI (Winter 1960-1961).

pp. 35-55: "Hemingway's Ambiguity: Symbolism and Irony" by E. M. Halliday, reprinted from *American Literature*, XXVIII (March 1956).

pp. 56-82: "The Snows of Ernest Hemingway" by Bern Oldsey, reprinted from the *Wisconsin Studies in Contemporary Literature*, IV (Spring-Summer 1963).

pp. 83-91: "Hemingway Achieves the Fifth Dimension" by F. I. Carpenter, reprinted from *American Literature and the Dream*, New York, 1955, pp. 185-193.

pp. 92-111: "Ernest Hemingway, Literary Critic" by Daniel Fuchs, reprinted from *American Literature*, XXXVI (Jan. 1965).

pp. 112-126: "Hemingway and the Pale Cast of Thought" by Robert Evans, reprinted from *American Literature*, XXXVIII (May 1966).

pp. 127-140: "The World and an American Myth" by Philip Young, reprinted from *EH: A Reconsideration*, University Park, Pennsylvania, 1966, pp. 242-260.

pp. 141-149: Selected Bibliography.

419 Walker, Gerald, ed. *Best Magazine Articles: 1968*. New York: Crown, 1968. pp. 236-248.

"Indian Camp Camp" by Donald St. John, reprinted from the *Carleton Miscellany*, IX (Winter 1968). An interview with Hemingway's sister, Sunny [Mrs. Ernest Miller], at the family's summer home overlooking Walloon Lake in northern Michigan.

420 Walker, William E., and Robert L. Welker, eds. *Reality and Myth: Essays in American Literature in Memory of Richmond Croom Beatty*. Nashville: Vanderbilt University Press, 1964. pp. 83, 192, 199, 212, 213, 218-220, 246.

pp. 212-236: "The New Orleans *Double Dealer*" by Francis Bowen Durrett. pp. 219-220: Hemingway's fable "A Divine Gesture" is reprinted from the *Double Dealer*, III (May 1922). See (C85).

421 Warfel, Harry R. *American Novelists of Today*. New York: American, 1951. pp. 200-202.

"Ernest Hemingway."

422 Watkins, Floyd C. *The Flesh and the Word: Eliot, Hemingway, Faulkner*. Nashville: Vanderbilt University Press, 1971. pp. 95-166.

pp. 95-108: Ch. 7: "*The Sun Also Rises* and the Failure of Language." pp. 109-126: Ch. 8: "World Pessimism and Personal Cheeriness in *A Farewell to Arms*." pp. 127-136: Ch. 9: "Hemingway's First 'Big Writing.'" Regarding *DIA* and *GHOA*. pp. 137-151: Ch. 10: "Garrulous Patriot." Regarding *THAHN* and *FWBT*. pp. 152-166: Ch. 11: "The Iceberg and the Cardboard Box." Regarding *OMATS* and *ARIT*.

423 Watt, William W. *An American Rhetoric*. New York: Holt, Rinehart & Winston, 1970. Fourth edition. pp. 6, 17, 178, 219-222, 375, 398, 453, 457.

pp. 219-222: Discussion on Hemingway's style.

424 Watts, Emily Stipes. *Ernest Hemingway and the Arts*. Urbana: University of Illinois Press, 1971. xvi + 243 pages. Illustrations.

A study of Hemingway's interest in the arts and "how the poetry and prose of Hemingway might have been enriched and deepened by the paintings and sculpture and architecture which he saw being created around him, which he owned, and which he had viewed in museums." pp. 227-234: "An index of references to the arts in the works of Ernest Hemingway and of his biographies and critics."

425 Wegelin, Christof, ed. *The American Novel: Criticism and Background Readings*. New York: Free Press, 1972. pp. 425-452.

Part XII: "*The Sun Also Rises* (1926) by Ernest Hemingway." pp. 427-431: "Ernest Hemingway's *The Sun Also Rises*" by James T. Farrell, reprinted from the *N.Y. Times Book Review* (Aug. 1, 1943). pp. 432-437: "Death and Transfiguration" by Philip Young, reprinted from *EH: A Reconsideration*, University Park, Pennsylvania, 1966, pp. 82-88. pp. 438-452: "The Death of Love in *The Sun Also Rises*" by Mark Spilka, reprinted from *Twelve Original Essays on Great American Novels* edited by Charles Shapiro, Detroit, 1958, pp. 238-256.

426 Weintraub, Stanley. *The Last Great Cause: The Intellectuals and the Spanish Civil War*. New York: Weybright and Talley, 1968. pp. 10, 156, 166-167, 179-221, 229-232, 251-252, 256, 260, 269-270, 274-276, 279, 281-285, 324-326.

pp. 179-220: Ch. 7: "Things Unsimple: 'Hemingstein' at War."

427 Wellershoff, Dieter. *Der Gleichgültige: Versuche über Hemingway, Camus, Benn und Beckett*. Berlin: Kiepenheuer & Witsch, 1963. pp. 15-39.

"Hemingway."

428 West, Ray B., Jr. *The Writer in the Room: Selected Essays.* East Lansing: Michigan State University Press, 1968. pp. 142-174, 236-252.

pp. 142-157: "Ernest Hemingway: The Failure of Sensibility," reprinted from the *Sewanee Review,* LIII (Jan.-March 1945). pp. 158-174: "*A Farewell to Arms,*" reprinted from *The Art of Modern Fiction* edited by Ray B. West, Jr. and Robert W. Stallman, New York, 1949, pp. 622-634. pp. 236-252: "Three Methods of Modern Fiction: Ernest Hemingway, Thomas Mann, Eudora Welty," reprinted from *College English,* XII (Jan. 1951).

429 Westbrook, Max, ed. *The Modern American Novel: Essays in Criticism.* New York: Random House, 1966. pp. 90-130.

pp. 90-92: "Ernest Hemingway." pp. 93-113: "Tristan or Jacob: The Choice of *The Sun Also Rises*" by Robert W. Lewis, Jr., reprinted from *Hemingway on Love,* Austin, 1965, pp. 19-35. pp. 113-118: "Criticism and *A Farewell to Arms*" by Norman Friedman, reprinted from the *Antioch Review,* XVIII (Fall 1958). pp. 118-130: "*The Old Man and the Sea*: Hemingway's Tragic Vision of Man" by Clinton S. Burhans, Jr., reprinted from *American Literature,* XXXI (Jan. 1960).

430 White, Ray Lewis, ed. *The Achievement of Sherwood Anderson: Essays in Criticism.* Chapel Hill: University of North Carolina Press, 1966. pp. 14, 120-121, 196, 202-210, 220, 234-236, 254-255.

pp. 202-210: "Sherwood Anderson's Two Prize Pupils" by William L. Phillips. Essay on Hemingway and Faulkner, reprinted from the *University of Chicago Magazine,* XLVII (Jan. 1955).

431 White, Ray Lewis, ed. *Sherwood Anderson/Gertrude Stein: Correspondence and Personal Essays.* Chapel Hill: University of North Carolina Press, 1972. pp. 3, 10-11, 18, 19, 36-38, 43, 44, 46, 49, 52, 54, 72-76, 81, 93, 113.

p. 11: Sherwood Anderson's letter of December 3, 1921, introducing the Hemingways to Gertrude Stein, is quoted. p. 43*n.*: Anderson's blurb for the dust jacket of *IOT* is quoted.

432 White, William, ed. *The Merrill Studies in The Sun Also Rises.* Columbus, Ohio: Merrill, 1969. [Charles E. Merrill Studies.] vi + 106 pages.

Contents: pp. iii-iv: Preface by William White.

Part 1: Contemporary Reviews

pp. 2-4: "Expatriates," review of *SAR* by Conrad Aiken, reprinted from the *N.Y. Herald Tribune Books* (Oct. 31, 1926).

pp. 5-8: "Readers and Writers," review of *SAR* by Ernest Boyd, reprinted from the *Independent,* CXVII (Nov. 20, 1926).

pp. 9-11: "Out of Little, Much," review of *SAR* by Cleveland B. Chase, reprinted from the *Saturday Review of Literature,* III (Dec. 11, 1926).

pp. 12-14: "Warfare in Man and among Men," review of *SAR* by Lawrence S. Morris, reprinted from the *New Republic,* LXIX (Dec. 22, 1926).

pp. 15-16: "Fiction [*Fiesta*]," review of *SAR* by Edwin Muir, reprinted from the *Nation and Athenaeum,* XLI (July 2, 1927).

pp. 17-19: "Hard-Boiled," review of *SAR* by Allen Tate, reprinted from the *Nation,* CXXIII (Dec. 15, 1926).

pp. 20-21: "Sad Young Man," review of *SAR,* reprinted from *Time,* VIII (Nov. 1, 1926).

pp. 22-23: "Fiesta," review of *SAR,* reprinted from the *Times Literary Supplement* (June 30, 1927).

Part II: Essays

pp. 26-36: "The Way It Was" by Carlos Baker, reprinted from *Hemingway: The Writer as Artist,* Second edition, Princeton, 1956, pp. 48-59.

pp. 37-52: "Jake Barnes and Spring Torrents" by Sheridan Baker, reprinted from *EH: An Introduction and Interpretation,* New York, 1967, pp. 40-55.

pp. 53-57: "*The Sun Also Rises*" by James T. Farrell, reprinted from the *N.Y. Times Book Review* (Aug. 1, 1943).

pp. 58-72: "*The Sun Also Rises*: An Essay in Applied Principles" by Earl Rovit, reprinted from *Ernest Hemingway,* New York, 1963, pp. 147-162.

pp. 73-85: "The Death of Love in *The Sun Also Rises*" by Mark Spilka, reprinted from *Twelve Original Essays on Great American Novels* edited by Charles Shapiro, Detroit, 1958, pp. 238-256.

pp. 86-90: [*The Sun Also Rises*: A Commentary] by Philip Young, reprinted from *Ernest Hemingway,* New York, 1952, pp. 54-60.

pp. 91-106: "Commencing with the Simplest Things" by Malcolm Cowley, reprinted from the Introduction to *SAR* in *Three Novels of Ernest Hemingway.* See (A29).

433 White, William. *The Merrill Guide to Ernest Hemingway.* Columbus, Ohio: Merrill, 1969. [Charles E. Merrill Guides.] 44 pages.

A bio-bibliographical essay. Hemingway's Nobel prize acceptance speech is reprinted on pp. 28-29.

434 White, William, compiled by. *The Merrill Checklist of Ernest Hemingway.* Columbus, Ohio: Merrill, 1970. [Charles E. Merrill Checklists.] 45 pages.

A checklist of books by Hemingway and books and articles about him.

435 Wickes, George. *Americans In Paris*. Garden City, N.Y.: Doubleday, 1969. [Paris Review Editions.] pp. 7, 51-52, 56, 88, 90, 91, 94,
149-187, 206, 261, 286-288. Photographs.

> pp. 149-187: Part IV: "Ernest Hemingway in Montparnasse."

436 Wilhelm, Bernard. *Hemingway et Malraux devant la guerre
d'Espagne*. Berne: University of Berne, 1966. 240 pages.

437 Wilson, Colin. *Eagle and Earwig*. London: John Baker, 1965. pp.
113, 115, 121-127.

> pp. 113-127: "The Swamp and the Desert: Notes on Powys and
Hemingway."

438 Wilson, Edmund. *The Devils and Canon Barham: Ten Essays on
Poets, Novelists and Monsters*. New York: Farrar, Straus & Giroux,
1973. pp. xii, 105-111, 115. Foreword by Leon Edel.

> pp. 105-111: "An Effort at Self-Revelation," review of *Islands*, re-
printed from the *New Yorker*, XLVI (Jan. 2, 1971).

439 Wilson, James R. *Responses of College Freshmen to Three Novels*.
Champaign, Illinois: National Council of Teachers of English, 1966.
[NCTE Research Report, No. 7.]

> *FTA* is one of the three novels considered. See (H1479).

440 Wilson, Robert Forrest. *Paris on Parade*. Indianapolis: Bobbs-Merrill, 1925. pp. 244, 246, 248.

> p. 248: Discusses Hemingway's position in the "bookshop circle"
in Paris, and comments that "his friends expect him to go far." Note:
Only *iot* and *TSTP* had been published at the time this was written.

441 Witham, W. Tasker. *The Adolescent in the American Novel, 1920-
1960*. New York: Frederick Ungar, 1964. pp. 2, 24, 25, 34-36, 94, 225,
235, 262, 270, 303.

> Discusses Nick Adams in *IOT*.

442 Wolfe, Don M. *The Image of Man in America*. Dallas: Southern
Methodist University Press, 1957. [New York: Crowell, 1970. Second edition.] pp. 344-360.

> Ch. XVII: "Faulkner and Hemingway: Image of Man's Desolation."

443 Woolf, Virginia. *Collected Essays*. Volume Two. London: Hogarth
Press, 1966. [New York: Harcourt, Brace & World, 1967.] pp. 252-
258.

> "An Essay in Criticism," review of *MWW* (with a preliminary
study of *SAR*), reprinted from the *N.Y. Herald Tribune Books*
(Oct. 9, 1927).

444 Wylder, Delbert E. *Hemingway's Heroes*. Albuquerque: University of New Mexico Press, 1969. x + 256 pages. Selected Bibliography on pp. 245-[252].

Hemingway's novels are discussed in separate chapters: *TOS* in "A Parody of the Sentimental Hero," revised from an article in the *South Dakota Review*, v (Winter 1967-1968); *SAR* in "The Wounded Anti-Hero"; *FTA* in "The Guilt-Ridden Anti-Hero"; *THAHN* in "The Self-Destructive Anti-Hero"; *FWBT* in "The Mythic Hero in the Contemporary World"; *ARIT* in "The Tyrant Hero"; and *OMATS* in "The Hero as Saint and Sinner."

445 Young, Philip. *Ernest Hemingway: A Reconsideration*. University Park and London: Pennsylvania State University Press, 1966. x + 297 pages. [Paperback edition: New York: Harcourt, Brace & World, 1966. (A Harbinger Book, H 064.)]

"Revised extensively in minor ways" from *Ernest Hemingway*, New York, 1952. See (G460). With a new foreword, on pp. 1-28, "Author and Critic: A Rather Long Story," an expanded version of an essay which first appeared in the *Kenyon Review*, xxviii (Jan. 1966); and an afterword, on pp. 261-290, "Touching Down and Out," reprinted from the *Kenyon Review*, xxvi (Autumn 1964). The foreword was reprinted in *Three Bags Full*, see next entry. Note: Incompletely entered as (G460d).

446 Young, Philip. *Three Bags Full: Essays in American Fiction*. New York: Harcourt Brace Jovanovich, 1972. pp. xi-xiii, 3-75, 155, 157, 158, 168, 175. [Paperback edition: Harcourt Brace Jovanovich, 1973. (A Harvest Book, HB 265.)]

pp. 3-29: "Hemingway and Me: A Rather Long Story," reprinted with revisions from the *Kenyon Review*, xxviii (Jan. 1966). This essay served as the foreword to *EH: A Reconsideration*, see above entry. pp. 30-54: "The End of Compendium Reviewing," reprinted from the *Kenyon Review*, xxvi (Autumn 1964). See (H1551). pp. 55-67: "I Dismember Papa," review of A. E. Hotchner's *Papa Hemingway*, reprinted from the *Atlantic*, ccxviii (Aug. 1966). pp. 68-75: "Locked in the Vault," regarding the making of *The Hemingway Manuscripts*, reprinted from the *N.Y. Times Book Review* (Sept. 29, 1968). For reprints of this article, see (S-H470).

447 Young, Philip, and Charles W. Mann. *The Hemingway Manuscripts: An Inventory*. University Park and London: Pennsylvania State University Press, 1969. xiv + 138 pages. Facsimiles.

An inventory of the manuscripts of published and unpublished work (books, short fiction, journalism and other non-fiction, poetry, and fragments), letters, and miscellaneous items in the possession of Mary Hemingway. 332 items. For previously unpublished work by Hemingway and a description of this book, see (S-B11). For fac-similes of manuscript pages, see (S-F33).

448 Zentner, Karl. *Ernest Hemingway in der Anekdote.* Munich: Heimeran Verlag, 1969. [Kleine Anekdotensammlung, VI.] 69 pages. Illustrated by Luis Murschetz.

SECTION H

NEWSPAPER AND

PERIODICAL MATERIAL

ON HEMINGWAY

THROUGH 1973

The items in this section have been culled from many sources, including the *MLA International Bibliography, Book Review Digest, Book Review Index, American Literary Scholarship, British Humanities Index,* and *Readers' Guide to Periodical Literature.* Three new reference works were particularly helpful: *An Index to Literature in The New Yorker: Volumes I-XV, 1925-1940* by Robert Owen Johnson, Metuchen, N.J.: Scarecrow Press, 1969; *The Contemporary Novel: A Checklist of Critical Literature on the British and American Novel Since 1945* by Irving Adelman and Rita Dworkin, Metuchen, N.J.: Scarecrow Press, 1972, pp. 254-281; and *Articles on Twentieth-Century Literature: An Annotated Bibliography, 1954 to 1970* by David E. Pownall, New York: Kraus-Thomas, 1973, Vol. 3, pp. 1476-1553. Supplements to three reference works consulted earlier for the bibliography were also very helpful: *Articles on American Literature: 1950-1967* compiled by Lewis Leary with the assistance of Carolyn Bartholet and Catharine Roth, Durham, N.C.: Duke University Press, 1970, pp. 262-279; *The American Novel: Vol. II: Criticism Written 1960-1968* by Donna Gerstenberger and George Hendrick, Chicago: Swallow Press, 1970, pp. 164-177; and *Twentieth-Century Short Story Explication: Supplement I: 1967-1969* compiled by Warren S. Walker, Hamden, Conn.: Shoe String Press, 1970, pp. 97-112.

The greatest help came, of course, from those publications devoted solely to Hemingway: Maurice Beebe and John Feaster's bibliography in the special Hemingway number of *Modern Fiction Studies,* XIV (Autumn 1968); William White's bibliography in the first issue of *Hemingway notes,* I (Spring 1971); the checklists by Taylor Alderman, Kenneth Rosen, and William White in subsequent issues of *Hemingway notes;* and the checklist in the *Fitzgerald/Hemingway Annual 1972.*

The foreign listings were greatly enlarged by items from José María Iribarren's bibliography in *Hemingway y los Sanfermines,* Pamplona, 1970; Valentina Libman's *Russian Studies of American Literature: A Bibliography,* Chapel Hill, N.C., 1969; the bibliographical footnotes in Yuri Prizel's "Hemingway in Soviet Literary Criticism," *American Literature,* XLIV (Nov. 1972); and Wayne Kvam's selected bibliography in *Hemingway in Germany,* Athens, Ohio, 1973. All of these sources bear checking for additional items of interest in their particular language.

S-H1 "Dare Girls Rescued," *Oak Leaves* (Feb. 3, 1917).
Three girls who were riding the dumbwaiter in the lunchroom of the Oak Park and River Forest Township High School "were flying to destruction when Ernest Hemingway . . . saw and realized the danger. He grabbed the rope and was jerked off his feet and his

bare hands engaged and blocked the pulley at the top" until four other boys ran to his assistance and pulled the girls back to safety. Reprinted in *Trapeze* (June 9, 1967), p. 7.

2 "Lieutenant Hemingway, convalescing from 237 wounds, being driven around Milan by an Italian Officer," *American Red Cross Central Division Bulletin*, I, xlix (Dec. 7, 1918). Photograph of Hemingway in the sidecar of a motorcycle.

The accompanying article mentions Hemingway's being cited to receive the Silver Medal of Valor, the second highest award of the Italian command, for carrying a helpless comrade to safety before he collapsed from his own wounds. A letter from Hemingway, describing his wounds, is quoted.

3 Ebersold, Frederick. "Hanna Club Has Rousing First Meeting with 'Ernie' Hemingway as Speaker," *Trapeze*, VIII (Feb. 7, 1919), 2.
Hemingway spoke on war.

4 Stein, Gertrude. Review of *TSTP*, *Chicago Tribune* [Paris edition] (Nov. 27, 1923).
"Three stories and ten poems is very pleasantly said. So far so good, further than that, and as far as that, I may say of Ernest Hemingway that as he sticks to poetry and intelligence it is both poetry and intelligent. . . . I should say that Hemingway should stick to poetry and intelligence and eschew the hotter emotions and the more turgid vision. Intelligence and a great deal of it is a good thing to use when you have it, it's all for the best." Reprinted in *The Left Bank Revisited* edited by Hugh Ford, University Park, Pennsylvania, 1972, p. 257.

5 [Mencken, H. L.] Check List of New Books column, brief review of *iot*, *American Mercury*, V (Aug. 1925), xxxviii.
"The sort of brave, bold stuff that all atheistic young newspaper reporters write. Jesus Christ in lower case. A hanging, a carnal love, and two disembowelings. Here it is set forth solemnly on Rives hand-made paper, in an edition limited to 170 copies, and with the imprimatur of Ezra Pound." Quoted in toto. Note: Reprinted, with authentication of Mencken's authorship by Charles Angoff, in Frank Luther Mott's *A History of American Magazines*, Vol. V, Cambridge, 1968, p. 11.

6 Check List of New Books column, brief review of *IOT*, *American Mercury*, VII (Feb. 1926), xxx.
"It is made up of sketches and stories in the bold, bad manner of the Café Dôme."

7 Dounce [Harry Esty]. Review of *SAR*, *New Yorker*, II (Nov. 20, 1926), 88, 90.

"*The Sun Also Rises* . . . is a new novel by that already almost legendary figure in the Parisian group of young, American authors. This is a story of exquisite simplicity built on the sensational theme of a love affair between an American who has been sexually incapacitated during the war, and a credible and living counterpart of the jejune Iris March. The author of *The Torrents of Spring*, who has only to publish to be read by a certain circle of the intelligentsia, and not even to publish to be discussed, has written wittily and with a smooth deliberateness astonishingly effective in numerous passages of nervous staccato. An unconscious sense of security in the author carries the reader from episode to episode with mounting curiosity and no fatigue. The story is told in a crisp procession of events in which no scene is quite without poignancy, however brutal, nor quite without wit, however poignant. Under the hard, flat glass of Mr. Hemingway's virtuosity the ever-present yet unmentionable tragedy ebbs and flows like dark water."

8   Emmett, Elizabeth. "A Reader in Revolt," *McNaught's Monthly,* VII (April 1927), 114-115.

A complaint against favorable reviews of *SAR*. See also the letter, signed "Reader," endorsing this article, "The Sun Also Rises," *MM*, VII (May 1927), 160.

9   Thurber, James. "A Visit from Saint Nicholas (In the Ernest Hemingway Manner)," *New Yorker*, III (Dec. 24, 1927), 17-18.
Parody.

10   Constant Reader [Dorothy Parker]. "Excuse It, Please," *New Yorker,* III (Feb. 18, 1928), 76-77.

A reassessment of her statement in her review of *MWW* (H81) that Hemingway was "the greatest living writer of short stories." After being reminded of Max Beerbohm and Rudyard Kipling, she changed her assessment to "the greatest living American short-story writer." Reprinted in *Constant Reader*, New York, 1970, pp. 66-68; in *The Portable Dorothy Parker*, New York, 1973, pp. 495-496.

11   Jordan, Philip. "Ernest Hemingway: A Personal Study," *Everyman,* II (Dec. 12, 1929), 541. Cover drawing of Hemingway by Joseph Simpson.

A "personal impression" by a friend who met Hemingway at one of Ford Madox Ford's parties at the Bal Musette in Paris.

12   Calverton, V. F. "Ernest Hemingway and the Modern Temper," *Book League Monthly,* III (Jan. 1930), 165-166.

The author differs with the claim that Hemingway "has already won a secure and lasting place in our literature."

13   "R.M.C." [Robert M. Coates]. Brief review of *IOT* (Scribner's edition), *New Yorker*, VI (Nov. 22, 1930), 116.

"Ernest Hemingway's first book, *In Our Time*, so long out of print in its American edition and so expensive a collector's item in its European, has just now been issued in a new printing. It was heartily kicked about when it first came out six years ago (I remember Hemingway murderously wondering what Mencken meant by calling it 'cloacal'), but if you've missed it, you missed some of the finest writing he's done."

14 Alajalov. "*Vanity Fair's* own paper dolls. No. 5: Ernest Hemingway, America's own literary cave man; hard-drinking, hard-fighting, hard-loving—all for art's sake," *Vanity Fair,* XLII (March 1934), 29.

Paper doll of Hemingway as the Neanderthal Man, surrounded by costumes of the Lost Generation (complete with café table), Izaak Walton, Don José the toreador, and the unknown soldier (with a Red Cross armband and wounded knee).

15 "E.B.W." [E. B. White]. "The Law of the Jungle," *New Yorker,* X (April 14, 1934), 31.

Verse parody. Subtitled: "Mr. Hemingway said that he shot only lions that were utter strangers to him."—*The Herald Tribune.*

16 Koven, Joseph. "The Liberal Literary Legion," *Monthly Review,* I (June 1934), 44-45. General article.

Hemingway is described as "artist-in-ordinary to America's pseudo-intelligenzia [*sic*] to whom the cock-and-bull struggles of neurotic adventurers are infinitely more important than the life and death conflicts of humanity."

17 Cotton, W. "Mr. Dickens Meets His Rival Best-Sellers," *Vanity Fair,* XLII (June 1934), 20. Drawing of Charles Dickens with Sinclair Lewis, Kathleen Norris, Hervey Allen, Hemingway, and Dashiell Hammett.

18 Broun, Heywood. It Seems to Me column, *N.Y. World-Telegram* (Aug. 18, 1934), p. 13.

Regarding Hemingway's *Esquire* letters.

19 Seldes, Gilbert. "The Prize-fighter and the Bull: Evaluating Hemingway and Lardner in the light of the former's now-famous phrase," *Esquire,* II (Nov. 1934), 52, 173-174.

Regarding Hemingway's remarks on Ring Lardner in "Defense of Dirty Words," *Esquire,* II (Sept. 1934).

20 Harrison, Charles Yale. "Story for Mr. Hemingway," *Modern Monthly,* VIII (Feb. 1935), 731-737.

A story by the author of *Generals Die in Bed.* The headnote, on p. 731, quotes Hemingway's reference to this book in "A Natural History of the Dead": "writers are mistaken who write books called

Generals Die in Bed . . . the titles of all such books should be *Generals Usually Die in Bed*, if we are to have any sort of accuracy in such things."

21 Briefer Mention column, review of *GHOA, American Mercury,* XXXVI (Dec. 1935), 503.

"Hemingway has never written better than this and few men ever as well. His style, simple and pure, has almost attained perfection. He is authentic: every sound, smell, and sight is described with lucid accuracy. His thinking is adult. He has humor: the dialogue is fresh and rich. And he is human. . . . Subject matter and form are not important to a writer of Hemingway's distinction. . . . What is important is the fact that he has written truthfully and supremely well."

22 Hansen, Harry. The First Reader column, *N.Y. World-Telegram* (Feb. 15, 1936), p. 15.

Sinclair Lewis's "Lines to a College Professor," on Hemingway's use of four-letter words, is reprinted from the *Yale Literary Magazine,* CI (Feb. 1936). See (H274).

23 The Talk of the Town column, *New Yorker,* XIII (Aug. 28, 1937), 7.

A satire on the Hemingway-Eastman encounter in Maxwell Perkins's office, on August 11, 1937.

24 Editorial Comment, "Editing Hemingway," *New Masses,* XXVI (Feb. 1, 1938), 10.

Regarding the omission of the last sentence of Hemingway's cablegram praising Herbert Matthews's *Two Wars and More to Come* in Carrick & Evans's ad in the *N.Y. Times* (Jan. 24, 1938), p. 21. See also Matthews's *A World in Revolution* (S-G289).

25 Fagin, Bryllion. "The Psychological Moment," *Step Ladder,* XXIV (May 1938), 101-107. General article. Discussion of Hemingway's work on pp. 101-103.

26 "Mr. Hemingway in Spain," review of "The Spanish War," *TLS* (Aug. 6, 1938), p. 514.

Review of Hemingway's NANA dispatches in *Fact,* No. 16 (July 15, 1938). See (S-C18).

27 Anisimov, I. "V Amerike" [In America], *Oktiabr',* No. 11 (Nov. 1938), pp. 186-196.

Essay on Upton Sinclair and Hemingway.

28 Phelps, William Lyon. *Esquire*'s Five-Minute Shelf column, "While fellow critics, thousands of readers applaud *For Whom the Bell Tolls,* your columnist won't dance," review of *FWBT, Esquire,* XV (Feb. 1941), 76, 135.

"I do not believe Mr. Hemingway is a great writer; I do not believe *For Whom the Bell Tolls* is a literary masterpiece. . . . Its deficiencies and limitations should be painfully apparent. . . . In voluminous verbiage, I suggest that the book has an excess of about 150 pages." The reviewer also criticizes the "superfluous obscenities."

29 Church, Richard. Review of *FWBT, John O'London's Weekly* (March 21, 1941), p. 653.
    "*For Whom the Bell Tolls* . . . is likely to be [Hemingway's] *magnum opus*. [Discussion of the plot.] Now consider that situation: love snatched a moment before annihilation. Hemingway has chosen it as the vehicle of his most mature creative effort. I believe that reveals the whole man. All his previous work has been leading up to this. He has chosen this theme inevitably, because he is the creature of his time and people. His time is the present, which includes the post-war years. His people is the American, still at the frontier of civilization. . . ."

30 *Look* Examines series, "Ernest Hemingway," *Look,* v (April 8, 1941), 18, 20-21. Photographs.

31 Lawson, Edna B. "On the Road to Honolulu," *Paradise of the Pacific,* LV (Dec. 1941), 75.
    Brief mention of a visit by Hemingway and Martha Gellhorn on their way to cover the war in China for *Collier's* magazine.

32 Davis, Bob. Bob Davis Reveals column, "Ernest Hemingway, as He Seems to His Hunting Companion," *N.Y. Sun* (Oct. 1, 1942), p. 16.
    Interview with Taylor Williams in Sun Valley, Idaho.

33 "Ernest Hemingway: He Is One of America's Greatest Novelists," *Victory,* II, iii [1944], 72-74. Photographs.
    Biographical essay. Note: *Victory* was published from 1943 to 1945 by the Crowell-Collier Publishing Company in collaboration with the U.S. Office of War Information. There were editions in Afrikaans, Dutch, English, French, Italian, Portuguese, and Spanish. According to a label affixed to the cover, it was not distributed in the United States or to American civilian or military personnel overseas.

34 "Hemingway Looks at the War in Europe," *Hulton's National Weekly Picture Post,* XXIV (July 15, 1944), 20-21. Photographs.
    Interview with Hemingway in "Southern England."

35 [The Editors]. "Hemingway's *A Farewell to Arms,*" *Explicator,* III (Nov. 1944), Item 11.
    Reply to the query in *Explicator,* II (June 1944), regarding the title of *FTA*.

36 Gierasch, Walter. "Hemingway's 'Snows of Kilimanjaro,'" *Explicator*, IV (Feb. 1946), Query 9.

   Regarding the relationship of the epigraph to the body of Hemingway's story.

37 Guérard, Albert-J. "Lettre d'Amerique," *Le Magasin du spectacle* (Dec. 7, 1946), pp. 123-124. General article. Includes a discussion of Hemingway's work.

38 Chamberlain, John. "American Writers," *Life*, XXIII (Sept. 1, 1947), 82-92. Caricature of Hemingway on p. 82. General article.

39 Crane, R. S. "Ernest Hemingway: 'The Short Happy Life of Francis Macomber,'" *English "A" Analyst*, No. 16 (Nov. 1, 1949). For reprints of this essay, see *The Idea of the Humanities and Other Essays Critical and Historical* (S-G96).

40 Prause, Gerhard. "Ernest Hemingway," *Welt und Wort*, VI (Feb. 1951), 49-51.

41 Carlson, Eric W. "Questions on *Murder in the Cathedral* and *The Sun Also Rises*," *Exercise Exchange*, I (1952), 6-8.

42 Yndurain Hernández, Francisco. "España en la obra de Hemingway," *Revista Universidad de Zaragoza*, Nos. 3 and 4 (1952).

43 Howard, Milton. "Hemingway and Heroism," review of *OMATS*, *Masses & Mainstream*, V (Oct. 1952), 1-8.

   "This is Hemingway's best piece of writing, for it works up to the maximum the literary effects and the morals implicit in his view of life and society—the aloneness, the splendor of hard energy and courage, all operating in a social vacuum and therefore an art which cannot hide its terrible hollowness. Being the best that this social and literary attitude can produce it only accentuates the more the bitterness of its inhumanity."

44 Fenton, Charles A. "Hemingway's Kansas City Apprenticeship," *New World Writing*, Second number (Nov. 1952), pp. 316-326. A revised version of this essay appears in *The Apprenticeship of Ernest Hemingway*, New York, 1954, pp. 28-49.

45 Knöller, Fritz. "Hemingways Weltbild und Werkform," *Welt und Wort*, VII (Dec. 1952), 411-412.

46 Lilje, Hanns. "Gnadenlosigkeit und Gnade im Werke Hemingways," *Zeitwende*, XXIV (1953), 5-13.

47 Baur, Josef. "Ein Stück Epos: Zu Hemingways letztem Erzählerwerk," *Welt und Wort*, VIII (March 1953), 81-82.

   On *Der alte Mann und das Meer (OMATS)*.

48 Burke, Jackson. "Ernest Hemingway—Muy Hombre!" *Blue Book* (July 1953), pp. 6-10.
An interview with Hemingway conducted in the Café Floridita, in Havana.

49 Gronke, Erich. "Das jüngste Buch Hemingways," review of *OMATS*, *Zeitschrift für Anglistik und Amerikanistik*, II, i (1954), 119-123.

50 Thurber, James. "How to Be Sixty," *Bermudian*, xxv (June 1954), 25, 51, 53-54.
Commentary on Hemingway's article in *Look*, IX (May 4, 1954), regarding his dreams. See (C381).

51 Zappone, Domenico. "Incontro con Hemingway," *Galleria*, IV (Dec. 1954), 210-213.

51₁ Crovi, Raffaele. "Vittorini, l'America e la giovane letteratura italiana," *ibid.*, pp. 307-313.
Discusses Hemingway's influence on Elio Vittorini.

52 Piontek, Heinz. Review of *Die grünen Hügel Afrikas (GHOA)*, *Welt und Wort*, IX (Dec. 1954), 413.

53 "Hemingway Tells of Early Career; States That He 'Won't Quit Now,' " *Daily Princetonian* (April 14, 1955), p. 3.
On April 6, 1955, four Princeton sophomores, Jack Goodman, John Milton, Alan Graber, and Bill Tangney, interviewed Hemingway at Finca Vigia. They included his comments on writing and literature in this article.

54 Eisinger, Chester E. "The American War Novel: An Affirming Flame," *Pacific Spectator*, IX (Summer 1955), 272-287. General article.

55 "Romane im Safe," interview with Hemingway, *Der Spiegel*, IX (Nov. 23, 1955), 59.

56 Owen, John. "Inside Hemingway: His Strange Search for Love and Death," *See*, xv (May 1956), 28-31.

57 Škvorecký, Josef. "Literární názory Ernesta Hemingwaye," *Světová literatura*, I (June 1956), 190-195.

58 Mertens, Gerard M. "Hemingway's *The Old Man and the Sea* and Mann's *The Black Swan*," *Literature and Psychology*, VI (Aug. 1956), 96-99.

59 Feuchtwanger, Lion. "Laxness a Hemingway," *Host do domu*, III (Dec. 1956), 559.
Essay on Halldór Laxness and Hemingway.

60 Vala, Josef [pseudonym of Josef Škvorecký]. "Zamyšlení nad Hemingwayem" [Some thoughts on Hemingway], *Květen*, III, xiii (1957), 740-744.

61 Lucas, Christopher. "Ernest Hemingway's temper also rises," *Sunday Dispatch*, London (Oct. 27, 1957). Excerpted in Dennis Pepper's *A Hemingway Selection*, London, 1972, p. 195.

62 Boal, Sam. "The Hemingway I Know," *Gent*, II (Dec. 1957), 7-10, 55-57.

63 Schwerin, Christoph. "Hemingways Parodie," review of *TOS*, *Deutsche Rundschau*, LXXXIV (April 1958), 403-404.

64 Fukuma, Kin-ichi. Review, *Kyushu American Literature*, No. 1 (June 1958), p. 35.
   Review of Shigetaka Ban's "A Study of Ernest Hemingway's *A Farewell to Arms*" in the *Fukuoka Liberal Arts College Treatises*, 1956.

65 Fritzsch, Robert. "Der Hemingway'sche Held und die Frau: Zur 'Sexualfrivolität' im Werk Ernest Hemingways," *Welt und Wort*, XIII (July 1958), 197-201.

66 Review and Outlook column, "The Old Man and the Fee," *Wall Street Journal* (Aug. 8, 1958), p. 4.
   Parody on Hemingway's refusal to permit *Esquire* to reprint three Spanish Civil War stories in an anthology. Reprinted in Arnold Gingrich's "Scott, Ernest and Whoever," *Esquire*, LXVI (Dec. 1966); and *Esquire*, LXXX (Oct. 1973).

67 Kauffmann, Stanley. "Hollywood and Hemingway," review of the film *The Old Man and the Sea*, *New Republic*, CXXXIX (Oct. 6, 1958), 21-22.

68 Stevenson, David L. "Fiction's Unfamiliar Face," *Nation*, CLXXXVII (Nov. 1, 1958), 307-309. General article.
   Discusses *OMATS* as possibly the last of the novels "of formal structure, with a solidly presented central character, and a definite conclusion."

69 Morgan, Raleigh, Jr. "Stylistic Devices and Levels of Speech in the Works of Hemingway," *Sprache und Literatur Englands und Amerikas*, III (1959), 145-154.

70 Gräf, Gerhard. "*In* und *out* als Richtungspräpositionen in U.S.-English," *Zeitschrift für Anglistik und Amerikanistik*, VII (Jan. 1959), 64-71. General article.

71 O'Hara, John. "Anecdote Amended," *Holiday*, xxvi (Dec. 1959), 4.
Letter to the editor regarding the shillelagh incident described in Joe McCarthy's "Costello's: The Wayward Saloon," *Holiday*, xxvi (Oct. 1959), 112.

72 "Dva interv'iu Khemingueia" [Two interviews with Hemingway], *Inostrannaya Literatura*, No. 1 (Jan. 1960), 267-269.

73 Rubinstein, Annette T. "Brave and Baffled Hunter," *Mainstream*, xiii (Jan. 1960), 1-23. Note: The cover title is "Ernest Hemingway: His Art and Scope."

74 [Plimpton, George]. "Ernest Kheminguei o svoei rabote" [Ernest Hemingway about his work], *Voprosy Literatury*, No. 1 (Jan. 1960), pp. 153-156.
Interview by George Plimpton translated into Russian, by M. Landora, from the *Paris Review*, v (Spring 1958).

75 Pendleton, Harold Edmen. "Ernest Hemingway: A Theory of Learning," *Dissertation Abstracts*, xx (Feb. 1960), 3302-3303.
Abstract from a doctoral dissertation, University of Illinois, 1959.

76 Alekseev, A. "Don Ernesto zhivet pod Gavanoi. A. I. Mikoian v gostiakh u E. Khemingueia," *Izvestia* (Feb. 14, 1960).
Reports on a visit to Hemingway, at his home near Havana, by Anastas Mikoyan.

77 Moknachev, M. "Kheminguei govorit: 'Liudi dolzhny zhit' bez voiny'" [Hemingway says: "People ought to live without war"], *Izvestia* (March 19, 1960).

78 Mikoyan, Sergo. "Vstrecha s Khemingueem" [A meeting with Hemingway], *Literaturnaya Gazeta* (May 7, 1960), p. 5. Photograph of Hemingway and Anastas Mikoyan.

79 Kuppuswamy, B. "Hemingway on Insomnia," *Literary Half-Yearly*, 1 (July 1960), 58-60.
On "Now I Lay Me."

80 Lyons, Leonard. "Ma vie avec 'Papa,' " *Candide*, No. 10 (July 6-13, 1960), pp. 9-10.

81 Heilborn, Franz. "Hemingway no crepúsculo," *Senhor*, ii, No. 21 (Nov. 1960), 60-61.
On Hemingway's career in his later years.

82 "Papas Fiesta," *Der Spiegel*, xiv (Nov. 9, 1960), 75-78.
Regarding "The Dangerous Summer."

83 Spilka, Mark. "The Necessary Stylist: A New Critical Revision," *Modern Fiction Studies*, vi (Winter 1960-1961), 283-297. General

article. Regarding Warren Beck's essay "The Shorter Happy Life of Mrs. Macomber" (H967), on pp. 289-297.

84 Poenaru, Ioana. "Creația literară a lui Hemingway," *Analele Universitații București*, x (1961).

85 Takigawa, Motoo. "A Study of Hemingway—The World War I and II Novels," *Journal of the Society of English and American Literature* (Kwansei Gakuin University), No. 5 (1961), 1-12.

86 Poenaru, Ioana. "Umanismul lui Ernest Miller Hemingway," *Studii de literatura universală*, III (1961), 287-297.

87 Blonski, Jan. "Americans in Poland," *Kenyon Review*, XXIII (Winter 1961), 32-51. General article. Mentions, on p. 45, that "Polish readers see Hemingway as a marvelous upholder of human liberty."

88 Souchere, Elena de la. "La corrida y la muerte: Variaciones sobre un tema de Hemingway," *Cultura Universitaria*, No. 74-75 (Jan.-June 1961), pp. 56-68; No. 76-77 (July-Dec. 1961), pp. 65-79.

89 Stern, Edith M. "Papa's Flops," *Esquire*, LV (Feb. 1961), 16.
Letter to the editor, giving details of Hemingway's relationship with Boni & Liveright, in reply to Lester Cohen's remark "Mr. Hemingway had a flop and was dismissed" in his article on Horace Liveright, *Esquire*, LIV (Dec. 1960), 108.

90 Murphy, Michael. "Ernest Miller Hemingway," *Inland*, No. 30 (Spring 1961), pp. 10-15.

91 Borovik, Genrikh. "Serdtse Khemingueia" [Hemingway's heart], *Ogoniok*, No. 28 (July 1961), p. 29.

92 Pennington, Phil. "Hemingway's Letters to L. A. Man Released," *Los Angeles Mirror* [Home Edition] (July 5, 1961), pp. 1, 8. Facsimile of complimentary closing and signature. For excerpts from Hemingway's letters to Russ Burton, a young writer, see (S-F111) and (S-F125).

93 Klie, Barbara. "Bevor die Sonne Aufgeht: Zum Tode von Ernest Hemingway," *Christ und Welt* (July 7, 1961), p. 13.

94 McCabe, Charles. "Requiem for an Immortal," *San Francisco Sunday Chronicle* (July 9, 1961), This World section, pp. 3-4.

95 Ledig-Rowohlt, H. M. "Der Tod am Morgen," *Die Zeit*, XVI (July 14, 1961), 9.
Essay by Hemingway's German publisher. Includes excerpts from three letters from Hemingway to Ernst Rowohlt. See (S-F68), (S-F70), and (S-F97). For English translation, see Ledig-Rowohlt's *Meeting Two American Giants*, Reinbek, 1962.

96 Mathias, Paul, and Paul Slade. "Le même jour ils se sont tus," *Paris Match*, No. 640 (July 15, 1961), pp. 28, 34-35. Cover photograph.

96₁ Sabathier, Jean-Marc. "Journaliste, boxeur, soldat, prix Nobel, il courait là où les obus tombent. Comme son père il est mort foudroyé par son fusil," *ibid.*, pp. 36-40.

97 Přidal, Antonin. "Hrana Hemingwayovi," *Host do domu*, VIII (Aug. 1961), 372.

98 Lania, Leo. "Hemingway," *Welt und Wort*, XVI (Aug. 1961), 240.

99 Kim, Suk-Choo. "Stoicism in Hemingway," *English Language and Literature*, X (Sept. 1961), 292-306. In Korean.

100 Eisner, A. "On byl s nami v Ispanii" [He was with us in Spain], *Novyi Mir*, No. 9 (Sept. 1961), pp. 169-173.

100₁ Orlova, R. "Posle smerti Khemingueia. Po stranitsam zarubezhnoi pressy" [After Hemingway's death. On the pages of the foreign press], *ibid.*, pp. 173-178.

101 Finchley, Peter. "Ernest Hemingway, the Bell Tolls for Thee," *Astrology* (Oct. 1961), pp. 18-20.
   Analysis of Hemingway's career based on the stars and planets.

102 Hotchner, A. E. "A Note from the Playwright," *The Playgoer* (Oct. 4, 1961), p. 12.
   On "A Short Happy Life," presented at the Huntington Hartford Theatre.

103 Varenne, René. "Hemingway e il romanticismo dell' azione," *Fiera Letteraria*, XVI (Oct. 8, 1961), 1, 2.

104 Quintanilla, Luis. "Hemingway en mi recuerdo," *Cuadernos del Congreso por la Libertad de la Cultura*, LIV (Nov. 1961), 45-51.
   Drawing of Hemingway on p. 47 by the artist-author.

105 Allen, John J. "The English of Hemingway's Spaniards," *South Atlantic Bulletin*, XXVII (Nov. 1961), 6-7. Reprinted in Sheldon Norman Grebstein's *The Merrill Studies in For Whom the Bell Tolls*, Columbus, Ohio, 1971, pp. 91-93.

106 Elliston, Stephen. "Hemingway and the Next Generation," *University College Quarterly* (Michigan State University), VII (Nov. 1961), 23-27.

107 Schafer, William J. "Ernest Hemingway: Arbiter of Common Numerality," *Carleton Miscellany*, III (Winter 1962), 100-104.
   A re-examination of "The Light of the World."

108 Matsuyama, Nobunao. "A Note on Hemingway's *In Our Time,*" *Doshisha Literature,* No. 22 (Jan. 1962), pp. 20-28.

109 Stevenson, Philip. "A Note on Ernest Hemingway," *Monthly Review,* XIII (Feb. 1962), 475-479.
Discusses the Hemingway heroes and their fate.

110 "Als ob," review of the film *Adventures of a Young Man, Der Spiegel,* XVI (Feb. 7, 1962), 84-85.

111 Morioka, Sakae. "Huck Finn and *A Farewell to Arms,*" *Kyushu American Literature,* No. 5 (April 1962), pp. 27-35. In English.

112 Takigawa, Motoo. "A Study of Ernest Hemingway: *Men Without Women,*" *Journal of the Society of English and American Literature* (Kwansei Gakuin University), No. 4 (May 1962), pp. 41-66.

113 Krock, Arthur. In the Nation column, "Previous Veto of a Pulitzer Board Award," *N.Y. Times* (May 11, 1962), p. 30.
Regarding the Pulitzer prize advisory board's recommendation of *FWBT,* in 1941, and Nicholas Murray Butler's veto of their selection.

114 Campoamor, Fernando G. " 'Papa': Good Bye," *Secolul 20,* II (July 1962), 91-92. In Rumanian. Special number dedicated to Hemingway. See also (S-C42).

114₁ Ehrenburg, Ilya. "Amintiri despre Hemingway," *ibid.,* pp. 93-98. Translated into Rumanian by Madeleine Fortunescu.

114₂ Kaskin, Ivan. "Ernest Hemingway," *ibid.,* pp. 115-131.

114₃ Sidorovici, Alexandra. "Scriitorul despre viață și moarte," *ibid.,* pp. 132-138.

114₄ Cabrera Infante, Guillermo. "Hemingway, Cuba și revoluția," *ibid.,* pp. 139-149.

115 Fratini, Gaio. "Il 'rovescio' di Hemingway," *Fiera Letteraria,* XVII (July 15, 1962), 6.

116 Rossky, William. "Sudden Love: An Approach to *A Farewell to Arms,*" *English Record,* XII (Sept. 1962), 4-6.

117 Takigawa, Motoo. "From Anderson to Hemingway and Faulkner," *Journal of the Society of English and American Literature* (Kwansei Gakuin University), No. 7 (Oct. 1962), pp. 68-75.

118 Nakamura, Junichi. "A Study of *For Whom the Bell Tolls,*" *Studies* (Kobe), IX (Oct. 1962), 1-10.

119 Mailer, Norman. "The Big Bite," *Esquire*, LVIII (Nov. 1962), 134.
Thoughts on the deaths of Hemingway and Marilyn Monroe.

120 Goldhurst, William. "Literary Anti-Semitism in the 20's," *Congress Bi-Weekly* (American Jewish Congress), XXIX (Dec. 24, 1962), 10-12. General article.
Discusses Hemingway's treatment of Robert Cohn in *SAR*.

121 Hoffman, Frederick J. "Hemingway and Fitzgerald," *American Literary Scholarship: An Annual | 1963*, pp. 81-91. (Durham, N.C.: Duke University Press, 1965. Edited by James Woodress.)

122 Joyner, Charles W. "Ernest Hemingway's Retreat from Pacifism," *The Proceedings of the South Carolina Historical Association* (1963), pp. 4-11.

123 Saroyan, William. "Americans in Paris, 1929," review of Morley Callaghan's *That Summer in Paris*, *New Republic*, CXLVIII (Feb. 9, 1963), 26-28. Reprinted in *I Used to Believe I Had Forever Now I'm Not So Sure*, New York, 1968, pp. 85-90.

124 Woodward, Robert H. "Hemingway's 'On the Quai at Smyrna': An Exercise in Irony," *Exercise Exchange*, X (March 1963), 11-12.

124₁ Lagios, Socrates A. "*The Old Man and the Sea*—1932 and 1952," *ibid.*, pp. 12-13.
The paragraph that was the nucleus of *OMATS* is quoted from "On the Blue Water," which first appeared in *Esquire*, V (April 1936)—not 1932 as stated in this title and article. See (C243).

125 Broadus, Robert N. "The New Record Set by Hemingway's Old Man," *Notes and Queries*, X [New Series] (April 1963), 152-153.
Regarding the 84 days that the old man (in *OMATS*) went without taking a fish, and the previous record of 83 days held by Zane Grey.

126 Kim, Byung-Chol. "Hemingway's Dualism," *English Language and Literature*, XIV (June-Oct. 1963), 56-77. In Korean.

127 Childs, Barney. "Hemingway and the Leopard of Kilimanjaro," *American Notes & Queries*, II (Sept. 1963), 3. For reply, see R. W. Bevis et al., *AN&Q*, VI (April 1968).

127₁ Bennett, J. Q. "Dust Jacket of *For Whom the Bell Tolls*," *ibid.*, p. 3.
Regarding the omission of the photographer's name under the photograph of Hemingway on the back cover of the first state of the dust jacket. The credit line on the second state reads: "Photograph by Arnold—Sun Valley."

128 Hoffman, Frederick J. "Hemingway and Fitzgerald," *American Literary Scholarship: An Annual / 1964*, pp. 82-88.

129 "50 Pounds of Hemingway," *Newsweek*, LXIII (Jan. 6, 1964), 67.
Interview with Mary Hemingway regarding the unpublished manuscripts.

130 Brief review of Earl Rovit's *Ernest Hemingway, Choice*, I (March 1964), 23.

131 [Bruccoli, Matthew J.]. Review of *A Moveable Feast, Fitzgerald Newsletter*, No. 25 (Spring 1964). Reprinted in the bound volume of the *Fitzgerald Newsletter*, Washington, D. C.: Microcard Editions, 1969, p. 149.

132 Connolly, Cyril. "Bully of the Left Bank," review of *AMF, Sunday Times*, London (May 24, 1964), p. 36.
"Posthumous works are seldom well written, *A Moveable Feast* is an exception. . . . It is one of the best books Hemingway wrote, and one which he had to write. Having read it one could not imagine the oeuvre of Hemingway without it. . . . Not a word is wasted, not an emphasis misplaced; a magical directness flowers in the first sentence: 'Then there was the bad weather.' . . . One must not think of this as a sentimental, nostalgic book; much of it is about as sentimental as a Mafia-killing. When Hemingway says what he really thinks of someone it becomes a verdict against which there is no appeal. . . . Perhaps he uses his knife too freely." Reprinted in *The Evening Colonnade*, London, 1973, pp. 303-306.

133 Thompson, Hunter S. "What Lured Hemingway to Ketchum?" *National Observer* (May 25, 1964), pp. 1, 13.

134 Phillips, Perrott. "Hemingway in the 'twenties," review of *AMF, Books and Bookmen*, IX (June 1964), 16-17. Facsimiles of *Toronto Star* articles.
"Although there is much lean and beautiful writing (the opening sentence is particularly evocative), one cannot escape the impression of a muted hand at work. . . . The nostalgia in the book is of a strange and yearning kind. Was it the world-weariness of a man who was tired of today? We shall never know."

135 Review of *AMF, Choice*, I (June 1964), 133.
"Though a memoir, the book somewhat resembles a novel—its theme a young writer's struggle to master his art, its mood a lyrical love for Paris recollected in tranquility, its story-line his respectful but cautious relationships with his mentors, its climax his friendship with Scott Fitzgerald. Notably different from the brutal callousness suggested by some already published letters. Hemingway's attitude

toward Fitzgerald mingles amused exasperation with affection and pity. . . . Hemingway at 60 recalled his younger self with tenderness and restraint. As a human being he appears to better advantage than in anything heretofore written by or about him."

136 Fulford, Robert. "On Hemingway: his last sad book gives him back his early stature," review of *AMF, Maclean's,* LXXVII (June 6, 1964), 47-48.

"It contains passages of great bitterness and it shows that generosity was not one of Hemingway's dominant characteristics. But it evokes the young Hemingway so palpably, so effectively, that all he did and wrote is restored to its original value. . . . *A Moveable Feast* is a diverse and absorbing book. . . . But it is never more striking than when it describes how the young Ernest Hemingway came to see himself as a romantic hero and came to make demands upon himself that were so harsh even he could never begin to satisfy them."

137 Foster, Malcolm. Letter, *Times Literary Supplement* (June 11, 1964), p. 511.

Regarding the review of *AMF* in *TLS* (May 21, 1964). Reprinted in *T.L.S.: Essays and Reviews of The Times Literary Supplement, 1964,* London, 1965, p. 61.

138 Gresset, Michel. "Après la fête: derniers échos des grands écrivains américains des années 20," *Mercure de France,* No. 351 (July-Aug. 1964), pp. 513-520.

Essay on William Faulkner, F. Scott Fitzgerald, Erskine Caldwell, John Dos Passos, and Hemingway.

139 Macauley, Robie. "A Moveable Myth," *Encounter,* XXIII (Sept. 1964), 56-58.

Regarding Hemingway's recollections of Ford Madox Ford in *AMF.*

140 Larsen, Erling. "Making the Seney Scene," *Carleton Miscellany,* V (Fall 1964), 50-74.

On "Big Two-Hearted River."

141 Beach, Sylvia. Excerpt on Hemingway, *Argosy* [London], XXV [New Series] (Oct. 1964), 93-96.

Excerpt from *Shakespeare and Company,* New York, 1959, pp. 77-83. This excerpt follows Hemingway's chapter on Sylvia Beach reprinted from *AMF.* See (S-C43).

142 Wark, Bob. "Ernest Hemingway and the Club Fighters," *Argosy,* CCCLIX (Dec. 1964), 40-41, 116-118.

Based in part on a 1959 interview with Hemingway in Idaho.

143 Tanner, Tony. "Hemingway y Fitzgerald," *Casa de las Américas,* IV (Dec. 1964), 99-105. Translated into Spanish, by José Rodriguez Feo, from *Encounter,* XXIII (July 1964). See (H1539).

144 Mudrick, Marvin. "A Farewell to Spring and Paris," review of *AMF, Hudson Review,* XVII (Winter 1964-1965), 572-579.

"*A Moveable Feast*, recognizably Hemingway as it is, makes a new beginning. It is the first book by the old master, and full of pride, amusement, melancholy, and—of all things—love. . . . For Hemingway at the very end wrote his authentic love story. . . . The heroine—Hemingway's only live and persuasive heroine—of *A Moveable Feast* is the first Mrs. Hemingway. The book is in praise of her and what he lost when he let her go. . . . That Hemingway could have come to such a candor of private regret and love and longing against the grain of his so carefully cultivated reputation, less than a year before his death, is the proof of the health he died in. There are no charging lions or leaping marlin in *A Moveable Feast*, or wars or rumors of wars. The book is not only a new beginning for one of the greatest American writers, but his masterpiece." Reprinted, in revised form, in *On Culture and Literature*, New York, 1970, pp. 117-127.

145 Hoffman, Frederick J. "Hemingway and Fitzgerald," *American Literary Scholarship: An Annual / 1965*, pp. 90-103.

146 Hoffmann, Gerhard. "Kontrast und Parallelität in den Kurzgeschichten Ernest Hemingways," *Anglia,* LXXXIII (1965), 199-224.

147 Damp, Waldemar. "Zu Ernest Hemingway als weltliterarischen Phänomen," *Wissenschaftliche Zeitschrift der Ernst-Moritz-Arndt Universität Greifswald,* XIV, iv (1965), 445-450.

148 Wickes, George. "Ernest Hemingway Pays His Debts," review of *AMF, Shenandoah,* XVI (Winter 1965), 46-54.

"*A Moveable Feast* is the book that Harry in 'The Snows of Kilimanjaro' wanted to write before he died: a writer's memories of places he'd been and things he'd done. There is a close connection between that story of Hemingway's middle years and this posthumous book of reminiscence, so close that one echoes the other at times. In both we get a closeup of the writer that may be a likeness but is also a work of fiction. . . . *A Moveable Feast* is not autobiography, then, nor yet a portrait of the artist, but a collection of somewhat fictionalized reminiscences. If it has any model, it is Turgenev's *A Sportsman's Sketches*, a book which Hemingway refers to with admiration. . . . Here we have the old writer looking back at the young writer that he was and finding himself very much in sympathy with that character."

149 Gado, Frank. "The Curious History of the Hemingway Hero," *Symposium* (Union College), IV (Winter 1965), 18-22.

150 Watt, F. W. "The One True Sentence," review of *AMF, Tamarack Review*, No. 34 (Winter 1965), pp. 78-81.

"Hemingway's search for a clear, simple reality carried on in a spirit of absolute ruthless honesty is in the end self-defeating. . . . And the last irony is that the spare, flexible, transparent language Hemingway created to let his reality shine through had become, long before these late memoirs, itself a style, a manner, an instantly recognizable and easily parodied rhetorical mode, an eloquent pose in defiance of the nothingness of the non-verbal universe."

151 Hemingway, Mary. "Havana," *Saturday Review*, XLVIII (Jan. 2, 1965), 40-41, 70, 72, 74.

Recollections on the Havana that she and Hemingway knew.

152 Takigawa, Motoo. "The Development of Hemingway's View of Death," *Studies in English Literature* (English Literary Society of Japan, University of Tokyo), XLI (March 1965), 183-194.

153 Viertel, Peter. "Luis Miguel Dominguín," *Gentlemen's Quarterly*, XXXIV (April 1965), 72-73, 125, 126, 128, 133.

Discusses Hemingway's partiality for Dominguín's brother-in-law, Antonio Ordóñez. A letter from Hemingway is quoted, see (S-F134).

154 Aldridge, John W. "Two poor fish on one line," review of *OMATS, N.Y. Herald Tribune Book Week* (June 20, 1965), pp. 16, 19.

"Rereading [*The Old Man and the Sea*] is not a very happy experience, particularly when one recalls the high hopes one had for it when it first appeared, and considers how nice it would be if one could feel that it is really terribly good. But one cannot feel this, not even in deference to the memory of a much loved and great writer. It is, of course, nowhere near so bad a book as *Across the River*, a disaster no writer, however great, could conceivably perpetrate twice. . . . The action of the novel is . . . to my mind, a façade, a classic parable in stone, terribly picturesque and *meaningful*, but quite dead. One must question the vitality of a story that becomes a myth too quickly, that is accepted as universal before it has been felt as particular." Note: This review was occasioned by the Scribner Library paperback edition of *OMATS*. It was reprinted in *Time to Murder and Create*, New York, 1966, pp. 185-191; *The Devil in the Fire*, New York, 1972, pp. 86-90.

155 Steiner, George. "La retraite du mot," *Preuves*, XV (July 1965), 12-26. General article. Discusses Hemingway on pp. 23-25.

156 Cowley, Malcolm, and Robert Cowley, edited by. "Memoranda of

a Decade," *American Heritage*, XVI (Aug. 1965), 33-40. General article.

F. Scott Fitzgerald's first letter to Maxwell Perkins (ca. Oct. 10, 1924) regarding Hemingway is quoted on p. 37. Also the passage from *FTA* (p. 196) regarding "the words sacred, glorious, and sacrifice" is quoted, on p. 37, as "an epitome of Twenties disillusionment with war."

157 Slabey, Robert M. "The Structure of *In Our Time*," *South Dakota Review*, III (Autumn 1965), 38-52. Reprinted in *Moderna språk*, LX, iii (1966), 273-285.

158 Hoffmann, Gerhard. " 'The Gambler, the Nun, and the Radio': Untersuchung zur Gestaltungsweise Hemingways," *Germanisch-Romanische Monatsschrift*, XV (Oct. 1965), 421-429.

159 Sander, Oscar. "Hemingway in Vorarlberg," *Vorarlberg*, IV (Oct. 1965), 6-9. See also (S-C45).

160 Kim, Byung-chull. "Hemingway's Nihilism," *English Language and Literature*, XVII (Nov. 1965), 102-137. In Korean.

161 "A *Redbook* Dialogue: Mary Hemingway and Robert Morley," *Redbook*, CXXVI (Nov. 1965), 62-63, 146-149, 151-153.

Mary Hemingway discusses Hemingway's Russian royalties, horse racing in Paris in the early 1950s, hunting, and other topics with the actor-dramatist, Robert Morley.

162 Skipp, Francis E. "What Was the Matter with Jacob Barnes?" *The Carrell*, VI (Dec. 1965), 17-22.

163 Bigsby, C.W.E. "Two Types of Violence," *University Review* (Kansas City), XXXII (Winter 1965), 129-136. General article. Discusses the distinction between formal and informal violence in Hemingway's work, on pp. 132-136.

164 LeBost, Barbara. " 'The Way It Is': Something Else on Hemingway," *Journal of Existentialism*, VI (Winter 1965-1966), 175-180.

An analysis of certain central themes in Hemingway's work that reveal his "existential apprehension of the world, a complex confrontation of reality that goes below surface events to the ambiguities at the core of man's predicament. Hemingway's revelation is a truthful and authentic statement of life 'the way it is.' "

165 Hoffman, Frederick J. "Hemingway and Fitzgerald," *American Literary Scholarship: An Annual / 1966*, pp. 85-94.

166 Gordon, David. "The Son and the Father: Patterns of Response to Conflict in Hemingway's Fiction," *Literature and Psychology*, XVI, iii-iv (1966), 122-138.

167 Harlow, Benjamin C. "Some Archetypal Motifs in *The Old Man and the Sea*," *McNeese Review*, XVII (1966), 74-79.

168 Wood, Cecil. "On the Tendency of Nature to Intimate Art," *Minnesota Review*, VI, ii (1966), 133-148.

On pp. 140-148, the author compares Kafka's *Ein Hungerkünstler* and *The Old Man and the Sea*, which are "addressed to different subcultures of Western culture, written in different languages, but treating the same basic concept: the role of the idealist in a materialistic society." Note: The editor's footnote states that "Intimate" is not a misspelling.

169 Kashkeen, I. A. "Kheminguei," *Prometey,* No. 1 (1966), pp. 72-169. Photographs.

An unfinished biography of Hemingway.

169₁ Lorie, Maria. ["On I. A. Kashkeen,"] *ibid.*, pp. 170-173.

On Kashkeen's books and articles on Hemingway. An English translation appeared in *Sputnik*, No. 7 (July 1967), pp. 40-47.

170 Amiran, Minda Rae. "Hemingway as Lyric Novelist," *Scripta Hierosolymitana* (Hebrew University, Jerusalem), XVII (1966), 292-300.

171 Stephens, Rosemary. " 'In Another Country': *Three* as Symbol," *University of Mississippi Studies in English*, VII (1966), 77-83.

172 Cooperman, Stanley. "Hemingway's Blue-eyed Boy: Robert Jordan and 'Purging Ecstasy,' " *Criticism*, VIII (Winter 1966), 87-96.

173 Strandberg, Victor H. "A Palm for Pamela: Three Studies in the Game of Love," *Western Humanities Review*, XX (Winter 1966), 37-47.

A defense of Richardson's *Pamela* by showing "that the game of love endures unchanging, codified and ritualistic as the peacock's dance, through all time and mutability." The three works used in the defense are: Kalidasa's Hindu play *Shakuntala, Romeo and Juliet*, and *FTA*.

174 White, William. "Hemingway Hunting in Scandinavia," *American Book Collector*, XVI (Jan. 1966), 22-24.

On Hemingway translations in Norwegian, Swedish, and Danish.

175 Miner, Ward L. Review of Roger Asselineau's *The Literary Reputation of Hemingway in Europe, American Literature*, XXXVII (Jan. 1966), 501-502.

176 Young Philip. "Hemingway and Me: A Rather Long Story," *Kenyon Review*, XXVIII (Jan. 1966), 15-37.

The author gives an account of the delays in publication of his book *Ernest Hemingway* (G460), caused by Hemingway's belief that it was a biographical study rather than a critical study. See Young's *Three Bags Full* (S-G446) for reprint notes.

177 White, William. "*The Old Man and the Sea* as a German Text-book," *Papers of the Bibliographical Society of America*, LX (Jan.-March 1966), 89-90. See note under (A24a).

178 "Mrs. Hemingway Sues to Stop Book," *N.Y. Times* (Jan. 15, 1966), p. 25.
Mary Hemingway filed suit in the New York State Supreme Court to prevent the distribution and sale of A. E. Hotchner's *Papa Hemingway* on the grounds that the book infringed on her right of privacy. Random House planned to publish the book on March 7th.

179 Baker, Carlos. Speaking of Books column, "Hemingway's Italia," *N.Y. Times Book Review* (Jan. 23, 1966), p. 2. Photograph.
Regarding the author's research trips to Hemingway's "adopted Italian domain." Reprinted in Francis Brown's *Page 2*, New York, 1969, pp. 197-201.

180 "Hemingway's Widow Sues to Stop New Book of Memoirs," *Publishers' Weekly*, CLXXXIX (Jan. 24, 1966), 274.
Regarding Mary Hemingway's request for an injunction to stop publication of A.E. Hotchner's *Papa Hemingway*.

181 "Hemingway-Biographie: Vertrauen verletzt," *Der Spiegel*, XX (Jan. 24, 1966), 93-94.
Regarding A. E. Hotchner's *Papa Hemingway*.

182 Tomasson, Robert E. " 'Papa Hemingway' Brought to Court," *N.Y. Times* (Jan. 29, 1966), p. 22.
New York State Supreme Court Justice Harry B. Frank heard the argument on Mary Hemingway's suit against A. E. Hotchner's *Papa Hemingway*, but he reserved his decision.

183 Dudar, Helen. "Hemingway Called Her Durable," *N.Y. Post* (Jan. 30, 1966), Weekend Magazine, Section 2, p. 1.
On Mary Hemingway.

184 Johnson, Ron D. "The House Hemingway Called Home," *Minnesota Motorist* (Feb. 1966), p. 10. Drawing of Hemingway.
Regarding Hemingway's Key West house at 907 Whitehead Street.

185 The Law column, "Literary Property," *Time*, LXXXVII (Feb. 11, 1966), 50.
Regarding Mary Hemingway's suit against A. E. Hotchner's *Papa Hemingway*.

186 Moravia, Alberto. "Il mito di Hemingway," *Corriere della Sera* (Feb. 13, 1966), p. 3. Datelined: L'Avana. An English translation, titled "The Ghost of Hemingway: The Tragic Conflict of a Great Man Haunts a House on a Hill Outside Havana," appeared in *Atlas,* XI (June 1966), 337-340.

187 Young, Philip. Review of Robert W. Lewis's *Hemingway on Love, N.Y. Times Book Review* (Feb. 13, 1966), p. 38.

188 Tomasson, Robert E. "Mrs. Hemingway Loses Book Plea," *N.Y. Times* (Feb. 22, 1966), p. 7.
New York State Supreme Court Justice Harry B. Frank rejected Mary Hemingway's suit for an injunction against A. E. Hotchner's *Papa Hemingway.*

189 "Mrs. Hemingway Loses Court Action," *Times,* London (Feb. 23, 1966), p. 10. See above item.

190 White, William. "Hemingway in the Red Cross," *American Red Cross Journal,* XLII (March 1966), 28-29.
Regarding Hemingway's experiences as a Red Cross ambulance driver in Italy in World War I.

191 Sylvester, Bickford. "Hemingway's Extended Vision: *The Old Man and the Sea,*" *Publications of the Modern Language Association,* LXXXI (March 1966), 130-138.

192 Gastwirth, Donald E. "Can Life Have Meaning?: A Study of *The Sun Also Rises,*" *Yale Literary Magazine,* CXXXIV (March 1966), 36-41.

193 "Hemingway's Views Disclosed by Friend," *N.Y. Times* (March 1, 1966), p. 33.
Regarding serialization of A. E. Hotchner's *Papa Hemingway* in the *Saturday Evening Post.*

194 "Mrs. Hemingway Denied Injunction on Memoirs," *Publishers' Weekly,* CLXXXIX (March 7, 1966), 52-53.
Regarding the ruling, on February 21st, on Mary Hemingway's suit against A. E. Hotchner's *Papa Hemingway.*

195 Hotchner, A. E. *Papa Hemingway* serialized in three installments, *Saturday Evening Post,* CCXXXIX (March 12, 1966), 32-41, 45-48; (March 26, 1966), 36-44, 48, 52, 77-78, 83; (April 9, 1966), 34-47, 50. Photographs, and cover drawings on first installment. See (G198). Also excerpted in the *Sunday Times Magazine,* London (Sept. 11, 1966), pp. 8-13, 15-17, 19, 21. Translated into Italian in *L'Europeo,* XXII (May 5, 1966), 30-39; (May 12, 1966), 78-85; (May 26, 1966), 64-69. An excerpt was translated into Rumanian by Ilona Vasilescu-Somesan, in *Magazin,* II, No. 518 (Sept. 9, 1967), 4-5.

196 Fallaci, Oriana. "Mio marito Hemingway: intervista con la vedova del grande scrittore americano," *L'Europeo*, XXII (March 17, 1966), 30-37. Photographs. An English translation, titled "An Interview with Mary Hemingway: 'My Husband, Ernest Hemingway,'" appeared in *Look*, XXX (Sept. 6, 1966), 62-68. Reprinted, with slight revisions, in *The Egotists*, Chicago, 1968, pp. 141-158.

197 "Appeal on Hemingway Book," *N.Y. Times* (March 18, 1966), p. 41.
The Appellate Division upheld the State Supreme Court decision that rejected Mary Hemingway's suit to block publication of A. E. Hotchner's *Papa Hemingway*.

198 Pilpel, Harriet F. "But Can You Do That?" *Publishers' Weekly*, CLXXXIX (March 28, 1966), 40-42.
The case of the *Estate of Ernest Hemingway v. Random House, Inc.* is discussed, on p. 42, under "Privacy Cases versus Freedom of Expression." Random House was the publisher of A. E. Hotchner's *Papa Hemingway*.

198₁ "Mrs. Hemingway's Appeal Denied in Privacy Case," *ibid.*, p. 46.

199 Akmakjian, Hiag. "Hemingway and Haiku," *Columbia University Forum*, IX (Spring 1966), 45-48.
A study of the connection between Hemingway's prose and haiku, based on "the deep love both reveal for the more common things and events of nature."

200 Moses, W. R. "Victory In Defeat: 'Ad Astra' and A Farewell to Arms," *Mississippi Quarterly*, XIX (Spring 1966), 85-89.
Examines the influence of *FTA* on William Faulkner's short story "Ad Astra."

201 Anderson, David D. "Ernest Hemingway, The Voice of an Era," *Personalist*, XLVII (Spring 1966), 234-247.

202 Glasser, William A. "*A Farewell to Arms*," *Sewanee Review*, LXXIV (Spring 1966), 453-469.
Frederic Henry is presented as one "who transcends his paganism to achieve a Christian awareness of life." The author differs with critics who have arrived at negative views of the ending of *FTA*.

203 Wasserstrom, William. "Hemingway, the *Dial*, and Ernest Walsh," *South Atlantic Quarterly*, LXV (Spring 1966), 171-177.
On *A Moveable Feast*. Note: See Carlos Baker's note in *EH: A Life Story*, pp. 587-588, regarding the probability of an error in *AMF* (p. 125/line 11) in the reference to Walsh and the *Dial*: "this quarterly" should read "*This Quarter*."

204 Hays, Peter L. "Hemingway and the Fisher King," *University Review* (Kansas City), XXXII (Spring 1966), 225-228.

Discusses "God Rest You Merry, Gentlemen" and the Fisher King legend.

205 Brown, John Mason. Review of A. E. Hotchner's *Papa Hemingway, Book-of-the-Month Club News* (April 1966), pp. 1-5. Photographs.

The book was the May selection of the Book-of-the-Month Club. Note: A special bulletin was laid in the *B-O-M C News* regarding Mary Hemingway's court case against the book.

205₁ "A. E. Hotchner," *ibid.*, pp. 6, 16.

206 Bourjaily, Vance. "Good Times Before Dark," review of A. E. Hotchner's *Papa Hemingway, N.Y. Times Book Review* (April 3, 1966), pp. 1, 32. Photograph.

206₁ Nichols, Lewis. In and Out of Books column, "Case of Papa Hemingway," *ibid.*, p. 8.

Regarding Mary Hemingway's court case against A. E. Hotchner.

207 Barkham, John. "Hemingway . . . A Portrait of Aging Greatness," review of A. E. Hotchner's *Papa Hemingway, N.Y. World Telegram* (April 5, 1966), p. 23.

208 Hicks, Granville. "No Compromise with Life," review of A. E. Hotchner's *Papa Hemingway* and Philip Young's *EH: A Reconsideration, Saturday Review*, XLIX (April 9, 1966), 29-30.

208₁ Tebbel, John. "Papa's Troubled Legacy," *ibid.*, pp. 30-31, 91-92.

Regarding Mary Hemingway's court case against A. E. Hotchner.

209 Galbraith, John Kenneth. "The Old Man at Sea: A skillful if larger than life portrait of the writer as hero," review of A. E. Hotchner's *Papa Hemingway, N.Y. Herald Tribune Book Week* (April 10, 1966), pp. 1, 11.

210 Newquist, Roy. Review of A. E. Hotchner's *Papa Hemingway, N.Y. Post* (April 10, 1966), p. 49.

211 Dolbier, Maurice. "With Hemingway to the End: A Friend's Moving Memoir," review of A. E. Hotchner's *Papa Hemingway, N.Y. Herald Tribune* (April 11, 1966), p. 23.

212 "The Torment of a Master," review of A. E. Hotchner's *Papa Hemingway, Newsweek*, LXVII (April 11, 1966), 111.

213 Fuller, Edmund. "Portrait of Hemingway is Skillful, Revealing," review of A. E. Hotchner's *Papa Hemingway, Wall Street Journal* (April 11, 1966), p. 18.

214 Ferris, John. "Hemingway Is the Star in His Own Tragedy," review of A. E. Hotchner's *Papa Hemingway, Life*, LX (April 15, 1966) 10.

215 Review of A. E. Hotchner's *Papa Hemingway, Time,* LXXXVII (April 15, 1966), 107.

216 Kihss, Peter. "Hemingway Lost Pulitzer in 1941," *N.Y. Times* (April 20, 1966), pp. 49, 95.

Regarding Robert Bendimer's article, "The Truth About the Pulitzer Prize Awards," *McCall's,* XCIII (May 1966). The Advisory Board's nomination of *For Whom the Bell Tolls* was vetoed by Nicholas Murray Butler, and no award for fiction was made in 1941.

217 Wickes, George. "Hemingway to His Boswell," review of A. E. Hotchner's *Papa Hemingway, New Republic,* CLIV (April 23, 1966), 24-27.

218 Thompson, John. "Poor Papa," review of A. E. Hotchner's *Papa Hemingway, New York Review of Books,* VI (April 28, 1966), 6-7. Drawing of Hemingway by David Levine.

219 White, William. "For Hemingway Buffs," *American Book Collector,* XVI (May 1966), 27-28.

Regarding recent books on and by Hemingway.

220 Evans, Robert. "Hemingway and the Pale Cast of Thought," *American Literature,* XXXVIII (May 1966), 161-176.

A study on the nature of Hemingway's anti-intellectualism.

221 Weeks, Edward. Review of A. E. Hotchner's *Papa Hemingway, Atlantic,* CCXVII (May 1966), 122, 124.

222 Archer, William H. Review of A. E. Hotchner's *Papa Hemingway, Best Sellers,* XXVI (May 1, 1966), 44-45.

223 Barnes, Daniel R. "Ritual and Parody in 'A Clean, Well-Lighted Place,'" *Cithara: Essays in the Judaeo-Christian Tradition,* V (May 1966), 15-25.

224 Friedman, Ralph. "Hemingway: 'the hills that he loved,'" *Mainliner,* X (May 1966), 9-11. Photograph of Robert Berks's bronze head of Hemingway.

On Hemingway in Ketchum, Idaho.

225 Hemingway, Mary. "That Magnificent Man and His Converter Machine," *fact,* III (May-June 1966), 62-64.

Enumerates the errors that she found in A. E. Hotchner's *Papa Hemingway.*

226 White, William. Review of Hans W. Bentz's *Ernest Hemingway in Übersetzungen, Bulletin of Bibliography,* XXIV (May-August 1966), 241-242.

227 Sheed, Wilfrid. "Hemingway Si, Papa No: Hotchner's Echo," review of A. E. Hotchner's *Papa Hemingway, Commonweal,* LXXXIV (May 13, 1966), 221-223.

228 Muggeridge, Malcolm. Review of A. E. Hotchner's *Papa Hemingway, Esquire,* LXV (June 1966), 34, 36.

229 Hatch, Robert. "Hemingway Gossip," review of A. E. Hotchner's *Papa Hemingway, Harper's* CCXXXII (June 1966), 101-102.

230 Palievsky, Pyotr. "Hemingway and Faulkner: A Russian View," *Soviet Life,* No. 6 (June 1966), pp. 58-59.

231 "American Hero," review of Philip Young's *EH: A Reconsideration, Times Literary Supplement* (June 2, 1966), p. 496.

232 Bannerman, James. "The Old Man and the Biographer: Nothing's spared in this account of the fall of Papa Hemingway," review of A. E. Hotchner's *Papa Hemingway, Maclean's,* LXXIX (June 4, 1966), 50.

233 Funke, Lewis. "Hemingway Hero," *N.Y. Times* (June 19, 1966), Sec. 2, p. 1.
     Regarding A. E. Hotchner's play *The Hemingway Hero.*

234 "A Hemingway Fund Set Up," *N.Y. Times* (June 22, 1966), p. 3.
     Mary Hemingway set up a fund in Yugoslavia to aid students of literature. The fund will be financed by royalties from Hemingway's works published in Yugoslavia.

235 Hovey, Richard B. "*The Old Man and the Sea*: A New Hemingway Hero," *Discourse,* IX (Summer 1966), 283-294.

236 Hovey, Richard B. "*The Sun Also Rises*: Hemingway's Inner Debate," *Forum* [Houston], IV (Summer 1966), 4-10.

237 Lisca, Peter. "The Structure of Hemingway's *Across the River and Into the Trees,*" *Modern Fiction Studies,* XII (Summer 1966), 232-250.

237₁ Hattam, Edward. "Hemingway's 'An Alpine Idyll,'" *ibid.,* pp. 261-265.

238 Howell, John M. "Hemingway and Fitzgerald in Sound and Fury," *Papers on Language and Literature,* II (Summer 1966), 234-242.
     A study of William Faulkner's parody in *The Sound and the Fury* of "the romantic despair and cynicism" of Hemingway and F. Scott Fitzgerald.

239 Brief review of A. E. Hotchner's *Papa Hemingway, Virginia Quarterly Review,* XLII (Summer 1966), ciii.

240 Grimes, Sister Richard Mary. "Hemingway: The Years with *Esquire*," *Dissertation Abstracts*, xxvii (July 1966), 204-A.

Abstract from a doctoral dissertation, Ohio State University, 1965.

241 Levine, M. H. "Hemingway and the 'Lost Generation,'" *Kyushu American Literature*, No. 9 (July 1966), pp. 19-26.

241₁ Uchida, Shigeharu. "The Nada Theme of *A Farewell to Arms* and Its Significance to the Code," *ibid.*, pp. 27-33.

242 Burgess, Anthony. "He Wrote Good," review of A. E. Hotchner's *Papa Hemingway, Spectator*, ccxvii (July 8, 1966), 47.

This review also includes mention of Penguin editions of *GHOA, ARIT, TOS, TFC*, and *AMF*. Reprinted in *Urgent Copy*, New York, 1968, pp. 121-126.

243 Lyons, Leonard. The Lyons Den column, *N.Y. Post* (July 21, 1966), p. 31.

Anecdotes about Hemingway.

244 "Memorial to Hemingway Dedicated at Sun Valley," *N.Y. Times* (July 22, 1966), p. 32. Datelined: July 21.

Robert Manning was the main speaker at ceremonies for the dedication of a bronze head of Hemingway.

245 "Hemingway's Widow Allowed Jury Trial," *N.Y. Times* (July 23, 1966), p. 22.

Mary Hemingway's assertion that Random House and A. E. Hotchner had infringed on the Hemingway estate's literary property rights was dismissed by New York State Supreme Court Justice Francis P. Murphy, Jr. She won the right to have a jury trial determine whether the book *Papa Hemingway* had violated her right of privacy.

246 Item, *Time*, lxxxviii (July 29, 1966), 27.

Regarding the dedication of a bronze bust of Hemingway in Idaho.

247 Young, Philip. "On Dismembering Hemingway," review of A. E. Hotchner's *Papa Hemingway, Atlantic*, ccxviii (Aug. 1966), 45-49. Reprinted, under the title "I Dismember Papa," in *Three Bags Full*, New York, 1972, pp. 55-67.

248 Fuson, Ben W. Review of Philip Young's *EH: A Reconsideration, Library Journal*, xci (Aug. 1966), 3733.

249 Photograph of Robert Berks's bronze head of Hemingway, *Valley Sun*, xxix (Aug. 1966), [1]. Special Hemingway Memorial Edition.

249₁ "The Hemingway Memorial," *ibid.*, p. [3]. Photograph.
   Regarding the bronze head of Hemingway, by Robert Berks, set "in a copse of alder, willow and red birch on a high point of land overlooking Trail creek." The lines from Hemingway's eulogy to Gene Van Guilder, which are inscribed on the pedestal, are quoted. See (S-C21).

249₂ Taylor, Dorice. "Ernest Hemingway's Sun Valley Visits," *ibid.*, p. [3].
   An account of Hemingway's visits to Sun Valley, which began in September 1939, and the "nice, shy, friendly side of Hemingway that all Sun Valley and Ketchum loved."

249₃ Program for the Dedication of the Ernest Hemingway Memorial, July 21, 1966, Sun Valley, Idaho, *ibid.*, p. [3].

249₄ "The Meaning of Hemingway's Achievement," *ibid.*, p. [4]. From the address of Robert Manning at the dedication of the Hemingway memorial.

249₅ Photographs of Hemingway in Sun Valley, *ibid.*, p. [5].

249₆ "The Last Letter of Ernest Hemingway," *ibid.*, p. [6].
   Facsimiles of Hemingway's two-page letter, written June 15, 1961, to Fritz Saviers. See (F147).

250 Zolotow, Sam. "New Play to Tell About 2 Authors," *N.Y. Times* (Aug. 5, 1966), p. 15.
   Regarding Trevor Reese's *The Story of Two Afternoons,* a two-character drama about Hemingway and F. Scott Fitzgerald.

251 Gilroy, Harry. "Widow Believes Hemingway Committed Suicide," *N.Y. Times* (Aug. 23, 1966), p. 36.
   Interview with Mary Hemingway in which she discusses her statements in Oriana Fallaci's interview in *Look,* xxx (Sept. 6, 1966), about her acceptance of Hemingway's death and A. E. Hotchner's *Papa Hemingway.* See (S-H196).

252 "Hemingway's Suicide," *Times,* London (Aug. 24, 1966), p. 7.
   Regarding Oriana Fallaci's interview with Mary Hemingway in *Look,* xxx (Sept. 6, 1966). See (S-H196).

253 Review of A. E. Hotchner's *Papa Hemingway, Choice,* iii (Sept. 1966), 520.

253₁ Review of Philip Young's *EH: A Reconsideration, ibid.*, p. 524.

254 Davis, Robert Murray. "Hemingway's 'The Doctor and the Doctor's Wife,' " *Explicator,* xxv (Sept. 1966), Item 1.

255 Grenzmann, Wilhelm. "Ernest Hemingway und seine Dichtung," *Universitas,* xxi (Sept. 1966), 903-913.

256 White, William. "Hemingway, Boy and Youth," review of Constance Cappel Montgomery's *Hemingway in Michigan, Providence Journal* (Sept. 11, 1966), p. H-9.

257 "Much larger than life," review of A. E. Hotchner's *Papa Hemingway* and Nelson Algren's *Notes from a Sea Diary: Hemingway All the Way, Times,* London (Sept. 22, 1966), p. 14.

258 Ellmann, Richard. "Hemhotch," review of A. E. Hotchner's *Papa Hemingway, New Statesman,* LXXII (Sept. 23, 1966), 446-447.

259 Daley, Arthur. Sports of The Times column, *N.Y. Times* (Sept. 29, 1966), p. 63.
Michael Burke describes a football game he played with Hemingway in Paris during World War II.

260 "All the Way with Hemingway," review of A. E. Hotchner's *Papa Hemingway* and Nelson Algren's *Notes from a Sea Diary, Times Literary Supplement* (Sept. 29, 1966), p. 891.

260₁ "Off-campus," *ibid.,* p. 899.
The lead article depicts Hemingway as an off-campus writer who lived dangerously.

261 White, William. "Hemingway as Reporter: An Unknown News Story," *Journalism Quarterly,* XLIII (Autumn 1966), 538-542.
Authenticates an article by Hemingway, on the Yokohama Quake, in the *Toronto Daily Star* (Sept. 25, 1923). See (C427).

262 White, William. "Why Collect Ernest Hemingway—or Anyone?" *Prairie Schooner,* XL (Falls 1966), 232-246.
Reprinted in *American Book Collector,* XVII (Dec. 1966), 4-15.

263 Stavrou, C. N. "Nada, Religion, and Hemingway," *Topic: 12,* VI (Fall 1966), 5-20.

264 Linderoth, Leon Walter. "The Female Characters of Ernest Hemingway," *Dissertation Abstracts,* XXVII (Oct. 1966), 1060-A.
Abstract from a doctoral dissertation, Florida State University, 1966.

265 Hand, Harry E. "Transducers and Hemingway's Heroes," *English Journal,* LV (Oct. 1966), 870-871.
Makes an analogy between a transducer, with an input and output, and the Hemingway hero responding to the world and acting out a code.

266 Di Donato, Pietro. "Tropic of Cuba," *Playboy,* XIII (Oct. 1966), 149, 190, 192, 194, 196.
Relates an encounter with Hemingway during a visit to Cuba.

267 "Record Prices for Hemingway," *Antiquarian Bookman,* XXXVIII (Oct. 24, 1966), 1603.

Regarding the Swann auction, on Oct. 6, 1966, of a collection of books and articles by and about Hemingway. See (G406).

268 Turner, E. S. "Mortal Ballet," review of books on bullfighting, including *DIA* (Penguin edition), *New Statesman,* LXXIII (Oct. 28, 1966), 640.

269 Eby, Cecil D. "The Real Robert Jordan," *American Literature,* XXXVIII (Nov. 1966), 380-386.

Regarding Robert Merriman. Reprinted in Sheldon Norman Grebstein's *The Merrill Studies in For Whom the Bell Tolls,* Columbus, Ohio, 1971, pp. 43-49.

270 Miron, Charles. "Ernest Hemingway—the Truth," *Cavalcade* (Nov.-Dec. 1966), pp. 8-10.

271 "A Sister of Hemingway Is an 'Apparent Suicide,'" *N.Y. Times* (Nov. 1, 1966), p. 3.

Mrs. Ursula Hemingway Jepson, an artist, died at her home in Honolulu of an overdose of medicine. She had established the Ernest Hemingway Memorial Award for creative writing at the University of Hawaii.

272 Nichols, Lewis. In and Out of Books column, "Work in Progress," *N.Y. Times Book Review* (Nov. 6, 1966), p. 8.

Item regarding Carlos Baker's research for his biography of Hemingway.

273 Fitch, Robert E. Review of the first six booklets in the Contemporary Writers in Christian Perspective series, including Nathan A. Scott's *Ernest Hemingway, N.Y. Times Book Review* (Nov. 13, 1966), pp. 46-47. Painting of Hemingway by Henry Strater. For letters from Roderick Jellema, Nathan A. Scott, Jr., John Killinger, Giles Gunn, Roger L. Shinn, and Amos N. Wilder, and a reply by Robert Fitch, see the *NYTBR* (Dec. 11, 1966), pp. 62, 64.

273₁ Slonim, Marc. European Notebook column, "Hemingway's Renata," *ibid.,* p. 54.

Regarding Hemingway's "portrait" of Adriana Ivancich as Renata in *ARIT.* See (H1591).

274 Sylvester, Bickford. "Hemingway's Extended Vision: *The Old Man and the Sea,*" *Dissertation Abstracts,* XXVII (Dec. 1966), 1841-A.

Abstract from a doctoral dissertation, University of Washington, 1966.

275 Gingrich, Arnold. "Scott, Ernest and Whoever," *Esquire,* LXVI (Dec. 1966), 186-189, 322-325. Drawing by David Levine.

Regarding the various stages of the author's friendship with Hemingway, and the relationship of Hemingway and F. Scott Fitzgerald. Reprinted in *Esquire,* LXXX (Oct. 1973).

276 Dörfel, Hanspeter. "Der alternde Hemingway: A. E. Hotchners zweifelhafter Freundschaftsdienst," *Die Zeit* (Dec. 2, 1966), p. VI.
Review of A. E. Hotchner's *Papa Hemingway.*

277 Eller, Vernard. "A Theology of Nonresistance," *Christian Century,* LXXXIII (Dec. 14, 1966), 1534-1537. General article.
Discusses Anselmo's "revulsion toward war" in *FWBT.*

277₁ Drake, Robert. "The *Nada* and the Glory," review of Nathan A. Scott's *Ernest Hemingway, ibid.,* pp. 1539-1540.

278 Robichon, Jacques. "Hemingway face à la mort," *Nouvelles Littéraires,* XLIV (Dec. 29, 1966), 1, 11.
Regarding A. E. Hotchner's *Papa Hemingway.*

279 Lewis, Robert W., Jr., and Max Westbrook. "The Texas Manuscript of 'The Snows of Kilimanjaro,' " *Texas Quarterly,* IX (Winter 1966), 65-101. Facsimiles.
Part I: "Text and Critic," on pp. 66-74. Part II: "Vivienne de Watteville: Hemingway's Companion on Kilimanjaro," on pp. 75-88, by Robert W. Lewis, Jr. Part III: "The Stewardship of Ernest Hemingway," on pp. 89-101, by Max Westbrook. For facsimiles of the typescript of "The Snows of Kilimanjaro," from the Ernest Hemingway Collection at the University of Texas, see (S-F29).

280 Hayes, Curtis W. "A Study in Prose Styles: Edward Gibbon and Ernest Hemingway," *Texas Studies in Literature and Language,* VII (Winter 1966), 371-386. Reprinted in *Statistics and Style* edited by Lubomír Doležel and Richard W. Bailey, New York, 1969, pp. 80-91.

281 Hovey, Richard B. "*A Farewell to Arms*: Hemingway's Liebestod," *University Review* (Kansas City), XXXIII (Winter 1966), 93-100; Part II (Spring 1967), 163-168.

282 Lupan, Radu. "The Old Man and the World: Some Final Thoughts on Ernest Hemingway," *Literary Review,* X (Winter 1966-1967), 159-165. Translated into English from *Hemingway, Scriitorul,* Bucharest, 1966.

283 Sylvester, Bickford. " 'They Went Through This Fiction Every Day': Informed Illusion in *The Old Man and the Sea*," *Modern Fiction Studies,* XII (Winter 1966-1967), 473-477.

284 White, William. "Hemingway and Fitzgerald," *American Literary Scholarship: An Annual / 1967*, pp. 96-112.

285 Naik, M. K. "Thematic Structure in *A Farewell to Arms*," *Indian Journal of English Studies*, VIII (1967), 79-82.

286 Wertheim, Stanley. "The Conclusion of Hemingway's *The Sun Also Rises*," *Literature and Psychology*, XVII, i (1967), 55-56.

287 Corona, Mario. "Considerazioni sull'ordine di successione dei racconti di Hemingway," *Studi Americani*, XIII (1967), 325-337.

288 Finkel'shtein, I. L. "K problematike rasskazov Khemingueya" [The problems of Hemingway's short stories], *Uchenye zapiski Gor'kovskogo Universiteta* (Gorki Institute), No. 29 (1967), pp. 138-142.

289 Vasil'eva, L. I. "Vstuplenie Khemingueya v literaturu" [Hemingway's entry into literature], *Uchenye zapiski Leningradskii Pedagogicheskii Institut* (Leningrad Institute), No. 308 (1967), pp. 303-326.

290 Damp, Waldemar. "Individuum und Gesellschaft in Hemingways Romanen," *Wissenschaftliche Zeitschrift der Ernst-Moritz-Arndt-Universität*, XVI (1967), 189-192.

291 Simonov, K. "Ispanskaya tema v tvorchestve Khemingueya" [The Spanish theme in Hemingway's works], *Zvezda vostoka*, No. 3 (1967), pp. 194-201.

292 Kruse, Horst H. "Ernest Hemingway's 'The End of Something': Its Independence as a Short Story and Its Place in the 'Education of Nick Adams,' " *Studies in Short Fiction*, IV (Winter 1967), 152-166.

292₁ Howell, John M. "The Macomber Case," *ibid.*, pp. 171-172.
On the mystery of Francis Macomber's death.

293 Stein, William Bysshe. Review of Roger Asselineau's *The Literary Reputation of Hemingway in Europe, Western Humanities Review*, XXI (Winter 1967), 83.

294 Auction Sales column, "Hemingway," *American Book Collector*, XVII (Jan. 1967), 23; (Feb. 1967), 7-8.
List of prices paid for Hemingway items in the Swann Auction, in New York, October 6, 1966. See (G406).

295 Umbach, Herbert H. Review of Nathan A. Scott's *Ernest Hemingway: A Critical Essay, Cresset*, XXX (Jan. 1967), 25.

296 Scoville, Samuel. "The *Weltanschauung* of Steinbeck and Hemingway: An Analysis of Themes," *English Journal*, LVI (Jan. 1967), 60-63, 66.

297 Walz, Lawrence A. "Hemingway's 'The Killers,' " *Explicator*, XXV (Jan. 1967), Item 38.

298 Bisol, Gaetano. "Hemingway, uomo e personaggio," review of A. E. Hotchner's *Papa Hemingway, Letture,* XXII (Jan. 1967), 40-42.

299 Kanters, Robert. "Hemingway, l'homme et l'oeuvre," *Figaro Littéraire,* No. 1082 (Jan. 12, 1967), p. 5.

300 Calta, Louis. " 'Hemingway Hero' Begins Rehearsal," *N.Y. Times* (Jan. 28, 1967), p. 18.
   Reports that A. E. Hotchner's play, *The Hemingway Hero,* was scheduled to open on Broadway, in March, after trial runs in New Haven and Boston. The play "is a chronological amalgam of virtually all Hemingway's heroes. The theme of the two-act play is man's courage."

301 Robinson, Forrest Dean. "The Tragic Awareness of Hemingway's First-Person Narrators: A Study of *The Sun Also Rises* and *A Farewell to Arms,*" *Dissertation Abstracts,* XXVII (Feb. 1967), 2543-A.
   Abstract from a doctoral dissertation, Ohio University, 1966.

302 Beatty, Jerome, Jr. "Hanging Up on Hemingway," *Esquire,* LXVII (Feb. 1967), 116.
   Regarding the author's telephone interview with Hemingway, in 1958, about the three Spanish Civil War stories that Hemingway had denied *Esquire* permission to reprint in an anthology. See (H1079).

303 Burgess, Anthony. "Soft-Shelled Classics," *Spectator* (Feb. 10, 1967), p. 171. Includes a brief review of *DIA* (Penguin edition).

304 Hoffman, Frederick J. Review of Constance Cappel Montgomery's *Hemingway in Michigan, American Literature,* XXXIX (March 1967), 123-124.

305 Sbârcea, George. "Reîntîlnire cu Hemingway" [Meeting Hemingway again], *Argeș,* II (March 1967), 13.

305₁ Manu, Paraschiva. "Hemingway in Românâ: Bibliografie," *ibid.,* p. 13.

306 White, William. "Collected Hemingway: A Japanese Translation," *Serif,* IV (March 1967), 30-32.
   Full description of the nine-volume collected works of Hemingway published in Tokyo by Mikasa-Shobo. See (D214) and (S-G401).

307 " 'Hemingway Hero' to Close in Boston," *N.Y. Times* (March 4, 1967), p. 15.
   Regarding A. E. Hotchner's play, *The Hemingway Hero,* which had been scheduled for Broadway.

308 Hemingway, Mary. "Hemingway's Spain," *Saturday Review,* L (March 11, 1967), pp. 48-49, 102-104, 107.

243

An Italian translation, titled "La Madrid di Hemingway," appeared in *Fiera Letteraria*, XLII (May 11, 1967), 11-12.

308₁ Cowley, Malcolm. "The Twenties in Montparnasse," *ibid.*, pp. 51, 55, 98-101. General article.

309 Slonim, Marc. European Notebook column, "Hemingway," *N.Y. Times Book Review* (March 12, 1967), p. 22.
Regarding the 296-page monograph on Hemingway by Ivan Kashkin published in Moscow, and the Pléiade Library edition of Hemingway's work published by Gallimard in Paris.

310 Gilroy, Harry. "Scribner's Is Giving Archives to Princeton," *N.Y. Times* (March 31, 1967), p. 33.
Charles Scribner's Sons gave Princeton University the archives of its 121 years of book publishing. The archives include correspondence with Hemingway, who became a Scribner author in 1926.

311 Davis, Robert Murray. Review of Philip Young's *EH: A Reconsideration, Books Abroad*, XLI (Spring 1967), 220.

312 Coven, Carol. "Through the Eyes of Simplicity," *Crest*, LXXIII (Spring 1967), 10. Cover drawing of Hemingway by Jeff Varilla. See also (S-C48).

312₁ Davenport, Ben. " 'None are to be found more clever than Ernie,' " *ibid.*, p. 11. Photograph of Hemingway and list of his high-school activities reproduced from the *Senior Tabula* (June 1917).

312₂ Gottfried, Ralph. "The Unity of the Old Man and His Sea," *ibid.*, p. 15.

313 Stephens, Robert O. "Some Additions to the Hemingway Check-List," *American Book Collector*, XVII (April 1967), 9-10.

313₁ White, William. "More on Hemingway," *ibid.*, pp. 10-11.
Regarding Hemingway's articles in the *Toronto Star Weekly* and the *Toronto Daily Star*.

314 Daniels, Howell. "Literary Perspectives," includes a review of Roger Asselineau's *The Literary Reputation of Hemingway in Europe, Journal of American Studies*, I (April 1967), 113-119.

315 Gadda Conti, Giuseppe. "Sui Campi di Verdun, Hemingway e Fitzgerald," *Fiera Litteraria*, XLII (April 6, 1967), 10-11.

316 Zasurskii, Ya. "Tak nachinalsya khudozhnik . . ." [This was how an artist began], *Literaturnaya Gazeta*, No. 16 (April 19, 1967), p. 13.

317 Anania, Valeriu. "Aşezămintul Hemingway" [The Hemingway endowment], *Gazeta Literară*, XIV, No. 17 (April 27, 1967), 8.

244

318 Toole, William B., III. "Religion, Love and Nature in *A Farewell to Arms*: The Dark Shape of Irony," *CEA Critic* (College English Association), XXIX (May 1967), 10-11.

319 Wittkowski, Wolfgang. "Gekreuzigt im Ring: Zu Hemingways '*The Old Man and the Sea,*'" *Deutsche Vierteljahrsschrift für Literaturwissenschaft und Geistesgeschichte,* XLI (May 1967), 258-282.

320 Benson, Jackson Jerald. "Ernest Hemingway and the Doctrine of True Emotion," *Dissertation Abstracts,* XXVII (May 1967), 3862-A.
Abstract from a doctoral dissertation, University of Southern California, 1966.

321 Thompson, Richard J. Review of *By-Line* (edited by William White), *Library Journal,* XCII (May 1, 1967), 1834.
"This potpourri of Hemingway's journalism from the 1920's to the 1950's will be interesting to Papa-cultists ever searching for new sources of anecdote and biographical fillip; more important, it will be required reading for scholars who want to locate original accounts of the Pamplona afternoons and Parisian dusks that were to be caught in the amber of his novels. But chiefly this worthy book is for the so-called general reader who will be charmed and moved and astonished by Hemingway's talent for *teaching* about wine, food, shooting, fishing, travel, writing, and European customs and pastimes."

322 "Hemingway Story for Auction," *Times,* London (May 2, 1967), p. 4.
Regarding Hemingway's 26-page unpublished short story, "Black Ass at the Cross Roads," to be auctioned by Charles Hamilton, in New York, on May 24th. The story concerns "a group of allied soldiers in the Second World War who murder retreating Germans and loot their bodies." See (S-B18).

323 Callaghan, Morley. "La Parigi di Scott Fitzgerald," *Fiera Letteraria* (May 4, 1967), pp. 10-11.
Regarding the late 1920s when Fitzgerald, Hemingway, and Callaghan were in Paris.

324 "Hero as Celebrity," review of *By-Line* (edited by William White), *Time,* LXXXIX (May 19, 1967), 133-134, 136.
"Although *By-Line: Ernest Hemingway* is really source material for Hemingway biographers and thesis hunters in the Eng. Lit. factories, the book does have intrinsic value for non-academic readers. Hemingway told good yarns. . . . But always the book's main interest is the author. It traces the rise, the peaking out and the decline of Ernest Hemingway as stylist."

325 Prescott, Peter S. Review of *By-Line* (edited by William White), *Women's Wear Daily* (May 19, 1967), p. 36.

"Much of the best of what Hemingway wrote about what he saw and thought of life has been brought together by William White in *By-Line: Ernest Hemingway.* . . . The best of his journalism, like the best of his fiction, was written in the 1920's and 1930's, and reads as well today as it did when originally published. . . . Whatever the experience of which he wrote, he wrapped it in his own mystique. Hemingway is forever pronouncing on the best beer, the best bait, the mysterious and undefined code of Ndege people, the especially daring elite of which he was certainly one. He writes with humor about his accident in which he shot himself through both legs and about his two plane crashes in Africa and always with an understatement which underlines his authority. In the 1940's and 1950's Hemingway had become an institution. His writing reflected his recognition and acceptance of it. Prior to his fossilization, however, Hemingway wrote not so much about himself as about what he saw and knew. Reading it now, a generation later, is a tremendously exciting experience."

326 Poore, Charles. "Portrait of a Man and Some Pieces of Paper," review of *By-Line* (edited by William White), *N.Y. Times* (May 25, 1967), p. 45.

"In these pages you share Hemingway's enjoyment of living. As such things go, he had a short life in the saddle, but it was far better than many a longer one by the fire."

326₁ Knox, Sanka. "2 Hemingway MSS. Bought for $7,650," *ibid.*, p. 57.

The entire Hemingway collection auctioned by Charles Hamilton, in New York, was bought by Maury A. Bromsen, rare-book dealer of Boston, for $16,700. The collection included two unpublished short stories, "Black Ass at the Cross Roads" and "The Bubble Illusion," and 18 letters to N. M. Davis. "The Bubble Illusion" is described as "a hilarious autobiographical account of a brush with American military authorities while the author was working as a war correspondent." See (S-B18).

327 "Hemingway Items Make $16,700," *Times*, London (May 26, 1967), p. 6. See above item.

328 Hicks, Granville. "The Novelist as Newspaperman," review of *By-Line* (edited by William White), *Saturday Review*, L (May 27, 1967), 23-24.

"[Hemingway's] journalism taken as journalism is almost always first-rate, and sometimes it is as truly literature as anything he ever wrote. . . . This is a volume that could be enjoyed if the by-line were Joe Doakes, but it inevitably has a special interest for students of Hemingway and for all his admirers . . . the volume can only enhance his reputation."

329 Young, Philip. "Hemingway by Moonlight," review of *By-Line* (edited by William White), *Chicago Tribune Book Week* (May 28, 1967), p. 6.

"Now the whole range of Hemingway's mostly-foreign correspondence, selected by a reputable professor of Journalism and built to last, is going to get around a lot. All that's needed is that those who read it should read it for what it is: writing that was at first the meal ticket, before long the moonlighting, of a man who really had a different job."

330 Baker, Carlos. "His Beat Was the World," review of *By-Line* (edited by William White), *N.Y. Times Book Review* (May 28, 1967), pp. 1, 16.

"This generous volume, which reprints 77 of his journalistic articles, is a welcome addition to the slowly expanding shelf of posthumous books by Hemingway. . . . Rescued from piles of yellowing newsprint and files of superannuated magazines, these selections shine like a hoard of gold pieces brought newly to light and still bearing the coin-maker's inimitable imprimatura. Mint-fresh, too, most of them, after all these years. For the Hemingway personality, flaws and all, is memorably revived and made visible and audible in these thoroughly readable articles."

331 Kennedy, William. "The 'Clear Heart' of Reporter Hemingway," review of *By-Line* (edited by William White), *National Observer* (May 29, 1967), p. 19.

"Even as a journalist Hemingway had what someone once called a 'clear heart,' which made for an almost instant point of view, and he put his personality, his tastes, even his prejudices into his articles. In the early years the story was refracted through Hemingway; in later years the story became a means of listening to the Hemingway mind. . . . True, this journalism is not topdrawer Hemingway. But it is fascinating, for here in raw form are the bulls running in Pamplona's streets, the pseudo artists in Paris, the cowardly lion hunters, the old fisherman who loses his great catch to sharks, and much more that Hemingway transformed so magically into stories and novels."

332 "Hemingway-Manuskripte: Keine Widerrede," *Der Spiegel*, XXI (May 29, 1967), 144.

Regarding Charles Hamilton's auction, on May 24, 1967, of Hemingway's letters to Bill Davis and the unpublished manuscript "Black Ass at the Cross Roads." See (S-B18).

333 Cowley, Malcolm. "Papa and the Parricides," *Esquire*, LXVII (June 1967), 100-101, 103, 160, 162. Drawing by Ann Weisman.

A protest against the "recent attacks on Hemingway's reputation."

334 Helwig, Werner. "Als ihm die Stunde schlug," review of A. E. Hotchner's *Papa Hemingway, Merkur,* XXI (June 1967), 596-598.

335 Kirshner, Sumner. "From the Gulf Stream into the Main Stream: Siegfried Lenz and Hemingway," *Research Studies* (Washington State University), XXXV (June 1967), 141-147.

336 Bisol, Gaetano ˙ "Iemingway postumo e autobiografico," *Civiltà Cattolica,* CXVIII (June 3, 1967), 468-473.

337 Brief review of *By-Line* (edited by William White), *New Yorker,* XLIII (June 3, 1967), 145-146.
"The quality of Hemingway's journalism tends to ⋅⋅n parallel to that of his imaginative writing. That is to say, the pieces written in the twenties and thirties are, with one or two exceptions, much the best. Some of the early [Toronto] *Star* pieces are immediately reminiscent of the earliest stories, and the writing in many of the *Esquire* articles (and a description of a Wyoming wilderness written for *Vogue*) is inimitably quick, sharp, and rich. . . . The Second World War correspondence . . . is somewhat dated, and more general pieces are often loud and flat."

338 Havighurst, Walter. "A generous sampling of journalism," review of *By-Line* (edited by William White), *Chicago Tribune* (June 4, 1967), Books Today section, p. 1.
"*By-Line: Ernest Hemingway* is a generous and judicious sampling of his journalism. . . . The best pieces have a personal center, showing Hemingway's response to people and places. The most interesting portion of the book is a selection culled from his 'Reporting' years, 1920 to 1924. . . . His dispatches show a young reporter with a shrewd eye and a skeptical independent mind. . . . At 25 Hemingway could unmask political pretensions, and he could see the hollowness of generalities."

339 Maloff, Saul. "Farewell to Arms," review of *By-Line* (edited by William White), *Newsweek,* LXIX (June 5, 1967), 102.
"Hemingway was a journalist all his life, from the time of his obscurity to the time when he was the world's most famous writer. The 77 articles and dispatches over four decades collected in this volume are, inevitably, wildly uneven, so much so that Hemingway's name would have been better served by far more rigorous selection."

340 Coven, Carol. Editorial, *Trapeze,* LVI (June 9, 1967), 1. Photographs and facsimiles.
Regarding the special Hemingway section in honor of the fiftieth anniversary of his graduation from Oak Park and River Forest High School in Oak Park, Illinois.

340₁ Meyerson, Holly. " 'We Knew Him When' Panel of Six Recalls School Days of Ernest Hemingway in Oak Park," *ibid*, pp. 5, 8.

The panel members were Miss Edith Stryker, John Gehlmann, Frank Platt, Mrs. Carl Kesler (Sue Lowrey), Frank Kohler, and Lewis Clarahan. The moderator was Van Allen Bradley.

340₂ "Series of Four Programs Tells of Hemingway's Life and Work," *ibid.*, pp. 5, 8.

340₃ Cooke, Jackie. "School Exciting for a Student Like Hemingway," *ibid.*, pp. 5, 7.

Regarding humorous incidents that happened during Hemingway's high-school years.

340₄ Varilla, Jeff. Pencil sketch of Hemingway, *ibid.*, p. 5.

340₅ Dardick, Nathan. " 'Senator' Hemingway Debates 'Shipping' at Burke Club," *ibid.*, p. 7.

Report on the minutes of the Burke Debating Society for December 6, 1916.

340₆ "Hemingway's Houses," *ibid.*, p. 7. Photographs.

340₇ "Dare Girls Rescued," *ibid.*, p. 7.

Article reprinted from *Oak Leaves* (Feb. 3, 1917). See (S-H1). A facsimile of the story is also reproduced.

340₈ Davenport, Ben. " 'Trap' On Display at Key West," *ibid.*, p. 8.

Report on a teacher's visit to the Hemingway Museum in Key West.

340₉ Grippe, Charles. "Books," review of Leicester Hemingway's *My Brother, Ernest Hemingway, ibid.*, p. 8.

341 Kauffmann, Stanley. "Before and After Papa," review of *By-Line* (edited by William White), *New Republic*, CLVI (June 10, 1967), 18, 35.

"The prime effect of this collection—both parts, before and after the Papa figure—is to confirm for me the value of his posthumous book *A Moveable Feast*. . . . The journalism of the early 20's, with its combined feelings of power and insouciance, underscores the daring of the plunge he took from that platform of security; and the later journalism, most of it, emphasizes the gap between the young man and the old—and it is the consciousness of that gap that generates the pathos of *A Moveable Feast*. His last book shows us that he knew what had happened; much of this collection shows it happening. Read in conjunction, these two books illuminate an artistic tragedy."

342 Review of *Oeuvres romanesques*, Vol. 1 (Paris: Gallimard, 1966), *Times Literary Supplement* (June 22, 1967), p. 557.

"The 'Bibliothèque de la Pléiade' is well known as one of the most attractive and compendious series of texts ever to have appeared. The works chosen for it have all a good reason for being called 'classic.' . . . Ernest Hemingway is the only writer in English to be included. There is not a single British writer in the list. Hemingway's inclusion is a remarkable tribute to his standing in France, and this edition 'de la Pléiade' is bound to enhance his reputation." See (S-D34).

343 Weeks, Robert P. Reviews, *American Quarterly*, XIX (Summer 1967), 260-265.

Reviews of Roger Asselineau's *The Literary Reputation of Hemingway in Europe*, Carlos Baker's *Hemingway: The Writer as Artist* (3rd edition), Sheridan Baker's *EH: An Introduction and Interpretation*, A. E. Hotchner's *Papa Hemingway*, Robert W. Lewis's *Hemingway on Love*, and Philip Young's *EH: A Reconsideration*. "In the six books reviewed here—all but one published since 1965— Hemingway is looked at from various points of view: as pal, confidant, drinking companion—and gold mine (Hotchner); as American phenomenon with powerful impact on European fiction (Asselineau); as agreeable means to Ph.D. (Lewis); as *leo Maximus*, the giant of American literature (Carlos Baker); and as fruitful subject of psycho-biographical criticism (Young, Sheridan Baker). . . . It is a sad commentary that Hotchner's book, although by far the least respectable intellectually, will be read more widely than the other five combined."

344 Schneider, Daniel J. "The Symbolism of *The Sun Also Rises*," *Discourse*, X (Summer 1967), 334-342.

345 Wyatt, Bryant N. "Huckleberry Finn and the Art of Ernest Hemingway," *Mark Twain Journal*, XIII (Summer 1967), 1-8.

346 Galligan, Edward L. "Hemingway's Staying Power," *Massachusetts Review*, VIII (Summer 1967), 431-439.

The author bases his thesis that "our best writers are still finding strength in Hemingway's vision" on Nelson Algren's *Notes from a Sea Diary*, Norman Mailer's *Cannibals and Christians*, and Vance Bourjaily's *The Unnatural Enemy*.

347 Bradford, M. E. "On the Importance of Discovering God: Faulkner and Hemingway's *The Old Man and the Sea*," *Mississippi Quarterly*, XX (Summer 1967), 158-162.

Regarding William Faulkner's review of *OMATS* in *Shenandoah*, III (Autumn 1952). See (H757).

348 White, Ray Lewis. "Hemingway's Private Explanation of *The Torrents of Spring*," *Modern Fiction Studies*, XIII (Summer 1967), 261-263.

A digest of five unpublished letters from Hemingway in the Sherwood Anderson Collection of the Newberry Library, in Chicago.

349 Costa, Richard Hauer. Review of Philip Young's *EH: A Reconsideration*, *Quartet*, III (Summer 1967), 27-28.

350 Lanoux, Armand. "Un homme nommé Hemingway," *À la Page*, No. 37 (July 1967), pp. 1008-1014.

351 Weeks, Edward. " 'Captain' Hemingway," review of *By-Line* (edited by William White), *Atlantic*, CCXX (July 1967), 109-110.

352 Henss, Herbert. "Eine verbindende Interpretation auf der Oberstufe als Teil des Themenkomplexes 'Amerika': Edgar Allan Poe, 'The Masque of the Red Death,' Ernest Hemingway, 'A Clean, Well-Lighted Place,' " *Neueren Sprachen*, XVI [New Series], (July 1967), 327-338.

353 Lorie, Maria. "Hemingway and Kashkeen," *Sputnik*, No. 7 (July 1967), 40-47. Facsimile and photographs.

On Ivan Kashkeen's books and articles on Hemingway. Translated into English from *Prometey*, No. 1 (1966). For facsimile of a Hemingway letter, regarding Kashkeen, see (S-F96).

353₁ Lazarev, Lazar, and Stanislav Rassadin. Parody of *OMATS*, *ibid.*, pp. 48-49. In English. Caricature of Hemingway by Joseph Igin.

353₂ "Hemingway and Faulkner in the USSR," *ibid.*, p. 49.

Hemingway's books have been printed "in 17 languages in the USSR in 57 editions totalling over 2,582,000 copies." In English, "70,000 copies of *Green Hills of Africa* and 150,000 copies of *The Old Man and the Sea* have been printed."

354 "Hemingway Works Given to the Houghton Library," *N.Y. Times* (July 4, 1967), p. 17.

Regarding the gift of Hemingway letters, written to Harvey Breit, and other items presented to Houghton Library, at Harvard University, by Dr. and Mrs. Edmundo Lassalle.

355 Reta, Javier Esteban. "Pamplona es una fiesta: Hemingway universalizó los Sanfermines," *La Voz de España* (July 7, 1967).

356 Brief review of *The Short Stories of Ernest Hemingway* (Scribner Library Omnibus edition). *Publishers' Weekly*, CXCII (July 10, 1967), 188.

357 Turnbull, Andrew. Speaking of Books column, "Perkins's Three Generals," *N.Y. Times Book Review* (July 16, 1967), pp. 2, 25-27.
   Regarding F. Scott Fitzgerald, Thomas Wolfe, and Hemingway, and their "common parent" Maxwell Perkins. Reprinted in Francis Brown's *Page 2*, New York, 1969, pp. 245-251.

358 Gorbunov, A. "Kheminguei—chelovek i pisatel' " [Hemingway—man and writer], *Novyi Mir*, No. 8 (Aug. 1967), pp. 251-254.
   Review of Ivan Kashkin's two books on Hemingway, which were published in Moscow in 1966.

359 Finkel'shtein, I. L. "Sovetskaya kritika o Kheminguee" [Hemingway in Soviet criticism], *Voprosy Literatury*, No. 8 (Aug, 1967), 174-190.

360 Bocca, Geoffrey. "Hemingway's Havana—Today," *This Week* (Aug. 6, 1967), pp. 6-7. Photographs and cover photograph.
   An account of a visit to the Hemingway Museum (formerly Finca Vigía) and the Café Floridita.

361 Cort, David. Review of *By-Line* (edited by William White), *Commonweal*, LXXXVI (Aug. 11, 1967), 499-500.

362 Le Clec'h, Guy. "Hemingway, l'homme qui détestait la guerre et la racontait si bien," *Figaro Littéraire* (Aug. 14-20, 1967), p. 25.
   On *By-Line* (edited by William White).

363 Baker, Carlos. Speaking of Books column, "The Relevance of a Writer's Life," *N.Y. Times Book Review* (Aug. 20, 1967), pp. 2, 31. General article. Discusses "The Battler." Reprinted in Francis Brown's *Page 2*, New York, 1969, pp. 217-221.

364 Sanders, Barry. "An Unsolved Hemingway Enigma," *American Book Collector*, XVIII (Sept. 1967), 8-9.
   Regarding the source of Hemingway's title *A Moveable Feast*.

365 Stephens, Robert O., and James Ellis. "Hemingway, Fitzgerald and the Riddle of 'Henry's Bicycle,' " *English Language Notes*, V (Sept. 1967), 46-49.
   On the allusion to "Henry's bicycle" in the Burguete scene in *The Sun Also Rises*.

366 Magee, John D. "Hemingway's 'Cat in the Rain,' " *Explicator*, XXVI (Sept. 1967), Item 8.

367 Bogdan, Mihail. "Hemingway," review of Radu Lupan's *Hemingway, scriitorul, Steaua*, XVIII (Sept. 1967), 115-117. In Rumanian.

368 "Hemingway: Jeden Tag Geschichte," *Der Spiegel*, XXI (Sept. 4, 1967), 130-132.
   Regarding publication of *By-Line* (edited by William White).

369 Maynard, Reid. "The Decay Motif in 'The Snows of Kilimanjaro,'"
Discourse, x (Autumn 1967), 436-439.

370 Pickett, Calder M. Review of *By-Line* (edited by William White),
Journalism Quarterly, XLIV (Autumn 1967), 579-580.
This "uneven" book . . . "is extremely absorbing, sometimes exciting, sometimes embarrassing. Anybody in journalism should read
it, but don't expect to find out what separates journalistic man from
literary man. Some of the journalism reads like literature, and Hemingway, as he got older . . . slipped a lot."

371 Wiegand, William. "The 'Non-fiction' Novel," *New Mexico Quarterly*, XXXVII (Autumn 1967), 243-257.
Examines Truman Capote's *In Cold Blood*, Hemingway's *Green
Hills of Africa*, and other works on the borderline between fiction
and journalism.

372 Baker, Carlos. "The Slopes of Kilimanjaro: A Biographical Perspective," *Novel: A Forum on Fiction*, 1 (Fall 1967), 19-23. Adapted for
American Heritage, XIX (Aug. 1968), 40-43, 90-91.

373 Wickes, George. "Hemingway's Journalism," review of *By-Line*
(edited by William White), *Shenandoah*, XIX (Autumn 1967), 73-78.
"For the student of Hemingway's fiction the most interesting section of White's anthology is the earliest, which reflects the writer in
the making between the ages of twenty and twenty-four. . . . Much
of his early reporting reflects Hemingway's growing mastery of the
craft of fiction. Some of the stories, carefully controlled and
rounded, reveal his sense of form. . . . The final section is . . . a mix-
ture of good and bad. The best article is Hemingway's account of
his two plane crashes in Africa in 1954. . . . His writing for *Esquire*
suffers by comparison."

374 Stone, Edward. "Some Questions About Hemingway's 'The Killers,'"
Studies in Short Fiction, v (Fall 1967), 12-17. See reply by Bayne
Freeland in *SSF*, v (Spring 1968), iii-v.

374₁ Dussinger, Gloria R. "'The Snows of Kilimanjaro': Harry's Second
Chance," *ibid.*, pp. 54-59.

375 Loeb, Harold. "Hemingway's Bitterness," *Connecticut Review*, 1
(Oct. 1967), 7-24.
Relates the events in Paris and Pamplona, in 1925, on which *SAR*
was based, and discusses Hemingway's use of friends as "disagree-
able fictive characters." The author was portrayed as "Robert
Cohn." Reprinted in Bertram D. Sarason's *Hemingway and The Sun
Set*, Washington, D.C., 1972, pp. 111-135. See Comment by the editor, Bertram D. Sarason, in *CR*, 1 (April 1968), 144, regarding comments received on this article.

376 Long, Madeleine J. "Sartrean Themes in Contemporary American Literature," *Dissertation Abstracts,* XXVIII (Oct. 1967), 1439-A.

Abstract from a doctoral dissertation, Columbia University, 1967. Examines the application of Sartre's themes in *OMATS*.

377 Korn, Barbara. "Form and Idea in Hemingway's 'Big Two-Hearted River,'" *English Journal,* LVI (Oct. 1967), 979-981, 1014.

378 Oldsey, Bernard S. "Always Personal," review of *By-Line* (edited by William White), *Journal of General Education,* XIX (Oct. 1967), 239-243.

"*By-Line: Ernest Hemingway* is a collection of journalistic pieces written between 1920 and 1956. It acts as a short history of the man, his work, and the times. Much of what Hemingway put into his fiction came from his journalism. So the book is also a kind of writer's notebook or journal. . . . If you read closely from beginning to end, you get some idea of how Hemingway's style started fresh, gained in almost lyric compression, staggered in self-parody, and then came back to the exact and piercing thing made of it in *A Moveable Feast*—which is probably a collaboration of the young man who made the observations in the twenties and of the old man who brought them firmly together when he himself was going to pieces in the fifties and sixties. . . . Perhaps what is most noticeable in the reporting is that it is always personal—freshly and humorously in the earliest pieces, more knowingly and self-seekingly in the later ones."

379 Melland, Amicia. "Casa memorială 'Hemingway' din Havana," *Secolul 20,* No. 10 (Oct. 1967), pp. 131-132. Photographs. See also (S-C50).

380 Reardon, John. "Hemingway's Esthetic and Ethical Sportsmen," *University Review* (Kansas City), XXXIV (Oct. 1967), 13-23.

381 Nemy, Enid. "Mary Hemingway: 'I'm Never Bored,'" *N.Y. Times* (Oct. 19, 1967), p. 54.

Interview with Mary Hemingway in New York.

382 Tanner, Tony. "Tony Tanner writes about some remarkable letters shortly to be sold in London: the aging Hemingway to Adriana Ivancich, dear friend, dream-girl and Venetian muse," *Times,* London (Oct. 21, 1967), Saturday Review section, p. 17.

Includes excerpts from the "67 letters, or fragments of letters," written by Hemingway between 1950 and 1955, auctioned at Christie's, in London, November 29, 1967. See (S-F105).

383 Raymont, Henry. "Widow of Hemingway Protests Use of His Letters," *N.Y. Times* (Oct. 22, 1967), p. 72.

Regarding publication of excerpts from Hemingway's letters to Adriana Ivancich in the London *Times*. See above item. Hemingway's request, dated May 20, 1958, that none of his letters be published, is quoted.

384 LaRoque, Geraldine E. Review of *By-Line* (edited by William White), *English Journal*, LVI (Nov. 1967), 1216-1217.

384₁ Fuller, James F. Review of *FTA* (Scribner School Edition, with Introduction and Study Guide by John C. Schweitzer), *ibid.*, pp. 1225-1226.

385 Zasurskii, Ya. "Ot sobstvennogo korrespondenta Ernesta Khemingueya" [From our own correspondent Ernest Hemingway], *Literaturnaya Gazeta*, No. 48 (Nov. 29, 1967), p. 13.

386 Shuster, Alvin. ["Einstein Letters in London Auction"], *N.Y. Times* (Nov. 30, 1967). p. 42.
    Regarding the purchase, at Christie's in London, of 65 Hemingway letters to Adriana Ivancich by Lew David Feldman, rare-book dealer in New York, for $16,800. Note: These letters are among the holdings of the Humanities Research Center of the University of Texas.

387 Vandiver, Samuel Earl. "The Architecture of Hemingway's Prose," *Dissertation Abstracts*, XXVIII (Dec. 1967), 2268-A.
    Abstract from a doctoral dissertation, University of Texas, 1967.

388 Tamke, Alexander. "Jacob Barnes' 'Biblical Name': Central Irony in *The Sun Also Rises*," *English Record*, XVIII (Dec. 1967), 2-7.

389 White, William. "*Ernest Hemingway: The Wild Years*," *AB* [*Antiquarian Bookman*] *Bookman's Weekly*, XL (Dec. 4, 1967), 1988.
    Regarding the similarities in the cover of the reissued paperback edition of *The Wild Years*, edited by Gene Z. Hanrahan, and the dust jacket of *By-Line*, edited by White.

390 Gorlier, Claudio. "Hemingway giornalista," review of *Dal nostro inviato Ernest Hemingway* (*By-Line*), *Corriere della Sera* (Dec. 10, 1967), p. 11.

391 Tarbox, Raymond. "Blank Hallucinations in the Fiction of Poe and Hemingway," *American Imago*, XXIV (Winter 1967), 312-343.

392 Kobler, Jasper F. "Confused Chronology in *The Sun Also Rises*," *Modern Fiction Studies*, XIII (Winter 1967-1968), 517-520.

393 Wylder, Delbert E. "*The Torrents of Spring*," *South Dakota Review*, V (Winter 1967-1968), 23-25.

Examines Hemingway's parody of Sherwood Anderson's *Dark Laughter*. Reprinted, in a revised version, in *Hemingway's Heroes*, Albuquerque, 1969, pp. 11-30.

394 Severino, Alex. "O Papel da Personagem: O Herói do Código nos Romances de Ernest Hemingway," *ALFA*, Nos. 13 and 14 (1968), 163-235.
Examines the anti-hero in Hemingway's novels.

395 White, William. "Hemingway and Fitzgerald," *American Literary Scholarship: An Annual / 1968*, pp. 107-117.

396 Fisher, Marvin. "More Snow on Kilimanjaro," *Americana Norvegica*, II (1968), 343-353.
On similarities and dissimilarities between "Harry" in "The Snows of Kilimanjaro" and Hemingway.

397 Vargas, Germán. "Un libro de crónicas de Hemingway," *Boletín Cultural y Bibliográfico*, XI, No. 12 (1968), 55-56.
Review of *By-Line* (edited by William White).

398 Takamura, Katsuji. "Hemingway no Rojin to Shonen," *Eigo Seinen*, CXIV (1968), 300-301.

398₁ Kawasaki, Toshihiko. "Hemingway to futatsu no Bunseki Hihyo," *ibid.*, pp. 498-500.

399 Kukharenko, V. A. "E. Kheminguei v perevode A. Voznesenskogo," *Filologičeskie Nauki*, No. 6 (1968), pp. 40-49.

400 Trenev, Blagoj. "Sense Appeals as a Means of Expresson in Hemingway's Early Short Stories," *Godisnik na Sofijskiya universitet: Fakutet po zapadni filolgii*, LXII , No. 1 (1968), 133-151.

401 Nicolaisen, Peter. Review of Audre Hanneman's *EH: A Comprehensive Bibliography*, *Literatur in Wissenschaft und Unterricht*, I, i (1968), 154-155.

402 Hagood, Thomas Neal. "Humor in Hemingway's Toronto Articles," *McNeese Review*, XIX (1968), 48-58.
On Hemingway's work for the *Toronto Daily Star* and the *Toronto Star Weekly* in the early 1920s.

403 Koskimies, Rafael. "Notes on Ernest Hemingway's *For Whom the Bell Tolls*," *Orbis Litterarum*, XXIII (1968), 276-286.

403₁ Gillespie, Gerald. "Hemingway and the Happy Few," *ibid.*, pp. 287-299.
Regarding Stendhal's use of the phrase "the happy few" and the problem in Hemingway's novels of "how to be true to oneself in a world of hypocrisy and moral ugliness."

404 Yu, Beongcheon. "The Still Center of Hemingway's World," *Phoenix* (Korea University), XII (1968), 15-44.

405 Cowley, Malcolm. "American Writers and the First World War," *Proceedings of the American Academy of Arts and Letters and the National Institute of Arts and Letters,* Second Series, No. 18 (1968), pp. 25-46. General article.

406 St. John, Donald. "Indian Camp Camp," *Carleton Miscellany,* IX (Winter 1968), 95-109.
   An interview with Hemingway's sister, Sunny [Mrs. Ernest Miller], at Walloon Lake in Upper Michigan, and a visit to the scene of "Indian Camp." Reprinted in *Best Magazine Articles: 1968,* edited by Gerald Walker, New York, 1968, pp. 236-248.

407 Ganzel, Dewey. "*Cabestro* and *Vaquilla*: The Symbolic Structure of *The Sun Also Rises,*" *Sewanee Review,* LXXVI (Winter 1968), 26-48.

408 Williams, Wirt. "Hemingway as Tragic Writer," *Statement Magazine,* XXIV (Winter 1968), 11-20.

409 Holland, Robert B. "Macomber and the Critics," *Studies in Short Fiction,* V (Winter 1968), 171-178.

409₁ Atkins, Anselm. "Ironic Action in 'After the Storm,' " *ibid.,* pp. 189-192.

410 Matsuda, Sumio. "Symbolism and the Rhetoric of Fiction in Hemingway's Novels," *Dissertation Abstracts,* XXVIII (Jan. 1968), 2689-A.
   Abstract from a doctoral dissertation, University of Southern California, 1967.

411 Yakovlev, Yegor. "Skazhite: po kom zvonil kolokol," *Zhurnalist,* No. 1 (Jan. 1968), pp. 56-61.
   An interview with Colonel-General Haji Mamsurov "who lived through the events of Hemingway's *For Whom the Bell Tolls.*" An English translation, titled "Can You Say for Whom the Bell Tolls?", appeared in *Soviet Life,* No. 7 (July 1968), pp. 52-55.

412 White, William. "Notes on Hemingway . . . ," *American Book Collector,* XVIII (Jan.-Feb. 1968), 30.
   Regarding paperback reprints of books by and about Hemingway.

413 Curran, Ronald T. "The Individual and the Military Institution in Hemingway's Novels and *Collier's* Dispatches," *Revue des Langues Vivantes,* XXXIV (Jan.-Feb. 1968), 26-39.

414 "E. T." "When a Hemingway Edition Was a Total of 300 Copies," review of Audre Hanneman's *EH: A Comprehensive Bibliography, Washington Sunday Star* (Jan. 21, 1968), p. C-2.

415 Collections column, *Library Journal*, XCIII (Feb. 1, 1968), 504.
Item regarding A. E. Hotchner's collection of typescripts, galley proofs, and legal papers for *Papa Hemingway* being acquired by the Washington University Libraries in St. Louis, Missouri.

416 Murray, Donald. "Hong Kong Letter: Bombs, Books, and Hemingway," *American Book Collector*, XVIII (March 1968), 16-21.
Includes a list of 20 titles of Hemingway in Chinese translation, prepared by Wong Tak-Wai.

417 Silhol, Robert. "Étude: *L'Adieu aux armes*, Fantasme et Littérature ou Hemingway et Oedipe," *Langues Modernes*, II (March-April 1968), 211-219.

417₁ Hily, Geneviève. "Étude: *L'Adieu aux armes*, Hemingway et la Perspective," *ibid.*, pp. 220-227.

418 Penland, Patrick R. Review of Audre Hanneman's *EH: A Comprehensive Bibliography*, *Library Journal*, XCIII (March 1, 1968), 977.

419 Fleming, Peter. "Bygones," review of *By-Line* (edited by William White, with Commentaries by Philip Young), *Spectator*, CCXX (March 1, 1968), 266.
"*By-Line* is somehow a sad book. I cannot think that his editors have done the memory of a great story-teller a service by republishing material of which, as one of them jauntily reminds us, Hemingway himself told a biographer: 'no one has any right to dig this stuff up and use it against the stuff you have written to write the best you can.' "

420 Haskell, Henry C. Scanning the Arts column, "—Or Perhaps Hemingway Was in Love With Love," *Kansas City Star* (March 3, 1968).
Regarding Hemingway's purported "engagement" to Mae Marsh, a star of the silent films, in May 1918. Note: See Carlos Baker's *EH: A Life Story*, pp. 39, 571, regarding Hemingway's letter to Dale Wilson about his alleged meeting with the actress in New York. See (S-F14H).

421 "Big enough to hit," review of *By-Line* (edited by William White, with Commentaries by Philip Young) and *TFC* (Cape edition), *Times Literary Supplement* (March 7, 1968), p. 219.
"*By-Line* is chiefly fascinating as a notebook crammed full of vignettes and ideas which turn up again in his fiction. . . . [*The Fifth Column*] is academically interesting as an adjunct to *For Whom the*

Bell Tolls but it is hyper-romantic, and for the most part is without either action or words of a quality necessary to compensate for that fault. Compared even with the Spanish Civil War dispatches the play is thin stuff and should serve only to send the reader back to the superb Spanish War novel and to the reports in *By-Line* which are, at their best, models of war reporting." Note: This review includes a discussion of Hemingway's reputation since his death.

422 Jacobson, Dan. "Private Risks," review of *By-Line* (edited by William White, with Commentaries by Philip Young), *Listener*, LXXIX (March 14, 1968), 340.

"Considering how long the book is, and how well Hemingway could sometimes write, it is really very surprising how few of the pieces can begin to bear comparison with the reporting of someone like George Orwell—let alone with that of such other contenders as Mark Twain, Tolstoy and Turgenev, whom Hemingway himself used to speak of as his sparring-partners."

423 Nolan, William F. The Book Report column, "Bibliography of Works by and About Hemingway," review of Audre Hanneman's *EH: A Comprehensive Bibliography, Los Angeles Times* (March 15, 1968), Part IV, p. 4. Reprinted in the *International Herald Tribune* (March 23-24, 1968), under the title "How Far and Wide Hemingway Ranged as a Writer."

424 Bradbury, Malcolm. "Sad Voyage," review of *By-Line* (edited by William White, with Commentaries by Philip Young) and *TFC* (Cape edition), *New Statesman*, LXXV (March 22, 1968), 386.

"What both books do is to illuminate a man whose life was so crucially a part of his art—illuminate the steady search for the right life-style, and the paradox that goes along with it: that when it comes, when the style is achieved, when Hemingway is his own hero, the work falls off."

425 Butcher, Maryvonne. "Occasional Pieces," review of *By-Line* (edited by William White, with Commentaries by Philip Young), *Tablet,* CCXXII (March 23, 1968), 285.

"As one might have expected, the standard of writing shows a wide range of variation over those thirty-odd years of packed and passionate living. What one might not so easily have guessed is that the variation in quality does not all depend on date. By which I mean that some of Hemingway's best stuff can be found quite early in the book, cheek by jowl with examples of very amateur reporting; while right at the end of his career—tired and sick at heart as he was—he wrote some really terrible passages of near self-parody. . . . this book is a valuable help to the understanding of a writer who has wielded an almost disproportionate influence over his successors; and the very unevenness of the contents will provide ammunition for both friend and foe."

426 Klapper, Harold. "In Pursuit of Minutiae," review of Constance Cappel Montgomery's *Hemingway in Michigan, Prairie Schooner,* XLII (Spring 1968), 84-86.

427 Grimble, June A. "The *Revista Plaza* Talks to Mary Hemingway," *Revista Plaza* (Hotel Plaza Magazine), IV (Spring 1968), 20-22.
    Interview with Mary Hemingway, in Madrid, regarding Hemingway's love for Spain, and plans for the ABC television special. See (S-H481).

428 Waggoner, Hyatt H. "Hemingway and Faulkner: 'The End of Something,' " *Southern Review,* IV (Spring 1968), 458-466.
    Includes reviews of Roger Asselineau's *The Literary Reputation of Hemingway in Europe,* Carlos Baker's *Hemingway: The Writer as Artist* (3rd edition), Sheridan Baker's *Ernest Hemingway,* A. E. Hotchner's *Papa Hemingway,* Robert W. Lewis's *Hemingway on Love,* Philip Young's *EH: A Reconsideration,* and *By-Line* edited by William White.

429 Marin, Dave. "Seven Hours with Papa," *Southwest Review,* LIII (Spring 1968), 167-177.
    Relates an interview with Hemingway in Ketchum in the winter of 1958.

429₁ Gregory, Vahan. "Elegy: Hemingway," poem, *ibid.,* p. 178.

430 Ross, Danforth. Review of Nathan A. Scott's *EH: A Critical Essay, Studies in Short Fiction,* V (Spring 1968), 307-309.

431 White, William. "Books About Hemingway Abroad," *American Book Collector,* XVIII (April 1968), 23.

432 Bevis, R. W., M.A.J. Smith, Jr., and G. Brose. "Leopard Tracks in 'The Snows . . . ,' " *American Notes & Queries,* VI (April 1968), 115.
    Regarding the verbal similarities between the "frozen leopard" epigraph of "The Snows of Kilimanjaro" and H. W. Tilman's *Snow on the Equator.* Note: This is a reply to Barney Childs, *AN&Q,* II (Sept. 1963). See (S-H127).

433 Drawbell, James. "The Young Reporter," review of *By-Line* (edited by William White, with Commentaries by Philip Young), *Books and Bookmen,* XIII (April 1968), 39, 41. Cover drawing of Hemingway.
    "William White has dug it up and, with commentaries by Philip Young, Collins have published the book—'seventy-five articles and despatches recording the adventure that was Hemingway's life, and

the events from which he fashioned his masterpieces.' And a magnificent job all the parties have made of it. Particularly Hemingway. For here, in spite of his earlier disclaimer, you can trace through these pieces—some of them written when he was a very young reporter—that the old maestro disregarded his own credo. If he did not believe that his newspaper stuff was good enough, he certainly went on drawing heavily on it."

434 St. John, Donald. "Interview with Hemingway's 'Bill Gorton,'" *Connecticut Review,* I (April 1968), 5-12.
    Interview with Bill Smith, who was in Paris and Pamplona with the Hemingways in 1925, and served as one of the models for "Bill Gorton" in *SAR*. Part II of this interview appeared in *CR*, III (Oct. 1969). Both parts were reprinted in Bertram D. Sarason's *Hemingway and The Sun Set*, Washington, 1972, pp. 151-188.

435 Dussinger, Gloria R. "Hemingway's 'The Snows of Kilimanjaro,'" *Explicator,* XXVI (April 1968), Item 67.
    Regarding the lack of evidence that "Helen" and "Harry" are married.

436 Joost, Nicholas. "Ernest Hemingway and *The Dial*," *Neophilologus,* LII (April 1968), 180-190; (July 1968), 304-313.
    Hemingway submitted three manuscripts to the *Dial* during 1924 and 1925, and all three were rejected.

437 Nolan, William F. "Papa's Planet," *Playboy,* XV (April 1968), 131, 182-183. Drawing of Hemingway by Eugene Karlin. Short story.

438 McDonough, Jean. "In Hemingway's Footsteps Through Spain," *International Herald Tribune* (April 6-7, 1968), p. 14.

439 "Moscow to Publish a Hemingway Novel," *N.Y. Times* (April 7, 1968), p. 5.
    For Whom the Bell Tolls to be published, for the first time in Russian, in a four-volume edition of Hemingway's collected works.

440 Henson, Clyde. "Hemingway: Craftsman in our time," *Collage* (Michigan State University) (April 18, 1968), p. 5. Cover drawing of Hemingway by Doug Houston.

441 Hagemann, E. R., and Margaret C. Lewis. "A Critique of *Ernest Hemingway: A Comprehensive Bibliography*," *American Book Collector,* XVIII (May 1968), 5-6.

442 Griffin, Gerald R. "Hemingway's Fictive Use of the Negro: 'the curious quality of incompleteness,'" *Husson Review,* I (May 1968), 104-111.

443 Tanner, Tony. Review of *By-Line* (edited by William White, with Commentaries by Philip Young), *London Magazine,* VIII [New Series] (May 1968), 90-95.

"It is easy to point to the limitations of Hemingway's prose, and some of the later pieces reveal the grace stiffening into a stilted posture. But there is enough in this book to remind us once again that he was one of the important writers of our time. . . . One final comment on this welcome collection: it reveals more of the humour in Hemingway than his books do. There are a number of passages which read like Mark Twain, who developed clowning into a deliberate strategy in *Innocents Abroad.* Hemingway plays the clown too, on many occasions, and for similar reasons. It was a way of surviving in unfamiliar and possibly threatening territories; it is also a way of coping with fear. And this surviving and this coping Hemingway made his own particular business. It is this underlying seriousness and tension which redeems most of his journalism from the ephemerality and contingency usually inherent in this activity."

444 Hagemann, E. R. Review of *By-Line* (edited by William White), *American Book Collector,* XVIII (June 1968), 6.

The reviewer quotes Joseph Conrad's famous statement: "My task which I am trying to achieve is, by the power of the written word to make you hear, to make you feel—it is, before all, to make you *see.* That—and no more, and it is everything."

"*By-Line,* a generous sampling of his journalism from 1920 to 1956, intelligently edited by Professor William White . . . reminds us forcibly that Hemingway for a good part of his life also achieved this task as a first-rate working reporter and correspondent."

444₁ White, William. "Errors in *By-Line: Ernest Hemingway,*" *ibid.,* p. 24. See note under (S-A14).

445 Serravalli, Luigi. "Ernest Hemingway inviato speciale," *Cristallo,* X (June 1968), 142-164.

On *Dal nostro inviato Ernest Hemingway (By-Line).*

446 Hemingway, Mary. "Harry's Bar in Venice," *Holiday,* XLIII (June 1968), 62-63, 106.

Mary Hemingway recalls her first visit to Harry's Bar with Hemingway, in 1948, and their later visits in the 1950s.

447 Cecil, L. Moffitt. "The Color of *A Farewell to Arms,*" *Research Studies* (Washington State University), XXXVI (June 1968), 168-173.

Examines the predominance of "red and black, then white, and finally gray" in *FTA.*

448 Irwin, Richard. " 'Of War, Wounds, and Silly Machines': An Examination of Hemingway's 'In Another Country,' " *Serif,* V (June 1968), 21-29.

449 Weeks, Lewis E., Jr. "Mark Twain and Hemingway: 'A Catastrophe' and 'A Natural History of the Dead,' " *Mark Twain Journal,* xiv (Summer 1968), 15-17.

450 Young, Philip. "Scott Fitzgerald on His Thirtieth Birthday Sends a Small Gift to Ernest Hemingway," *Modern Fiction Studies,* xiv (Summer 1968), 229-230.

Quotes a letter to Hemingway from F. Scott Fitzgerald [September 24, 1926] spoofing Hemingway's prose in *in our time.*

451 Smith, Julian. " 'A Canary for One': Hemingway in the Wasteland," *Studies in Short Fiction,* v (Summer 1968), 355-361.

451₁ Leiter, Louis H. "Neural Projections in Hemingway's 'On the Quai at Smyrna,' " *ibid.,* pp. 384-386.

452 Review of Audre Hanneman's *EH: A Comprehensive Bibliography, Virginia Quarterly Review,* xliv (Summer 1968), cxii.

453 Bagchi, Krishna. "The Hemingway Hero," *Banasthali Patrika,* No. 11 (July 1968), pp. 91-94. Special number on American Literature edited by Rameshwar Gupta.

454 Bellman, Samuel Irving. "Hemingway, Faulkner, and Wolfe . . . and the Common Reader," *Southern Review,* iv (July 1968), 834-849.

Includes reviews of Philip Young's *EH: A Reconsideration,* Robert W. Lewis's *Hemingway on Love,* and Roger Asselineau's *The Literary Reputation of Hemingway in Europe.*

455 Review of Audre Hanneman's *EH: A Comprehensive Bibliography, Choice,* v (July-August 1968), 607.

456 Liedloff, Helmut. "Two War Novels: A Critical Comparison," *Revue de Littérature Comparée,* xlii (July-Sept. 1968), 390-406.

Comparison of *FTA* and Erich Maria Remarque's *All Quiet on the Western Front.*

457 "A Hemingway Street is Dedicated in Spain," *N.Y. Times* (July 7, 1968), p. 2.

A bronze bust [by Luis Sanguino] and a street named after Hemingway were dedicated in Pamplona at the beginning of the annual San Fermin celebrations.

458 "Hemingway Avenue, Pamplona," *International Herald Tribune* (July 8, 1968), p. 3. Photograph.

459 Pett, Saul. "Key West Remembers Hemingway," *Chicago Sun-Times* (July 14, 1968), p. 82.

Includes reminiscences of Hemingway by Toby and Betty Bruce.

460 Menn, Thorpe. "Everything About Hemingway—Almost," review of Audre Hanneman's *EH: A Comprehensive Bibliography, Kansas City Star* (July 20, 1968).

461 Foor, Mel. "Remembering Hemingway's Kansas City Days," *Kansas City Star* (July 21, 1968), Section D, pp. 1-2. Drawings and photographs.

Four articles attributed to Hemingway, which appeared in the *K. C. Star* in 1917 and 1918, are reprinted. See (S-C56).

462 Nash, Jay Robert. "Ernest Hemingway: The Young Years and the Chicagoans Who Knew Him," *ChicagoLand Omnibus*, v (Aug. 1968), 19-25. Photographs.

463 Kobler, Jasper Fred, III. "Journalist and Artist: The Dual Role of Ernest Hemingway," *Dissertation Abstracts*, xxix (Aug. 1968), 606-A to 607-A.

Abstract from a doctoral dissertation, University of Texas, 1968.

464 Ross, Frank. "The Assailant-Victim in Three War-Protest Novels," *Paunch*, No. 32 (Aug. 1968), pp. 46-57.

Examines *FTA*, John Dos Passos' *Three Soldiers*, and Norman Mailer's *The Naked and the Dead*.

465 "Reputations," review of Jackson R. Bryer's *The Critical Reputation of F. Scott Fitzgerald* and Audre Hanneman's *EH: A Comprehensive Bibliography*, *Times Literary Supplement* (Aug. 1, 1968), p. 826.

466 Solov'ëv, E. "Tsvet tragedii: O tvorčestve E. Khemingueya," *Novyi Mir*, xliv (Sept. 1968), 206-235.

467 "Hemingway's Idaho," *Venture,* v (Sept. 1968), 50-55. Photographs by Jack Ward.

467₁ Wardlow, Jean. "At Home with Miss Mary," *ibid.*, pp. 56-62.
Describes a visit with Mary Hemingway in Ketchum, Idaho.

468 Fuson, Ben W. Review of Robert O. Stephens' *Hemingway's Non-fiction, Library Journal*, xciii (Sept. 15, 1968), 3142.

468₁ Bender, Rose S. Review of Leo Gurko's *Ernest Hemingway and the Pursuit of Heroism, ibid.*, p. 3316.

469 Traver, Robert. "A Memorial for Hemingway," *Detroit News Sunday Magazine* (Sept. 29, 1968), pp. 16-20.

470 Young, Philip. Speaking of Books column, "In the Vault With Hemingway," *N.Y. Times Book Review* (Sept. 29, 1968), pp. 2, 28.

Regarding Philip Young and Charles W. Mann's inventory of the unpublished Hemingway manuscripts. See (S-B11). An Italian translation, titled "Il mio Hemingway," appeared in *Panorama*, viii (Oct. 9, 1969), 72-75. Reprinted in an updated and revised form, under the title "Locked in the Vault with Hemingway," in *Ren-*

dezvous, v (Winter 1970), 1-5. Reprinted in *Three Bags Full,* New York, 1972, pp. 68-75.

See also Donald S. Heines's Letter to the Editor in the *NYTBR* (Oct. 27, 1968), p. 72, regarding the general principles that should determine future publication of Hemingway manuscripts.

471 Munson, Gorham. "A Comedy of Exiles," *Literary Review,* XII (Fall 1968), 41-75.
On *SAR.*

472 Gifford, William. "Ernest Hemingway: The Monsters and the Critics," *Modern Fiction Studies,* XIV (Autumn 1968), 255-270. Special number on Hemingway.

472₁ Farquhar, Robin H. "Dramatic Structure in the Novels of Ernest Hemingway," *ibid.,* pp. 271-282.

472₂ Schneider, Daniel J. "Hemingway's *A Farewell to Arms*: The Novel as Pure Poetry," *ibid.,* pp. 283-296.

472₃ Cochran, Robert W. "Circularity in *The Sun Also Rises,*" *ibid.,* pp. 297-305.

472₄ Green, James L. "Symbolic Sentences in 'Big Two-Hearted River,' " *ibid.,* pp. 307-312.

472₅ Burhans, Clinton S., Jr. "The Complex Unity of *In Our Time,*" *ibid.,* pp. 313-328.

472₆ Ryan, William James. "Uses of Irony in *To Have and Have Not,*" *ibid.,* pp. 329-336.

472₇ Beebe, Maurice, and John Feaster. "Criticism of Ernest Hemingway: A Selected Checklist," *ibid.,* pp. 337-369. In two parts: Part I: General. Part II: Studies of Individual Works of Fiction.

473 Nolan, William F. "Hemingway: Now Never There," poem, *Prairie Schooner,* XLII (Fall 1968), 208-211.

474 Cannell, Kathleen. "Scenes With a Hero," *Connecticut Review,* II (Oct. 1968), 5-9.
Reminiscences of Hemingway in Paris in the 1920s. The character "Frances Clyne" in *The Sun Also Rises* was based on the author. Reprinted in Bertram D. Sarason's *Hemingway and The Sun Set,* Washington, D.C., 1972, pp. 145-150.

474₁ St. John, Donald. "Hemingway and the Girl Who Could Skate," *ibid.,* pp. 10-19.
Dorothy Connable, who met Hemingway in Petoskey, Michigan, in the winter of 1919-1920, reminisces about the two periods that Hemingway spent in Toronto in the early 1920s.

475 Slattery, Sister Margaret Patrice. "Hemingway's *A Farewell to Arms*," *Explicator*, XXVII (Oct. 1968), Item 8.

On the structural pattern of motion in *FTA*.

476 "P. H." [Paul Heins]. Review of Leo Gurko's *Ernest Hemingway and the Pursuit of Heroism, Horn Book*, XLIV (Oct. 1968), 569.

477 Yevish, Irving A. "The Sun Also Exposes: Hemingway and Jake Barnes," *Midwest Quarterly*, X (Oct. 1968), 89-97.

478 Hotchner, A. E. "I Remember 'Papa' Hemingway," *Reader's Digest*, XCIII (Oct. 1968), 148-153. Small drawing of Hemingway by David Levine.

479 White, William. "Addendum to Hanneman: Hemingway's *The Old Man and the Sea*," *Papers of the Bibliographical Society of America*, LXII (Oct.-Dec. 1968), 613-614.

Describes an abridged version of *OMATS* that was published in English as a textbook for Dutch students. See note under (S-A9H).

480 Sullivan, Dan. "Theater: Tale of Scotty and Papa Opens in 'Village,'" *N.Y. Times* (Oct. 14, 1968), p. 56.

Review of Trevor Reese's play *Before I Wake*, based on the friendship of F. Scott Fitzgerald and Hemingway.

481 Gould, Jack. "'Hemingway's Spain,'" *N.Y. Times* (Oct. 22, 1968), p. 95. Review of the American Broadcasting Company's television special "Hemingway's Spain: A Love Affair," produced by Lester Cooper.

482 White, William. "Hemingway's Spain," *American Book Collector*, XIX (Nov. 1968), 22. Regarding the television special in the above item.

483 Mahony, Patrick J. "Hemingway's 'A Day's Wait,'" *Explicator*, XXVII (Nov. 1968), Item 18.

484 Cheney, Frances Neel. Review of Audre Hanneman's *EH: A Comprehensive Bibliography*, *Wilson Library Bulletin*, XLIII (Nov. 1968), 285, 289.

485 Tannenbaum, Earl. Review of Lloyd Arnold's *High on the Wild with Hemingway*, *Library Journal*, XCIII (Nov. 1, 1968), 4131.

486 "Russians Now Leading Visitors to Hemingway's Cuban House," *N.Y. Times* (Nov. 24, 1968), p. 116.

Reports that 18,000 visitors a year tour Hemingway's former home, now a museum maintained by the National Council of Culture.

487 Hungerford, Edward B. Review of Leo Gurko's *Ernest Hemingway and the Pursuit of Heroism*, *Washington Post Book World* (Nov. 24, 1968), p. 20.

488 Review of Leo Gurko's *Ernest Hemingway and the Pursuit of Heroism, Choice,* v (Dec. 1968), 1306.

489 Fukumoto, Takako. "Hemingway's Women: Anima Mother," *Kyushu American Literature,* No. 11 (Dec. 1968), pp. 98-102.
   The author uses the term "anima mother" as the equivalent to "life or ego to be given to a hero." Note: This was the *KAL* prize winning essay for 1968.

490 Hemingway, Patrick, "My Papa, Papa," *Playboy,* xv (Dec. 1968), 197-198, 200, 263-264, 268.
   A loving portrait of Hemingway by his second son.

491 Ortiz, Sergio. "Your friend, Ernest Hemingway," *Los Angeles Herald-Examiner* (Dec. 1, 1968), California Living section, pp. 8, 10-11. Drawing of Hemingway by Bryon Robley. Facsimile of Hemingway letter.
   Regarding correspondence between Hemingway and Russ Burton, a young writer. For facsimile and excerpted letters, see (S-F111), (S-F112), and (S-F125).

492 Lidman, David. Stamps column, "New Items from the U.N.," *N.Y. Times* (Dec. 1, 1968), Sec. 2, p. 44. Reproduction of a 15-haleru Czechoslovakian stamp with a caricature of Hemingway.

493 Hood, Robert. Review of Leo Gurko's *Ernest Hemingway and the Pursuit of Heroism, N.Y. Times Book Review* (Dec. 8, 1968), p. 54.

494 "State Court Clears Book on Hemingway," *N.Y. Times* (Dec. 13, 1968), p. 55.
   The New York Court of Appeals affirmed the rulings of a lower court and dismissed Mary Hemingway's suit to block the sale of A. E. Hotchner's *Papa Hemingway.*

495 Baker, Carlos. Review of Lloyd Arnold's *High on the Wild with Hemingway, N.Y. Times Book Review* (Dec. 15, 1968), pp. 7, 29.

496 "Impala Sculpture to Mark Hemingway Grave in Idaho," *N.Y. Times* (Dec. 22, 1968), p. 54.
   Mary Hemingway commissioned the sculpture of an impala by Jonathan Kenworthy for a graveside monument.

497 "Hemingway giorno per giorno," *L'Espresso,* No. 52 (Dec. 29, 1968), p. 25.
   Regarding Carlos Baker's biography of Hemingway.

498 Sharma, D. R. "Vision and Design in Hemingway," *Literary Criterion,* VIII (Winter 1968), 42-51.

499 Hill, John S. "Robert Wilson: Hemingway's Judge in 'Macomber,'" *University Review* (Kansas City), XXXV (Winter 1968), 129-132.

267

500 White, William. "Hemingway and Fitzgerald," *American Literary Scholarship: An Annual / 1969*, pp. 122-136.

501 Kondratjuk, Andrij. "Heminguej hovoryt' po-ukrajins' komu," *Dnipro: Literaturne-xudožnij Žurnal*, XLIII, x (1969), 148-151.

502 Takigawa, Motoo. " 'The Short Happy Life of Francis Macomber' no Shusei," *Eigo Seinen*, cxv (1969), 98-100.

502₁ Hamada, Seijiro. "Kilimanjaro e no Hisho," *ibid.*, pp. 699-701.

503 Wells, Elizabeth. "A Comparative Statistical Analysis of the Prose Style of F. Scott Fitzgerald and Ernest Hemingway," *Fitzgerald/ Hemingway Annual: 1969*, pp. 47-67. (Washington, D.C., NCR Microcard Editions. Edited by Matthew J. Bruccoli and C. E. Frazer Clark, Jr.) See also (S-C58).

503₁ Facsimile of the wedding announcement (Sept. 3, 1921) of Elizabeth Hadley Richardson and Ernest Miller Hemingway, *ibid.*, p. 69.

503₂ Torchiana, Donald T. "*The Sun Also Rises*: A Reconsideration," *ibid.*, pp. 77-103.

503₃ Clark, C. E. Frazer, Jr. "Hemingway at Auction: A Brief Survey," *ibid.*, pp. 105-124. Includes Appendix: Auction record of *TSTP* and *iot* for 1930 to 1968.

503₄ Bruccoli, Matthew J. " 'The Light of the World': Stan Ketchel as 'My Sweet Christ,' " *ibid.*, pp. 125-130.

503₅ Unrue, John. "Hemingway and the *New Masses*," *ibid.*, pp. 131-140.

503₆ Facsimile of Hemingway's *Who's Who in America* form for 1928, *ibid.*, p. 141.

503₇ Long, Robert Emmet. "Fitzgerald and Hemingway on Stage," review of Trevor Reese's play *Before I Wake*, *ibid.*, pp. 143-144.

504 Noland, Richard W. "A New Look at Hemingway," review of Richard B. Hovey's *Hemingway: The Inward Terrain*, *Hartford Studies in Literature*, I, ii (1969), 140-145.

505 Egri, Péter. "The Relationship Between the Short Story and the Novel: Realism and Naturalism in Hemingway's Art. Part I: 1923-1929," *Hungarian Studies in English*, IV (1969), 105-126.

506 Gotkharde, R. "The Evolution of Hemingway's 'Weltanschauung' and the Development of His Hero During the Twenties and Thirties," *Latviiskii Gosudarstvennyi Universitet*, No. 110 (1969), pp. 64-88. In English.

507 Orlova, R. " 'Zadacha Pisatelya Neizmenna': K 70-letiyu (So Dnya

Rozhdeniya Amerikanskogo Pisatelya) E. Khemingueya" [The invariable goal of a writer: in honor of Hemingway's seventieth birthday], *Literature v Shkole,* No. 4 (1969), pp. 83-92.

508 D'Avanzo, Mario L. "The Motif of Corruption in *A Farewell to Arms,*" *Lock Haven Review,* No. 11 (1969), pp. 57-52.

509 Gribanov, B. "Zhizn' Khemingueya" [The life of Hemingway], *Pamir,* No. 5 (1969), pp. 76-84.

510 Sallnäs, Hilding. "Studie i Hemingway," *Studiekamraten,* LI (1969), 23-26.

511 Nikitin, V. "O povesti *Starik i more* E. Khemingueya," *Vestnik Moskovskovo Universiteta: Filologiya,* No. 1 (1969), pp. 41-52.
On *The Old Man and the Sea.*

512 Marsden, Malcolm M. "Hemingway's Symbolic Pattern: The Basis of Tone," *Discourse: A Review of the Liberal Arts,* XII (Winter 1969), 16-28.

513 Strandberg, Victor H. "Eliot's Insomniacs," *South Atlantic Quarterly,* LXVIII (Winter 1969), 67-73.
Examines Hemingway's "disdain" for T. S. Eliot and the "parallel studies in morbid psychology" provided by the work of both writers.

514 Light, Martin. "Of Wasteful Deaths: Hemingway's Stories about the Spanish Civil War," *Western Humanities Review,* XXIII (Winter 1969), 29-42.

515 Bruccoli, Matthew J. Review of Audre Hanneman's *EH: A Comprehensive Bibliography, American Literature,* XL (Jan. 1969), 571-572.

515₁ Baker, Carlos. Review of Nicholas Joost's *Ernest Hemingway and the Little Magazines, ibid.,* pp. 572-574.

516 Wycherley, H. Alan. "Hemingway's 'The Sea Change,' " *American Notes & Queries,* VII (Jan. 1969), 67-68.

516₁ Howell, John M. "What the Leopard Was Seeking," *ibid.,* p. 68.
A reply to R. W. Bevis et al., *AN&Q,* VI (April 1968), regarding the epigraph of "The Snows of Kilimanjaro."

517 Baker, Carlos. "Ernest Hemingway: Living, Loving, Dying," *Atlantic,* CCXXIII (Jan. 1969), 45-67; (Feb. 1969), 91-95, 100-116, 118. Cover photograph by John Bryson on Part I.
Drawn from *EH: A Life Story.* Part I from pp. 292-357; Part II from pp. 464-529. For letters from Milton Wolff and Jonathan Latimer, see The Mail column, *Atlantic,* CCXXIII (March 1969), 29-30, 32.

518 D'Avanzo, Mario L. "Hemingway's *A Farewell to Arms*, Chapter xxxv," *Explicator*, XXVII (Jan. 1969), Item 39.

Regarding the "meaningful relationship" between Frederic Henry and Count Greffi.

519 Chesworth, Jo. "Inside Hemingway," *Town & Gown*, IV (Jan. 1969), 12-15, 23, 34. Drawing of Hemingway by Larry Krezo.

Interview with Charles Mann and Philip Young regarding their inventory of Hemingway's unpublished manuscripts.

520 Gadda Conti, Giuseppe. "Hemingway e la pace dei nostri giorni," *Vita e Pensiero*, LII (Jan. 1969), 3-20.

521 Glanville, Brian. Speaking of Books column, "Silence, Exile and Cunning," *N.Y. Times Book Review* (Jan. 5, 1969), pp. 2, 24. General article.

Discusses Hemingway's "authentic and substantial" relationship to France, Italy, and Spain while still remaining the "most quintessentially American of writers."

522 Whitman, Alden. "Biographer Evaluates Unpublished Hemingway," *N.Y. Times* (Jan. 10, 1969), p. 35.

Interview with Carlos Baker regarding his research for *EH: A Life Story* and Hemingway's unpublished manuscripts.

523 Callaghan, Morley. Review of Robert O. Stephens's *Hemingway's Nonfiction, N.Y. Times Book Review* (Jan. 12, 1969), p. 32.

524 Hart, Jeffrey. "Fitzgerald and Hemingway: The Difficult Friend," *National Review*, XXI (Jan. 14, 1969), 29-31.

525 Carlin, Stanley A. "Anselmo and Santiago: Two Old Men of the Sea," *American Book Collector*, XIX (Feb. 1969), 12-14.

Regarding Anselmo Hernandez's claim that he was the original of "Santiago" in *The Old Man and the Sea*.

526 Kann, Hans-Joachim. Review of Audre Hanneman's *EH: A Comprehensive Bibliography, Neueren Sprachen*, No. 18 [New Series] (Feb. 1969), pp. 96-98.

527 Caprariu, Al. "Eu stiu ca Hemingway s-a reintors . . ." [I know Hemingway will return . . .], *Tribuna*, No. 7 (Feb. 1969), p. 8.

528 Yglesias, José. "Key West: Of Sailors, Shrimps and the Way It Was," *Venture*, VI (Feb. 1969), 67-70, 73, 75-76.

Includes reminiscences of Hemingway in Key West in the 1930s.

529 Le Clec'h, Guy. "Hemingway: avait-il gardé pour lui son chef-d'oeuvre?" *Figaro Littéraire*, No. 1189 (Feb. 17-23, 1969), p. 26.

Regarding Hemingway's unpublished manuscripts.

530 Fadiman, Clifton. Report on Carlos Baker's *EH: A Life Story, Book-of-the-Month Club News* (March 1969), pp. 1-6. Note: This book was the Book-of-the-Month Club selection for April. The report was reprinted in an eight-page booklet (a single sheet folded twice), which was sent with the book club edition.

530₁ Baker, Carlos. "Telling a Storyteller's Story," *ibid.*, pp. 7, 15.

531 Hagood, Thomas Neal. "Elements of Humor in Ernest Hemingway," *Dissertation Abstracts,* xxix (March 1969), 3139-A.
Abstract from a doctoral dissertation, Louisiana State University, 1968.

532 Nagle, John M. "A View of Literature Too Often Neglected," *English Journal,* lviii (March 1969), 399-407.
Analyzes *OMATS* to illustrate *"how* and *why* a writer deliberately chooses his language so that it not only *expresses* his intended meaning, but *intensifies* or *reinforces* the importance of his particular meaning."

533 Lebowitz, Alan. "Hemingway in Our Time," *Yale Review,* lviii (March 1969), 321-341.

533₁ Hoffman, Michael J. "From Cohn to Herzog," *ibid.*, pp. 342-358.
A comparison of the Jewish literary character as portrayed in *SAR* and Saul Bellow's *Herzog.*

534 Marques, Nelson Salasar. "Hemingway e a 'Geração Perdida,'" *A Tribuna* (March 1, 1969), p. 1.
On Hemingway and the Lost Generation.

535 Marques, Nelson Salasar. "O sentido da dignidade humana em Hemingway," *A Tribuna* (March 8, 1969), p. 1.
On Hemingway's *angst* and existential themes.

536 "Taking the Beard Off Hemingway," *Chicago Tribune Book World* (March 16, 1969), pp. 1, 3-6. Previously unpublished photographs of Hemingway with biographical captions by Carlos Baker.

537 "R.H.S." [Roger H. Smith]. Authors and Editors column, *Publishers' Weekly,* cxcv (March 31, 1969), 15-17.
Interview with Carlos Baker regarding *EH: A Life Story.*

538 Smith, Julian. "Christ Times Four: Hemingway's Unknown Spanish Civil War Stories," *Arizona Quarterly,* xxv (Spring 1969), 5-17.
A study of "The Denunciation," "The Butterfly and the Tank," "Night Before Battle," and "Under the Ridge."

539 White, W. M. "The Crane-Hemingway Code: A Reevaluation," *Ball State University Forum,* x (Spring 1969), 15-20.

539₁ McCarthy, Paul. "Chapter Beginnings in *A Farewell to Arms*," *ibid.*, pp. 21-30.

540 Lisca, Peter. "Steinbeck and Hemingway: Suggestions for a Comparative Study," *Steinbeck Newsletter*, II (Spring 1969), 9-17.

541 Kopf, Josephine Z. "Meyer Wolfsheim and Robert Cohn: A Study of a Jewish Type and Stereotype," *Tradition: A Journal of Orthodox Jewish Thought*, X (Spring 1969), 93-104.
   Examines the Jewish literary character as portrayed in F. Scott Fitzgerald's *The Great Gatsby* and in *SAR*.

542 Sarason, Bertram D. "Lady Brett Ashley and Lady Duff Twysden," *Connecticut Review*, II (April 1969), 5-13. Reprinted in *Hemingway and The Sun Set*, Washington, D.C., 1972, pp. 228-240.

542₁ Moss, Arthur H. "The Many Ways of Hemingway," *ibid.*, pp. 14-16.
   The editor of the *Boulevardier* recalls Hemingway's reactions to editorial changes in "The Real Spaniard." See (C183).

543 Broer, Lawrence Richard. "The Effects of Ernest Hemingway's Identification with Certain Aspects of Spanish Thinking on His Rendering of Character," *Dissertation Abstracts*, XXIX (April 1969), 3606-A.
   Abstract from a doctoral dissertation, Bowling Green State University, 1968.

544 Brøgger, Fredrik Chr. "Hemingway—der kjaelighet og religion møtes," *Kirke og Kultur*, LXXIV (April 1969), 224-231.

545 Shourds, Raymond. "Hemingway's Key West Home," *Mainliner*, XIII (April 1969), 14-17. Drawing and Photographs.

546 Benson, Jackson J. "Literary Allusion and the Private Irony of Hemingway," *Pacific Coast Philology*, IV (April 1969), 24-29.

547 White, William. Review of Richard B. Hovey's *Hemingway: The Inward Terrain, American Book Collector*, XIX (April-May 1969), 4.

548 Moore, Harry T. "Ambitious Biography of Ernest Hemingway," review of Carlos Baker's *EH: A Life Story, Chicago Daily News* (April 5, 1969), p. 11. Drawing of Hemingway in the 1940s. Reprinted, under the title "Hemingway and a Chronology without Characterization," in *Age of the Modern and Other Literary Essays*, Carbondale, Illinois, 1971, pp. 89-91.

548₁ Haas, Joseph. "Papa: a small boy 'fraid a nothing,' " review of Carlos Baker's *EH: A Life Story, ibid.*, p. 11.

549 Kazin, Alfred. "He sensed the disenchantment in our time," review of Carlos Baker's *EH: A Life Story, Chicago Tribune Book World* (April 13, 1969), pp. 1, 3.

550 "Reise abwärts," review of Carlos Baker's *EH: A Life Story, Der Spiegel,* XXIII (April 14, 1969), 169-170.

551 Fuson, Ben W. Review of Jackson J. Benson's *Hemingway: The Writer's Art of Self-Defense, Library Journal,* XCIV (April 15, 1969), 1632-1633.

552 "Ernest, Good and Bad," review of Carlos Baker's *EH: A Life Story, Time,* XCIII (April 18, 1969), 102-104. Photographs.

553 Hicks, Granville. "Hemingway: The Complexities That Animated the Man," review of Carlos Baker's *EH: A Life Story, Saturday Review,* LII (April 19, 1969), 31-33, 43. Cover portrait of Hemingway by Henry Strater in 1922.

This review includes commentary on Lloyd Arnold's *High on the Wild with Hemingway* and William Seward's *My Friend Ernest Hemingway,* and brief mention of other current books about Hemingway.

554 Gingrich, Arnold. Review of Carlos Baker's *EH: A Life Story, Chicago Sun-Times Book Week* (April 20, 1969), pp. 1, 10.

555 Lehmann-Haupt, Christopher. "A Replica of Hemingway So Real It Moves," review of Carlos Baker's *EH: A Life Story, N.Y. Times* (April 21, 1969), p. 45.

556 Goldman, Albert. "Hemingway: Papa as King Lear," review of Carlos Baker's *EH: A Life Story, Newsweek,* LXXIII (April 21, 1969), 112, 112A, 112D.

557 Fuller, Edmund. "Demythologizing Hemingway," review of Carlos Baker's *EH: A Life Story, Wall Street Journal* (April 21, 1969), p. 18.

558 Hart, Jeffrey. "Hemingway: Sunlight and Night-Face," review of Carlos Baker's *EH: A Life Story, National Review,* XXI (April 22, 1969), 390-391.

559 Samuels, Charles Thomas. "The Heresy of Self-Love," review of Carlos Baker's *EH: A Life Story, New Republic,* CLX (April 26, 1969), 28-32.

560 "The Critics Are Saying . . . ," excerpts from reviews of Carlos Baker's *EH: A Life Story, N.Y. Post* (April 26, 1969), p. 47.

561 O'Leary, Theodore M. "Hemingway: A Moralist of Sorts," review of Carlos Baker's *EH: A Life Story, Kansas City Star* (April 27, 1969), p. 3F.

561₁ "H.C.H." [Henry C. Haskell]. Scanning the Arts column, "Hemingway's Subtle Talent Runs Away . . . at Times," *ibid.*

A long excerpt from Schuyler Ashley's review of *SAR* is reprinted from the *Kansas City Star* (Dec. 4, 1926). See (H58).

562 Bourjaily, Vance. "Hemingway on trial, Judge Baker presiding," review of Carlos Baker's *EH: A Life Story, N.Y. Times Book Review* (April 27, 1969), pp. 5, 38.

563 Coffey, Raymond R. "They still remember 'Ernie': Boyhood friends of Hemingway in Oak Park tell of bully with grin who never liked to be bested," *Chicago Daily News* (April 29, 1969), pp. 3, 4.

564 Prescott, Peter S. "Hemingway: The Whole Truth and Nothing But," review of Carlos Baker's *EH: A Life Story, Look,* XXXIII (April 29, 1969), 6. Drawing by David Levine. Reprinted in *Soundings*, New York, 1972, pp. 241-244.

565 Yokelson, Joseph B. "A Dante-Parallel in Hemingway's 'A Way You'll Never Be,' " *American Literature,* XLI (May 1969), 279-280.

565₁ White, William. Review of Robert O. Stephens's *Hemingway's Nonfiction, ibid.,* pp. 298-299.

565₂ White, William. Review of Lloyd Arnold's *High on the Wild with Hemingway, ibid.,* pp. 299-300.

565₃ Baker, Sheridan. Review of Richard B. Hovey's *Hemingway: The Inward Terrain, ibid.,* pp. 300-301.

566 White, William. "Hemingway's 'Suppressed Poems,' " *American Notes & Queries,* VII (May 1969), 135-136.
Regarding a possibly unique variant edition of *The Collected Poems*, titled *The Suppressed Poems*, in the collection of Stanley A. Carlin of Melrose, Massachusetts. See note under (S-A10G).

567 Review of Richard B. Hovey's *Hemingway: The Inward Terrain, Choice,* VI (May 1969), 366.

568 Wylder, Delbert E. "Faces of the Hero: A Study of the Novels of Ernest Hemingway," *Dissertation Abstracts,* XXIX (May 1969), 4029-A to 4030-A.
Abstract from a doctoral dissertation, University of Iowa, 1968.

569 Petrarca, Anthony J. "Irony of Situation in Ernest Hemingway's 'Soldier's Home,' " *English Journal,* LVIII (May 1969), 664-667.

569₁ Reichard, Daniel P. "None are to be found more clever than Ernie," *ibid.,* pp. 668-672.
Regarding Hemingway's activities and writings during his high-school days.

570 Howe, Irving. "The Wounds of All Generations," review of Carlos Baker's *EH: A Life Story, Harper's* CCXXXVIII (May 1969), 96-102.
This review ends with a paean to "A Clean, Well-Lighted Place."

571 Andrews, Larry. " 'Big Two-Hearted River': The Essential Hemingway," *Missouri English Bulletin*, XXV (May 1969), 1-7.

572 Cannell, Kathleen. "Bully boy to artist," review of Carlos Baker's *EH: A Life Story, Christian Science Monitor* (May 1, 1969), p. B-10.

573 Schroth, Raymond A. "Hemingway's Truth," review of Carlos Baker's *EH: A Life Story*, America, CXX (May 3, 1969), 534.

574 Maloff, Saul. "The Impotence of Being Ernest," review of Carlos Baker's *EH: A Life Story, Commonweal*, XC (May 9, 1969), 235-236, 238. See also letters from James J. Kirschke and Bruce McCabe, and a reply by Saul Maloff, in *Commonweal*, XC (July 25, 1969), 451, 470-471.

575 Light, James F. "Between Legend and Man," review of Carlos Baker's *EH: A Life Story, Nation*, CCVIII (May 26, 1969), 671-674.

576 White, William. "Hemingway's Animals of Farmer Johns,' " *American Notes & Queries*, VII (June 1969), 151-152.
Regarding Hans W. Bentz's inclusion of a Swedish children's book in *Ernest Hemingway in Übersetzungen*. See (G41).

577 Weeks, Edward. Review of Carlos Baker's *EH: A Life Story, Atlantic*, CCXXIII (June 1969), 110, 112.

578 Grant, Naomi M. "The Role of Women in the Fiction of Ernest Hemingway," *Dissertation Abstracts*, XXIX (June 1969), 4456-A.
Abstract from a doctoral dissertation, University of Denver, 1968.

579 Barnes, Clive. On the Scene column, "Late notes on camp plus Papa Hemingway," *Holiday*, XLV (June 1969), 8, 10-11. Includes a review of Carlos Baker's *EH: A Life Story*.

580 Ross, Mary Lowrey. Review of Carlos Baker's *EH: A Life Story, Saturday Night*, LXXXIV (June 1969), 41.

581 Hardwick, Elizabeth. "Dead Souls," review of Carlos Baker's *EH: A Life Story, New York Review of Books*, XII (June 5, 1969), 3-4.
Drawing of Hemingway by David Levine.

582 Allen, Gay Wilson. Review of Jackson J. Benson's *Hemingway: The Writer's Art of Self-Defense, Saturday Review*, LII (June 21, 1969), 54.

583 Sprague, Claire. "*The Sun Also Rises*: Its 'Clear Financial Basis,' " *American Quarterly*, XXI [No. 2, Pt. 1] (Summer 1969), 259-266.

584 Johnston, Kenneth G. "Counterpart: The Reflective Pattern in Hemingway's Humor," *Kansas Quarterly*, I (Summer 1969), 51-57.

Regarding the three key humorous scenes in *FTA* and their very serious counterparts later in the story.

585 Crane, John Kenny. "Crossing the Bar Twice: Post-Mortem Consciousness in Bierce, Hemingway and Golding," *Studies in Short Fiction*, VI (Summer 1969), 361-376.

Discusses Hemingway's use of "post-mortem consciousness" in "The Snows of Kilimanjaro."

585₁ Flora, Joseph M. "Hemingway's 'Up in Michigan,'" *ibid.*, 465-466.

586 Wasserstrom, William. "The Hemingway Problem," *Virginia Quarterly Review*, XLV (Summer 1969), 531-537.

Review of Carlos Baker's *EH: A Life Story*, Lloyd Arnold's *High on the Wild with Hemingway*, Robert O. Stephens's *Hemingway's Nonfiction*, and Richard B. Hovey's *Hemingway: The Inward Terrain*.

587 "Portret Khemingueya: K 70-letiyu so Dnya Rozhdeniya" [A portrait of Hemingway: on the 70th anniversary of his birth], *Don*, XIII (July 1969), 188-192.

588 Kinnamon, Keneth. Review of Audre Hanneman's *EH: A Comprehensive Bibliography*, *Journal of English & Germanic Philology*, LXVIII (July 1969), 556-560. Includes a corrigenda and addenda to the bibliography.

589 Hill, John S. "*To Have and Have Not*: Hemingway's Hiatus," *Midwest Quarterly*, X (July 1969), 349-356.

590 Pardo Pérez, Gastón. "Siguiendo los pasos de Ernest Hemingway," *Revista de la Universidad de México*, XXIII (July 1969).

591 Hily, Geneviève. "Langage et Communication: Un Aspect inédit de la pensée de Hemingway," *Études Anglaises*, XXI (July-Sept. 1969), 279-292. Cover photograph of Hemingway.

591₁ Hily, Geneviève. Review of Richard B. Hovey's *Hemingway: The Inward Terrain*, *ibid.*, pp. 324-325.

592 McCormick, John. "The Sound of Hooves," *Sports Illustrated*, XXXI (July 7, 1969), 60-64, 69-71.

Regarding the dedication in Pamplona, on July 6, 1968, of a bronze bust of Hemingway, by Luis Sanguino, and a street adjoining the bullring, which was named the Paseo de Hemingway.

593 Cromie, Robert. Authors and Books column, review of William Seward's *My Friend Ernest Hemingway*, *Chicago Tribune* (July 17, 1969), p. 30.

594 Mikoyan, Sergo. "Kheminguei: Kakim on Byl?" [Hemingway: What was he like?], *Ogoniok*, No. 29 (July 19, 1969), pp. 22-24.

595 "Soviet Sailors Visit Hemingway's Home," *N.Y. Times* (July 24, 1969), p. 11.

Regarding the visit to the Hemingway Museum in San Francisco de Paula, Cuba, by a group of sailors from the Soviet fleet visiting Havana.

596 Nucci, Joseph Charles. "The Poetry of Time and Place in the Fiction of Ernest Hemingway," *Dissertation Abstracts International*, xxx (Aug. 1969), 733-A to 734-A.

Abstract from a doctoral dissertation, University of Pittsburgh, 1968.

597 Smirnov, Nik. "Kheminguei i Okhota" [Hemingway and hunting], *Okhota i Okhotnich'ye Khozyaǐstvo*, No. 8 (Aug. 1969), pp. 36-37.

598 Borch, Herbert von. "Hemingway," *Universitas*, xxiv (Aug. 1969), 801-807.

599 "P.H.S." The Times Diary column, *Times*, London (Aug. 5, 1969), p. 8.

Item regarding Air Marshal Sir Peter Wykeham's reminiscences of Hemingway during World War II as reported in Carlos Baker's *EH: A Life Story.*

600 Weatherby, W. J. "Hemingway's Manuscripts," *Times Literary Supplement* (Aug. 7, 1969), p. 883.

Letter to the editor urging the publication of all Hemingway manuscripts in order that posterity can be the final judge rather than any contemporary critics. For Robert Wright's reply, see *TLS* (Aug. 14, 1969), p. 906.

601 Connolly, Cyril. "Living in Earnest," review of Carlos Baker's *EH: A Life Story, Sunday Times*, London (Aug. 10, 1969), p. 41. Reprinted in *The Evening Colonnade*, London, 1973, pp. 307-310.

602 Bradbury, Malcolm. "Hemingway's Luck," review of Carlos Baker's *EH: A Life Story, Listener*, LXXXII (Aug. 14, 1969), 219-220.

603 Dewhurst, Keith. "Poor, wounded pioneer Papa," *Manchester Guardian* (Aug. 14, 1969), p. 11.

Discusses Hemingway's reputation and the "gift of words, which Hemingway possessed to an extraordinary degree."

604 Ellmann, Richard. "The Hemingway Circle," review of Carlos Baker's *EH: A Life Story, New Statesman*, LXXVII (Aug. 15, 1969), 213-214.

605 Bradley, Van Allen. Bookman's Briefcase column, "A New Hemingway bibliography," review of Audre Hanneman's *EH: A Comprehensive Bibliography, Chicago News* (Aug. 16, 1969), p. 7.

606 Potter, Dennis. "Hemingway: the taxidermist takes over," review of Carlos Baker's *EH: A Life Story, Times*, London (Aug. 16, 1969), Saturday Review, p. 2.

607 Whitman, Alden. "Short Story by Fitzgerald Is Discovered," *N.Y. Times* (Aug. 20, 1969), p. 42.
Regarding the first issue of the *Fitzgerald/Hemingway Annual*. Reprinted in the *Times*, London (Aug. 21, 1969), p. 4.

608 Boston, Richard. "The Importance of Being Ernest," *New Society* (Aug. 21, 1969), pp. 295-296.

609 Wycherley, H. Alan. Review of Carlos Baker's *EH: A Life Story, American Notes & Queries*, VIII (Sept. 1969), 15-16.

610 Review of Carlos Baker's *EH: A Life Story, Choice*, VI (Sept. 1969), 810.

611 Kvam, Wayne Eugene. "The Critical Reaction to Hemingway in Germany, 1945-1965," *Dissertation Abstracts International*, XXX (Sept. 1969), 1139-A to 1140-A.
Abstract from a doctoral dissertation, University of Wisconsin, 1969.

612 Shepherd, Allen. "Taking Apart 'Mr. and Mrs. Elliot,' " *Markham Review*, II (Sept. 1969), 15-16.
Comparison of the version published in *IOT* (1925) and the version in *TFC & First 49*.

613 Paul, Kenneth. "Vintage Hemingway," review of *TFC & 4 Stories, Newsweek*, LXXIV (Sept. 8, 1969), 88.
"The play is an unresolved period piece. Dorothy Bridges, a correspondent more at home at Vassar than in a war zone, and her lover, a rollicking Hemingway cliché, are talky and shallow. Its quirky dialogue makes *The Fifth Column* less dramatic than much of Hemingway's fiction. 'Night Before Battle' stands out among the stories . . . as vintage Hemingway. Staccato, wine-clouded conversation is transformed to poetry. . . . Lightheaded fear bubbles beneath bravado in all the stories. One is called 'The Butterfly and the Tank,' metaphors for the 'misunderstood gaiety' of men at war and their 'deadly seriousness.' "

614 "Big two-hearted liver," review of Carlos Baker's *EH: A Life Story, Times Literary Supplement* (Sept. 11, 1969), p. 997.

615 Gheorghe, Fănică N. "Hemingway şi sentimentul tragic al exis-
tenţei," *Contemporanul* (Sept. 12, 1969), p. 9.

616 Steiner, George. "Across the River and Into the Trees," review of
Carlos Baker's *EH: A Life Story, New Yorker*, XLV (Sept. 13, 1969),
147-150.

617 Bach, Bert C. Review of *TFC & 4 Stories, Library Journal*, XCIV
(Sept. 15, 1969), 3083.
". . . decidedly second-drawer Hemingway. . . . Of the four stories,
only 'The Denunciation' deserves attention."

618 Heise, Hans-Jürgen. "Ernests Kram: Reportagen des legendären
Hemingway," review of *By-Line, Christ und Welt* (Sept. 19, 1969),
p. 13.

619 Baker, Carlos. Review of *TFC & 4 Stories, Saturday Review*, LII
(Sept. 20, 1969), 36-37.
"The reappearance of the play reminds us once again that Hemingway's forte was fiction rather than drama. . . . The appearance
in book form of these four stories ought to add appreciably to our
sense of Hemingway's stature as a writer of short fiction."

620 Young, Philip. "Immediate, unmistakable Hemingway in besieged
Madrid," review of *TFC & 4 Stories, N.Y. Times Book Review*
(Sept. 21, 1969), p. 6.
"The book is unified . . . in time, place, and action. It is unified
even more by the dominating presence of the author, who is to be
found alive on every page. That presence slants the focus, but also
gives the book its sharp distinction. . . . He nowhere appears entirely without disguise, but the leading character in all these pieces is
clearly the writer of them."

621 Raymont, Henry. "Hemingway Papers Yield Surprises," *N.Y. Times*
(Sept. 22, 1969), pp. 1, 36. Facsimile.
Regarding Philip Young and Charles Mann's *The Hemingway
Manuscripts: An Inventory*. For facsimile of manuscript page, see
(S-F33₁).

622 Knipe, Michael. "The novel left in Joe's bar," *Times*, London
(Sept. 23, 1969), p. 1.
Regarding Philip Young and Charles Mann's *The Hemingway
Manuscripts: An Inventory*.

623 Spender, Stephen. "Writers and Revolutionaries: The Spanish War,"
New York Review of Books, XIII (Sept. 25, 1969), 3-6, 8.
Includes a review of *TFC & 4 Stories*. " 'The Denunciation' is ob-
viously a story with a moral, horrid as it is. Yet in another story,
'Under the Ridge,' where Hemingway is using his experience and

his imagination and not preaching toughness, there is a truth which undermines any moralizing. . . . Comparing these two stories I can only conclude that when Hemingway was justifying war and toughness, he could be maudlin with a hideous inverted sentimentality, but that when he was simply observing and experiencing, war did move him to truthful observation and deep imaginative insight."

624 Murphy, Michael E. "Hemingway: Rod & Gun," *Inland: The Magazine of the Middle West*, No. 64 (Autumn 1969), pp. 2-5. Drawing of Hemingway.

On Hemingway's fishing and hunting in the fields and streams of Illinois and Michigan.

624₁ "S.A.M." [Sheldon A. Mix]. Minor matters column, *ibid.*, inside front cover.

On the Hemingway family home in Oak Park.

625 Leary, Lewis. Review of Carlos Baker's *EH: A Life Story*, *South Atlantic Quarterly*, LXVIII (Autumn 1969), 556-558.

626 Davis, Robert Murray. "Entering Literary History: Hemingway," *Southern Humanities Review*, III (Fall 1969), 382-395.

Review of Richard B. Hovey's *Hemingway: The Inward Terrain*, Robert O. Stephens's *Hemingway's Nonfiction*, Nicholas Joost's *Ernest Hemingway and the Little Magazines*, and Carlos Baker's *EH: A Life Story*.

627 Loeb, Harold. Review of Carlos Baker's *EH: A Life Story*, *Southern Review*, V [New Series] (Autumn 1969), 1214-1225.

628 Carlin, Stanley. Review of William Seward's *My Friend Ernest Hemingway* and Carlos Baker's *EH: A Life Story*, *American Book Collector*, XX (Oct. 1969), 7-8.

628₁ White, William. "Frederic or Frederick Henry in *A Farewell to Arms*," *ibid.*, p. 22.

Discusses the variations in the spelling of Lt. Henry's first name, and points out that it appears in Chapter 13 (p. 90) when he is asked his name at the hospital and replies: "Henry. Frederic Henry."

629 Review of Jackson J. Benson's *Hemingway: The Writer's Art of Self-Defense*, *Choice*, VI (Oct. 1969), 1008.

630 St. John, Donald. "Interview with Hemingway's 'Bill Gorton.' Part II," *Connecticut Review*, III (Oct. 1969), 5-23.

Interview with Bill Smith, who was one of the models for 'Bill Gorton' in *SAR* and a protagonist in two short stories, "The End of Something" and "The Three-Day Blow." Part I of this interview appeared in *CR*, I (April 1968). Both parts were reprinted in Bertram D. Sarason's *Hemingway and The Sun Set*, Washington, D.C., 1972, pp. 151-188.

630₁ Sarason, Bertram D. "Hemingway in Havana, Two Interviews," *ibid.*, pp. 24-31.

Interviews with Armondo Chardiet, who knew Hemingway in Cuba in the 1950s, and Robert T. E. Schuyler, who met Hemingway in Havana in August 1943.

630₂ Simpson, Claude M., Jr. Review of Carlos Baker's *EH: A Life Story, ibid.*, pp. 32-34.

630₃ St. John, Donald. Review of Carlos Baker's *EH: A Life Story, ibid.*, pp. 35-42.

630₄ Moss, Arthur H. "More Ways of Hemingway," *ibid.*, pp. 43-44.

A letter from the editor of the *Boulevardier*, with additional comments to his article in *CR*, II (April 1969).

631 Bigsby, C.W.E. "Hemingway en de Amerikaanse traditie van de mens als Christus," *Nieuw Vlaams Tijdschrift*, XXII (Oct. 1969), 826-839.

632 "Owen Wister Papers," *Quarterly Journal of the Library of Congress*, XXVI (Oct. 1969), 244.

Regarding letters from Hemingway and Maxwell Perkins to Owen Wister. A check for $500 intended as a gift from Owen Wister to Hemingway, in 1929, is reproduced. Hemingway returned the check with a six-page covering letter, dated March 1, 1929.

633 Vanderbilt, Kermit. "*The Sun Also Rises*: Time Uncertain," *Twentieth-Century Literature*, XV (Oct. 1969), 153-154.

"By Chapter XV, neither the calendar of Hemingway's 1925 summer nor the chronology of a fictional timetable accords properly with the time of the happenings that unfold in the novel."

634 Williams, Wirt. "How Author Kept His Cool with Hemingway," review of William Seward's *My Friend Ernest Hemingway, Los Angeles Times Calendar* (Oct. 5, 1969), p. 46.

635 Braem, Helmut M. "Journalismus, unvergilbt: Ernest Hemingways *49 Despeschen*," review of *By-Line, Die Zeit* (Oct. 10, 1969), Literary section, p. 3.

636 McNamara, Eugene. Review of *TFC & 4 Stories, America*, CXXI (Oct. 18, 1969), 333.

"This play, *The Fifth Column*, comes off as a kind of self-parodying romantic melodrama, uncertain as to whether it should be comedy or somber social comment. . . . John Steinbeck thought 'The Butterfly and the Tank' one of the finest short stories ever written. . . . it is certainly a fine story of its kind. It has immediacy, irony, a deft handling of minor characters and setting, and a subtle interworking of the war story with a writer's problem of turning everyday reality into enduring fictional art. 'Under the Ridge' is possibly the best of the four stories in the volume. It is tight and controlled, with little posturing and no self-consciousness, and uses the same materials: the war, the tangled political motives, the bitterness of the Spanish people. . . ." Note: For the reference to John Steinbeck, see Carlos Baker's *EH: A Life Story*, p. 337.

637 Simmons, Michael K. "A Look into *The Glass Mountain*," *American Literature*, XLI (Nov. 1969), 422-425.

Discusses Joseph Warren Beach's use of Hadley Richardson Hemingway and Hemingway as models for his *roman à clef*.

638 Stevenson, Elizabeth. Review of Carlos Baker's *EH: A Life Story*, *Commentary*, XLVIII (Nov. 1969), 92-96.

639 Murphy, George D. "Hemingway's *The Sun Also Rises*," *Explicator*, XXVIII (Nov. 1969), Item 23.

Regarding the symbolism in the references to water in *SAR*.

640 Mösslang, Monika. "Er begann als Reporter in Toronto," review of *By-Line, Welt der Literatur* (Nov. 6, 1969), pp. 4-5.

641 ["A Letter by Lincoln is Sold for $3,600], *N.Y. Times* (Nov. 8, 1969), p. 37.

Article on Charles Hamilton Galleries auction that includes mention of a Hemingway letter, "about his romantic conquests," that was acquired by the Carnegie Book Shop for $1,100.

642 Nesbitt, Scott R. "Sorts Out Hemingway Legend," *Kansas City Times* (Nov. 17, 1969), p. 16A.

Interview with Carlos Baker.

643 Cordry, Harold V. "Competitive Spirit Spurred Hemingway," *Kansas City Times* (Nov. 18, 1969), p. 16B.

Excerpts from an interview with Carlos Baker.

644 Wolf, Jacob H. "The Unpublished Hemingway Papers," review of Philip Young and Charles Mann's *The Hemingway Manuscripts: An Inventory*, *St. Louis Post-Dispatch* (Nov. 23, 1969), p. 4F.

645 Latham, Aaron. "Fitzgerald-Hemingway Letters," *Washington Post* (Nov. 30, 1969), pp. F1, F3.

Regarding F. Scott Fitzgerald's letter to Hemingway, in 1925, advising him to omit the opening chapters in the manuscript of *The*

Sun Also Rises. Note: See Philip Young and Charles Mann's article in *F/HA: 1970*, pp. 7-8 (S-H651), regarding Latham's "misreading" of the Fitzgerald-Hemingway correspondence.

645₁ Martin, Judith. "The Difficult Legacy of Mrs. Ernest Hemingway," *ibid.*, pp. K1, K2.

Interview with Mary Hemingway, in New York. Partially reprinted, under the title "Mary Hemingway: For Her, a Time to Write," in the *N.Y. Post* (Dec. 20, 1969), p. 25.

646 Aiken, William. "Hemingway's 'Ten Indians,' " *Explicator*, XXVIII (Dec. 1969), Item 31.

647 "J. H." [John Hollander]. Review of *TFC & 4 Stories, Harper's Magazine,* CCXXXIX (Dec. 1969), 146.

"These four stories are all a bit long-winded. . . . They propound a world of desperation, military blunders, a senseless slaying of a civilian in a café, the necessary dirtiness of turning in a spy, and the crippling aspects of the International presence on the Loyalist side. Within that world, familiar Hemingwayan acts of grace occur, in a kind of low-keyed way, and the genuine people are mostly being hurt. The Spaniards all speak the patented Hemingway dialect, no contractions and *muy formal.* But the stories are authentic enough, and are quite better than the worst of those in the collected volume."

648 Baker, Carlos. [Excerpts from *EH: A Life Story*], *Inostrannaya Literatura*, No. 11 (Nov. 1969), pp. 234-252; No. 12 (Dec. 1969), pp. 235-243. Translated into Russian by Maria Lorie. An afterword, by A. Startsev, appears in *IL*, No. 12 (Dec. 1969), pp. 243-245.

649 El'sberg, Ia. "Golosa narodnye . . . ," *Znamya*, No. 12 (Dec. 1969), pp. 145-157.

Draws a distinction between the epic and lyrical in Hemingway's work.

650 White, William. "Hemingway and Fitzgerald," *American Literary Scholarship: An Annual / 1970*, pp. 132-148.

651 Young, Philip, and Charles W. Mann. "Fitzgerald's *Sun Also Rises*: Notes and Comment," *Fitzgerald / Hemingway Annual: 1970*, pp. 1-9. Facsimile of Hemingway inscription on back endpaper. See also (S-C59), (S-F34).

Commentary on the letter from F. Scott Fitzgerald criticizing *SAR* (see next entry) and the proofs of the omitted original opening chapters of *SAR*, which were found by the authors during their inventory of the Hemingway manuscripts. Reprinted in Bertram D. Sarason's *Hemingway and The Sun Set*, Washington, D.C., 1972, pp. 247-255.

651₁ Fitzgerald, F. Scott. "Letter to Ernest Hemingway," *ibid.*, pp. 10-13.

A previously unpublished ten-page letter, written in 1926, criticizing the final typescript of *SAR*. See the above entry and Philip Young and Charles Mann's *The Hemingway Manuscripts: An Inventory*, University Park, Pa., 1969, Item 305[H]. This letter was reprinted in Bertram D. Sarason's *Hemingway and The Sun Set*, Washington, D.C., 1972, pp. 256-259. Note: For newspaper articles about the publication of this letter, see *F/H A: 1971*, pp. 372-373.

651₂ Drew, Fraser. "April 8, 1955 with Hemingway: Unedited Notes on a Visit to Finca Vigia," *ibid.*, pp. 108-116.

651₃ Stewart, Lawrence D. "Hemingway and the Autobiographies of Alice B. Toklas," *ibid.*, pp. 117-123.

651₄ Smith, William B. "A Wedding Up in Michigan," *ibid.*, pp. 124-126.

Reminiscences by the best man of Hadley and Ernest's wedding, on September 3, 1921, at Horton Bay, Michigan.

651₅ Sarason, Bertram D. "Pauline Hemingway: In Tranquillity," *ibid.*, pp. 127-135.

Relates a trip to Key West, late in 1950, and two visits with Pauline Hemingway.

651₆ Goldhurst, William. "The Hyphenated Ham Sandwich of Ernest Hemingway and J. D. Salinger: A Study in Literary Continuity," *ibid.*, pp. 136-150.

651₇ Healey, Winifred. "When Ernest Hemingway's Mother Came to Call," *ibid.*, pp. 170-172.

Relates a visit from Mrs. Grace Hall Hemingway to a family across Walloon Lake, in Michigan.

651₈ Mai, Robert P. "Ernest Hemingway and Men Without Women," *ibid.*, pp. 173-186.

651₉ Clark, C. E. Frazer, Jr. "The Beginnings of Dealer Interest in Hemingway," *ibid.*, pp. 187-194. Illustrated with facsimiles, including the Ulysses Book Shop catalogue, see (F57); the Bastard Note issued by Louis Henry Cohn, see (F150); and the galley proofs of *Four Poems by Ernest Hemingway*, see (F149).

651₁₀ Hanneman, Audre. "Hanneman Addenda," *ibid.*, pp. 195-218.

A checklist of omissions in *EH: A Comprehensive Bibliography* and work published since 1965, with a prefatory note.

651₁₁ Jackson, Thomas J. "The 'Macomber' Typescript," *ibid.*, pp. 219-222. Facsimiles of p. 1 and p. 37 of the typescript of "The Short Happy Life of Francis Macomber," from the holdings of Morris Library at Southern Illinois University.

651₁₂ "M.J.B." [Matthew J. Bruccoli]. "Francis Macomber and Francis Fitzgerald," *ibid.*, p. 223.

651₁₃ McClellan, David M. "Hemingway's Colonel Appropriately Quotes Jackson," *ibid.*, p. 234.
On *ARIT*.

651₁₄ Drake, Constance. " 'A Lake Superior Salmon Fisherman,' " *ibid.*, p. 235.
Comments on a letter from Hemingway to F. Scott Fitzgerald, written in 1926.

651₁₅ "M.J.B" [Matthew J. Bruccoli]. " 'Oh, Give Them Irony and Give Them Pity,' " *ibid.*, p. 236.
The source of Bill Gorton's "irony and pity" phrase in *SAR* is traced to Gilbert Seldes' review of *The Great Gatsby*.

651₁₆ Linebarger, J. M. "Eggs As Huevos in *The Sun Also Rises*," *ibid.*, pp. 237-239.

651₁₇ Crosby, Caresse. "The Last Time I Saw Hemingway," *ibid.*, p. 240.
Excerpt from a letter, dated January 7, 1970, from the publisher of the Crosby Continental Editions of *IOT*, see (A3c), and *TOS*, see (A4b).

651₁₈ Bruccoli, Matthew J. Review of *Islands, ibid.*, pp. 245-246.
"There are no surprises in *Islands in the Stream*—no new techniques or themes. The writing, especially in the conversations, is wordy for Hemingway, but then he did not have the chance to revise and cut. There is no strong thematic line, although *Islands* reaffirms the Hemingway code of discipline and integrity. . . . Probably the final importance of *Islands in the Stream* lies in its clearly autobiographical basis. It should help Hemingway pros to understand what he was like in the late fifties."

651₁₉ Cagle, William. Review of Philip Young and Charles Mann's *The Hemingway Manuscripts: An Inventory, ibid.*, pp. 257-259.

651₂₀ Gingrich, Arnold. Review of *Ernest Hemingway, Cub Reporter*, edited by Matthew J. Bruccoli, *ibid.*, pp. 263-264.
"There are only the most fleeting glimpses, or the faintest of hints, of anything like real literary distinction in these routine reportings. But they make fascinating reading nevertheless, because the yield of any intimations of immortality in this journeyman prose is so low that the few that are indubitably there stand out more strikingly than they would in a setting of more finished work. . . . A small book, *Ernest Hemingway, Cub Reporter* is none the less seminal, for no serious student of the Hemingway canon will want to miss

these relatively few but extremely significant examples of how, in literature too, coming events cast their shadows before."

652 Finkel'shtein, I. L. "O Romane Khemingueya *I Voskhodit Sointse*" [On Hemingway's Novel *The Sun Also Rises*], *Gor'kovskii Pedagogicheskii Institut Inostrannykh Yakykov* (Gorki Institute), No. 30 (1970), pp. 144-152.

653 Davies, Phillips G., and Rosemary R. Davies. " 'A Killer Who Would Shoot You for the Fun of It': A Possible Source for Hemingway's 'The Killers,' " *Iowa English Yearbook*, xv (1970), 36-38.
Regarding the murder of a heavyweight boxer in New York in 1924.

654 Kann, Hans-Joachim. "Ernest Hemingway's Knowledge of German," *Jahrbuch für Amerikastudien*, xv (1970), 221-232.

655 Kruse, Horst. "Hemingway's 'Cat in the Rain' and Joyce's *Ulysses*," *Literatur in Wissenschaft und Unterricht*, iii, i (1970), 28-30.

656 Petrov, Dimităr. "Havana, Kaza de Heminguej," *Plamăk*, xiv (1970), No. 13, pp. 58-63; No. 14, pp. 74-81.

657 Sheremet'ev, N. " 'Papa Kheminguei Tol'ko Chto Voshel' (Vpechatleniya ot Poseshcheniya Papyatnykh Mest, Svyazannykh s Zhizn'yu Amerikanskogo Pisel'ya na Kube)" ['Papa Hemingway Just Entered' (Impressions from a visit to memorials connected with the life of an American author in Cuba)], *Sibirskie Ogni*, No. 1 (1970), pp. 145-154.

658 Finkel'shtein, I. L. "Obrazy Revolyutsionerov v Tvorchestve Khemingueya" [Images of Revolutionaries in Hemingway's Work], *Uchenye Zapiski Gor'kovskogo Universiteta* (Gorki Institute), No. 93 (1970), pp. 80-103.

659 Jones, Edward T. "Hemingway and Cézanne: A Speculative Affinity," *Unisa English Studies*, viii, ii (1970), 26-28.

660 Wüstenhagen, Heinz. Review of Audre Hanneman's *EH: A Comprehensive Bibliography*, *Zeitschrift für Anglistik und Amerikanistik*, xviii (1970), 214-215.

661 Heaton, C. P. "Style in *The Old Man and the Sea*," *Style*, iv (Winter 1970), 11-27.

662 Benson, Jackson J. Review of Richard B. Hovey's *Hemingway: The Inward Terrain*, *Western Humanities Review*, xxiv (Winter 1970), 84-85.

663 Schorer, Mark. Review of Carlos Baker's *EH: A Life Story*, *American Literature*, xli (Jan. 1970), 592-594.

664 Gutwinski, Waldemar Franciszek. "Cohesion in Literary Texts: A Study of Some Grammatical and Lexical Features of English Discourse," *Dissertation Abstracts International,* XXX (Jan. 1970), 2990-A.

Abstract from a doctoral dissertation, University of Connecticut, 1969. Compares selected passages from the fiction of Henry James and Hemingway for cohesion.

664₁ Morrison, Robert William. "The Short Stories of Ernest Hemingway: A Search for Love and Identity," *ibid.,* pp. 3018-A to 3019-A.

Abstract from a doctoral dissertation, Washington State University, 1969.

665 Miller, Evelyn E. "A Trilogy of Irony," *English Journal,* LIX (Jan. 1970), 59-62.

An analysis of "Old Man at the Bridge."

666 Hayashi, Tetsumaro. "*A Farewell to Arms*: The Contest of Experience," *Kyushu American Literature,* No. 12 (Jan. 1970), pp. 14-19.

666₁ Tanaka, Keisuke. "The Bipolar Construction in the Works of Ernest Hemingway," *ibid.,* pp. 32-44.

667 "Young Discovers New Hemingway Manuscripts," *Research in the College of Liberal Arts* (Pennsylvania State University) (Jan. 1970), pp. 9-10. Facsimile of typescript page of "The Killers." See (S-F33₂).

Regarding Philip Young and Charles Mann's examination of the Hemingway manuscripts, which resulted in *The Hemingway Manuscripts: An Inventory.*

668 Griffin, Lloyd W. Review of Philip Young and Charles Mann's *The Hemingway Manuscripts, Library Journal,* XCV (Jan. 15, 1970). 146.

668₁ Fuson, Ben W. Review of the *Fitzgerald/Hemingway Annual: 1969, ibid.,* p. 160.

669 White, William. "Hemingway's (?) Kilimanjaro," *Literary Sketches,* I (Feb. 1970), 11.

670 Bass, Eben. "Hemingway at Roncesvalles," *NEMLA Newsletter* (Northeast Modern Language Association), II (Feb. 1970), 1-7.

On the resemblances between Robert Jordan in *FWBT* and Count Roland in *The Song of Roland.* Also, commentary on the visit to the monastery at Roncesvalles in *SAR.*

671 Bennett, Warren. "Character, Irony, and Resolution in 'A Clean, Well-Lighted Place,'" *American Literature,* LXII (March 1970), 70-79.

Regarding the emended text in Scribner's 1965 edition of *The Short Stories of Ernest Hemingway.* See (S-A7F).

671₁ Longmire, Samuel E. "Hemingway's Praise of Dick Sisler in *The Old Man and the Sea*," *ibid.*, pp. 96-98.

Hemingway met the Philadelphia ball player in Havana during the winter of 1945-1946.

672 Steiner, Paul. "Intimately Yours—But Don't Quote Me," *Escapade* (March 1970), p. 36.

Regarding a Hemingway letter to John Austin Parker, in 1949. See (S-F103).

673 Harder, Kelsie B. "Hemingway's Religious Parody," *New York Folklore Quarterly*, XXVI (March 1970), 76-77.

Examines Hemingway's parody of the Paternoster and Ave Maria in "A Clean, Well-Lighted Place."

674 Joost, Nicholas. "Ernest Hemingway," *Contemporary Literature*, XI (Spring 1970), 293-302.

Reviews of Carlos Baker's *EH: A Life Story*, Robert O. Stephens' *Hemingway's Nonfiction*, Jackson J. Benson's *Hemingway: The Writer's Art of Self-Defense*, and Richard B. Hovey's *Hemingway: The Inward Terrain*.

675 DeMarr, Mary Jean. "Hemingway's Narrative Methods," *Indiana English Journal*, IV (Spring 1970), 31-36.

675₁ Shepherd, Allen. "Hemingway's 'A Day's Wait': Biography and Fiction," *ibid.*, pp. 37-39.

676 Vorpahl, Ben M. "Ernest Hemingway and Owen Wister: Finding the Lost Generation," *Library Chronicle* (University of Pennsylvania), XXXVI (Spring 1970), 126-137.

677 Von Ende, Frederick. "The Corrida Pattern in *For Whom the Bell Tolls*," *Re: Arts and Letters*, III (Spring 1970), 63-70.

678 Thomaneck, Jurgen K. A. "Hemingway's Riddle of Kilimanjaro Once More," *Studies in Short Fiction*, VII (Spring 1970), 326-327.

678₁ Patrick, W. R. Review of Leo Gurko's *Ernest Hemingway and the Pursuit of Heroism*, *ibid.*, pp. 354-355.

679 Seward, William W., Jr. Review of Jackson J. Benson's *Hemingway: The Writer's Art of Self-Defense*, *Western Humanities Review*, XXIV (Spring 1970), 194-195.

680 St. John, Donald, "Leicester Hemingway, Chief of State," *Connecticut Review*, III (April 1970), 5-19.

Interview with Hemingway's brother, the founder-president of New Atlantis, who comments on the Hemingway family, books about Hemingway, and the Michigan origins of the short stories.

680₁ Sarason, Bertram D. Review of the *Fitzgerald/Hemingway Annual: 1969* edited by Matthew J. Bruccoli, *ibid.*, pp. 20-23.

680₂ Charters, James. "Pat and Duff, Some Memories," *ibid.*, pp. 24-27.
Reminiscences of Pat Guthrie and Lady Duff Twysden. Reprinted in Bertram D. Sarason's *Hemingway and The Sun Set*, Washington, D.C., 1972, pp. 241-246.

681 Walker, Emma Clement. "A Study of the Fiction of Hemingway and Faulkner in a College Sophomore English Class," *Dissertation Abstracts International*, xxx (April 1970), 4212-A.
Abstract from a doctoral dissertation, Ohio State University, 1969.

681₁ Byrd, Lemuel Brian. "Characterization in Ernest Hemingway's Fiction: 1925-1952, With a Dictionary of the Characters," *ibid.*, p. 4444-A.
Abstract from a doctoral dissertation, University of Colorado, 1969.

681₂ Raeburn, John Hay. "Ernest Hemingway: The Writer as Object of Public Attention," *ibid.*, p. 4462-A.
Abstract from a doctoral dissertation, University of Pennsylvania, 1969.

682 Rogers, Jean Muir, and Gordon Stein. "Bibliographical Notes on Hemingway's *Men Without Women*," *Papers of the Bibliographical Society of America*, LXIV, ii (April-June 1970), 210-213.
An analysis of copies of *MWW* for 1927, 1928, 1932, 1938, 1946, and 1955 for determination of weight differences and textual changes. See note under (S-A2G).

683 Fuson, Ben W. Review of *Ernest Hemingway, Cub Reporter* edited by Matthew J. Bruccoli, *Library Journal*, xcv (April 1, 1970), 1371.
"These columns (most of which had been identified as Hemingway's before Bruccoli did his editing) involve prize fights, a police raid, ambulance runs, an auto accident, Navy recruitment, and a dance for soldiers one winter night at the city YWCA. . . . students of style will be able here and there to detect Hemingwayese in embryo."

684 Raymont, Henry. "11 Hemingway Stories—'Cub' to 'Giant,' " *N.Y. Times* (April 7, 1970), p. 47. Facsimile of the assignment sheet of the *Kansas City Star* of Jan. 3, 1918.
Regarding *Ernest Hemingway, Cub Reporter* edited by Matthew J. Bruccoli. Reprinted in the *Kansas City Times* (April 11, 1970), p. 16-C.

685 Fuson, Ben W. Review of Delbert Wylder's *Hemingway's Heroes*, *Library Journal*, xcv (April 15, 1970), 1483.

686 "Bloomfield Hills Collector Finds Early Hemingway," *Birmingham Eccentric* (April 23, 1970), p. 4-B.

Regarding C. E. Frazer Clark's collection of *Kansas City Star* stories that Hemingway had sent to his family in 1917-1918. "Battle of Raid Squads" is partially reprinted, see Matthew J. Bruccoli's *EH, Cub Reporter* (S-A16).

687 Borovik, G. "Pravila Khemingueya" [The Rules of Hemingway], *Sovetskaya Estoniya* (April 24, 1970), p. 6. Reprinted in *Literaturnaya Gazeta* (June 17, 1970), p. 15.

688 "Out of the Vault," *Newsweek*, LXXV (April 27, 1970), 91-92.

Regarding the plans for publication of *Islands*, with references to other "vaulted works."

689 Raymont, Henry. "Book Left by Hemingway Will Be Published in Fall," *N.Y. Times* (April 29, 1970), p. 47.

Regarding the announcement by Mary Hemingway and Charles Scribner, Jr. of the plans for publication of *The Islands and the Stream* [*sic*].

690 "G. M." "Hemingway's 'The Light of the World,'" *Explicator*, XXVIII (May 1970), Query 2.

Query on Hemingway's use of the initials "C. and M."

691 "New Novel by Hemingway," *Publishers' Weekly*, CXCVII (May 11, 1970), 16.

Regarding the press conference at Scribner's, on April 28, 1970, to announce the publication of *Islands*.

691₁ "Books in the Bank," *ibid.*, p. 16.

Regarding Hemingway's unpublished manuscripts.

692 Singer, Kurt. "Señor Hemingway's House Near Havana," *Chicago Tribune Book World* (May 31, 1970), p. 8.

Interview with René Villareal, the caretaker of the Hemingway Museum in Cuba.

693 Mack. Caricature of Hemingway, *N.Y. Times Book Review* (May 31, 1970), p. 18. Caricatures of Pearl Buck, Carl Sandburg, Robert Frost, and Hemingway in an ad for the bound volumes of the *N.Y. Times Book Review*.

694 Garraty, John A. "A Century of American Realism," *American Heritage*, XXI (June 1970), 12-15, 86-90. Interview with Alfred Kazin. General article.

695 Rosen, Kenneth Mark. "Ernest Hemingway: The Function of Violence," *Dissertation Abstracts International*, XXX (June 1970), 5456-A.

Abstract from a doctoral dissertation, University of New Mexico, 1969.

696 Bradshaw, Hank. "Out in Hemingway Country," *Field & Stream,* LXXV (June 1970), 70-71, 152-153, 156, 158, 160, 162-165.
Regarding a fishing trip in Idaho with Jack and Patrick Hemingway.

697 Barba, Harry. "The Three Levels of 'The End of Something,' " *West Virginia University Philological Papers,* XVII (June 1970), 76-80.

698 Skipp, Francis E. "Nick Adams, Prince of Abissinia," *Carrell,* XI (June and Dec. 1970), 20-26.

699 Amory, Cleveland. Trade Winds column, *Saturday Review,* LIII (June 6, 1970), 12.
Item regarding Mary Hemingway's press conference announcing the publication of *Islands.*

700 Photograph, *N.Y. Times* (June 26, 1970), p. 84. Full-page photograph of Hemingway in the ad for the October 1970 issue of *Esquire.*

701 Adams, Sam. "The Sun Also Sets," *Sports Illustrated,* XXXII (June 29, 1970), 57-60, 62-64.
Regarding Cayetano Ordóñez, the bullfighter Niño de la Palma, who was Hemingway's model for "Pedro Romero" in *SAR.* Reprinted in Bertram D. Sarason's *Hemingway and The Sun Set,* Washington, D.C., 1972, pp. 212-221.

702 Koster, Donald N. Review of Carlos Baker's *EH: A Life Story, American Quarterly,* XXII, ii, Part 2 (Summer 1970), 262.

703 Srivastava, Ramesh. "Hemingway's 'Cat in the Rain': An Interpretation," *Literary Criterion,* IX (Summer 1970), 79-84.

704 Rodgers, Paul C., Jr. "Levels of Irony in Hemingway's 'The Gambler, the Nun, and the Radio,' " *Studies in Short Fiction,* VII (Summer 1970), 439-449.

704₁ Martine, James J. "A Little Light on Hemingway's 'The Light of the World,' " *ibid.,* pp. 465-467.

705 Lewis, Robert W., Jr., and Max Westbrook. " 'The Snows of Kilimanjaro' Collated and Annotated," *Texas Quarterly,* XIII (Summer 1970), 67-143. Facsimiles, see (S-F35).
A textual study of "The Snows of Kilimanjaro" based on the typescript in the Ernest Hemingway Collection at the University of Texas.

706 Kimball, William J. "Hemingway and the Code," *Venture* (University of Karachi), VI (Summer 1970), 18-23.

707 Alderman, Taylor. "Ernest Hemingway: Four Studies in the Competitive Motif," *Dissertation Abstracts International*, XXXI (July 1970), 380-A.
Abstract from a doctoral dissertation, University of New Mexico, 1969.

707₁ Nelson, Jon Eric. "Religious Experience in the Fiction of Ernest Hemingway," *ibid.*, p. 396-A.
Abstract from a doctoral dissertation, University of North Carolina at Chapel Hill, 1969.

708 Vaidyanathan, T. G. "Did Margot Kill Francis Macomber?" *Indian Journal of American Studies*, I (July 1970), 1-13.

708₁ Jain, S. P. " 'Hills Like White Elephants': A Study," *ibid.*, pp. 33-38.

709 Montgomery, Marion. "Emotion Recollected in Tranquility: Wordsworth's Legacy to Eliot, Joyce, and Hemingway," *Southern Review*, VI [New Series] (July 1970), 710-721. Reprinted in *The Reflective Journey Toward Order*, Athens, Georgia, 1973, pp. 283-295.
Examines *A Moveable Feast*.

710 Carlucci, Carlo. "Ernest Hemingway dieci anni dopo," *Cenobio*, XIX (July-Aug. 1970), 219-228. Reprinted in book form, Lugano, 1970.

711 Paige, Whitney. "Hemingway's Michigan," *Travel & Camera*, XXXIII (July-Aug. 1970), 32-37. Photographs by Rus Arnold.
Includes short excerpts from Hemingway's stories.

712 Lewis, Clifford. "The Short Happy Life of Francis Scott Macomber," *Études Anglaises*, XXIII (July-Sept. 1970), 256-261. In English.
A study of the "skillfully planned" parallels, including domestic similarities, between F. Scott Fitzgerald and "Francis Macomber."

713 Pólvora, Hélio. "Notas de um Diário Crítico," *Journal do Brasil* (July 22, 1970), p. 2. Entry for Feb. 4, 1965, regarding *First 49*.

714 White, William. Review of Richard K. Peterson's *Hemingway: Direct and Oblique*, *Library Journal*, XCV (Aug. 1970), 2682-2683.

715 Bonet, Laureano. "Los dos rostros de Ernest Hemingway," *Revista de Occidente*, XXX (Aug. 1970), 176-199.

716 Review of *Islands*, *Publishers' Weekly*, CXCVIII (Aug. 10, 1970), 47. Scribner's ad for *Islands* on the front cover and the inside cover. The cover quotes the first five lines under the heading: "These are

the opening lines of one of the best books Ernest Hemingway ever wrote."

"The question everyone in publishing is asking is, how good is the 'new' Hemingway in the final analysis? The answer, in the opinion of this reviewer, is that the first section is absolutely first rate; the second and third sections, somewhat disappointing. . . . The action of the first of the three sections of the novel revolves around the summer visit to Bimini of Hudson's three young sons (time: the Thirties). The four of them do some fine fishing and talking—the deep sea fishing passages are as fine as any writing Hemingway did. . . . Hemingway's delineations of the boys' separate personalities is tenderly and movingly done. The Bimini section ends with Hudson learning of the death of two of his sons, and includes a brilliant vintage-Hemingway passage on bereavement. The second section, set in Cuba during the war, deals with Hudson's loneliness and the death of his last son. The big disappointment here is an alcoholic dialog between Hudson and a lachrymose prostitute—funny in places, but overlong. The final section, dealing with tracking down the survivors of a German submarine, is all action, lacks overtones of any kind and could have been written by any topflight adventure writer."

717 Lingeman, Richard. American Notebook column, *N.Y. Times Book Review* (Aug. 30, 1970), pp. 10, 12.

Regarding *Islands* as one of the five most important books of the publishers' fall announcements.

718 Fleissner, R. F. "The Macomber Case: A Sherlockian Analysis?" *Baker Street Journal,* xx (Sept. 1970), 154-156, 169.

On "The Short Happy Life of Francis Macomber."

719 Palmer, Barbara Dallas. "The Guide and Leader: Studies in a Narrative Structural Motif," *Dissertation Abstracts International,* xxxi (Sept. 1970), 1236-A to 1237-A.

Abstract from a doctoral dissertation, Michigan State University, 1969. Examines *FWBT.*

719₁ Gebhardt, Richard Coate. "Denial and Affirmation of Values in the Fiction of Ernest Hemingway," *ibid.,* pp. 1274-A to 1275-A.

Abstract from a doctoral dissertation, Michigan State University, 1969.

720 De Cadaval, Rudy. "Hemingway letterato e personaggio nella leggenda," *Cenobio,* xix (Sept.-Oct. 1970), 294-297.

721 Mann, Charles W., Jr. "Once again the familiar Hemingway is with us," review of *Islands, Library Journal,* xcv (Sept. 1, 1970), 2827.

"Those who wish to can find flaws, can complain that the three divisions are not perfectly wed, that some of the scenes verge on self-parody, that a blonde ex-wife is all Dietrich . . . and that Thomas Hudson is more often Ernest Hemingway than a painter. But they would be wrong. This is a big, impressive, and haunting book; it may not be the masterpiece we wanted, but the peculiar world of Hemingway is much with us in these pages."

722 Raymont, Henry. "Mrs. Hemingway Recalls 'Island in the Stream,'" *N.Y. Times* (Sept. 12, 1970), p. 32.

Interview with Mary Hemingway regarding Hemingway's working on *Islands*, and her interpretation of the ending.

723 Lehmann-Haupt, Christopher. "The Case of the Missing Annotations," review of *Islands, N.Y. Times* (Sept. 30, 1970), p. 41.

"The first and by far the best section, 'Bimini,' in which Thomas Hudson is visited at his island retreat by his three sons, has something of the old Hemingway polish and control. But even 'Bimini' is tainted by excesses of sentiment, mannered dialogue . . . and a pervasive tone of pity for its Hemingway-surrogate hero. . . . And after 'Bimini,' all semblance of finished work vanishes. . . . Yet to read it against the background of Hemingway's life is not without interest. To learn how he selected, rearranged and transmuted actual incidents and people from his experience . . . to observe how he splits himself into two characters, the painter Thomas Hudson and his writer friend, and then to watch him comparing the two media; to know finally that *The Old Man and the Sea* was written during the same period . . . and then to compare the two works—all this is most useful to understanding both Hemingway's life and his art."

724 Fadiman, Clifton. Report of *Islands, Book-of-the-Month Club News* (Fall 1970), pp. 2-4. Cover photograph of Hemingway. *Islands in the Stream* was the Book-of-the-Month Club's special selection for Fall 1970.

"To read it is a moving experience. As a whole it should rank well up in the Hemingway canon. And if one singles out its finest episodes, it is fair to say that they are at least as good as any comparable ones to be found in his entire body of work. . . . [In Part I] Hudson's three boys . . . visit their father. . . . An infrequently glimpsed side of Hemingway is revealed in these passages: a tender and humorous human being, gentle and charming. . . . [In Part II] The drunken dialogues with a group of bar flies and especially the Chaucerian whore Honest Lil are superbly done, funny and sad. . . . For this reader the most moving passages in the final section deal not with the technicalities of the pursuit of the Germans but with poor Hudson's dreamy memories of a happier time, when he was poor and in love and in Paris. Here the factual record which readers will remember from *A Moveable Feast* undergoes a transmutation into art."

725 Hemingway, Mary. "Ernest's Homework," *ibid.,* pp. 5, 12.

Regarding Hemingway's early morning work habits and the tower workroom that Mary Hemingway had built for him, which turned out to be "too lonely" to work in.

726 Farnham, James F. "Hemingway: The Myth of Crucified Man," review of *Islands, Cross Currents,* xx (Fall 1970), 481-483.

"*Islands in the Stream* continues the writer's concern with the destruction by impersonal forces of the individual's sense of meaning and of his relationships to others. Life is absurd, Hemingway tells us, if life can be crushed so easily. Therefore, life must get its meaning primarily from the attitude—specifically, from the bravery—with which one looks destruction in the eye . . . the way one dies becomes the core of meaning for his life. . . . Regardless of what one knows or does not know of Hemingway's rather tortured personal story, *Islands in the Stream* can and should, first of all, be read as a narrative of human life and as an ethical and philosophic probing into the heart of that life."

727 Thomas, Peter. "A Lost Leader: Hemingway's 'The Light of the World,'" *Humanities Association Bulletin* [Canada], xxi (Fall 1970), 14-19.

728 Sears, Donald A., and Margaret Bourland. "Journalism Makes the Style," *Journalism Quarterly,* xlvii (Autumn 1970), 504-509.

Hemingway is one of eight authors studied for the influence of a journalistic background.

729 Davis, Robert Murray. " 'If You Did Not Go Forward': Process and Stasis in *A Farewell to Arms," Studies in the Novel,* ii (Fall 1970), 305-311.

729₁ Etulain, Richard W. Review of Delbert E. Wylder's *Hemingway's Heroes, ibid.,* pp. 382-383.

730 Anderson, Paul Victor. "Nick's Story in Hemingway's 'Big Two-Hearted River,' " *Studies in Short Fiction,* vii (Fall 1970), 564-572.

730₁ Smith, Julian. "More Products of the Hemingway Industry," *ibid.,* pp. 638-646.

Reviews of Carlos Baker's *EH: A Life Story,* Audre Hanneman's *EH: A Comprehensive Bibliography,* and Philip Young and Charles Mann's *The Hemingway Manuscripts: An Inventory.*

731 Brief review of *EH, Cub Reporter* edited by Matthew J. Bruccoli, *Virginia Quarterly Review,* xlvi (Autumn 1970), cxxxvii.

732 Barrett, Mary Ellin. Review of *Islands, Cosmopolitan*, CLXIX (Oct. 1970), 6.

"I fell in love with the book at first sight. From the initial sun-lit, sea-sprayed pages describing an American painter's fishing vacation on the island of Bimini with his three young sons, I was gone . . . caught up by the Hemingway voice (never truer nor more relaxed), by his hero, Thomas Hudson, by those charming, gutsy boys. . . . *Islands* is a lovely, loving work, deeply sad and deeply felt."

733 "A. G." [Arnold Gingrich]. Publisher's Page, "Notes on *Bimini*," *Esquire*, LXXIV (Oct. 1970), 6, 12. Facsimile of manuscript page superimposed over photograph of Hemingway on cover. See (S-F36).

Regarding the publication of "Bimini," Part One of *Islands*. See (S-C64).

734 Howe, Irving. "Great man going down," review of *Islands, Harper's*, CCXLI (Oct. 1970), 120-125.

"[Thomas Hudson] is a grossly self-indulgent and pompous fellow. His crippling limitation is that he deeply reflects his creator yet isn't a deeply created figure. One looks through him toward the Hemingway psyche, but not into him, as a man interesting in his own right. . . . [In the first part] Hudson gets mixed up in a local brawl. . . . What strikes one, in reading these flaccid and rather ugly pages, is how painful it is that the great master of narrative pacing, the Hemingway who could make tightness of phrase into a moral virtue, should now write so slackly, as if he must hang on to an incident for pages of chatter simply because he doesn't quite know what to do next. There follows, nevertheless, a quite charming section in which Hudson's three sons come to visit, and here the talk is bright, the feeling pure, and the action vibrant. . . . Part II, a complete disaster . . . [has] a long, dragging bar conversation. . . . Part III, 'At Sea,' constitutes a notable recovery. It is a tense and exciting story. . . . These pages I found myself reading with a happy surrender to primitive suspense, as well as with pleasure at seeing Hemingway once again in command of his material."

735 Stafford, William T. "Hemingway/Faulkner: Marlin and Catfish?" *Southern Review*, VI [New Series] (Oct. 1970), 1191-1200.

Includes reviews of Richard B. Hovey's *Hemingway: The Inward Terrain* and Jackson J. Benson's *Hemingway: The Writer's Art of Self-Defense.*

736 Golyseva, E. "Kheminguei—Esseist," *Voprosy Literatury*, No. 10 (October 1970), 201-207.

737 Barkham, John. Review of *Islands, N.Y. Post* (Oct. 2, 1970), p. 44.

"You will not soon forget the right cross to the heart with which

Hemingway closes [Part I, 'Bimini'] . . . [In Part II, 'Cuba'] Two women appear—one an aging Cuban whore, the other a beautiful American. Both are essentially the archetypal Hemingway woman —big hearted, affectionate, made for men. . . . [Part III, 'At Sea'] is compounded of classic Hemingway ingredients—physical courage, expertise (in this case seamanship) and masculine emotion concealed in hairy-chested humor."

738 Geismar, Maxwell. "Hemingway's 'lost' novel: Illuminating self-portrait," review of *Islands, Chicago Sun-Times Showcase* (Oct. 4, 1970), pp. 1, 19.

"*Islands in the Stream* may be hailed as the literary sensation of the fall season, but it is not major fiction. It is not even good Hemingway if you know Hemingway at his best. But it is fascinating to read as a kind of illuminating self-portrait and as revelatory fiction. . . . The novel's real theme—and perhaps the real reason why the novel has been held back so long—is the disintegration of its hero. . . . If, in his later years, we know that Hemingway had lost so much of the lyrical, tender, ironical poetry of youth which his early writing exemplified . . . *Islands in the Stream* does show that he could still pull himself together to do certain things superbly."

739 Macauley, Robie. "100-proof Old Ernest, most of it anyway," review of *Islands, N.Y. Times Book Review* (Oct. 4, 1970), pp. 1, 51.

"Hudson . . . is splendidly realized both as a man and as a painter. Hemingway's brilliant descriptive talent frames one small, superb picture after another in Hudson's eyes, to make him that rare thing in literature, a believable artist. As a man, he is efficient and capable, but he always falls just a little short of the heroic effort that events demand of him. The verge of failure is always close—and this gives the story much of its quiet tension. . . . One of the delights of reading Hemingway is to watch the familiar done all over again with just as much verve and force as if it had never been done before."

740 Norris, Hoke. "Hemingway's Life and Work Reflected in His Last Novel," review of *Islands, Philadelphia Inquirer* (Oct. 4, 1970), p. 6.

"Lesser men than Ernest Hemingway will no doubt have their fun with this book. God knows it is vulnerable, as others of Hemingway's have been, and as he himself was: and having fun helps small men gain stature, or so they believe. . . . But Hemingway remains, and one can still cherish and enjoy him and his novels, even this last one. He did as much to rescue American literature from the Jamesians as any writer ever did; he brought to it his characteristic economy, his passion for the most in the least, his devotion to both craft and art (which he would say are both essential to the writing of literature worth the name), and in *Islands in the Stream* he tried again. His failure would be a lesser man's triumph."

741 Hogan, William. "Hemingway's Unfinished Novel," review of *Islands, San Francisco Examiner & Chronicle* (Oct. 4, 1970), This World section, pp. 34, 40. Caricature of Hemingway, by David Levine, on the cover.

"The thing that must be said right off about this posthumous novel is that it is unfinished. . . . Yet it is Hemingway and there are moments deep-sea fishing off Bimini in the Gulf Stream, for instance, that soar and reach the emotional heights of his classic *The Old Man and the Sea*. In the second and third parts of this three-part sea adventure there are depths as well that are especially bad Hemingway. . . . Yet I read it with much of the old feeling for this mighty spellbinder, wishing he had had 'better luck,' as he sometimes put it."

742 Rubin, Louis D., Jr. "New Hemingway Novel Poses Questions," review of *Islands, Washington Sunday Star* (Oct. 4, 1970), p. E-1.

"Let me say at once that I think *Islands in the Stream* is mediocre work. The novel has few high points, a number of low points, and a great deal of barren, lusterless writing in between. . . . Hemingway was, therefore, very wise, from all the fictional material he was working on in the 1950s to have published only *The Old Man and the Sea*, for that narrative has what the episodes of *Islands in the Stream* lack: the metaphysical dimension that gives deep human significance to an elemental situation."

743 Cook, Bruce. "A Posthumous Hemingway Novel Yields Both Gold and Platitude," review of *Islands, National Observer*, IX (Oct. 5, 1970), 19.

". . . [Hemingway] mattered, not just to his own generation but to the one that followed, in a total way that no writer does or can today. . . . The book's three parts are not only at markedly different stages of completion, but the transitions between them are also missing; there is no flow to the book. Nevertheless, there is a progression, which leads directly to that fight with the sub crew on the key. . . . The entire Bimini section, 200 pages of it, is pure gold. . . . What follows, in the book's second and third sections, tends only to dissipate, even falsify, the effects achieved in those fine first 200 pages."

744 Foote, Timothy. "Papa Watching," review of *Islands, Time*, XCVI (Oct. 5, 1970), 90, 92.

"*Islands in the Stream* is not a novel in any well-made sense of the word. It is more like a muted literary *son et lumière* in which the aging author reviews and reflects upon the preoccupations of a working lifetime—death and love, work and action. It is all too easy, especially in the digressive anecdotes, to find him at his easy-to-parody worst. There are the mock heroics . . . the self-indulgent garrulity. . . . But there is also the Hemingway who could sometimes sustain a moment of humor long enough for it to edge toward comedy, and the Hemingway who could write about the things of this world so that, without having to explain, he could convey his love for them."

745 Nordell, Roderick. "The Sea As a Mirror: Hemingway's View of Himself," review of *Islands, Christian Science Monitor* (Oct. 8, 1970), p. 13.

"After all the caveats have been entered, *Islands in the Stream* remains as likable and heartbreaking a book as Ernest Hemingway ever wrote. An inescapable part of this impression lies in the resonance between the novel's hero and a reader's memories of the author's own finally tragic life. . . . But there are also, along with much that is unworthy of Papa, many passages that stand firmly on their own. . . . If the book is a testament, it is sad as well as sunny. . . . for all its faults, this book leaves one feeling closer to the man than before."

746 Ricks, Christopher. "At Sea with Ernest Hemingway," review of *Islands, New York Review of Books*, XV (Oct. 8, 1970), 17-19. Caricature of Hemingway by David Levine.

"Devious and secretive, *Islands in the Stream* is an elaborate refusal to say what is the matter with Thomas Hudson. It calls him Thomas Hudson throughout, which makes the reader's relationship with him at once utterly stable and aloofly unadvancing. The book makes it impossible for us to know what is the matter with him (and so at the same time to know what was the matter with Hemingway) by an ingenious circumvention: it proliferates good reasons for him to be in a bad way. . . . his creator, with that kindliest of protectings which is usually a self-protecting, decides against any painful exploration of what is the matter."

747 Broyard, Anatole. "Papa's disappointing 'big one,'" review of *Islands, Life*, LXIX (Oct. 9, 1970), 10.

"Less disciplined than *The Old Man and the Sea*, less disastrous than *Across the River and Into the Trees*, the book is unlikely to affect Hemingway's standing. . . . The line ['You never understand anybody that loves you.'] sums up not only Hudson, but Hemingway himself, for he certainly did not understand either love or people. What he did understand was that life is rich in proportion to what we put into it. This affirmation, this anguished, old-fashioned faith, reaches and moves us in spite of the book's many shortcomings. In fact, it may be precisely this—Hemingway's insatiable hunger for experience—that flawed his rendering of it."

748 "Hemingway the Obscure," review of *Islands, Economist*, CCXXXVII (Oct. 10, 1970), 55.

"Hemingway's famous cryptic style here amounts to obscurantism or even a closed mind; there are too many things Hemingway-Hudson just won't think about. There are too many gaps; it might be kinder to accept this book as scraps of rich Hemingway embedded in a background of unpolished nonsense and be content with it as a literary oddity. But that would also be unfair. *Islands in the Stream* is not unpolished. Nor is the story incomplete. . . . The gaps are not in the narrative but in Hudson's character. Whether Hemingway could have filled them in, or would ever have wanted to, is another matter: such doubts make this a fidgeting book to read. But the publishers have not cheated either Hemingway or us. Even an odd lot of Hemingway is worth a fit of the fidgets."

749 Yardley, Jonathan. "How Papa Grew," review of *Islands, New Republic*, CLXIII (Oct. 10, 1970), 25-26, 30.

"As much as anything else, *Islands in the Stream* seems to have been motivated by an urge to shore up, magnify and embroider the [Hemingway] legend. . . . Artistically it is ordinary postwar Hemingway, with dialogue which parrots Hemingwayisms . . . and prose which lacks the care and resilience of the best short stories. There are some very good passages in the first section, 'Bimini'; the second, 'Cuba,' is a bore; and the third, 'At Sea,' is a diverting adventure tale."

750 Aldridge, John W. "Hemingway Between Triumph and Disaster," review of *Islands, Saturday Review*, LIII (Oct. 10, 1970), 23-26, 39.

". . . the book is neither very good nor very bad. . . . it is both, in some places downright wonderful, in others as sad and embarrassingly self-indulgent as the work of any sophomore. . . . There is a marvellous ocean-fishing sequence in Part I. . . . There are some nicely comic scenes in a Havana bar that are reminiscent of the better moments of *To Have and Have Not*, and the best sustained piece of writing in the book, the long story of the search for the German submariners ending in the gun battle. This is one of the most impressive descriptions of physical action to be found in Hemingway, comparable to the finest of them all, the account of El Sordo's last stand on the hilltop in *For Whom the Bell Tolls*. Yet in spite of the high quality of individual episodes, one still senses a deficiency in the whole. . . ." Reprinted in *The Devil in the Fire*, New York, 1972, pp. 91-100.

751 Raymond, John. "Hemingway: Papa's Sea Epic Is Merely a Draft," review of *Islands, Atlanta Journal and Constitution* (Oct. 11, 1970), p. 8-D.

"To tell the truth, I had to force myself through most of this novel. . . . Not that there is nothing good in the book. The last of its three sections is a tense and exciting sea chase. . . . This new book is Hemingway's writing—sometimes at its best, mostly at its worst—but it is not his novel. . . . I believe he would have cut at least half, maybe two thirds of what we have here. In short, *Islands in the Stream* is more an early draft than a finished novel."

752 Wain, John. "No surprises," review of *Islands, London Observer Review* (Oct. 11, 1970), p. 33.

". . . one thing should be made clear at once. There is nothing new in it—nothing that a seasoned reader of Hemingway has not met before. . . . Each of the three sections ends tragically. This gives the novel its thematic structure—a triple hammer-blow—and also its unifying atmosphere. It is a portrait of a man who feels that his life is going down into a cold sea of disappointment and regret and loneliness. Against them all he has to set is his work and his few remaining physical pleasures. . . . There are a few glutinous passages in the dialogue—Hemingway didn't know how to make children talk, but then neither did Shakespeare. And always there is the sense of *déjà vu*. But that never matters much if you liked what was *vu* in the first place."

753 Connolly, Cyril. "The missing magic," review of *Islands, Sunday Times*, London (Oct. 11, 1970), p. 41.

"Hudson is an unreal character, except in so far as he is Hemingway whom he becomes more and more unashamedly, until in the later chapters he is his Poppa's old intolerable self. The episodes do not achieve the mounting tension at which they aim as Hudson is gradually stripped of everything but his pride. . . . in everything connected with nature—the sky, the shore, above all the sea and its denizens, the reef, boats and boatmen, fish and fisherman—Hemingway's observation is acute, his touch sure."

754 Epstein, Joseph. "The Sun Also Sets: Starring Papa," review of *Islands, Washington Post Book World* (Oct. 11, 1970), pp. 1, 3. Drawing of Hemingway by James McMullan.

"In *Islands in the Stream* one finds very few surprises but most of the old Hemingway moves intact. Although this ample, somewhat rambling, posthumously published novel offers no radical departures from the body of Hemingway's work, its appearance, nonetheless, is salutary for his reputation. . . . What is so useful about the novel's appearance is that it allows us to gauge afresh his achievement and his faults—and in a way that rereading his earlier books, which have all been filmed, discussed, and 'explicated' half to death, no longer allows. . . . as it stands the novel contains all of Hemingway's strengths and weaknesses—his worst, which can be terrible, and his very best, which can be no less than wonderful." Note: This review includes an assessment of Hemingway's present reputation.

754₁ "Papa revisited," *ibid.*, p. 19.

Regarding publication of the Bantam paperback edition of Carlos Baker's *EH: A Life Story.*

755 Wolff, Geoffrey. "Out of the Desk," review of *Islands, Newsweek,* LXXVI (Oct. 12, 1970), 118, 120.

"It is a very bad novel with a few bright moments. Its central character, Thomas Hudson, is a persona for Hemingway. . . . Hemingway's prose is uncharacteristically loose-gaited, as though the author let his attention to it wander. . . . *Islands in the Stream* should be taken for what it is, a curiosity, an unfinished draft whose circumstances are untidy and ambiguous. . . . The first section . . . is much the best. There is a description of a fight against a swordfish that is superb; there are a few passages of inspired comic dialogue. But Thomas Hudson himself is a shadow, a talking machine, an instrument of rote memory, a palimpsest upon which Hemingway writes and erases."

756 Borovik, G. [Foreword to the Russian translation of *Islands,*] *Literaturnaya Gazeta* (Oct. 14, 1970), p. 13. See (S-C65).

757 Mayne, Richard. "Salvage from the Wreck," review of *Islands, Listener,* LXXXIV (Oct. 15, 1970), 522-523.

"In *Islands in the Stream,* Thomas Hudson remains too blank, all lonely pain and no identity, save for the one we suspect. . . . The deep-sea fishing in the first section, on that last golden holiday that Hudson spent with his sons; the pursuit through the *cayos* at the end; the warmth of that 'real discipline without the formalities of discipline which was the rule of the ship'; even some of the wise-cracking in the bars, which largely fills the middle section—these are as good, in isolation, as any similar passages that Hemingway wrote. They don't add up to a novel; but there's treasure trove among the salvage."

758 "Hemingway's unstill waters," review of *Islands, Times Literary Supplement* (Oct. 16, 1970), pp. 1193-1194. Photograph.

"In many obvious ways *Islands in the Stream* is not a good novel —'Cuba,' indeed, is the very worst piece of writing we have seen by Hemingway so far. It is colourless and boring, completely unfunny in the places where the author tries for comedy, and permeated with a particularly unattractive kind of self-pity. 'Bimini' . . . is formless . . . and leaves many loose ends. However, it does contain occasional flashes of good writing, and one or two passages of painful self-analysis, which prevent its being wholly unrewarding. 'At Sea' is much the best section. . . . it is an efficient and at times beautifully written narrative of violent action. . . . It is easy to make damaging criticisms of *Islands in the Stream*, yet it is, with all its weaknesses, the most interesting Hemingway novel to appear since *For Whom the Bell Tolls*. It is free of the grotesque self-parody of *Across the River*, and of the rather wooden heroics of *The Old Man and the Sea*."

759 Updike, John. "Papa's Sad Testament," review of *Islands, New Statesman*, LXXX (Oct. 16, 1970), 489.

"'Bimini' is a collection of episodes that show only a groping acquaintance with one another; 'Cuba' is a lively but meandering excursion in local colour that, when the painter's first wife materialises, weirdly veers into a dark and private region; and 'At Sea' is an adventure story of almost slick intensity. . . . this book opens in a mood of tonic breadth and humour, and closes with a sharp beatific version of himself, Hudson, dying and beloved . . . Hemingway speaks across the Sixties as strangely as a medieval saint; I suspect few readers younger than myself could believe, from this sad broken testament, how we *did* love Hemingway and, after pity feels merely impudent, love him still."

760 Kirsch, Robert. "*Islands in the Stream* a Worthy Addition to the Hemingway Canon," *Los Angeles Times Calendar* (Oct. 18, 1970), p. 46.

"There is no question that it is autobiographical. But then how much of Hemingway's work was not? His favorite themes are here as well. War and the sea, courage and the meaning of life, love and the complexity of relationships. Hemingway is here at his clearest understanding of his world and himself. . . . There are no oversimplifications here. Life is complex and people even more so. Great scenes of deep-sea fishing become parables of experience. . . . Now we know the real power of the novel, not to be judged solely in literary terms but rather as a testament of a man who for all his faults, his occasional childishness, his posturings, was one of the best we ever had, and through his art made us a part of his search."

761 Oldsey, Bernard. "The Novel in the Drawer," review of *Islands, Nation*, CCXI (Oct. 19, 1970), 376, 378.

"For though it is a pleasure to hear Hemingway's voice once again, *Islands in the Stream* is too often mawkish, sentimental and tasteless—particularly in the long dialogue between the protagonist, Thomas Hudson, and a Cuban prostitute called 'Honest Lil,' but also in love scenes between Hudson and his cat Boise, and Hudson and his first wife. . . . From the very beginning the prose is familiarly good, and consistent with the kind of description Hemingway said he learned to do from painters. . . . Ernest Hemingway's semi-professional knowledge of the sea and his novelist's knowledge of men at war make this last section ['At Sea'] worthy of canonization among his battle pieces."

762 Bell, Pearl K. "Hemingway's Abortive Resurrection," review of *Islands, New Leader,* LIII (Oct. 19, 1970), 16-17.

"Only in the final section of the novel does any of the bilge begin to rise above mean water level and seem even dimly recognizable as the work of the master who wrote *A Farewell to Arms* and the wonderfully crafted stories in *In Our Time.* . . . Here the focus is on the action of pursuit, and on the treacherously beautiful coastline—rather than, as earlier, on the stupefyingly sententious narcissism of the Hudson-Hemingway catechism. The prose is readable and, on rare occasion, sinewy and vigorous. . . . it is a pity that *Islands in the Stream*, his dull, pathetic worst, will only obscure Hemingway's true greatness still more."

763 Prescott, Peter S. "Anglers in the Lakes of Darkness," review of *Islands, Look,* XXXIV (Oct. 20, 1970), 24, 26. Caricature of Hemingway by David Levine.

"Hemingway presumably would not have wanted the stories published in this form, but it is good to have them anyway. None is comparable to the story of the old fisherman and his giant marlin, but two of them are interesting and the dreadful middle story has good scenes. What the stories lack as art they gain as autobiography. We must be careful here: This is not autobiography—though perhaps it is closer to it than any of Hemingway's other fiction—but it does show us Hemingway unrevised, almost naked. Amid the fussiness and gaseous banalities, the aging warrior finally is defeated." Reprinted in *Soundings,* New York, 1972, pp. 74-76.

764 Long, Robert Emmet. Review of *Islands, Commonweal,* XCIII (Oct. 23, 1970), 99-100.

"*Islands in the Stream* has without doubt, and perhaps even as its chief pleasure, the grand Hemingway manner—the sharp, chiseled style that has been one of the most admired and imitated in the world and is what one means when one speaks of American prose fiction as 'modern.' . . . Hemingway drifts off at times into lengthy memoire-like recollections which not only do not move the novel along, but give the impression of an imperfect fusion of literary forms. The only thing that really is 'happening' in *Islands in the Stream* is style, style as an end and pleasure in itself and related weakly, if at all, to a compelling human drama. It is as if, in *Islands in the Stream*, Hemingway's art had survived intact and failed only of a subject."

765 Monteiro, Ezio Pinto. "Aproveitomento da paisagem," *O Estado de São Paulo* (Oct. 24, 1970), Suplemento literário, p. 1.

On the use of memory and dream in depicting Santiago's odyssey in *OMATS*.

766 Bradbury, Malcolm. "Broken Stoic," review of *Islands, Manchester Guardian Weekly* (Oct. 24, 1970), p. 18.

"Certainly *Islands in the Stream* should have been published. It's a major addition to the Hemingway canon: worse than the best, but better than the worst. . . . It romanticises (women, male-friends, sons, servants); it aggrandises (Hemingway himself); it justifies some dubious actions. It is also affecting, tragic, suffused with a profound sense of loneliness and loss. What, in part, it lacks is his basic power: the power to contain, through literary and moral controls all the materials to produce an exact line. Hemingway himself helped set that standard for us; and for that reason this book should have a preface indicating how finished Hemingway thought it, and how this text was arrived at."

766₁ Pearson, Anthony. "Hemingway's one that got away," *ibid.*, p. 18.

Regarding chapter IX in *Islands*, which is "devoted to the description of a battle with a big swordfish. It is an epic description. Hemingway writing of something he really understood. . . ."

767 Cosgrave, Patrick. "Religion without God," review of *Islands, Spectator*, CCXXV (Oct. 24, 1970), 476.

"The first episode is remarkable for an epic fight between David, the second son, and a giant swordfish; the third for the most moving and exacting writing about men at war since Hemingway's own *A Farewell to Arms*; the second for destructively self-indulgent writing and thought. . . . Hemingway was a crippled novelist, because his instinct often failed and he never found his absolute value. He was also a great one, for he never abandoned the search. He is certainly the greatest novelist in our language maturing in this century."

768 Igoe, W. J. "No Truck with Tragedy," review of *Islands, Tablet*, CCXXIV (Oct. 24, 1970), 1030.

"It contains his best writing since *To Have and Have Not* yet it is difficult to define simply as a novel. So much derives from the facts of his life, as we have been told them . . . the tragic awareness that was in the core of Hemingway's talent and which he felt heretical. He fought it to the death, his own death. The alternative to the tragic vision, the European thing, is sentimentality. Sustained by the illusion of vanquishing tragedy, he was the master when describing perilous action. . . . No writer of his generation could depict sea and landscapes with the artistry of Hemingway. . . . A very sad, and, with its flaws, rather splendid book."

769 Johnston, Kenneth G., "The Star in Hemingway's *The Old Man and the Sea,*" *American Literature,* XLII (Nov. 1970), 388-391.
Regarding the reference to the star Rigel in *OMATS.*

769₁ Baker, Carlos. Review of Delbert E. Wylder's *Hemingway's Heroes, ibid.,* pp. 417-418.

770 Thiébeauld, Sylvie. Brief review of Audre Hanneman's *EH: A Comprehensive Bibliography, Bulletin des bibliothèques de France,* XV (Nov. 1970), Item 2455.

771 Review of *EH, Cub Reporter* edited by Matthew J. Bruccoli, *Choice,* VII (Nov. 1970), 1223.
"This slim volume includes 11 previously uncollected Hemingway news stories. They are a small part of his seven months work (Oct. 1917-April 1918) for the Kansas City *Star.* The pieces illustrate Hemingway's early desire to go beyond straight reporting in his use of color and feeling. Here, too, are important examples of Hemingway's first attempts to deal with death and violence in terse prose and 'controlled sentiment.' The short works show some problems of syntax but otherwise an unusual amount of maturity for an 18-year-old writer."

772 Donadio, Stephen. "Hemingway," review of *Islands, Commentary,* L (Nov. 1970), 93-99.
"It was this last section which Hemingway had the most difficulty writing, but there is a quality of insomnia about the novel as a whole, an edge of desperation reminiscent of a man driving himself beyond exhaustion. The resulting combination of determination and distractedness probably accounts for the book's uneven momentum: the narrative often seems slightly out of control, as if it had begun growing with a life of its own, bulging out in strange and unexpected blossoms which are then cut back, only to reappear after a time like the heads of the Hydra. . . . The real interest of *Islands in the Stream* lies in the emotional life trapped but stirring restlessly beneath its surface, a life which it manages to convey through these passages of prose cut loose and flowing free of the particular events of the plot: the events themselves are often (especially in Part III) presented without conviction."

773 Lovering, J. Review of *Islands, Best Sellers*, xxx (Nov. 1, 1970), 321.

"The work is . . . composed of three distinct, and loosely ligated, narrative sequences. . . . The events in 'Bimini' bring overtones and suggestions of several other Hemingway works. There is the fighting and brawling of *To Have and Have Not*. There is the reminiscence of Parisian days [which has] a flavoring of *A Moveable Feast*. When a great broadbill strikes David's fishing line there is a long narrative sequence of the young man's desperate fight to land the fish and of his final failure, which suggests some of the movement and a little of the magic of *The Old Man and the Sea*. But all these resemblances to other Hemingway performances never come close to uniting 'Bimini' into a truly successful piece by itself. It is essentially an uneven work. . . . 'At Sea' picks up in narrative interest and pace and it brings to conclusion the death theme. But again there is a slackness about this section that reminds us that Hemingway has done it all so much better on so many other occasions."

774 Fuller, Edmund. "Hemingway: The Good and the Bad," review of *Islands, Wall Street Journal* (Nov. 3, 1970), p. 10.

". . . the 34-odd pages in which the young boy David, middle son of the book's central figure Thomas Hudson, fights a long battle at sea with a Goliath of a broadbill swordfish . . . might be called 'The Young Boy and the Sea.' Beautifully done, marred only by characteristic out-croppings of sentimentality, it is prime Hemingway. . . . What dismays one in the weak start of the book, and recurs from time to time, is the badness of much minor dialogue, some of which is unconscious self-parody of the most extreme sort. . . . In contrast, in description, especially of the sea and islands, he is good consistently. . . . What ultimately makes *Islands in the Stream* rewarding and worth publishing in spite of its flaws is the unique personal stamp on both its best and its worst. It is pure Hemingway, and there are scenes and passages as good as anything in his work. When he is bad it is the idiosyncratic badness of a great writer which is quite another thing than the badness of mediocrity."

775 Corbett, Edward P. J. Review of *Islands, America*, cxxiii (Nov. 7, 1970), 382-384.

"A fervent reader and admirer of Ernest Hemingway for over a quarter of a century, I find it painful to admit that this novel will do little to enhance Hemingway's reputation but may do a great deal to diminish it. . . . The finest piece in [Part i, 'Bimini']—in fact the best piece in the novel—is the 30-page account of young David's struggle to land a swordfish. . . . Part ii, 'Cuba,' is an utter bore. . . . Part iii, 'At Sea,' gets us back to what Hemingway was always able to manage best, muscular action. . . . Thomas Hudson is a thinly disguised *alter ego* for Ernest Hemingway. And that fact is probably the main reason for the weaknesses of this novel—not to mention its virtues. . . . Let us hold fast to our memories of the bright young Ernest and the unposturing heroes of *The Sun Also Rises* and the superb short stories."

776 Manfred, Frederick. Letters column, *"Islands in the Stream," N.Y. Times Book Review* (Nov. 8, 1970), p. 34.

Regarding adverse reviews of *Islands* by "turkey-buzzards" feeding on the "literary carcass" of Hemingway.

777 Davenport, Guy. "Hemingway as Walter Pater," review of *Islands, National Review*, xxii (Nov. 17, 1970), 1214-1215.

"Hemingway would have been the Walter Pater *de nos jours* if he had not committed himself for 35 years to a grey, low-voiced, plain prose of severely limited flexibility and puritanical restraint. . . . Using the same, the only prose he ever wrote, apparently not noticing that it is utterly inappropriate for the tale he's telling, Hemingway has scooped together a rigmarole of his favorite themes, and strung them out like so much washing on the line. And yet this late, wordy, shapeless novel is readable; it is still the old Hemingway of the battlefields, the cafés, the bitchy women, the mercurochrome. It is not Hemingway, but the world that has changed."

778 Cowley, Malcolm. "A Double Life, Half Told," review of *Islands, Atlantic*, ccxxvi (Dec. 1970), 105-106, 108.

"Having read most of the original manuscript, I can say with conviction that their [Mary Hemingway and Charles Scribner, Jr.] decisions have been wise ones: first to publish the stories together; then to make some omissions, the longest of which is an interlude in Florida, good enough in itself, that would have made the book less unified; and finally, to make no other changes except in Ernest's erratic spelling and punctuation. One is delighted to have the book in its present form. . . . it is a bold, often funny, always swashbuckling book that only Hemingway could have written. It gives one a new respect for the efforts of his later years. Handicapped as he was by injuries and admirers, he continued almost to the end a double life, playing the great man in public—and playing the part superbly—then standing alone at his worktable, humble and persistent, while he tried to summon back his early powers."

779 Review of Richard K. Peterson's *Hemingway: Direct and Oblique, Choice*, vii (Dec. 1970), 1377.

780 Kraus, W. Keith. "Ernest Hemingway's 'Hills Like White Elephants': A Note on a 'Reasonable Source,'" *English Record*, xxi (Dec. 1970), 23-27.

781 Hartwell, Ronald. "What Hemingway Learned from Ambrose Bierce," *Research Studies* (Washington State University), XXXVIII (Dec. 1970), 309-311.

782 Barry, Bill. "The Key West Days of Ernest Hemingway," *Boston Globe Sunday Magazine* (Dec. 13, 1970), pp. 16-26.

783 Kobler, J. F. "Hemingway's 'The Sea Change': A Sympathetic View of Homosexuality," *Arizona Quarterly*, XXVI (Winter 1970), 318-324.

783₁ Bunnell, Walter A. "Who Wrote the Paris Idyll? The Place and Function of *A Moveable Feast* in the Writing of Ernest Hemingway," *ibid.*, pp. 334-346.

784 Young, Philip. "Locked in The Vault with Hemingway," *Rendezvous*, V (Winter 1970), 1-5. Special Hemingway issue.
Essay on the Hemingway manuscripts, reprinted in an updated and revised form from the *N.Y. Times Book Review* (Sept. 29, 1968). Reprinted in *Three Bags Full*, New York, 1972, pp. 68-75.

784₁ Studebaker, William. "I Hemingway," a poem, *ibid.*, pp. 5-6.

784₂ "Father L. M. Dougherty Talks About Ernest Hemingway," *ibid.*, pp. 7-17.
Reminiscences of Hemingway in Idaho. Transcribed from tape recordings conducted by Waller and Rosemary Wigginton.

784₃ Berry, Frank W. "Looking for Hemingway," poem, *ibid.*, p. 18.

784₄ Lewis, Robert W., Jr. "Hemingway's Concept of Sport and 'Soldier's Home,' " *ibid.*, pp. 19-27.

784₅ Wampler, Martin. "Kilimanjaro Near Sun Valley," poem, *ibid.*, p. 28.

784₆ Wylder, D. E. "Hemingway's Satiric Vision—The High School Years," *ibid.*, pp. 29-35.

784₇ Obermayer, Lorna. Drawing of Hemingway, *ibid.*, p. 36.

784₈ Benson, Jackson J. "Patterns of Connection and Their Development in Hemingway's *In Our Time*," *ibid.*, pp. 37-52.

784₉ Etulain, Richard. "Ernest Hemingway and His Interpreters of The 1960's," *ibid.*, pp. 53-70.

785 Brenner, Gerry. "Epic Machinery in Hemingway's *For Whom the Bell Tolls*," *Modern Fiction Studies*, XVI (Winter 1970-1971), 491-504.

786 Smith, Julian. "Hemingway and The Thing Left Out," *Journal of Modern Literature*, I, ii (1970-1971), 169-182.

This essay concludes that "through omission Hemingway has succeeded in the goal he stated in *A Moveable Feast*: to 'make people feel something more than they understood.' "

787 Bryer, Jackson R. "Fitzgerald and Hemingway," *American Literary Scholarship: An Annual/1971*, pp. 120-145.

788 Meindl, Dieter. Review of Audre Hanneman's *EH: A Comprehensive Bibliography, Anglia*, LXXXIX, ii (1971), 276-279.

789 Ano, Fumio. "Hemingway and Politics," *Bulletin of the College of General Education of Tohoku University*, XII, ii (1971), 105-120. In Japanese, with a summary in English.

790 Bluefarb, Sam. "The Search for the Absolute in Hemingway's 'A Clean, Well-Lighted Place' and 'The Snows of Kilimanjaro,' " *Bulletin of the Rocky Mountain Modern Language Association*, XXV (1971), 3-9.

790₁ Bocaz, Sergio H. "*El ingenioso hidalgo Don Quijote de la Mancha* and *The Old Man and the Sea*: A Study of the Symbolic Essence of Man in Cervantes and Hemingway," *ibid.*, pp. 49-54.

791 Cordesse, Gérard. "De la castration dans *Le soleil se lève aussi*," *Caliban*, VIII (1971), 89-99.

792 Vančura, Zdeněk. "Současni američtí romanopisci, 4: Posmrtný Hemingway" [Some contemporary American novelists, 4: The posthumous Hemingway], *Časopis pro Moderní Filologii: Literatura*, LIII, iii (1971), 109-115. Summary in English, on pp. 114-115.

793 Stewart, Donald Ogden. "Recollections of Fitzgerald and Hemingway," *Fitzgerald/Hemingway Annual: 1971*, pp. 177-188.
Excerpts from the author's autobiography-in-progress.

793₁ Clark, C. E. Frazer, Jr. "La Vie est beau avec Papa," *ibid.*, pp. 189-193. Facsimiles of the front and back cover of the As Stable pamphlet *Today is Friday* and a two-page inscription.
Background information on the inscribed copy of *Today is Friday* that Hemingway sent to Gerald and Sara Murphy in 1926.

793₂ Kashkeen, Ivan. "Letters of Ernest Hemingway to Soviet Writers," *ibid.*, pp. 197-208. Reprinted from *Soviet Literature*, No. 11 (Nov. 1962). For Hemingway's letters, see (S-F79), (S-F88), (S-F91), and (S-F96).

793₃ Ficken, Carl. "Point of View in the Nick Adams Stories," *ibid.*, pp. 212-235.

793₄ Clark, C. E. Frazer, Jr. "The Crosby Copy of *In Our Time*," *ibid.*, pp. 237-258. Facsimile of Hemingway's inscription to Harry Crosby.

7935 Walz, Lawrence A. " 'The Snows of Kilimanjaro': A New Reading," *ibid.*, pp. 239-245.

7936 Greiner, Donald J. "Emerson, Thoreau, and Hemingway: Some Suggestions About Literary Heritage," *ibid.*, pp. 247-261.

7937 Mosher, Harold F., Jr. "The Two Styles of Hemingway's *The Sun Also Rises*," *ibid.*, pp. 262-273.

7938 Grenberg, Bruce L. "The Design of Heroism in *The Sun Also Rises*," *ibid.*, pp. 274-289.

7939 Drew, Fraser. "Recollections of a Hemingway Collector," *ibid.*, pp. 294-297.

793₁₀ Alexander, Archibald S. "Collecting Hemingway," *ibid.*, pp. 298-301.

793₁₁ Ewell, Nathaniel M., III. "Dialogue in Hemingway's 'A Clean, Well-Lighted Place,' " *ibid.*, pp. 305-306. See note under (S-A7F).

793₁₂ Monteiro, George. "Not Hemingway But Spain," *ibid.*, pp. 309-311.
   Regarding the silent truncation of the waiter's *nada* prayers in "A Clean, Well-Lighted Place" in *Relatos*, Barcelona, 1957. See (D326).

793₁₃ Nash, Ogden. "A Bunch of Bananas," *ibid.*, p. 313.
   A letter regarding the song Nash wrote at the time of Hemingway's two plane crashes in Africa in 1954.

793₁₄ "A Letter from Malcolm Cowley," *ibid.*, pp. 317-318.
   Regarding the Viking Portable *Hemingway*. See (A22).

793₁₅ Wilcox, Earl. "Jake and Bob and Huck and Tom: Hemingway's Use of *Huck Finn*," *ibid.*, pp. 322-324.
   On *SAR*.

793₁₆ Anderson, William R., Jr. "*Islands in the Stream*—The Initial Reception," *ibid.*, pp. 326-332. Includes a Checklist of Reviews, on pp. 330-332.

793₁₇ "M.J.B." [Matthew J. Bruccoli]. "Ole Anderson, Ole Andreson and Carl Andreson," *ibid.*, p. 341.
   A note on "The Killers."

793₁₈ Hanneman, Audre. "Hanneman Addenda," *ibid.*, pp. 343-346.
   A checklist of recently published work by Hemingway.

794 Kruse, Horst. "Ernest Hemingways Kunst der Allegorie: Zeitgenössische, literarische und biblische Anspielungen in 'God Rest You Merry, Gentlemen,' " *Jahrbuch für Amerikastudien*, XVI (1971), 128-150.

795 Johnston, Kenneth G. "Hemingway's 'Out of Season' and the Psychology of Errors," *Literature & Psychology*, XXI, i (1971), 41-46.

796 Baker, Carlos. "Hemingway and Princeton," *Princeton History*, No. 1 (1971), pp. 39-49. Photographs.

Discusses Hemingway's association with Princetonians, including William Horne, Mike Strater, F. Scott Fitzgerald, Edmund Wilson, Charles Scribner, Harold Loeb, Lee Samuels, Gelston Hardy, Andrew Turnbull, and Charles Scribner, Jr. Hemingway attended the Princeton-Yale game, with Fitzgerald, in November 1928.

797 Cor, Laurence W. "Hemingway, Montherlant, and 'Animal Tragedy,'" *Proceedings: Pacific Northwest Conference on Foreign Languages*, XXII (1971), 202-207.

798 Miller, Owen J. "Camus et Hemingway: pour une évaluation méthodologique," *Revue des Lettres Modernes*, No. 3 (1971), 9-42.

799 Review of *Islands*, *Virginia Quarterly Review*, XLVII (Winter 1971), viii.

"Hemingway's mesomorphic hero, as inescapably autobiographical as in all the previous books, has the simple appeal and force of a folk-figure battling fellow creatures or the forces of nature with grim fortitude."

800 Rovit, Earl. Review of Richard K. Peterson's *Hemingway, Direct and Oblique*, *American Literature*, XLII (Jan. 1971), 596-597.

801 Baldwin, Kenneth Huntress, Jr. "Autobiography as Art: An Essay Illustrated by Studies of the Autobiographies of Henry Adams, Ernest Hemingway, and Vladimir Nabokov," *Dissertation Abstracts International*, XXXI (Jan. 1971), 3538-A.

Abstract from a doctoral dissertation, Johns Hopkins University, 1970. Examines *AMF* as Hemingway's version of the theme of the education of the artist.

802 Gaillard, Theodore L., Jr. "The Critical Menagerie in 'The Short Happy Life of Francis Macomber,'" *English Journal*, LX (Jan. 1971), 31-35.

803 Lodge, David. "Hemingway's Clean, Well-lighted, Puzzling Place," *Essays in Criticism*, XXI (Jan. 1971), 33-56.

Discussion of the inconsistency in the dialogue between the two waiters in "A Clean, Well-Lighted Place," which Scribner's emended in their 1967 edition of *The Short Stories of Ernest Hemingway*. See note under (S-A7F). Reprinted in *The Novelist at the Crossroads*, Ithaca, New York, 1971, pp. 184-202.

804 Davison, Richard Allan. "Carelessness and the Cincinnati Reds in *The Old Man and the Sea*," *Notes on Contemporary Literature*, I (Jan. 1971), 11-13.

Regarding Hemingway's inaccuracy in Santiago's reference to the Cincinnati Reds as if they were in the American League.

805 Wilson, Edmund. "An Effort at Self-Revelation," review of *Islands*, *New Yorker*, XLVI (Jan. 2, 1971), 59-62.

". . . with all its preposterous elements, this imperfect work, *Islands in the Stream*, makes one feel the intensity of a crucial game played against invincible odds as one has not quite been able to do in connection with any of his last three finished novels—*For Whom the Bell Tolls, Across the River and Into the Trees, The Old Man and the Sea*. It has never been pulled tight or polished, as Hemingway would undoubtedly have done, for his sense of form was exacting. Everything goes on too long, even the most effective episodes. . . . These would all—if Hemingway had taken time to treat them with his characteristic technique—have surely been condensed to far fewer pages. . . . This book contains some of the best of Hemingway's descriptions of nature. . . . I do not agree with those who have thought it a disservice to Hemingway's memory to publish this uncompleted book. . . . I imagine that this book, in the long run, will appear to be more important than seems to be the case at present, and I believe that Mrs. Hemingway is to be encouraged to go on to publish further manuscripts." Reprinted in *The Devils and Canon Barham*, New York, 1973, pp. 105-111.

806 "Hemingway Help," *Washington Post* (Jan. 5, 1971), p. C6.

Regarding the publication of F. Scott Fitzgerald's letter to Hemingway, urging changes in *SAR*, in the *Fitzgerald/Hemingway Annual: 1970*.

807 Toop, Ronald Glenson. "Technique and Vision in the Fiction of Ernest Hemingway: A Chronological Study," *Dissertation Abstracts International*, XXXI (Feb. 1971), 4181-A to 4182-A.

Abstract from a doctoral dissertation, University of Toronto, 1969.

808 Theroux, Paul. "Lord of the Ring: Hemingway's 'Last Novel,' " review of *Islands, Encounter*, XXXVI (Feb. 1971), 62-66.

"The Hemingway stamp, that cauliflower earmark that characterises his worst fiction, is everywhere apparent. . . . [Thomas Hudson] is an embittered, heartless, unquestioning and deluded man. Physical superiority is what Hudson cares about, but he is old and life is unbearable for him. The disappointment and the sour regret give the novel the tone of a suicide note. It is sad to think that Hemingway wrote it, and understandable that he left it in a bottom drawer."

809 Livingston, Howard. "Religious Intrusion in Hemingway's 'The Killers,' " *English Record,* XXI (Feb. 1971), 42-45.

810 Davison, Richard Allan. "Hemingway's *A Farewell to Arms*," *Explicator,* XXIX (Feb. 1971), Item 46.
On religious symbolism in *FTA.*

811 Perelman, S. J. "The Machismo Mystique, or Some Various Aspects of Masculinity, as Demonstrated by Ernest Hemingway, Mike Todd, F. Scott Fitzgerald, and a Sensuous Shrimp from Providence, Rhode Island," *McCall's,* XCVIII (Feb. 1971), 88-89, 168-169.

812 Hess, John. "Jack Hemingway Remembers His Father," *National Wildlife,* IX (Feb.-March 1971), 12-15. Photographs.
Interview with Jack Hemingway in Sun Valley. Hemingway is described as "one of the early ecologists," and his conservation habits were passed on to his three sons.

813 Butwin, David. Booked for Travel column, "Turning the Keys," *Saturday Review,* LIV (Feb. 27, 1971), 38-40.
Regarding Hemingway's home in Key West. Includes reminiscences of Hemingway by Toby Bruce, "who served the writer as secretary, boat captain, traveling companion, and friend."

814 McLain, Charles Mansfield. "A Syntactic Study of Four Non-Fiction Books by John Steinbeck and Ernest Hemingway," *Dissertation Abstracts International,* XXXI (March 1971), 4726-A.
Abstract from a doctoral dissertation, University of Colorado, 1970. Examines *GHOA* and *AMF.*

814₁ Oliver, Charles Montgomery, II. "Principles of 'True Felt Emotion' in Hemingway's Novels," *ibid.,* p. 4787-A.
Abstract from a doctoral dissertation, Bowling Green State University, 1970.

815 Stone, Edward. "Hemingway's Mr. Frazer: From Revolution to Radio," *Journal of Modern Literature,* I (March 1971), 375-388.
Study of "The Gambler, the Nun, and the Radio."

815₁ Lewis, Robert W., Jr. "The Survival of Hemingway," *ibid.,* pp. 446-453.
Reviews of Jackson J. Benson's *Hemingway: The Writer's Art of Self-Defense,* Richard B. Hovey's *Hemingway: The Inward Terrain,* and Delbert E. Wylder's *Hemingway's Heroes.*

816 Gordon, David J. Review of *Islands, Yale Review,* LX (March 1971), 429-430.

"Hemingway's posthumously published *Islands in the Stream* was written for the most part between *For Whom the Bell Tolls* and *Across the River and Into the Trees*, and, though in most ways lamentable, is a better book than either. To be sure, its three long Caribbean episodes . . . are saturated in vanity and self-pity."

817   White, William. "Supplement to Hanneman: Articles, 1966-1970," *Hemingway notes*, I (Spring 1971), 3-12. Cover drawing of Hemingway, by Waldo Peirce, reproduced from the *Saturday Review of Literature*, VI (Oct. 12, 1929).

817₁   Monteiro, George. " 'Between Grief and Nothing': Hemingway and Faulkner," *ibid.*, pp. 13-15.
    Regarding Hemingway's "borrowing" from the ending of the title portion of William Faulkner's *The Wild Palms* for the ending of *FWBT*.

817₂   Ramsey, Paul. "Elegy for Ernest Hemingway," poem, *ibid.*, p. 16.

817₃   Warner, Fred. "Hemingway's Death: Ten Years Later," *ibid.*, pp. 16-19.

817₄   Murphy, George D. "Hemingway's *Waste Land*: The Controlling Water Symbolism of *The Sun Also Rises*," *ibid.*, pp. 20-26.

818   Cruttwell, Patrick. Review of *Islands, Hudson Review*, XXIV (Spring 1971), 180.
    "I found *Islands in the Stream* an appallingly depressing—indeed, in the end, an unreadable—volume: such a sad tired mechanical rehashing of what its author has done so often before, such a mindless round of drinking, fishing, killing, fornicating, and talking about nothing but these things. It is terrible to see what success and adulation had done to the man who wrote *In Our Time* and *The Sun Also Rises*. Yet I suppose the germs of the global disaster which Hemingway at last turned into were there from the start. . . . Hemingway *never* had it in him to be a great and lifelong novelist. For what he truly was, was a minor romantic poet. As much as Wordsworth's, all Hemingway's good work seems to have derived directly from certain vital experiences in childhood and early manhood; away from these, he stumbled and blustered and self-parodied himself into a creature that certainly tickled the groundlings but more and more made the judicious weep."

819   Hauger, B. A. "First Person Perspective in Four Hemingway Stories," *Rendezvous*, VI (Spring 1971), 29-38.
    Examines "My Old Man," "Fifty Grand," "Now I Lay Me," and "An Alpine Idyll."

820   Ditsky, John. "Hemingway, Plato and *The Hidden God*," *Southern Humanities Review*, V (Spring 1971), 145-147.

Regarding Cleanth Brooks' discussion in *The Hidden God* (New Haven, 1963) of the Christian concepts and Hemingway's "code of manhood."

821 May, Charles E. "Is Hemingway's 'Well-Lighted Place' Really Clean Now?" *Studies in Short Fiction*, VIII (Spring 1971), 326-330.

822 Review of *Islands, Choice,* VIII (April 1971), 224.
"This large novel contains the usual terse Hemingway dialogue and his sharply-etched characterizations. Like Hemingway's last two heroes, Cantwell and Santiago, Hudson now remembers as much as he acts."

823 Cody, Morrill. "*The Sun Also Rises* Revisited," *Connecticut Review,* IV (April 1971), 5-8.
Recalls the "real characters" behind Hemingway's novel. Reprinted in Bertram D. Sarason's *Hemingway and The Sun Set,* Washington, D.C., 1972, pp. 265-270.

823₁ Smith, Julian. "Eyeless in Wyoming, Blind in Venice—Hemingway's Last Stories," *ibid.*, pp. 9-15.
Examines "A Man of the World" and "Get a Seeing-Eyed Dog" as examples of Hemingway's "most powerful and typical theme: endurance under pressure."

823₂ Fitz, Reginald. "The Meaning of Impotence in Hemingway and Eliot," *ibid.*, pp. 16-22.

823₃ St. John, Donald. "Mr. and Mrs. Donald Ogden Stewart Abroad," *ibid.*, pp. 23-36.
Describes a visit with the Stewarts in London. Stewart was one of the models for Bill Gorton in *SAR.*

823₄ Bryer, Jackson R. Review of the *Fitzgerald/Hemingway Annual: 1970* edited by Matthew J. Bruccoli and C. E. Frazer Clark, Jr., *ibid.*, pp. 37-40.

824 Laurence, Frank Michael. "The Film Adaptations of Hemingway: Hollywood and the Hemingway Myth," *Dissertation Abstracts International,* XXXI (April 1971), 5411-A.
Abstract from a doctoral dissertation, University of Pennsylvania, 1970.

825 Farrington, Kip. "Remembering Great Men And Great Fish," *Field & Stream,* LXXV (April 1971), 54-55, 161-166.
Excerpts from *Fishing with Hemingway and Glassell,* New York, 1971. See also (S-B12) and (S-C69).

826 Cosgrave, Mary Silva. Review of *Islands, Horn Book,* XLVII (April 1971), 189.

"The old magic is still to be found in the novelist's humor, his descriptions, his ribaldry and bravado, his fantasies and anecdotes."

827 Gutkind, Lee Alan. "The Young Man and the Mountains," *Miami Herald* (April 4, 1971), *Tropic*, the Sunday Magazine section, pp. 12-16.

On Hemingway's trips to Wyoming in the late 1920s and the 1930s.

828 Bassett, Charles W. "Katahdin, Wachusett, and Kilimanjaro: The Symbolic Mountains of Thoreau and Hemingway," *Thoreau Journal Quarterly*, III (April 15, 1971), 1-10.

829 Bondy, Barbara. "Hemingway: *Wem die Stunde schlägt*: Schlafsack-Gespräche," *Süddeutsche Zeitung* (April 17-18, 1971).

829₁ Leicht, Robert. "Hemingway: *Wem die Stunde schlägt*: Von den Schönheiten eines Bürgerkriegs," *ibid.*

830 "G. C." [Guido Ceronetti]. "Ernest Hemingway: Per chi suona la campana," *L'Espresso*, No. 17 (April 25, 1971), pp. 10-11. Photograph in color on pp. 8-9. Note: The overall title for short articles on thirty novelists is "Freschi di stampa."

831 Coyne, John R., Jr. "Isn't it Pretty to Think So?" review of *Islands*, *Alternative*, IV (May 1971), 16-17. Cover caricature of Hemingway by Eric Lohnaas.

"*Islands in the Stream* is a first-rate piece of writing. *Islands* is actually a trilogy consisting of three loosely related novels. . . . Each novel shows a mature Hemingway doing the things he does best better than he ever did them before. The dialogue between Hudson and Honest Lil the whore as they sit drinking in Havana's Floridita Bar, is as good as any of the exchanges between Brett Ashley and Jake Barnes. But the conversations in 'Bimini' [Part One] between Hudson and his friend Roger Davis even top the wisecrackingly profound dialogue from the trout-fishing interlude in *The Sun Also Rises*—a dialogue I've always regarded as the single best piece of writing in American literature."

832 Schmidt, Dolores Barracano. "The Great American Bitch," *College English*, XXXII (May 1971), 900-905.

Study of the anti-heroine in the works of Hemingway, Sinclair Lewis, and F. Scott Fitzgerald.

833 O'Brien, Richard Michael. "The Thematic Interrelation of the Concepts of Time and Thought in the Works of Ernest Hemingway," *Dissertation Abstracts International*, XXXI (May 1971), 6066-A to 6067-A.

Abstract from a doctoral dissertation, New York University, 1969.

834 Johnston, Kenneth G. "Hemingway and Mantegna: The Bitter Nail Holes," *Journal of Narrative Technique*, I (May 1971), 86-94.

On Hemingway's allusions to Andrea Mantegna's painting, "The Dead Christ," in *FTA* and "The Revolutionist."

835 Bartlet, Norman. "Hemingway: The Hero as Self," *Quadrant*, xv (May-June 1971), 13-20.

836 Neyman, Mark. Review of S. Kip Farrington's *Fishing with Hemingway and Glassell, Library Journal*, xcvi (May 15, 1971), 1724.

837 Yalom, Irvin D., and Marilyn Yalom. "Ernest Hemingway—A Psychiatric View," *Archives of General Psychiatry*, xxiv (June 1971), 485-494.

838 Maynard, Reid Norris. "The Writer and Experience: Ernest Hemingway's Views on the Craft of Fiction," *Dissertation Abstracts International*, xxxi (June 1971), 6620-A.

Abstract from a doctoral dissertation, University of California at Davis, 1970.

838₁ Pearson, Roger Luke. "The Play-Game Element in the Major Works of Ernest Hemingway," *ibid.*, pp. 6625-A to 6626-A.

Abstract from a doctoral dissertation, University of Massachusetts, 1970.

838₂ Silverman, Raymond Joel. "The Short Story Composite: Forms, Functions, and Applications," *ibid.*, p. 6633-A.

Abstract from a doctoral dissertation, University of Michigan, 1970. Examines *IOT*.

839 Maynard, Reid. "Leitmotif and Irony in Hemingway's 'Hills Like White Elephants,' " *University Review* (Kansas City), xxxvii (June 1971), 273-275.

840 McCabe, Bruce. "JFK Library Prize: Hemingway Papers," *Boston Globe* (June 4, 1971), pp. 1, 5.

Interview with Mary Hemingway. The collection to be presented to the Kennedy Library, in Cambridge, "will include all of Hemingway's original manuscripts except *The Sun Also Rises*."

841 Weber, Ronald. "Hemingway's Michigan: Where Nature Became the Metaphor," *N.Y. Times* (June 6, 1971), Sec. 10, pp. 35, 45. Note: An article on D. H. Lawrence appeared on the same page, the overall heading was: "An Unlikely Twosome of Literary Tours: D.H.L. and 'Papa.' "

842 Howell, John M. "Hemingway's Riddle and Kilimanjaro's Reusch," *Studies in Short Fiction*, viii (Summer 1971), 469-470.

A letter from Richard Reusch, regarding the leopard carcass on Kilimanjaro, is reprinted from *Hemingway's African Stories*, New York, 1969, pp. 99-100.

843 Gottlieb, Carole Patricia. "The Armored Self: A Study of Compassion and Control in *The Great Gatsby* and *The Sun Also Rises*," *Dissertation Abstracts International*, XXXII (July 1971), 429-A to 430-A.
Abstract from a doctoral dissertation, University of Washington, 1970.

843₁ Pomeroy, Charles William. "Soviet Russian Criticism 1960-1969 of Seven Twentieth Century American Novelists," *ibid.*, p. 449-A.
Abstract from a doctoral dissertation, University of Southern California, 1971. Examines Soviet criticism of *FWBT* and the debate that preceded its first Russian publication in 1968.

844 Peckham, Morse. "Ernest Hemingway: Sexual Themes in Hemingway's Writing," *Sexual Behavior*, I (July 1971), 62-70.

845 Frazier, George. "Hemingway: July 2, 1961," *Boston Globe* (July 2, 1971), p. 36.

846 Starrett, Vincent. "Where's Papa: Ernest Hemingway, a Remembrance and Reevaluation," *Chicago Tribune Sunday Magazine* (July 18, 1971), pp. 26, 28, 30, 32, 39. Photographs.
A critical and biographical essay, in which the author recalls once meeting Hemingway, with Sherwood Anderson, in Chicago.

847 Newman, M. W. "The Earliest Hemingway: 'A born genius' at Oak Park High School," *Chicago Daily News* (July 31–Aug. 1, 1971), Panorama section, pp. 4-5. See also (S-C70).

848 Dean, Anthony Bruce. "Hemingway's Fiction: A Tragic Vision of Life," *Dissertation Abstracts International*, XXXII (Aug. 1971), 961-A.
Abstract from a doctoral dissertation, Temple University, 1971.

848₁ Somers, Paul Preston, Jr. "Sherwood Anderson and Ernest Hemingway: Influences and Parallels," *ibid.*, p. 985-A.
Abstract from a doctoral dissertation, Pennsylvania State University, 1970.

849 Sharma, D. R. "Moral Frontiers of Ernest Hemingway," *Panjab University Research Bulletin*, II (Aug. 1971), 49-59.

850 Weber, Ronald. "A Pilgrim Reports from Hemingway's Michigan (Have They Really Forgotten?)," *Detroit Free Press Magazine* (Aug. 22, 1971), pp. 19-22.

851 "'Häng dich auf, tapferer Hemingstein!'" *Der Spiegel*, XXV (Aug. 23, 1971), 96-97.

Regarding Irvin and Marilyn Yalom's psychoanalytic study in *Archives of General Psychiatry*, XXIV (June 1971).

852 Reynolds, Michael Shane. "A Historical Study of Hemingway's *A Farewell to Arms*," *Dissertation Abstracts International*, XXXII (Sept. 1971), 1525-A to 1526-A.

Abstract from a doctoral dissertation, Duke University, 1971.

853 Martine, James J. "Hemingway's 'Fifty Grand': The Other Fight(s)," *Journal of Modern Literature*, II (Sept. 1971), 123-127.

Argues that Hemingway's fictional Jack Brennan-Jimmy Walcott fight is "an amalgamation of at least two real-life bouts": the Siki-Carpentier fight, which Hemingway saw in Paris on September 24, 1922, and the Jack Britton-Mickey Walker fight, which took place in New York on November 1, 1922.

854 Crane, Joan St.C. "Rare or Seldom-Seen Dust Jackets of American First Editions: VI," *Serif*, VIII (Sept. 1971), 29-31.

Descriptions of dust jackets of *IOT* (Boni & Liveright, 1925) and *TOS* (Scribner's, 1926, and Crosby Continental Editions, 1932).

855 Hotchner, A. E. "The Guns of Hemingway," *True*, LII (Sept. 1971), 48-49, 51-52, 54.

On hunting in Cuba and Idaho with Hemingway. See This Is *True* column, p. 4, for background material on this article. See Forrest MacMullen's letter, reproduced in the *Fitzgerald/Hemingway Annual: 1972*, p. 289, regarding this article.

856 Nelson, Harry. "Hemingway and His Own Image," *Washington Post* (Sept. 2, 1971), p. 6-C.

857 Editorial. "Hemingway on the Couch," *Pittsburgh Post-Gazette* (Sept. 28, 1971), p. 10.

Regarding Irvin and Marilyn Yalom's theory in *Archives of General Psychiatry*, XXIV (June 1971), that Hemingway's masculine self-image was "so extreme that superhuman forces would have been required to satisfy it."

858 White, William. "Hemingway on Postage Stamps," *Hemingway notes*, 1 (Fall 1971), 3-4. Czechoslovakian stamp with caricature of Hemingway reproduced on front cover.

858₁ Doxey, William S. "The Significance of Seney, Michigan, in Hemingway's 'Big Two-Hearted River,' " *ibid.*, 5-6.

858₂ Photograph of a bust of Hemingway, which was sculpted by James Gardner for the Gale Research Company, *ibid.*, p. 6.

858₃ Johnston, Kenneth G. "The Great Awakening: Nick Adams and the Silkworms in 'Now I Lay Me,' " *ibid.*, pp. 7-9.

858₄ "T. A." [Taylor Alderman], "K. R." [Kenneth Rosen], and "W. W." [William White]. Current Bibliography, *ibid.*, pp. 10-13.

858₅ Greiner, Donald J. "The Education of Robert Jordan: Death with Dignity," *ibid.*, pp. 14-20.

858₆ Hays, Peter L. " 'Soldier's Home' and Ford Madox Ford," *ibid.*, pp. 21-22.

858₇ Review of *Ernest Hemingway's Apprenticeship* edited by Matthew J. Bruccoli, *ibid.*, pp. 22-23.

859 Kaufmann, Donald L. "The Long Happy Life of Norman Mailer," *Modern Fiction Studies*, XVII (Autumn 1971), 347-359.
A study of the similarities and dissimilarities between Mailer and Hemingway.

860 Ganzel, Dewey. "*A Farewell to Arms*: The Danger of Imagination," *Sewanee Review*, LXXIX (Autumn 1971), 576-597.
Argues that the book's real concern "is not 'war' or 'love' or the intellectual's 'quest for certitude' or 'Christian value,' but the discovery of death."

861 Monteiro, George. "Hemingway: Contribution Toward a Definitive Bibliography," *Papers of the Bibliographical Society of America*, LXV (Oct.-Dec. 1971), 411-414.
A checklist of work by and about Hemingway translated into Portuguese (addenda to Audre Hanneman's *EH: A Comprehensive Bibliography*).

862 Corodimas, Peter. Review of S. Kip Farrington's *Fishing with Hemingway and Glassell, Best Sellers*, XXX (Oct. 15, 1971), 321-322.

863 Shelby, J. E. "Home Town to Honor Ernest Hemingway," *Oak Leaves* (Oct. 20, 1971).
Regarding the Oak Park and River Forest Historical Society's program, "The Hemingways in Retrospect," on October 29, 1971. See *Ernest Hemingway as Recalled by His High School Contemporaries* edited by Ina Mae Schleden and Marion Rawls Herzog (S-G367).

864 Prigozy, Ruth. "A Matter of Measurement: The Tangled Relationship Between Fitzgerald and Hemingway," *Commonweal*, XCV (Oct. 29, 1971), 103-106, 108-109.
Regarding Hemingway's portrayal of F. Scott Fitzgerald in *AMF*. For letters from Thomas S. Klise and Robert Flaum, see *Commonweal*, XCV (Dec. 17, 1971), 267, 286-287.

865 Donaldson, Scott. "Hemingway's Morality of Compensation," *American Literature*, XLIII (Nov. 1971), 399-420.

865₁ McIlvaine, Robert M. "A Literary Source for the Caesarean Section in *A Farewell to Arms*," *ibid.*, pp. 444-447.

Regarding the resemblance in the death of Catherine Barkley to the death of Angela Witla following a Caesarean operation in Theodore Dreiser's novel *The "Genius."*

866 Thomsen, Christian W. "Liebe und Tod in Hemingways *Across the River and Into the Trees*," *Neueren Sprachen*, xx [New Series] (Dec. 1971), 665-674.

867 Munro, Dick. Letter from the Publisher column, *Sports Illustrated*, xxxv (Dec. 6, 1971), 11. Facsimile of portion of a manuscript page, see (S-F37).

Regarding the publication of Hemingway's "African Journal" in three installments in *Sports Illustrated*. See (S-C73).

868 Mann, Charles W., Jr. Review of Chaman Nahal's *The Narrative Pattern in Ernest Hemingway's Fiction*, *Library Journal*, xcvi (Dec. 15, 1971), 4096.

869 "Hemingway's unpublished African Journal. In Sports Illustrated," *N.Y. Times* (Dec. 16, 1971), p. 112.

A full-page ad for *Sports Illustrated*. Includes excerpts from the "African Journal."

870 Cave, Ray. "Introduction to An African Journal," *Sports Illustrated*, xxxv (Dec. 20, 1971), 40-41. Facsimile of portion of a manuscript page, see (S-F38).

Regarding the manuscript of Hemingway's journal of his 1953 safari, and the excerpting and editing of 55,000 words for three installments in *Sports Illustrated*. See (S-C73).

870₁ Munro, Dick. Letter from the Publisher column, *ibid.*, p. 5. Photograph of Mary Hemingway by Hemingway.

Regarding the "African Journal."

871 Goodman, Paul. "The Sweet Style of Ernest Hemingway," *New York Review of Books*, xvii (Dec. 30, 1971), 27-28. Caricature of Hemingway by David Levine.

A version of this essay was published in *Speaking and Language*, New York, 1971, pp. 181-190. Note: The cover title on the *NYRB* is "Hemingway's Sweetness."

872 Anderson, David M. "Basque Wine, Arkansas Chawin' Tobacco: Landscape and Ritual in Ernest Hemingway and Mark Twain," *Mark Twain Journal*, xvi (Winter 1971-1972), 3-7.

873 Hurwitz, Harold M. "Hemingway's Tutor, Ezra Pound," *Modern Fiction Studies*, xvii (Winter 1971-1972), 469-482.

A study of Hemingway's indebtedness to Pound.

873₁ Groseclose, Barbara S. "Hemingway's 'The Revolutionist': An Aid to Interpretation," *ibid.*, pp. 565-570.

873₂ Weeks, Robert P. Reviews, *ibid.*, pp. 634-639.
Reviews of *Ernest Hemingway's Apprenticeship* edited by Matthew J. Bruccoli, the *Fitzgerald/Hemingway Annual: 1970*, and Chaman Nahal's *The Narrative Pattern in Ernest Hemingway's Fiction.*

873₃ Rideout, Walter B. Reviews, *ibid.*, pp. 639-643.
Reviews of *Ernest Hemingway, Cub Reporter* edited by Matthew J. Bruccoli, the *Fitzgerald/Hemingway Annual: 1969*, Richard K. Peterson's *Hemingway: Direct and Oblique*, and Delbert E. Wylder's *Hemingway's Heroes.*

874 Winston, Alexander, "If He Hadn't Been a Genius He Would Have Been a Cad," *American Society Legion of Honor Magazine*, XLIII, i (1972), 25-40.
On Hemingway in Paris during the 1920s.

875 "Young Hemingway: A Panel," *Fitzgerald/Hemingway Annual: 1972*, pp. 113-144. Early photographs of Hemingway and facsimile of a poem, "The Ship" (1918), attributed to Hemingway.
Transcription of a panel discussion on the young Hemingway in Oak Park, Italy, and Chicago. The panelists were Mrs. Carl Kesler (Sue Lowrey), Frederick Spiegel, William Horne, Lewis Clarahan, and Raymond George. Charles Mann chaired the discussion, which was sponsored by the *F/H A* at the Modern Language Association meeting in Chicago, December 28, 1971.

875₁ Samsell, R. L. "Paris Days with Ralph Church," *ibid.*, pp. 145-147.
On Ralph Church's friendship with Sherwood Anderson and Hemingway in the 1920s.

875₂ Church, Ralph. "Sherwood Comes to Town," *ibid.*, pp. 149-156.
Regarding Sherwood Anderson and *TOS*.

875₃ Kroll, Ernest. "A Note on Victor Llona," *ibid.*, pp. 157-158.

875₄ Llona, Victor. "The Sun Also Rose for Ernest Hemingway," *ibid.*, pp. 159-171. Reminiscences from the French translator's uncompleted memoirs.

875₅ Grebstein, Sheldon Norman. "The Structure of Hemingway's Short Stories," *ibid.*, pp. 173-193.

875₆ Clark, C. E. Frazer, Jr. "Hemingway in Advance," *ibid.*, pp. 195-206. Includes a "Checklist of Pre-publication Printings of Hemingway," on pp. 201-206, and facsimiles of the title pages of the salesmen's dummy for *WTN* (A12A) and *THAHN* (A14A), and the title page and prologue to *Voyage to Victory* (A21).

875₇ Monteiro, George. "Hemingway's Christmas Carol," *ibid.*, pp. 207-213.
> On "God Rest You Merry, Gentlemen."

875₈ Grimes, Carroll. "Hemingway: 'Old Newsman Writes,'" *ibid.*, pp. 215-223.
> Examines Hemingway's letter in *Esquire,* ii (Dec. 1934) (C224), and gives the background of his feud with Heywood Broun.

875₉ Cass, Colin S. "The Love Story in *For Whom the Bell Tolls*," *ibid.*, pp. 225-235.

875₁₀ Gordon, Gerald T. "Hemingway's Wilson-Harris: The Search for Value in *The Sun Also Rises*," *ibid.*, pp. 237-244.

875₁₁ Vopat, Carole Gottlieb. "The End of *The Sun Also Rises*: A New Beginning," *ibid.*, pp. 245-255.
> On the "profound change" that Jake Barnes undergoes in *SAR.*

875₁₂ Sugg, Richard P. "Hemingway, Money and *The Sun Also Rises*," *ibid.*, pp. 257-267.

875₁₃ Clark, C. E. Frazer, Jr. "Kiki and Her 'Sympatique Montparnasseur,'" *ibid.*, pp. 269-271. Facsimile of Hemingway's inscription, to Edward W. Titus, in a copy of *TOS.*

875₁₄ Greco, Anne. "Margot Macomber: 'Bitch Goddess,' Exonerated," *ibid.*, pp. 273-280.

875₁₅ MacMullen, Forrest. "An Open Letter," *ibid.*, p. 289.
> Regarding "misleading and untrue" statements in A. E. Hotchner's article "The Guns of Hemingway," *True,* lii (Sept. 1971).

875₁₆ Kobler, J. F. "Francis Macomber as Four-Letter Man," *ibid.*, pp. 295-296.

875₁₇ Shepherd, Allen. "The Lion in the Grass (Alas?): A Note on 'The Short Happy Life of Francis Macomber,'" *ibid.*, pp. 297-299.

875₁₈ "Two Grace Hall Hemingway Letters," *ibid.*, pp. 301-302.
> A letter to a friend, Julia Stephenson, dated Nov. 8, 1929, regarding Dr. Hemingway's death, and a letter to Dutton's bookstore, dated Jan. 18, 1939, offering copies of Ernest's high-school writings for sale, are printed in full.

875₁₉ Weeks, Robert P. "Cleaning Up Hemingway," *ibid.*, pp. 311-313.
> Regarding typographical errors in "My Old Man," "Fifty Grand," "Big Two-Hearted River," and "A Clean, Well-Lighted Place."

875₂₀ Delaney, Paul. "Robert Jordan's 'Real Absinthe' in *For Whom the Bell Tolls*," *ibid.*, pp. 317-320.

875₂₁ Linebarger, J. M. "Symbolic Hats in *The Sun Also Rises*," *ibid.*, pp. 323-324.

875₂₂ Edelson, Mark. "A Note on 'One Reader Writes,' " *ibid.*, pp. 329-331.

875₂₃ McNalley, James. "A Hemingway Mention of *Gentlemen*," *ibid.*, pp. 333-334.

Regarding a possible source for "gentlemen" in Hemingway's expression "How do you like it now, gentlemen?" which was used as the title of Lillian Ross's *New Yorker* profile (H627).

875₂₄ Hemingway Checklist, *ibid.*, pp. 347-367.

875₂₅ Baker, Carlos. Review of *Ernest Hemingway's Apprenticeship* edited by Matthew J. Bruccoli, *ibid.*, pp. 383-385.

"The best argument for bringing out a volume like this over Hemingway's dead body is that its contents can be used to measure the degree of his later progress. Whether in journalism, poetry, or imaginative prose, the young writer of 1916-1917 had nowhere to go but up. The poems range from the simplest puppy-doggerel to parodies of Kipling, Longfellow, and James Whitcomb Riley. . . . Using these as a yardstick, one can see that the ten poems in his first published book showed at least some advance in sophistication and technical skill. The stories center, boy-like, on episodes of masculine violence. . . . Between these and the short stories of 1923 ("Up in Michigan," "My Old Man," and "Out of Season") the evidence of progress is enormous. . . . Some modest editorial annotation would have enhanced the value of this book. . . . Even so, it is a welcome addition to the Hemingway shelf . . . because it gathers and conveniently organizes materials hitherto scattered through yellowing old files."

875₂₆ Peckham, Morse. Review of Emily Stipes Watts's *Ernest Hemingway and the Arts, ibid.*, pp. 387-390.

875₂₇ Mann, Charles. Review of "African Journal," *ibid.*, pp. 395-396.

"The selections are judicious; they refer in the main to Miss Mary's pursuit of a Black Lion, Ernest's pursuit of a leopard, various conversations with natives, game wardens, and the author's nostalgic memories. This is not unfamiliar material where Ernest Hemingway is concerned; but there is, however, a wonderful difference, for the selections record the sensitive response of an aging man suddenly given a job to do—a real one, that of a game warden in a vast African park. It was work for which he was nobly suited, crammed with the minute need for attention to detail which he loved, and his handling of it left him with no shame. . . . The anecdotes are rather mystical; a touch of religion presumably in keeping with the Christmas season in which the events occur seems pervasive. Also in his characteristic way, Ernest Hemingway has stylized his material. As in *A Moveable Feast* it is a kind of fiction about true happenings."

875₂₈ Bruccoli, Matthew J. Review of *NAS, ibid.,* pp. 397-398.

"Of the new material, 'The Indians Moved Away' is perfect, though slight. . . . Philip Young's Foreword is inadequate. This collection requires a long introduction detailing the correspondences— or lack of them—between experience and fiction in Hemingway. . . . This volume also requires a map of the Walloon Lake area and a note on the order of the writing and publication of the stories."

875₂₉ Sarason, Bertram D. Review of John Graham's *Studies in A Farewell to Arms* and Sheldon Norman Grebstein's *Studies in For Whom the Bell Tolls, ibid.,* pp. 399-406.

875₃₀ Seigler, Milledge B. Review of S. Kip Farrington's *Fishing with Hemingway and Glassell, ibid.,* pp. 407-408.

876 Price, Reynolds. "For Ernest Hemingway," *New American Review,* No. 14 (1972), pp. 38-66. This essay was reprinted in *Things Themselves,* New York, 1972, pp. 176-213.

877 Howell, John M., and Charles A. Lawler. "From Abercrombie & Fitch to *The First Forty-Nine Stories*: The Text of Ernest Hemingway's 'Francis Macomber,'" *Proof: The Yearbook of American Bibliographical and Textual Studies,* II (1972), 213-281. Facsimiles.

The textual history of "The Short Happy Life of Francis Macomber" is traced from the original typescript (ribbon copy), with authorial revisions; through its appearance in *Cosmopolitan,* CI (Sept. 1936), with editorial alterations; its appearance in the *First 49,* with "more than 500 changes"; its republication in *Cosmopolitan,* CXXIII (Oct. 1947), with variants from its earlier appearance in the magazine; to its appearance in *The Short Stories of Ernest Hemingway* (1966). Appendix I, on p. 242, Checkpoints for Determining the Source of Editions of "Francis Macomber." Appendix II, on pp. 243-265, Emendations of the Original Typescript. Appendix III, pp. 266-267, 1936 *Cosmopolitan* Variants from the Typescript. Appendix IV, on pp. 268-279, Scribner's Variants from the Typescript. Appendix V, on pp. 280-281, 1947 *Cosmopolitan* Variants from the 1936 *Cosmopolitan.* Note: For facsimiles of the typescript, see (S-F39).

878 Reynolds, Michael S. "Two Hemingway Sources for *In Our Time,*" *Studies in Short Fiction,* IX (Winter 1972), 81-86.

Suggests that chapter six of *IOT* (concerning the execution of the Greek cabinet ministers) was derived from an event described in the *New York Times* (Dec. 1 and Dec. 20, 1922); and that chapter nine (concerning the cigar-store holdup) was derived from an event described in the *Kansas City Star* (Nov. 19, 1917). Note: There is no record of whether the *K.C. Star* article is by Hemingway.

879 MacDonald, Scott. "Implications in Narrative Perspective in Hemingway's 'The Undefeated,'" *Journal of Narrative Technique,* II (Jan. 1972), 1-15.

880 Bradbury, Ray. "The Parrot Who Met Papa," *Playboy,* XIX (Jan. 1972), 92, 126, 128, 218-219. Short story.

881 Anastasev, N. "Posle legendy," *Voprosy Literatury,* XVI (Jan. 1972), 119-134.
On the polemic elements in Hemingway's latest works.

882 Brian, Denis. "The Importance of Knowing Ernest," *Esquire,* LXXVII (Feb. 1972), 98-101, 164-166, 168-170.
Interviews with Lillian Ross, A. E. Hotchner, Malcolm Cowley, Truman Capote, Carlos Baker, George Plimpton, William Seward, John Hemingway, and Mary Hemingway. The interviews (except for the two with Lillian Ross and Carlos Baker) are excerpted from *Murderers and Other Friendly People,* New York, 1973, pp. 1-81, 107-109. Note: See also the Publisher's Page by A. G. [Arnold Gingrich], p. 6.

883 Lask, Thomas. "Readings and Writings," review of Philip Young's *Three Bags Full, N.Y. Times* (Feb. 5, 1972), p. 27.

884 Short review of *NAS, Publishers Weekly,* CCI (Feb. 7, 1972), 93.
"The last Nick Adams story appeared in 1933, and what surprises here, in these two dozen of varying length, quality and intent, is their freshness and immediacy."

885 Gurko, Leo. Review of Chaman Nahal's *The Narrative Pattern in Ernest Hemingway's Fiction, American Literature,* XLIV (March 1972), 165.

885₁ Donaldson, Scott. Review of Floyd Watkins's *The Flesh and the Word: Eliot, Hemingway, Faulkner, ibid.,* pp. 171-172.

886 Dunn, Charles William, Jr. "Ironic Vision in Hemingway's Short Stories," *Dissertation Abstracts International,* XXXII (March 1972), 5225-A.
Abstract from a doctoral dissertation, Kent State University, 1971.

887 Pardo, Hector Hernandez. "Hemingway's Cabin Cruiser 'Pilar' Being Restored," *Granma* (March 9, 1972). English edition.

888 Whitman, Alden. "Hemingway Letters Reproach Critics," *N.Y. Times* (March 9, 1972), p. 36.

Ten letters to Charles Poore, written between 1949 and 1953, are quoted from the catalogue of the Charles Hamilton Galleries, in New York, Catalogue Number 56 (March 9, 1972). Reproduced in *Hemingway at Auction*, pp. 165-171. See (S-F126) to (S-F133).

889 "10 Hemingway Letters Auctioned for $5,875," *N.Y. Times* (March 10, 1972), p. 44.

The letters to Charles Poore were sold at auction by the Charles Hamilton Galleries. See above entry.

890 Spang, Jean. Review of Emily Stipes Watts's *Ernest Hemingway and the Arts*, *Library Journal*, XCVII (March 15, 1972), 1017.

891 Hogan, William. " 'Autobiography' of Nick Adams," review of *NAS*, *San Francisco Chronicle* (March 23, 1972), p. 57.

"The whole thing . . . is arranged chronologically, Michigan, the war, the 1920s when Nick is husband, father, writer. I find the effect both startling and nostalgic, fresh and familiar, an 'autobiography' of the alter-ego. In a new entry, 'On Writing,' Nick wants to be a writer, a great writer, and is pretty sure he will be. . . . Hemingway and Nick both wrote like Cézanne painted."

892 Reynolds, Brad. "Afternoon With Mary Hemingway," *America*, CXXVI (March 25, 1972), 319-320.

The subtitle is: "A university student from nearby Spokane used his proximity—and Mary's kindness—to visit with Ernest's widow at the Hemingway home in Ketchum, Idaho."

893 Shepherd, Allen. " 'Other Things,' Unanswerable Question: Hemingway's *Islands in the Stream*," *Antigonish Review*, IX (Spring 1972), 37-39.

894 Schorer, Mark. "No Sporting Lion Here," review of *NAS* and *TFC & 4 Stories* (Scribner Library edition), *Berkeley Book Review* (Spring 1972), 2-3.

"The longest of the new pieces is called 'The Last Good Country,' a mawkish account of Nick's flight in the wilderness with his youngest sister, called Littless, from two game wardens who are no more unbelievable than the entire situation. . . . Most of the other new fragments or sketches are equally unsatisfactory. Only one of them, 'Summer People,' can be read as a complete entity, yet even if we stretch a point and call it a short story, we cannot call it a good one. . . . [regarding *TFC & 4 Stories*] 'The Butterfly and the Tank' is a nice story. The other three, if they do not damage the reputation as the new Nick Adams pieces do, clearly add nothing to it."

895 Allen, Michael J. B. "The Unspanish War in *For Whom the Bell Tolls*," *Contemporary Literature*, XIII (Spring 1972), 204-212.

896 Stephens, Robert O. "Language Magic and Reality in *For Whom the Bell Tolls*," *Criticism*, XIV (Spring 1972), 151-164.

897 Dowdy, Andrew. "Hemingway & Surrealism: A Note on the Twenties," *Hemingway notes*, II (Spring 1972), 3-6. Cover portrait of Hemingway reproduced from the *N.Y. Times Book Review* (Sept. 25, 1927).
Examines the surrealistic aspects of *TOS*.

897₁ Woodward, Robert H. "Robert Jordan's Wedding / Funeral Sermon," *ibid.*, pp. 7-8. A reply to George Monteiro's article on Hemingway and Faulkner in *Hn*, I (Spring 1971). See Professor Monteiro's reply in *Hn*, II (Fall 1972).

897₂ "T. A." [Taylor Alderman], "K. R." [Kenneth Rosen], and "W. W." [William White]. Current Bibliography, *ibid.*, pp. 9-13.

897₃ Davidson, Arnold E. "The Ambivalent End of Francis Macomber's Short, Happy Life," *ibid.*, pp. 14-16.

897₄ Monteiro, George. "Hemingway in Portuguese: More Hanneman Addenda," *ibid.*, pp. 17-19.

897₅ Steiner, Peter. Caricature of Hemingway, *ibid.*, p. 20.

897₆ Howell, John M. Review of "An African Journal," *ibid.*, pp. 21-22.
"As in *Green Hills*, Philip Percival appears as the white hunter, though a bit worse for the years and named 'Wilson Harris' instead of Jackson Philip. This is the only variation. The rest is sadly predictable. Though the edited narrative is always interesting and at times compelling, it seldom, if ever, lives up to the standard Hemingway establishes in the earlier work. Though there is a good emotional thrust to the actions leading up to the moments when Mary shoots her long-sought lion and Hemingway shoots his leopard, one looks in vain for the lovingly detailed pictures of animals and landscapes that are the poetry of *Green Hills*."

897₇ White, William. Review of Emily Stipes Watts's *Ernest Hemingway and the Arts*, *ibid.*, p. 22.

897₈ "T. A." [Taylor Alderman]. Review of Floyd Watkins's *The Flesh and the Word: Eliot, Hemingway, Faulkner*, *ibid.*, p. 23.

898 Hamilton, J. B. "Hemingway and the Christian Paradox," *Renascence*, XXIV (Spring 1972), 141-154.
On *OMATS*.

899 Bradford, M. E. Review of Floyd Watkins's *The Flesh and the Word: Eliot, Hemingway, Faulkner*, *South Atlantic Quarterly*, LXXI (Spring 1972), 277-278.

900 Larsen, Erling. "The End of Something Like Responsibility," review of *NAS, Carleton Miscellany*, XII (Spring/Summer 1972), 76-81.

The reviewer criticizes the arrangement of the stories and questions whether all of them are Nick Adams stories. "Out of place or not . . . 'The Last Good Country' is the longest of the new stories and perhaps the best. For one thing, it glows with a faint incestual phosphorescence that casts light on the later 'daughter' mystique."

901 Review of Chaman Nahal's *The Narrative Pattern in Ernest Hemingway's Fiction, Choice*, IX (April 1972), 215.

901₁ Review of Floyd Watkins's *The Flesh and the Word: Eliot, Hemingway, Faulkner, ibid.*, p. 218.

902 St. John, Donald. "Hemingway and Prudence," *Connecticut Review*, V (April 1972), 78-84.

Regarding the real-life counterparts of some of Hemingway's Indian characters.

903 Wiese, Glen James. "Moral Vision in Hemingway's Fiction," *Dissertation Abstracts International*, XXXII (April 1972), 5811-A.

Abstract from a doctoral dissertation, University of Utah, 1972.

904 Burnam, Tom. "The Other Ernest Hemingway," *Neuphilologische Mitteilungen*, LXXIII (April 1972), 29-36.

Regarding the sensitivity "which, at his best, Hemingway brought so movingly to his work."

905 Barkham, John. The Literary Scene, review of *NAS, N.Y. Post* (April 12, 1972), p. 28.

"Departed writers usually leave unfinished work, notes, fragments of this and that, but Hemingway's leavings are beginning to assume the proportions of a treasure trove. Was he indifferent to publication once the writing was done, or was he simply too severe a self-critic? . . . The unpublished 'Three Shots' . . . leads so naturally into the published 'Indian Camp' that one wonders why the two were ever separated. . . . The longest of the unpublished stories is 'The Last Good Country,' which is Hemingway in his prime."

906 Moore, Harry T. "Hemingway trove, Nick Adams back," review of *NAS, St. Louis Globe-Democrat* (April 15, 1972), p. 4-D.

"Even those [new stories] who are unfinished present interesting new views of Nick and his experiences. . . . Some of the stories deepen our knowledge of Nick, especially 'The Last Good Country,' which deals with Nick's attitudes to his family, with stress on his sister. One of the most revealing tales is 'Summer People.' The old favorite Nick Adams pieces appear in their own marvelous light— 'The Killers,' for example, that tense story of a boy's first acquaintance with the evil of the world. It stands among the great stories of our time."

907 Murray, G. E. "New Discoveries: Papa's tales of Nick Adams, his heroic alter ego," review of *NAS, Chicago Sun-Times Book Week* (April 16, 1972), p. 18.

"... Hemingway's reputation still is insurmountable in this country and elsewhere. ... Even the burghers of Oak Park, who have done little to boost their native son, have begun to come around; last spring a drawing of Hemingway graced the suburb's telephone directory. ... Of the eight new stories, three are little more than refugees from Hemingway's notebook or first drafts for later stories. ... The première selection of the group is 'Summer People,' a story that compares favorably with the best of Hemingway's early writing. ... The new fiction in this volume is, for the most part, second-rate. But even the worst of Hemingway deserves attention, and some interesting biographical notes can be garnered from this collection."

908 Elliott, Gerald A. "Revealing of the Creator," review of *NAS, Grand Rapids Press* (April 16, 1972), p. 2-H.

" 'The Last Good Country' contains some of the best writing in the book. Apparently it was intended to be the opening chapters of a novel, although there are no clues as to where Hemingway intended it to go. It seems plain enough that in the writing of it he reached a point where inspiration deserted him, and so the story ends abruptly, leaving the reader feeling as frustrated as Hemingway probably was at this point. Another of the new stories, 'Summer People,' is complete and sets forth in considerable detail a sexual adventure Nick has at Horton Bay with a girl named Kate. The story is sensitively told and contains some characteristic Hemingway humor (he could be outrageously funny in his writing). ... [The stories] reveal much of the creative process in one of the greatest writers the United States has produced in this century."

909 Diehl, Digby. "New Helping of Unissued Hemingway," review of *NAS, Los Angeles Times Calendar* (April 16, 1972), p. 45.

"There is no doubt that with each posthumous release of material from his unpublished manuscripts, the scope and literary brilliance of Ernest Hemingway dazzles us more. ... Of the 40% in this book that is new, at least one story leaps up as a powerful and finished (if not 'polished') story which stands with his best: 'Summer People.' ... Not all of the new Nick Adams material advances Hemingway's reputation. There are rough fragments and one eerie section called 'On Writing' in which the persona of Nick seems to slip away from Hemingway entirely and he careens out-of-control through memories and irrelevancies until he picks up a thread with Maile-resque abandon and brings us back to Nick."

910 Porterfield, Waldon R. "*The Nick Adams Stories*, Eight New Pieces by Ernest Hemingway," review of *NAS*, *Milwaukee Journal* (April 16, 1972), p. 4.

"The new stories, like the old ones, are not dated despite having been written all those years ago. They are fresh and sharp and, in the main, taut, and always replete with the crisp, incomparable Hemingway dialog."

911 "P.S.P." [Peter S. Prescott]. "Big Two-Hearted Writer," review of *NAS*, *Newsweek*, LXXIX (April 17, 1972), 100B, 104.

"The present collection assembles the sixteen published Nick Adams stories sequentially to show the progress of his life and fixes in appropriate positions eight unpublished sketches and fragments in which Nick Adams figures. It was a good idea . . . a sensible arrangement in which the parts retain their individual integrity yet benefit from our perception of the process of Nick's coming of age. . . . The hundred pages of new material, like the Nick Adams stories themselves, are of mixed quality. There are two important fragments—'Three Shots' and 'On Writing'—which Hemingway wisely pared from stories that could not support them, but which should not be lost."

912 King, George M. "New Light on Writer's Work, Personality," review of *NAS*, *Nashville Banner* (April 21, 1972), p. 50.

" 'The Killers' and 'Big Two-Hearted River' remain the best of the lot, the former illustrating Hemingway dialogue at its best and the latter containing his most beautiful descriptions. Both are classics. When it comes to the new material, only two 'pieces' stand out. 'The Last Good Country,' although not a complete story, is poignant and real. . . . The other new story, and it does qualify as a story, is called 'Summer People.' It comes after Nick has returned from war but takes place before his marriage. . . . Supposedly, this is Nick's last fling before matrimony, and Hemingway fills it with vivid detail."

913 Silverman, Burton. Drawing of Hemingway, *Saturday Review*, LV (April 22, 1972), 45. Note: Illustration for an article on Norman Mailer.

914 Donaldson, Scott. "Tales are Hemingway's 'coming-of-age novel,' " review of *NAS*, *Minneapolis Tribune* (April 23, 1972), pp. 8D, 9D.

"The appearance of this book containing 24 stories about Nick Adams, Hemingway's 20th-century Huckleberry Finn, constitutes a major event in American literature. . . . At least one of these eight [new stories], a long beginning-of-a-novel, called 'The Last Good Country,' ranks with the best prose Hemingway ever wrote, and all eight have their fascinations."

915 Rubin, Louis D., Jr. "A Portrait of Nick Adams and How He Happened," review of *NAS*, *Washington Sunday Star* (April 23, 1972), p. C-6. Caricature of Hemingway by Quinan.

"This is a fascinating collection. The fragmentary nature of the new pieces does not really interfere seriously with one's enjoyment. What we have is a more complete view of Hemingway as Nick Adams—and by this I mean the aesthetic experience of taking part in the writer's creation of himself in this guise. So much of reading Hemingway comes down to just that. No 20th-century writer ever projected himself more into his work, not merely with autobiographical material but in the sense of dramatizing, through style and attitude, the persona of the creator."

916 Manning, Margaret. "Nick Adams—a Reminder," review of *NAS*, *Boston Globe* (April 24, 1972), p. 23.

"The new things are really unfinished . . . and probably were simply abandoned because Hemingway decided he didn't care for them. There are sketches, snippets, a long, inconclusive and slightly soppy narrative about Nick as a boy running away from home, and a full scale story about Nick and a girl called 'Summer People.' Even these, however, are interesting bits with gorgeous nature writing. . . . No other writer in English has the same sensitivity to climate, to landscape, to natural physical things."

917 Lingeman, Richard R. "More Posthumous Hemingway," review of *NAS*, *N.Y. Times* (April 25, 1972), p. 41.

". . . many of the new ones are the literary equivalent of the cannibalization of spare parts—pieces of other stories that Hemingway cut out that have been resurrected on their own. . . . ['On Writing'] is a welter of new and unrelated thoughts that would have dragged 'Big Two-Hearted River' into the quicksands of irrelevancy. . . . *The Nick Adams Stories* neither add nor detract from Hemingway's memory, and it is good to have a collection of the good ones, but this present arrangement does not create any new synergism."

918 Higgins, George V. "Rooting In Papa's Closet To Discover . . . 14 Pages?!" review of *NAS*, *National Observer* (April 29, 1972), p. 21.

"Sixty per cent of [*The Nick Adams Stories*] is legit. Hemingway wanted it published, and he published it. Forty per cent he suppressed. Fourteen pages ('Summer People') he might, in my estimation, rightfully have let out. The rest? I think Hemingway was right about the rest. . . . The point, of course, lies not in my endorsement of Hemingway's wisdom in holding back the other fragments, nor in my respectful dissent from his decision to withhold 'Summer People.' The point is that while he lived, no one would have forcibly essayed to overrule his measured judgment about what ought to be offered for print under the byline Ernest Hemingway. Now he's dead, and they do."

919 Winner, Viola Hopkins. Review of Emily Stipes Watts's *Ernest Hemingway and the Arts, American Literature,* XLIV (May 1972), 335-336.

920 Robinson, Forrest D. "Frederick Henry: The Hemingway Hero as Storyteller," *CEA Critic,* XXXIV (May 1972), 13-16.

921 Adams, Phillip Duane. "Ernest Hemingway and the Painters: Cubist Style in *The Sun Also Rises* and *A Farewell to Arms," Dissertation Abstracts International,* XXXII (May 1972), 6311-A.
Abstract from a doctoral dissertation, Ohio University, 1971.

921₁ Shtogren, John Alexander, Jr. "Ernest Hemingway's Aesthetic Use of Journalism in His First Decade of Fiction," *ibid.,* 6454-A.
Abstract from a doctoral dissertation, University of Michigan, 1971.

922 Wagner, Linda W. *"The Sun Also Rises*: One Debt to Imagism," *Journal of Narrative Technique,* II (May 1972), 88-98.

923 Gottschalk, Klaus-Dieter. "Verkehrte Welt in Hemingways 'The Doctor and the Doctor's Wife,' " *Neueren Sprachen,* XXI [New Series] (May 1972), 285-293.

924 McHaney, Thomas L. "Anderson, Hemingway, and Faulkner's *The Wild Palms," PMLA,* LXXXVII (May 1972), 465-474.
An essay on the "complexly related allusions" to Sherwood Anderson and Hemingway in Faulkner's novel, and the philosophical and artistic differences between Hemingway and Faulkner.

925 Francis, William A. C. Review of *NAS, Best Sellers,* XXXII (May 1, 1972), 53.
"The strength of *The Nick Adams Stories* comes from the established masterpieces, despite the diluting effect of the new sketches. Many readers will be disappointed that the collection does not live up to its promise of coherence and impact, but scholars may delight in one hundred more pages of Nick."

926 Spang, Jean. Review of Arthur Waldhorn's *A Reader's Guide to Ernest Hemingway, Library Journal,* XCVII (May 1, 1972), 1719.

927 Skow, John. "A Moveable Fast," review of *NAS, Time,* XCIX (May 1, 1972), 81-82.

"There can be no pretense that the fragments are anything but rejects. Judged against the author's other work, none are much better than mediocre, and most are worse than that. They were written, and then written off, at the beginning of Hemingway's career. If he had wanted to change his mind about them, he had 30 years or more to do so."

928 Coppel, Alfred. "Hemingway Liberals and the Time Warp," review of *NAS*, *Peninsula Living* (May 13, 1972), pp. 31, 33.

"If he had lived to hone and polish the unfamiliar work in *The Nick Adams Stories* we would have been richer for it. But even in this unfinished and uneven state Papa's stuff is eminently readable. Which is simply another way of saying that Hemingway's discards are better than most writers' best efforts. His talent was monumental and if the values he held are presently unpopular, I would tend to suspect the times rather than the artist."

929 Marx, Leo. Review of Philip Young's *Three Bags Full*, *N.Y. Times Book Review* (May 14, 1972), pp. 4, 10, 14.

930 "SMC" [Sister M. Constance Melvin]. Brief review of Richard O'Connor's *Ernest Hemingway*, *Best Sellers*, XXXII (May 15, 1972), 98.

931 Anderson, Quentin. "Devouring the Hemingway Corpus," review of *NAS*, *New Leader*, LV (May 15, 1972), 13-15.

"The publication of *The Nick Adams Stories* is a case of insatiability pushed to the limit of indiscriminate greed; not simply commercial greed, but a desire to make Hemingway just the kind of imaginative commodity he is not. . . . [Philip] Young has interspersed eight unpublished Nick Adams pieces among those taken from the three earlier collections, reordering them to conform with what he believes to be their sequence in the 'life' of this character. In two instances the result is even worse than printing what Hemingway clearly did not wish to bring out; it is an undoing of what the author has done." Professor Anderson cites the "lopped-off" ending of "Big Two-Hearted River" and the "rejected opening" of "Indian Camp."

932 Lucid, Robert F. "Hemingway's Great Nick," review of *NAS*, *Philadelphia Bulletin* (May 21, 1972), Sec. 5, p. 11.

"Taken individually, the published stories are among the very best short fiction produced in the twentieth century and, just as importantly, they are among the best known. . . . By linking the stories together, [Philip] Young gives us the experience of discovering in three dimensions a place—the world of Nick Adams—which we have before seen only in flashes and fragments."

933 Abrahams, William. "Hemingway: The Posthumous Achievement," review of *NAS, Atlantic*, ccxxix (June 1972), 98, 100-101.

"The new stories in the present collection, set in italics to distinguish them from the ones already published, are recognizably lesser or apprentice work. It is quite obvious that the author knew this himself and put them aside, which is not to say that it was ill advised to bring them to light."

934 Hedge, G. C. Review of *NAS, Book-of-the-Month Club News* (June 1972), p. 11.

"The most substantial of the new lot, and probably the most noteworthy, is 'The Last Good Country,' an unfinished narrative about Nick aged about 15. . . . The story has most of the Hemingway stylistic earmarks and few of the Hemingway virtues; and much the same may be said of the other newly published ones, though surely it was an interesting idea to get them into print."

935 Review of Emily Stipes Watts's *Ernest Hemingway and the Arts, Choice*, ix (June 1972), 511.

936 Feeney, Joseph John. "American Anti-War Writers of World War I: A Literary Study of Randolph Bourne, Harriet Monroe, Carl Sandburg, John Dos Passos, E. E. Cummings, and Ernest Hemingway," *Dissertation Abstracts International*, xxxii (June 1972), 6972-A.

Abstract from a doctoral dissertation, University of Pennsylvania, 1971.

937 Vandervelde, Marjorie. "An Afternoon with Mary Hemingway," *Writer's Digest*, lii (June 1972), 28-30, 43.

An interview in Ketchum, Idaho.

938 Nolan, William F. "Papa as Nick," review of *NAS, WGAw News* (Writers Guild of America/West Newsletter) (June 1972), pp. 21-22.

"All of us, all writers, owe a solid debt of gratitude to Philip Young (who assembled these stories and wrote the Preface) for pushing his idea through to completion. Papa is dead, but here in these crystalline pages his young self still tramps the woods of Michigan, fishes its trout streams, camps on cricket-speaking night shore, meets violence, love and death—and, through it all, writes truly and wonderfully about 'the last good country.' Cézanne would have been proud of him." Note: The first printing of a section of the narration written by Hemingway to frame the action of the film *Adventures of a Young Man* is included in this review.

939 Spang, Jean. Review of *NAS, Library Journal*, xcvii (June 1, 1972), 2116.

"Interspersed with the familiar short stories, these [eight] new pieces don't appear as polished Hemingway, yet each presents a new perspective on his work. . . . An important addition to the Hemingway canon."

940 Madden, David. "Some early Hemingway," review of *NAS*, *Boston Herald-Traveler* (June 4, 1972), Sec. 5, p. 8. Drawing of Hemingway by David Stone Martin.

"The interrelationships among all these pieces give the collection the cohesiveness of an impressionistic novel. The best of the new pieces, 'The Last Good Country' introduces some interesting new characters. It contains many of the motifs developed throughout the rest of the book; whole passages turn up in other stories, especially 'Big Two-Hearted River,' to which it is most closely related. . . . Though the 64-page fragment is unfinished, the experience it offers is complete enough."

941 Harrison, Jim. "The Importance of Being Young—and Ernest," review of *NAS*, *Book World (Washington Post)* (June 4, 1972), p. 6.

"It is pleasant to see all the Nick Adams stories under one cover. . . . Now we have the additional delight of eight fragments and stories hitherto unpublished. Of the latter, I liked 'The Last Good Country' best. . . . It shows an enormously tender, almost maudlin side of Hemingway's character. . . . But it is most of all a summer idyll, the writing very relaxed and beautiful, and obviously a first draft—Hemingway with his guard down."

942 Fuller, Edmund. "Hemingway's Nick Adams Tales," review of *NAS*, *Wall Street Journal* (June 8, 1972), p. 10.

" 'The Last Good Country' . . . has the worst of Hemingway's characteristic sentimentality in Nick's relations with a younger sister, called 'Littless,' never met before or after. . . . 'Summer People' is the only really complete story. [Philip] Young thinks it may be the earliest piece written about Nick, which if true is mildly interesting because it is specifically erotic to a degree unusual in Hemingway. But it is not much of a story. 'On Writing' . . . is just awful —the worst unconscious self-parody."

943 Loesberg, Jonathan. "Nick Adams as a consistent hero," review of *NAS*, *Providence Sunday Journal* (June 11, 1972), p. H-21.

"All but one of [the eight new pieces] are fragments. Two of the fragments, 'Three Shots' and 'On Writing,' are quite clearly parts of other stories which Hemingway, correctly I think, saw fit to excise. 'On Writing,' in particular, is an almost intolerably boring fulmination on how Hemingway felt about his art. . . . 'Summer People' . . . is a welcome discovery, not as good as the best Nick Adams stories, but terse and effective."

337

944 Laurence, Frank M. "Hollywood Publicity and Hemingway's Popular Reputation," *Journal of Popular Culture*, VI (Summer 1972), 20-31.

945 Twitchell, James. "The Swamp in Hemingway's 'Big Two-Hearted River,' " *Studies in Short Fiction*, IX (Summer 1972), 275-276.

946 Moats, Alice-Leone. "A Day with Hemingway," *Paris Observer*, No. 1 (July 1972), pp. 3-8, 10-11.
   A tour of the Latin Quarter which, because of *AMF*, "will always be thought of as Hemingway territory."

947 Weinstein, Bernard. Review of Arthur Waldhorn's *A Reader's Guide to Ernest Hemingway*, *Best Sellers*, XXXII (July 15, 1972), 190-191.

948 Weber, Ronald. "Savoring the Hemingway of the Nick Adams Stories," review of *NAS*, *Detroit Free Press* (July 16, 1972), p. 5-B.
   "For the serious Hemingway reader the place to begin has always been the stories, and that's the best place to return as well. . . . Of the new stories, however, only one, 'Summer People,' can be considered a completed work and in any sense an important one, especially for its further development of the Michigan material that gave Hemingway the background for his first serious fiction. . . . But even arranged in sequence the stories never quite form a complete narrative, they retain a fragmented quality because of the nature of the short story itself . . . and because of Hemingway's special brand of story that was always meant to make the readers sense much more than was actually said."

949 Hitch, Gretchen. "Memories of Literary Greats Revived," *Birmingham Eccentric* (July 20, 1972), pp. 1-C, 11-C.
   Regarding the conference on Hemingway and F. Scott Fitzgerald held in Paris, June 23-24, 1972. See (S-G57).

950 Hart, Jeffrey. "Vintage Hemingway," review of *NAS*, *National Review*, XXIV (July 21, 1972), 801-802.
   " 'The Last Good Country' . . . is early and vintage Hemingway. . . . It does not even matter that the story is unfinished. The great themes are there, unrefined and uncriticized, but revealing the sources of energy. . . . It is a tremendous narrative, from the first line on, and all of Hemingway's power is present to suggest the deeper emotions and meanings beneath the simplest statements."

951 Flanner, Janet. "If either of us ever killed ourself, the other was not to grieve," *Life*, LXXIII (July 28, 1972), 17. Excerpt on Hemingway from *Paris Was Yesterday, 1925-1939*, New York, 1972, pp. vii-viii.

952 Koteskey, Joe. "He Remembers Hemingway as . . . 'Polite Kid,' " *Northern Michigan Graphic Resorter* (Aug. 21, 1972), pp. 24-25.

953 Brief review of Vernon (Jake) Klimo and Will Oursler's *Hemingway and Jake: An Extraordinary Friendship, Publishers Weekly,* CCII (Aug. 21, 1972), 78.

954 Clark, C. E. Frazer, Jr. "Having a Wonderful Time in Paris, Wish Scott and Papa Were Here," *Detroit Free Press Magazine* (Aug. 27, 1972), pp. 10-15.
 Regarding the conference on Hemingway and F. Scott Fitzgerald held in Paris, June 23-24, 1972. See (S-G57).

955 Carlin, Stanley A. "A Sun Rise on 'The Sun Set,' " review of Bertram Sarason's *Hemingway and The Sun Set, American Book Collector,* XXIII (Sept. 1972), 29.

956 Shepherd, Allen. "Hudson's Cats in Hemingway's *Islands in the Stream,*" *Notes on Contemporary Literature,* II (Sept. 1972), 3-6.

957 Forman, Jack. Review of Richard O'Connor's *Ernest Hemingway, Library Journal,* XCVII (Sept. 15, 1972), 2966.

958 Duffy, Martha. "Then and Now," review of *TOS* (Scribner's reprint edition), *Time,* C (Sept. 18, 1972), 98-100.
 "It is a brutal parody of Sherwood Anderson, a man who influenced Hemingway's prose and helped him materially early in his career. . . . Anderson had the last word however, 'It might have been humorous had Max Beerbohm condensed it to twelve pages,' he said—and he was right."

959 Pauly, Thomas H., and Thomas Dwyer. "Passing the Buck in *The Sun Also Rises,*" *Hemingway notes,* II (Fall 1972), 3-6. Cover portrait of Hemingway from a woodcut by Josef Bush.

959₁ "T. A." [Taylor Alderman], "K. R." [Kenneth Rosen], and "W. W." [William White]. "Current Bibliography," *ibid.,* pp. 7-12.

959₂ White, William. "Bill Gorton / Grundy in *The Sun Also Rises,*" *ibid.,* pp. 13-15.
 The publishing history of the "misprint" of Bill Gorton's name in the first edition of *SAR* (p. 91 / line 13) is traced through the Scribner Library Edition, printed in January 1972, where it again appears as "Grundy."

959₃ Monteiro, George. "Hemingway and Spain: A Response to Woodward," *ibid.,* pp. 16-17. A reply to Robert Woodward's article in *Hn,* II (Spring 1972).

959₄ Rovit, Earl. Review of *NAS, ibid.*, pp. 18-19.

"[Hemingway] knew precisely what he was doing by leaving the 'new' Nick Adams sketches unpublished; and he was clearly deliberate in scattering the published Nick Adams stories amongst the 'first forty-nine.' He was a short story writer par excellence and he had to be keenly aware of the need for each story to be definitely framed—each a self-sustained creation, ordering and resolving its own sense of space. . . . In all honesty, I cannot see that Hemingway's fine-honed artistry is particularly well served by this publication."

959₅ "T. A." [Taylor Alderman]. Review of Bertram Sarason's *Hemingway and The Sun Set, ibid.*, pp. 19-20.

959₆ White, Gertrude M. Review of Chaman Nahal's *The Narrative Pattern in Ernest Hemingway's Fiction, ibid.*, pp. 20-21.

959₇ "T. A." [Taylor Alderman]. An overview of recent memoirs and biographies in which Hemingway figures, *ibid.*, pp. 21-22.

960 Johnson, Russell I. Review of Emily Stipes Watts's *Ernest Hemingway and the Arts, Journal of Aesthetics and Art Criticism*, XXXI (Fall 1972), 138.

961 Hamalian, Leo. "Hemingway as Hunger Artist," *Literary Review*, XVI (Fall 1972), 5-13.

A study of Hemingway's "morality of hunger" in *AMF* and the short stories.

962 Young, Philip. " 'Big World Out There': *The Nick Adams Stories*," *Novel: A Forum on Fiction*, VI (Fall 1972), 5-19. Note: A footnote, on p. 5, states that this essay was initially conceived as an introduction to *NAS*; however, only a brief preface by Professor Young introduces the collection.

963 Langford, Gerald. Review of Floyd Watkins's *The Flesh and the Word: Eliot, Hemingway, Faulkner, Studies in the Novel*, IV (Fall 1972), 534-536.

964 Brief review of *NAS, Virginia Quarterly Review*, XLVIII (Autumn 1972), cxxi.

"Fully as fascinating as the constraint and anxiety deep in these stories is the consistency of their crafted style and, indeed, the constancy of Nick Adams himself despite the fact that, dating from the 1920's, these works span a crucial decade in Hemingway's development."

965 Fisher, Edward. "Lost Generations, Then and Now," *Connecticut Review*, VI (Oct. 1972), 13-25.

Recollections of Paris, in 1928, and Key West, in 1935. Claims that Hemingway "scrambled" the author and John Dos Passos "with a big dose of himself" to produce Richard Gordon, the proletarian writer in *THAHN*.

966 Item, *Newsweek*, LXXX (Oct. 9, 1972), 56.
Brief excerpts from Hemingway's letters to Arthur Mizener regarding F. Scott Fitzgerald, see (S-H969).

967 White, William. "Inelegant View of Hemingway," review of Vernon (Jake) Klimo and Will Oursler's *Hemingway and Jake, Detroit News* (Oct. 13, 1972), p. 5-E.

968 "Tanzania: The Son Also Rises," *Newsweek*, LXXX (Oct. 16, 1972), 48, 51.
Regarding Patrick Hemingway's work as an instructor at Tanzania's College of Wildlife Management.

969 Gent, George. "Hemingway's Letters Tell of Fitzgerald," *N.Y. Times* (Oct. 25, 1972), p. 38.
Eight letters to Arthur Mizener, written between 1949 and 1951, are excerpted from the Sotheby Parke Bernet catalogue, Sale Number 3428 (Oct. 31, 1972). Reproduced in *Hemingway at Auction*, pp. 172-175. See (S-F101), (S-F106) to (S-F109), (S-F113), and (S-F114).

970 "The Papa Papers," *New York Magazine*, V (Oct. 30, 1972), 64.
Regarding the Hemingway letters to Arthur Mizener being widely excerpted. See above item.

971 Martin, Judith. "The Importance of Being Ernest," *Washington Post* (Oct. 30, 1972), B1, B2. Facsimile, see (S-F109).
The eight Hemingway letters to Arthur Mizener are excerpted. See (S-H969).

972 Prizel, Yuri. "Hemingway in Soviet Literary Criticism," *American Literature*, XLIV (Nov. 1972), 445-456.
A study of Soviet literary criticism during the years 1955 to 1970, which concludes that "work in the mid-sixties shows increased preoccupation with the aesthetic side of Hemingway's art, as opposed to the political considerations of the late fifties and in 1934-1939."

973 Review of Arthur Waldhorn's *A Reader's Guide to Ernest Hemingway, Choice*, IX (Nov. 1972), 1134.

974 Pinsker, Sanford. "Rubbing Against the American Grain: Writing After Hemingway," *Quadrant*, XVI (Nov.-Dec. 1972), 48-54.

975 Spang, Jean. Review of Vernon (Jake) Klimo and Will Oursler's *Hemingway and Jake, Library Journal*, XCVII (Nov. 1, 1972), 3578.

976 Hemingway, Mary. "Ernest's Idaho and Mine," *World*, I (Nov. 7, 1972), 34-37.

977 Seymour, Gerald. Book News column, "Hemingway and O'Hara revisited," *Chicago Tribune Book World* (Nov. 26, 1972), p. 9.
Regarding the eight Hemingway letters to Arthur Mizener, which were auctioned at Sotheby Parke Bernet on October 31, and bought by William Young, a Boston dealer, for $12,000. See (S-H969).

978 Cowley, Malcolm. "The Lucky Generation: Neither lost, nor gone for good," *Atlantic*, ccxxx (Dec. 1972), 55-61. General article.

979 Carson, David L. "Symbolism in *A Farewell to Arms*," *English Studies*, LIII (Dec. 1972), 518-522.

980 Twitchell, James. "Hemingway's *The Sun Also Rises*," *Explicator*, xxxi (Dec. 1972), Item 24.
Regarding Jake Barnes and Bill Gorton's initiation of the Englishman Harris into their "club."

981 White, William. "So You're In a Book," review of Bertram Sarason's *Hemingway and The Sun Set, Literary Sketches*, xii (Dec. 1972), 10-11.

982 McLendon, James. "Hemingway: The Have Among the Have-Nots," *Miami Herald* (Dec. 10, 1972), *Tropic*, the Sunday Magazine section, pp. 10-12, 14, 17, 48-49.
On Hemingway in Key West during the 1930s.

983 Peirce, J. F. "The Car as Symbol in Hemingway's 'The Short Happy Life of Francis Macomber,'" *South Central Bulletin* (MLA), xxxii (Winter 1972), 230-232.

984 Ross, Morton L. "Bill Gorton, The Preacher in *The Sun Also Rises*," *Modern Fiction Studies*, xviii (Winter 1972-1973), 517-527.

985 Nakhdjavani, Erik. "Of Strength and Vulnerability: An Interview with Philip Young," *Dialogue: An Interdisciplinary Quarterly*, I (Winter 1973), 5-22.
The psychoanalytical aspect of Professor Young's early work on Hemingway and the misleading simplicity of Hemingway's style are discussed.

986 Cowley, Malcolm. "Hemingway: The Image and the Shadow," *Horizon*, xv (Winter 1973), 112-117. Photographs.

987 Wagoner, David. "At the Hemingway Memorial" *Ketchum, Idaho*, poem, *Southern Review*, ix (Winter 1973), 169-170.

988 Srivastava, Ramesh Kumar. "Hemingway's *For Whom the Bell Tolls*: A Critical Introduction with Annotations," *Dissertation Abstracts International,* xxxiii (Jan. 1973), 3674-A.
Abstract from a doctoral dissertation, University of Utah, 1972.

989 Konopa, Charles. "Hemingway's Royal Cats," *Cat Fancy,* xvi (Jan.-Feb. 1973), 6-7. Photograph by George Leavens.

990 O'Rourke, Matthew R. Review of James McLendon's *Papa: Hemingway in Key West, Best Sellers,* xxxii (Jan. 1, 1973), 459.

991 Mann, Charles, Jr. Review of James McLendon's *Papa: Hemingway in Key West, Library Journal,* xcviii (Jan. 15, 1973), 161.

992 Review of Bertram D. Sarason's *Hemingway and The Sun Set, Choice,* ix (Feb. 1973), 1592-1593.

993 Ciholas, Karin Nordenhaug. "Three Modern Parables: A Comparative Study of Gide's *L'Immoraliste,* Mann's *Der Tod in Venedig,* and Hemingway's *The Old Man and the Sea*," *Dissertation Abstracts International,* xxxiii (Feb. 1973), 4404-A.
Abstract from a doctoral dissertation, University of North Carolina at Chapel Hill, 1972.

993₁ Stephenson, Edward Roger. "Stephen Crane and Ernest Hemingway: A Study in Literary Continuity," *ibid.,* p. 4433-A.
Abstract from a doctoral dissertation, Brown University, 1972.

994 "Hemingway Letters Fetch $12,000," *N.Y. Times* (Feb. 21, 1973), p. 34.
Eight letters to Edward O'Brien, written between 1923 and 1927, were sold at auction by Sotheby Parke Bernet to [Mrs. Louis Henry Cohn] House of Books in New York.

995 Alderman, Taylor. Review of *NAS, Alternative,* vi (March 1973), 24-25. Caricature of Hemingway.
"The eight [new] pieces are . . . an odd lot. . . . 'On Writing' originally concluded 'Big Two-Hearted River.' The reader is not surprised to learn that Hemingway cut it from the story before publication; he is shocked to learn that Hemingway wrote it at all. . . . it bears no relationship to the ritualistic fishing trip which structures the more familiar tale. . . . The 'new' Nick Adams material in this book is decidedly inferior to the 'old'; once again one feels that Hemingway's editorial judgment was generally sound. But the reader who does not know the adventures of Nick Adams would do well to dip into this volume. The best of Nick Adams contains much of the best of Hemingway, and this volume is a good introduction to Hemingway's art."

996 Johnson, Robert O. "Hemingway's 'How Do You Like It Now, Gentlemen?': A Possible Source," *American Literature,* XLV (March 1973), 114-117.

Hemingway's oft-repeated phrase in Lillian Ross's profile in the *New Yorker,* XXVI (May 13, 1950), is traced to George Villiers' Restoration play *The Rehearsal* (1671).

997 Review of James McLendon's *Papa: Hemingway in Key West, Choice,* X (March 1973), 95.

998 White, William. "Hemingway," *Literary Sketches,* XIII (March 1973), 6-8.

Regarding new printings of *The Collected Poems.*

999 Stephens, Robert O. "Hemingway and Stendhal: The Matrix of *A Farewell to Arms,*" *PMLA,* LXXXVIII (March 1973), 271-280. For a reply by Stirling Haig, see *PMLA,* LXXXVIII (Oct. 1973), 1192-1193.

1000 Nagel, James. "The Narrative Method of 'The Short Happy Life of Francis Macomber,'" *Research Studies* (Washington State University), XLI (March 1973), 18-27.

1001 Mann, Charles W., Jr. Review of Alice Hunt Sokoloff's *Hadley: The First Mrs. Hemingway, Library Journal,* XCVIII (March 15, 1973), 863.

1002 "Twenty Years After," review of Carlos Baker's *Hemingway: The Writer as Artist,* Fourth edition, *Times Literary Supplement* (March 30, 1973), p. 357.

1003 Fox, Stephen D. "Hemingway's 'The Doctor and the Doctor's Wife,'" *Arizona Quarterly,* XXIX (Spring 1973), 19-25.

1003₁ Phillips, Steven R. "Hemingway and the Bullfight: The Archetypes of Tragedy," *ibid.,* pp. 37-56.

Discusses *DIA, SAR,* and "The Dangerous Summer."

1004 Monteiro, George. "The Limits of Professionalism: A Sociological Approach to Faulkner, Fitzgerald and Hemingway," *Criticism,* XV (Spring 1973), 145-155.

Includes an interpretation of "Indian Camp" in terms of Talcott Parsons' concepts "of affective neutrality and of the sick role."

1005 Presley, John W. " 'Hawks Never Share': Women and Tragedy in Hemingway," *Hemingway notes,* III (Spring 1973), 3-10. Caricature of Hemingway on the cover, reproduced from the *Alternative,* VI (March 1973).

1005₁ "T. A." [Taylor Alderman], "K. R." [Kenneth Rosen], and "W. W." [William White]. Current Bibliography, *ibid.,* pp. 11-13.

1005₂ White, William. "Two More Hanneman Addenda," *ibid.*, pp. 14-15.
    Describes the British edition of *The Writer in a Changing World*
    edited by Henry Hart, see (B26); and the Canadian school edition
    of *OMATS* with a Study Guide by Mary A. Campbell, see (A24D).

1005₃ Lewis, Robert W. "The Diary of a Mad Book Reviewer: Notes from
    At Sea Diary," review of Sheldon Norman Grebstein's *Hemingway's
    Craft, ibid.*, pp. 15-19.

1005₄ White, William. "Hemingway in Key West: Three New Books,"
    ibid., pp. 20, 22-23. Reviews of S. Kip Farrington's *Fishing with
    Hemingway and Glassell*, Vernon (Jake) Klimo and Will Oursler's
    Hemingway and Jake: An Extraordinary Friendship, and James
    McLendon's *Papa: Hemingway in Key West*.

1005₅ "T. A." [Taylor Alderman]. Review of Budd Schulberg's *The Four
    Seasons of Success, ibid.*, pp. 23-24.

1006 Watkins, Floyd C. "*The Nick Adams Stories*: A Single Work by
    Ernest Hemingway," review of *NAS, Southern Review*, IX (Spring
    1973), 481-491.
    "The cumulative effect of the story of Nick Adams is that he is
    initiated time and again and that he learns more and more. Each
    story therefore becomes more powerful and meaningful when taken
    along with others instead of separately."

1007 MacDonald, Scott. "The Confusing Dialogue in Hemingway's 'A
    Clean, Well-Lighted Place': A Final Word?" *Studies in American
    Fiction*, I (Spring 1973), 93-101.
    Cites examples in Hemingway's work where he ignored normal
    dialogue conventions, and argues against Scribner's change in the
    dialogue between the waiters in "A Clean, Well-Lighted Place." See
    note under (S-A7F).

1007₁ Martine, James J. Review of Fraser Sutherland's *The Style of In-
    nocence: A Study of Hemingway and Callaghan, ibid.*, pp. 118-120.

1008 Malin, Irving. Review of Philip Young's *Three Bags Full, Studies in
    the Novel*, V (Spring 1973), 148-149.

1009 Flora, Joseph M. "Biblical Allusion in *The Old Man and the Sea*,"
    Studies in Short Fiction, X (Spring 1973), 143-147.

1010 Schneiderman, Leo. "Hemingway: A Psychological Study," *Con-
    necticut Review*, VI (April 1973), 34-49.

1011 Minerbi, Marcello. "I Grandi Clienti di Favoloso Gritti di Venezia,"
    Oggi Illustrato, XXIX (April 12, 1973), 114-120. Photographs of Hem-
    ingway's room at the Gritti, on p. 116.

345

1012 "Hemingway committee seeks memorial stamp," *Oak Park-River Forest World* (April 22, 1973).

Regarding the plans of the Tribute to Hemingway committee for a celebration, on July 21, 1974, "to commemorate the 75th anniversary of the birth of Ernest Hemingway, Oak Park's most distinguished native son."

1012₁ Giammona, Vicki. "Seek to name Wright, Hemingway streets," *ibid.*

Regarding a petition to rename two streets in Oak Park, Illinois, after Hemingway and Frank Lloyd Wright.

1013 Loss, Archie K. Review of Arthur Waldhorn's *A Reader's Guide to Ernest Hemingway, American Literature*, XLV (May 1973), 309-310.

1014 Review of Vernon (Jake) Klimo and Will Oursler's *Hemingway and Jake: An Extraordinary Friendship, Choice*, X (May 1973), 458.

1015 Mikhail, Mona Naguib. "Major Existentialist Themes and Methods in the Short Fiction of Idris, Maḥfouz, Hemingway and Camus," *Dissertation Abstracts International*, XXXIII (May 1973), 6320-A.

Abstract from a doctoral dissertation, University of Michigan, 1972. Examines the affinities of two major contemporary Egyptian writers, Yūsuf Idris and Naguib Maḥfouz, with Hemingway and Albert Camus.

1016 Davidson, Arnold E. "The Dantean Perspective in Hemingway's *A Farewell to Arms,*" *Journal of Narrative Technique*, III (May 1973), 121-130.

1017 Agent, Dan. "The Hair on Hemingway's Chest," *Lost Generation Journal*, I (May 1973), 12-15. Drawing of Hemingway, by Tony Gresham, on the back cover.

1017₁ Pearson, Janet Lynne. "Hemingway's Women," *ibid.*, pp. 16-19.

1018 White, William. "Hemingway Items: What Are the Limits?" *American Book Collector,* XXIII (May-June 1973), pp. 18-20.

On books about bullfighting and their place in a Hemingway collection.

1019 Marsh, Robert C. "Hemingway's Paris Revisited," *Chicago Sun-Times Midwest Magazine* (May 13, 1973), pp. 43-47. See also Mary Hemingway's letter in the *CS-TMM* (July 1, 1973), p. 4.

1020 Moore, Robin. "Prof Hemingway expert," *Daily Collegian* (Pennsylvania State University) (May 18, 1973), p. 3.

Interview with Philip Young.

1021 Cooper, Arthur. "Life With Papa," review of Alice Hunt Sokoloff's *Hadley: The First Mrs. Hemingway, Newsweek,* LXXXI (May 28, 1973), 103-104, 106.

1022 Review of Carlos Baker's *Hemingway: The Writer as Artist,* Fourth edition, *Choice,* x (June 1973), 613.

1023 Mann, Charles W., Jr. Review of Sheldon Norman Grebstein's *Hemingway's Craft, Library Journal,* xcviii (June 1, 1973), 1820.

1024 Solomon, Albert J. Review of Alice Hunt Sokoloff's *Hadley: The First Mrs. Hemingway, Best Sellers,* xxxiii (June 15, 1973), 133-134.

1025 Review of Alice Hunt Sokoloff's *Hadley: The First Mrs. Hemingway, New Yorker,* xlix (June 16, 1973), 111.

1026 Barkham, John. Review of Alice Hunt Sokoloff's *Hadley: The First Mrs. Hemingway, N.Y. Post* (June 18, 1973), p. 35.

1027 White, William. "Recollections of Ernest's First Wife: Hemingway on the Way Up," review of Alice Hunt Sokoloff's *Hadley: The First Mrs. Hemingway, Detroit News* (June 24, 1973), p. 5-E.

1028 "Officials ponder using Hemingway, Wright as names of streets," *Oak Leaves* (June 27, 1973), p. 6.
On renaming streets in Oak Park, Illinois, after Hemingway and Frank Lloyd Wright.

1028₁ Shelby, J. E. "Ernest roamed the Des Plaines," *ibid.,* pp. 30-31, 33.
Reminiscences of Hemingway by an Oak Park schoolmate, Lewis A. Clarahan.

1029 Gertzman, Jay A. Review of *NAS, Studies in Short Fiction,* x (Summer 1973), 297-298.
"These stories are almost exclusively of a young man, and Hemingway's power in writing about youth and adolescence has been justly acclaimed in stories such as 'The Killers,' 'Ten Indians,' and 'An End To Something' [*sic*]. It is also strongly present in some of the new pieces, such as the fragment on Nick's first sight of the Mississippi, and especially in 'Three Shots,' the first story in the book, placed before 'Indian Camp,' of which it might once have been part. . . . 'Summer People' consists mainly of dialogue and soliloquy; with typical sureness and precision it describes events and attitudes which show more about the characters than they seem to. . . . Nick's preoccupation with wounding and suicide . . . clearly emerges as Nick's character develops. But, despite this 'morbidity' . . . there is much humor in these stories, always helping to restore the kind of balance good writers cannot go without. It is injected casually and naturally, just as happens when people desperately need it to face frustration, disappointment, and fear."

1030 Wilson, Douglas. "Ernest Hemingway, *The Nick Adams Stories,*" *Western Humanities Review,* xxvii (Summer 1973), 295-299.

1031 Traver, Robert. "Hemingway's Big Two-Hearted Secret," *Sports Afield,* CLXX (July 1973), 46-47, 82-84. Illustrated by John Groth.

Argues that Nick Adams never fished the Michigan trout stream called the Two Hearted River, and if Hemingway ever did "the only thing he found memorable about it was its romantic-sounding off-beat name."

1032 Facsimile of the title-page of *TSTP*, inscribed to Philip Jordan, *American Book Collector,* XXIII (July-Aug. 1973), 14.

1032₁ White, William. "On Hemingway and Others," *ibid.,* p. 15.

Includes a review of Sheldon Norman Grebstein's *Hemingway's Craft.*

1033 Briefs On The Arts column, "Joan Hemingway Publishes Novel," *N.Y. Times* (July 18, 1973), p. 34.

Hemingway's 23-year-old granddaughter (John Hemingway's daughter) collaborated with Paul Ronnecarrere on her first novel, *Rosebud,* which was published in France.

1034 Mosby, Aline. "Name hampers Hemingway's granddaughter," *Newark Star-Ledger* (July 22, 1973), Sec. 6, p. 1. Datelined: Paris (UPI). Photograph.

Interview with Joan Hemingway. See above entry.

1035 Wallach, John P. "The 'Old Man' Remembers Hemingway," *Genesis,* I (Aug. 1973), 22-24, 45, 118.

Interview with Gregorio Fuentes.

1036 Hahn, H. G. Review of Wayne Kvam's *Hemingway in Germany,* *Library Journal,* XCVIII (Aug. 1973), p. 2299.

1037 Thornton, Gene. "Why Hemingway with Man Ray?" *N.Y. Times* (Aug. 5, 1973), Sec. II, pp. 24, 27.

Regarding the photograph "of a herd of bulls running up a street in a Spanish town" which Hemingway took with Man Ray's camera, and which was included in an exhibition of Man Ray's photographs at the Metropolitan Museum of Art.

1038 Giniger, Henry. "Bulls Gone, Pamplona Gets Down to Business: Fiesta City Beloved of Hemingway Now Industrial Center," *N.Y. Times* (Aug. 7, 1973), p. 8.

1039 Burchard, Ruth Bagley. "Telling on Ernie: More Hemingway Lore," *Oak Leaves* (Aug. 8, 1973).

A former Oak Park resident recalls Dr. Hemingway's "triumphant trumpet call" announcing Ernest's birth, and Ernest's solo in the school play "Robin Hood."

1040 Winakor, Bess. Eye View column, *Women's Wear Daily* (Aug. 23, 1973), p. 10.
Interview with Mary Hemingway in Ketchum, Idaho.

1041 Review of Samuel Shaw's *Ernest Hemingway, Choice,* x (Sept. 1973), 985.

1042 Josephs, Mary Jim. "The Hunting Metaphor in Hemingway and Faulkner," *Dissertation Abstracts International,* xxxiv (Sept. 1973), 1282-A.
Abstract from a doctoral dissertation, Michigan State University, 1973. This study concludes with comparative readings of *OMATS* and Faulkner's "The Bear."

1043 Roberts, Dave. "Hemingway—Cupid in Michigan," *Motor News* (Automobile Club of Michigan), LVI (Sept. 1973), 16.

1044 "Fair commissions Hemingway bust," *Oak Park-River Forest World* (Sept. 2, 1973), p. 3.
The Oak Park Village Art Fair commissioned Egon Weiner to sculpt a bust of Hemingway to be placed in the Oak Park Public Library's Hemingway collection. The dedication of the bust was planned for July 21, 1974, during ceremonies commemorating Hemingway's 75th birthday.

1045 Holder, Robert C., Jr. "Counts Mippipopolous and Greffi: Hemingway's Aristocrats of Resignation," *Hemingway notes,* III (Fall 1973), 3-6. Caricature of Hemingway, by Eric Lohnaas, on the cover, reproduced from *Alternative,* IV (May 1971).
On Hemingway's "perfectly defined miniature portraits" in *SAR* and *FTA.*

1045₁ Davidson, Cathy N. "Laughter without Comedy in *For Whom the Bell Tolls,*" *ibid.,* pp. 6-9.
On the three types of laughter—"all hollow and humorless"—in *FWBT.*

1045₂ White, William. "Ernest Hemingway and Gene Tunney," *ibid.,* p. 10.
Gene Tunney's account of a visit with Hemingway in Havana, as related by John P. Marquand, is reprinted from *The Late John Marquand* by Stephen Birmingham, Philadelphia, 1972, p. 218.

1045₃ "T. A." [Taylor Alderman], "K. R." [Kenneth Rosen], and "W. W." [William White]. Current Bibliography, *ibid.,* pp. 12-16.

1045₄ "T. A." [Taylor Alderman]. Review of Arthur Waldhorn's *A Reader's Guide to Ernest Hemingway* and *EH: A Collection of Criticism* edited by Professor Waldhorn, *ibid.,* pp. 17-18.

1045₅ White, Gertrude M. Review of Alice Hunt Sokoloff's *Hadley: The First Mrs. Hemingway, ibid.*, pp. 18-19.

1045₆ White, William. Review of *Hemingway at Auction* compiled by Matthew J. Bruccoli and C. E. Frazer Clark, Jr., *ibid.*, pp. 19-21.

1046 Brasher, Jim. "Hemingway's Florida," *Lost Generation Journal*, I (Fall 1973), 4-8. Cover photograph of Hemingway and Charles Thompson.

1047 Howell, John M. "Hemingway's 'Metaphysics' in Four Stories of the Thirties: A Look at the Manuscripts," *ICarbS*, I, i (Fall-Winter 1973), 41-51. For facsimiles of the manuscripts, see (S-F41).

A study of Hemingway's symbolic syntheses, or "metaphysics," as they are revealed in "After the Storm," "Homage to Switzerland," "The Snows of Kilimanjaro," and "The Short Happy Life of Francis Macomber."

1048 Review of Alice Hunt Sokoloff's *Hadley: The First Mrs. Hemingway, Choice,* X (Oct. 1973), 1198.

1049 "The Fitzgerald/Hemingway Epoch," editorial headnote, *Esquire,* LXXX (Oct. 1973), 139. Fortieth Anniversary Issue. Photograph of Hemingway in hospital in London during World War II, on p. 140. See also (S-C79). Note: The drawing of Hemingway on the cover also appeared on the cover of the advertising insertion, announcing this issue, in the *N.Y. Times* (Oct. 8, 1972).

1049₁ Gingrich, Arnold. "Scott, Ernest and Whoever," *ibid.*, pp. 151-154, 374, 376, 380. Reprinted from *Esquire,* LXVI (Dec. 1966).

1050 Hipkiss, Robert A. "Ernest Hemingway's *The Things That I Know,*" *Twentieth Century Literature,* XIX (Oct. 1973), 275-282.

Essay on *ARIT*. "A careful reading of this work makes it evident that Papa Hemingway was letting his alter ego, Colonel Cantwell, sum up for us the meaning of Hemingway's lifetime experience." Note: *The Things That I Know* was one of the titles Hemingway considered for *ARIT*. See Carlos Baker's *EH: A Life Story*, p. 474.

1051 Meador, John M., Jr. "Addendum to Hanneman: Hemingway's *The Old Man and the Sea,*" *Papers of the Bibliographical Society of America,* LXVII, iv (Oct.-Dec. 1973), 454-457.

Regarding textual changes in both early and later editions of *OMATS*. For an error in the description of the first edition in the bibliography, see note following (S-A9h).

1052 Smith, Jack. "Across the River, Under the Table," *Los Angeles Times* (Oct. 31, 1973), Part IV, p. 1.

Regarding the frequent mention of wines, liquors, brandies, whiskies, and beers in Hemingway's books.

1053 "Seminars Open Hemingway Revival," *Oak Park Village Economist* (Oct. 31, 1973), p. 4.

Announcement of a series of seminars on Hemingway's works to be held at the Oak Park Public Library under the general direction of Daniel Reichard.

1054 Review of Sheldon Norman Grebstein's *Hemingway's Craft, Choice,* x (Nov. 1973), 1382.

1055 Dean, Sharon Welch. "Lost Ladies: The Isolated Heroine in the Fiction of Hawthorne, James, Fitzgerald, Hemingway, and Faulkner," *Dissertation Abstracts International,* xxxiv (Nov. 1973), 2616-A.

Abstract from a doctoral dissertation, University of New Hampshire, 1973. Includes a study of three Hemingway heroines: Lady Brett Ashley in *SAR*, Catherine Barkley in *FTA*, and Maria in *FWBT*.

1055₁ Elliott, Gary Douglas. "The Hemingway Hero's Quest for Faith," *ibid.,* p. 2621-A.

Abstract from a doctoral dissertation, Kansas State University, 1973.

1056 Oleson, Russ. "Hemingway's Cat Collection in 1973," *Cat Fancy,* xvi (Nov.-Dec. 1973), 12-15.

Regarding the descendants of Hemingway's cats in Key West.

1057 Waugh, Evelyn. "The Case of Mr. Hemingway," *Commonweal,* xcix (Nov. 16, 1973), 195-197.

Regarding the critics' reception to *ARIT*. Reprinted from *Commonweal,* liii (Nov. 3, 1950).

1058 St. John, Donald. Letters column, "The Paris Hemingway Knew," *N.Y. Times* (Dec. 16, 1973), Sec. 1C, p. 4.

Regarding Hemingway's Paris residences in the early 1920s, which have been torn down, or soon will be, to be replaced by modern apartment buildings.

1059 Ruhm, Herbert. "Hemingway in Schruns," *Commonweal,* xcix (Dec. 28, 1973), 344-345.

Describes a visit to the Hotel Taube in Schruns, in the Vorarlberg in Austria, where Hemingway spent the winters of 1925 and 1926.

1060 Gurko, Leo. Review of Sheldon Norman Grebstein's *Hemingway's Craft, Modern Fiction Studies,* xix (Winter 1973-1974), 600-601.

PART THREE

APPENDIX

LIST OF NEWSPAPERS AND PERIODICALS
CITED IN SECTIONS C AND H

NOTE: An asterisk has been used to indicate newspapers.

AB/Bookman's Weekly,
  Newark, New Jersey
  (formerly *Antiquarian
  Bookman*)
À la Page, Paris
ALFA, Marília, São Paulo,
  Brazil
Alternative, Bloomington,
  Indiana
America, New York
*American Academy of Arts and
  Letters and the National
  Institute of Arts and Letters,
  Proceedings,* New York
American Book Collector,
  Arlington Heights, Illinois
American Heritage, New York
American Imago, South
  Dennis, Massachusetts
*American Literary Scholarship:
  An Annual,* Durham, North
  Carolina
American Literature, Durham,
  North Carolina
American Mercury, New York
American Notes & Queries,
  New Haven, Connecticut
American Quarterly,
  Philadelphia
*American Red Cross Central
  Division Bulletin,* Chicago
American Red Cross Journal,
  Washington, D.C.
American Rifleman,
  Washington, D.C.
*American Society Legion of
  Honor Magazine,* New York
Americana Norvegica,
  Philadelphia
Analele Universității București,
  Bucharest, Rumania

Anglia, Tübingen,
  West Germany
Antigonish Review, Antigonish,
  Nova Scotia
Antiquarian Bookman,
  Newark, New Jersey
*Archives of General
  Psychiatry,* Chicago
Argeş, Bucharest, Rumania
Argosy, London (as noted)
Argosy, New York
Arizona Quarterly, Tucson,
  Arizona
Astrology, New York
**Atlanta Journal and
  Constitution,* Atlanta,
  Georgia
Atlantic, Boston
Atlas, New York

Baker Street Journal,
  New York
Ball State University Forum,
  Muncie, Indiana
Banasthali Patrika, Rajasthan,
  India
**Berkeley Book Review (Daily
  Californian),* Berkeley,
  California
Bermudian, Hamilton,
  Bermuda
Best Sellers, Scranton,
  Pennsylvania
*Birmingham Eccentric,
  Birmingham, Michigan
Blue Book, New York
*Boletín Cultural y
  Bibliográfico,* Bogotá,
  Colombia
Book League Monthly,
  New York

APPENDIX

Book-of-the-Month Club News, New York

*Book World (supplement to the *Washington Post* and *Chicago Tribune*)

Books Abroad, Norman, Oklahoma

Books and Bookmen, London

*Boston Globe, Boston

*Boston Herald-Traveler, Boston

Bulletin des bibliothèques de France, Paris

Bulletin of Bibliography, Boston

Bulletin of the College of General Education of Tohoku University, Sendai, Japan

Bulletin of the Rocky Mountain Modern Language Association, Boulder, Colorado

Caliban, Toulouse, France

Candide, Paris

Carleton Miscellany, Northfield, Minnesota

Carrell, The, Coral Gables, Florida

Casa de las Américas, Havana

Časopis pro Modern í Filologii: Literatura, Prague, Czechoslovakia

Cat Fancy, San Diego, California

Cavalcade, Canoga Park, California

CEA Critic (College English Association), Shreveport, Louisiana

Cenobio, Lugano, Switzerland

*Chicago News, Chicago

*Chicago Sun-Times, Chicago

*Chicago Tribune, Chicago

ChicagoLand Omnibus, Chicago

Choice, Middletown, Connecticut

Christ und Welt, Stuttgart, West Germany

Christian Century, Chicago

*Christian Science Monitor, Boston

Cithara: Essays in the Judaeo-Christian Tradition, St. Bonaventure, New York

Civiltà Cattolica, Rome

Collage, East Lansing, Michigan

College English, Urbana, Illinois

Columbia University Forum, New York

Commentary, New York

Commonweal, New York

Congress Bi-Weekly (American Jewish Congress), New York

Connecticut Review, Hartford, Connecticut

Contemporanul, Bucharest, Rumania

Contemporary Literature, Madison, Wisconsin

*Corriere della Sera, Milan, Italy

Cosmopolitan, New York

Cresset, Valparaiso, Indiana

Crest, Oak Park, Illinois

Cristallo, Bolzano, Italy

Criticism, Detroit, Michigan

Cross Currents, West Nyack, New York

Cuadernos del Congreso por la Libertad de la Cultura, Paris

Cultura Universitaria, Caracas, Venezuela

Daily Collegian (Pennsylvania State University), University Park, Pennsylvania

Daily Princetonian, Princeton, New Jersey

Daily Telegraph Magazine, London

Detroit Free Press, Detroit, Michigan

Detroit News, Detroit, Michigan

Deutsche Rundschau, Baden-Baden, West Germany

Deutsche Universitätszeitung, Bonn, West Germany

Deutsche Vierteljahrsschrift für Literaturwissenschaft und Geistesgeschichte, Stuttgart, West Germany

Dialogue: An Interdisciplinary Quarterly, Bradford, Pennsylvania

Discourse: A Review of the Liberal Arts, Moorhead, Minnesota

Dissertation Abstracts, Ann Arbor, Michigan (changed to *Dissertation Abstracts International* in July 1969)

Dnipro: Literaturne-xudožniz Žurnal, Kiev, USSR

Don, Saratov, USSR

Doshisha Literature, Kyoto, Japan

Economist, London

Eigo Seinen, Tokyo

êle ela, Rio de Janeiro

Ellery Queen's Mystery Magazine, New York

Encore, New York

Encounter, London

English "A" Analyst, Evanston, Illinois

English Journal, Urbana, Illinois

English Language and Literature, Seoul(?), Korea

English Language Notes, Boulder, Colorado

English Record, Oneonta, New York

English Studies, Amsterdam

Escapade, New York

Espresso, Rome

Esquire, New York

Essays in Criticism, Oxford

Estado de São Paulo, São Paulo, Brazil

Études Anglaises, Paris

Europeo, Milan, Italy

Everyman, London

Exercise Exchange, Burlington, Vermont

Ex Libris, Paris

Explicator, Richmond, Virginia

Fact, London (as noted)

fact, New York

Fiction Parade, New York

Field & Stream, New York

Fiera Letteraria, Rome

Figaro Littéraire, Paris

Filologičeskie Nauki: Nauchny e Doklady Vysshei Shkoly, Moscow

Fitzgerald/Hemingway Annual, Washington, D.C.

Fitzgerald Newsletter, Columbus, Ohio

Fontaine, Paris

Forum, Houston, Texas

Galleria, Turin, Italy

Gazeta Literară, Moscow (?)

Genesis, New York

Gent, New York

Gentlemen's Quarterly (GQ),
New York
Germanisch-Romanische
Monatsschrift, Heidelberg,
West Germany
Godisnik na Sofijskiya
universitet: Fakutet po
zapadni filologii, Sofia,
Bulgaria
Golden Book Magazine,
New York
Gor'kovskii Pedagogicheskii
Institut Inostrannykh
Yakykov (Gorki Institute),
Moscow
*Grand Rapids Press, Grand
Rapids, Michigan
Granma, Havana, Cuba

Harper's, New York
Hartford Studies in Literature,
West Hartford, Connecticut
Hemingway notes, Carlisle,
Pennsylvania
Holiday, Indianapolis, Indiana
Horizon, New York
Horn Book, Boston
Host do domu, Prague,
Czechoslovakia
Hudson Review, New York
Hulton's National Weekly
Picture Post, London
Humanities Association
Bulletin, Kingston, Ontario,
Canada
Hungarian Studies in English,
Debrecen, Hungary
Husson Review, Bangor, Maine

ICarbS, Carbondale, Illinois
*Idaho Statesman, Boise, Idaho
Indian Journal of American
Studies, Bombay

Indian Journal of English
Studies, Bombay
Indiana English Journal, Terre
Haute, Indiana
Inland: The Magazine of the
Middle West, Chicago
Inostrannaya Literatura,
Moscow
*International Herald Tribune,
Paris
Iowa English Yearbook, Iowa
City, Iowa
*Izvestia, Moscow

Jack London's Adventure
Magazine, New York
Jahrbuch für Amerikastudien,
Heidelberg, West Germany
John O'London's Weekly,
London
*Journal do Brasil,
Rio de Janeiro
Journal of Aesthetics and Art
Criticism, Baltimore,
Maryland
Journal of American Studies,
London
Journal of English and
Germanic Philology, Urbana,
Illinois
Journal of Existentialism,
New York
Journal of General Education,
University Park,
Pennsylvania
Journal of Modern Literature,
Philadelphia
Journal of Narrative
Technique, Ypsilanti,
Michigan
Journal of Popular Culture,
Bowling Green, Ohio

Journal of the Society of English and American Literature (Kwansei Gakuin University), Hyogo-ken, Japan

Journalism Quarterly, Minneapolis, Minnesota

*Kansas City Star, Kansas City, Missouri

*Kansas City Times, Kansas City, Missouri (morning edition of above entry)

Kansas Quarterly, Manhattan, Kansas

Kenyon Review, Gambier, Ohio

Kirke og Kultur, Oslo, Norway

Kvĕten, Prague, Czechoslovakia

Kyushu American Literature, Fukuoka City, Japan

Langues Modernes, Paris

Latviiskii Gosudarstvennyi Universitet, Riga, USSR

Letture, Milan, Italy

Library Chronicle (University of Pennsylvania), Philadelphia

Library Journal, New York

Life, New York

Lilliput, London

Listener, London

Literary Criterion, Mysore, India

Literary Half-Yearly, Mysore, India

Literary Review, Rutherford, New Jersey

Literary Sketches, Williamsburg, Virginia

Literatur in Wissenschaft und Unterricht, Kiel, West Germany

Literature and Psychology, Teaneck, New Jersey

Literature v Shkole, Moscow

*Literaturnaya Gazeta, Moscow

Livro de Cabeceira da Mulher, Rio de Janeiro

Lock Haven Review, Lock Haven, Pennsylvania

London Magazine, London

London Observer Review, London

Look, Des Moines, Iowa

*Los Angeles Herald-Examiner, Los Angeles, California

*Los Angeles Mirror, Los Angeles, California

*Los Angeles Times, Los Angeles, California

Lost Generation Journal, Tulsa, Oklahoma

McCall's, New York

Maclean's, Toronto

McNaught's Monthly, New York

McNeese Review, Lake Charles, Louisiana

Magasin du spectacle, Paris

Mainliner (United Air Lines), Chicago

Mainstream, New York

*Manchester Guardian Weekly, Manchester, England

Mark Twain Journal, Kirkwood, Missouri

Markham Review, Staten Island, New York

Massachusetts Review, Amherst, Massachusetts

Masses & Mainstream, New York

Mercure de France, Paris
Merkur, Stuttgart,
 West Germany
Mese, Il, London
*Miami Herald Tropic
 Magazine, Miami, Florida
Midwest Quarterly, Pittsburg,
 Kansas
*Milwaukee Journal,
 Milwaukee, Wisconsin
*Minneapolis Tribune,
 Minneapolis, Minnesota
Minnesota Motorist (AAA),
 Minneapolis, Minnesota
Minnesota Review,
 Minneapolis, Minnesota
Mississippi Quarterly,
 State College, Mississippi
Missouri English Bulletin,
 Columbia, Missouri
Modern Fiction Studies,
 Lafayette, Indiana
Modern Monthly, New York
Moderna språk,
 Saltsjö-Duvnäs, Sweden
Monthly Review, New York
Motor News (Automobile Club
 of Michigan), Detroit,
 Michigan

*Nashville Banner, Nashville,
 Tennessee
Nation, New York
*National Observer,
 Silver Springs, Maryland
National Review, New York
National Wildlife,
 Washington, D.C.
NCR World, Washington, D.C.
NEMLA Newsletter
 (Northeast Modern
 Language Association),
 Brockport, New York

Neophilologus, Groningen,
 The Netherlands
Neueren Sprachen, Frankfurt
 am Main, West Germany
Neuphilologische Mitteilun-
 gen, Helsinki, Finland
New American Review,
 New York
New Leader, New York
New Masses, New York
New Mexico Quarterly,
 Albuquerque, New Mexico
New Republic,
 Washington, D.C.
New Society, London
New Statesman, London
New World Writing, New York
New York Folklore Quarterly,
 Ithaca, New York
*N.Y. Herald Tribune,
 New York
New York Magazine,
 New York
*N.Y. Post, New York
New York Review of Books,
 New York
*N.Y. Sun, New York
*N.Y. Times, New York (also
 N.Y. Times Book Review)
*N.Y. World-Telegram,
 New York
New Yorker, New York
*Newark Star-Ledger, Newark,
 New Jersey
Newsweek, New York
Nieuw Vlaams Tijdschrift,
 Antwerp, Belgium
Northern Michigan Graphic
 Resorter, Petoskey, Michigan
Notes and Queries, London
Notes on Contemporary
 Literature, Carrollton,
 Georgia
*Nouvelles Littéraires, Paris

Novel: A Forum on Fiction,
Providence, Rhode Island
Novyi Mir, Moscow

Oak Leaves, Oak Park, Illinois
Oak Park-River Forest World,
Oak Park, Illinois
Oak Park Village Economist,
Oak Park, Illinois
Oggi Illustrato, Milan, Italy
Ogoniok, Moscow
*Okhota: Okhotnich'ye
Khozyaĭstvo,* Moscow
Oktiabr', Moscow
Orbis Litterarum,
Copenhagen, Denmark

Pacific Coast Philology,
Northridge, California
*Pacific Northwest Conference
on Foreign Languages,
Proceedings,* Victoria, B.C.,
Canada
Pacific Spectator, Palo Alto,
California
Pamir, Dushambe, USSR
*Panjab University Research
Bulletin,* Chandigarh, India
Panorama, Milan, Italy
*Papers of the Bibliographical
Society of America,*
New York
*Papers on Language and
Literature,* Edwardsville,
Illinois
Paradise of the Pacific,
Honolulu
Paris Match, Paris
Paris Observer, Paris
Paunch, Buffalo, New York
Peninsula Living, Redwood
City, California
Personalist, Los Angeles,
California

Philadelphia Bulletin,
Philadelphia
Philadelphia Inquirer,
Philadelphia
Phoenix (Korea University),
Seoul, Korea
Pittsburgh Post-Gazette,
Pittsburgh, Pennsylvania
Plamǎk, Sofia, Bulgaria
Playbill, New York
Playboy, Chicago
PMLA (Publications of the
Modern Language
Association), New York
Prairie Schooner, Lincoln,
Nebraska
Preuves, Paris
Princeton History,
Princeton, New Jersey
Prometey, Moscow
*Proof: The Yearbook of
American Bibliographical
and Textual Studies,*
Columbia, South Carolina
Providence Journal,
Providence, Rhode Island
Publishers Weekly, New York

Quadrant, Sydney, Australia
*Quarterly Journal of the
Library of Congress,*
Washington, D.C.
Quartet, Lafayette, Indiana

Re: Arts and Letters,
Nacogdoches, Texas
Reader's Digest, Pleasantville,
New York
Redbook, New York
Renascence, St. Mary-of-the-
Woods, Indiana
Rendezvous, Pocatello, Idaho

APPENDIX

Research in the College of the Liberal Arts (Pennsylvania State University), University Park, Pennsylvania

Research Studies (Washington State University), Pullman, Washington)

Revista de la Universidad de México, Mexico City

Revista de Occidente, Madrid

Revista Plaza (Hotel Plaza Magazine), Madrid

Revista Universidad de Zaragoza, Zaragoza, Spain

Revue des Langues Vivantes, Brussels

Revue des Lettres Modernes, Paris

Revue de Littérature Comparée, Paris

*St. Louis Globe-Democrat, St. Louis, Missouri

*St. Louis Post-Dispatch, St. Louis, Missouri

Sammlung, Die, Amsterdam

*San Francisco Examiner & Chronicle, San Francisco

Saturday Evening Post, Philadelphia

Saturday Night, Toronto

Saturday Review, New York

Scripta Hierosolymitana, Jerusalem

Secolul 20, Bucharest, Rumania

See, New York

Senhor, Rio de Janeiro

Serif, Kent, Ohio

Sewanee Review, Sewanee, Tennessee

Sexual Behavior, New York

Shenandoah, Lexington, Virginia

Sibirskie Ogni (Siberia)

South Atlantic Bulletin, Chapel Hill, North Carolina

South Atlantic Quarterly, Durham, North Carolina

South Carolina Historical Association, Proceedings, Columbia, South Carolina

South Central Bulletin (SCMLA), Houston, Texas

South Dakota Review, Vermillion, South Dakota

Southern Humanities Review, Auburn, Alabama

Southern Review, Baton Rouge, Louisiana

Southwest Review, Dallas, Texas

Sovetskaya Estoniya, Tallinn(?), Estonia

Soviet Life, Washington, D.C.

Spectator, London

Spiegel, Hamburg, West Germany

Sports Afield, New York

Sports Illustrated, New York

Sprache und Literatur Englands und Amerikas, Tübingen, West Germany

Sputnik, Moscow

SR. Uma Revista para o Senhor, Rio de Janeiro

Statement Magazine, Los Angeles, California

Steaua, Bucharest, Rumania

Steinbeck Newsletter, Muncie, Indiana

Step Ladder, Chicago

Studi Americani, Rome

Studiekamraten, Lund, Sweden

Studies (Kobe University), Kobe, Japan

Studies in American Fiction, Boston

Studies in English Literature
(University of Tokyo),
Tokyo
Studies in Short Fiction,
Newberry, South Carolina
Studies in the Novel, Denton,
Texas
Studii de literatura universală,
Bucharest, Rumania
Style, Fayetteville, Arkansas
* *Süddeutsche Zeitung,* Munich
* *Sunday Dispatch,* London
* *Sunday Times,* London
Světová literatura, Prague,
Czechoslovakia
Symposium (Union College)

* *Tablet,* London
Tamarack Review, Toronto
Tempo, Milan, Italy
Texas Quarterly, Austin, Texas
*Texas Studies in Literature and
Language,* Austin, Texas
* *This Week,* New York
(a nationally distributed
supplement in Sunday
newspapers)
Thoreau Journal Quarterly,
Old Town, Maine
Time, New York
* *Times,* London (as noted)
* *Times Literary Supplement
(TLS),* London
Topic:12, Washington,
Pennsylvania
Topper, Los Angeles,
California
* *Toronto Daily Star,* Toronto
Town & Gown, State College,
Pennsylvania
*Tradition: A Journal of
Orthodox Jewish Thought,*
New York

* *Trapeze,* Oak Park, Illinois
Travel & Camera, New York
Tribuna, Ljubljana,
Yugoslavia
* *Tribuna, A,* Santos, São Paulo,
Brazil
True, New York
Twentieth-Century Literature,
Los Angeles, California

*Uchenye Zapiski Gor'kovskogo
Universiteta* (Gorki
Institute), Moscow
*Uchenye Zapiski Leningradskii
Pedagogicheskii Institut,*
Leningrad
Unisa English Studies,
Pretoria, Union of South
Africa
Universitas, Stuttgart,
West Germany
University College Quarterly
(Michigan State University),
Lansing, Michigan
*University of Mississippi
Studies in English,*
University, Mississippi
University Review (Kansas
City) (as noted), Kansas
City, Missouri
* *University Times,* Pittsburgh,
Pennsylvania
U.S.A. (U.S. Office of War
Information), Washington,
D.C.

Valley Sun, Sun Valley, Idaho
Vanity Fair, New York
Venture (University of
Karachi) (as noted),
Karachi, West Pakistan
*Venture: The Traveler's
World,* New York

APPENDIX

Vestnik Moskovskovo universiteta: Filologiya, Moscow

Victory (U.S. Office of War Information), New York

Virginia Quarterly Review, Charlottesville, Virginia

Vita e Pensiero, Milan, Italy

Volontaires, Paris

Voprosy Literatury, Moscow

Vorarlberg, Bregenz, Austria

*Vorarlberger Landes-Zeitung, Bregenz, Austria

*Voz de España, La, San Sebastian, Spain

*Wall Street Journal, New York

*Washington Post, Washington, D.C.

*Washington Sunday Star, Washington, D.C.

*Welt der Literatur, Hamburg, West Germany

Welt und Wort, Tübingen, West Germany

West Virginia University Philological Papers, Morgantown, West Virginia

Western Humanities Review, Salt Lake City, Utah

WGAw News (Writers Guild of America/West Newsletter), Los Angeles

Wilson Library Bulletin, Bronx, New York

Wissenschaftliche Zeitschrift der Ernst-Moritz-Arndt Universität, Greifswald, East Germany

*Women's Wear Daily, New York

World, New York

Writer's Digest, Cincinnati, Ohio

Yale Literary Magazine, New Haven, Connecticut

Yale Review, New Haven, Connecticut

*Zeit, Die, Hamburg, West Germany

Zeitschrift für Anglistik und Amerikanistik, Leipzig, East Germany

Zeitwende, Munich

Zhurnalist, Moscow

Znamya, Moscow

Zvezda vostoka, Leningrad

INDEX

INDEX

INDEX

INDEX

INDEX

Friedman, Melvin J., S-G145
Friedman, Norman, S-G148, 429
Friedman, Ralph, S-H224
Friedrich, Otto, S-G161
Fritzsch, Robert, S-H65
Frohock, Wilbur M., S-G360
Frost, Robert, S-G293, S-H693
Fuchs, Daniel, S-G418
Fuentes, Gregorio, S-H1035
Fukuma, Kin-ichi, S-H64
Fukumoto, Takako, S-H489
Fulford, Robert, S-H136
Fuller, Edmund, S-H213, 557, 774, 942
Fuller, James F., S-H384₁
Funke, Lewis, S-H233
Fuog, Russell J., S-A18a
Fuson, Ben W., S-H248, 468, 551, 668₁, 683, 685

Gabdullin, Nyğymet, S-D99
Gabriel, Joseph F., S-G136
Gadda Conti, Giuseppe, S-G146, S-H315, 520
Gado, Frank, S-H149
Gahlot, Jai S., S-G287
Gaillard, Theodore L., Jr., S-H802
Galbraith, John Kenneth, S-H209
Galbraith, Robert E., S-E1
Gale, Charles Bolles, S-G367
Galinsky, Hans, S-G147
Galligan, Edward L., S-H346
Galloway, David, S-E96
Gamble, James, S-F25-Aa
Ganzel, Dewey, S-H407, 860
Garber, Frederick, S-E119
Garcia, Valentim, S-E19
Gardner, James, S-H858₂
Garnett, David, S-F16c
Garraty, John A., S-H694
Gary, Romain, S-G385
Gasiulis, P., S-D103
Gastwirth, Donald E., S-H192
Gaya, Ramón, S-C25
Gebhardt, Richard Coate, S-H719₁
Geduld, Harry M., S-B14
Gehlmann, John, S-G367, S-H340₁
Geismar, Maxwell, S-B7, S-G148, 317, 738
Gelfant, Blanche, S-G161
Gellens, Jay, S-G148
Gellhorn, Martha, S-F22d, S-G20, 247, S-H31
Gent, George, S-H969
George, Raymond, S-H875

Gerstenberger, Donna, S-E119
Gertzman, Jay A., S-H1029
Gheorghe, Fănică N., S-H615
Giammona, Vicki, S-H1012₁
Giannone, Richard, S-E161
Gibbon, Edward, S-G106, 137, S-H280
Gibson, Walker, S-G149
Gide, André, S-H993
Gierasch, Walter, S-H36
Gifford, Tommy, S-G345
Gifford, William, S-H472
Gil'dina, Z. M., S-G150
Gill, Brendan, S-G323
Gillespie, Gerald, S-H403₁
Gilmer, Walker, S-G151
Gilroy, Harry, S-H251, 310
Gingrich, Arnold, S-C64, S-E32, S-G48, 152, S-H275, 554, 651₂₀, 733, 882, 1049₁
Giniger, Henry, S-H1038
Gironella, José María, S-G158
Glanville, Brian, S-H521
Glassco, John, S-G153
Glassell, Alfred C., Jr., S-B12, S-G121
Glasser, William A., S-H202
Glazier, Teresa Ferster, S-E78
Glicksberg, Charles I., S-G154
Godolphin, Isabel Simmons, S-F14e
Goethals, Thomas, S-G155, 156
Gohdes, Clarence, S-G157, 258
Golden, Herbert H., S-G158
Goldhurst, William, S-H120, 651₆
Golding, William, S-H585
Goldman, Albert, S-H556
Golyševa, E., S-C34, S-D104, S-G221
Göncz, Arpád, S-D46, 50
Goodman, Jack, S-H53
Goodman, Paul, S-G159, S-H871
Goodman, Roger B., S-E120
Gorbunov, A., S-H358
Gordon, Caroline, S-G164, 203
Gordon, David J., S-H166, 816
Gordon, Gerald T., S-H875₁₀
Gordon, Walter K., S-E97
Gore, Gary, S-A16a
Gorlier, Claudio, S-H390
Gorrell, Robert M., S-E139, S-G160
Gotkharde, R. E., S-G150, S-H506
Gottfried, Ralph, S-H312₂
Gottlieb, Carole Patricia, see Vopat, Carole Gottlieb
Gottschalk, Klaus-Dieter, S-H923
Gould, Jack, S-H481
Graber, Alan, S-H53

INDEX

INDEX

INDEX

INDEX

INDEX

LIBRARY OF CONGRESS CATALOGING IN PUBLICATION DATA (REVISED)

Hanneman, Audre, comp.
    Ernest Hemingway, a comprehensive bibliography.

        Supplement.
    Includes index.
    1. Hemingway, Ernest, 1899-1961.—Bibl.
Z8396.3.H45 suppl [PS3515.E37] 016.813′5′2
ISBN 0-691-06284-6 (suppl.)   67-14409